REASSESSING
REVITALIZATION
MOVEMENTS

Edited by Michael E. Harkin

REASSESSING REVITALIZATION MOVEMENTS

Perspectives from
North America and
the Pacific Islands

UNIVERSITY OF NEBRASKA PRESS

LINCOLN AND LONDON

The publication of this book was supported by
funds provided by the Research Office
and the College of Arts and Sciences of
the University of Wyoming.

⊗

Library of Congress Cataloging-in-Publication Data
Reassessing revitalization movements: perspectives
from North America and the Pacific Islands / edited
by Michael E. Harkin.
p.   cm.
Based on an invited session at the 98th Annual
Meeting of the American Anthropological
Association in Chicago.
Includes bibliographical references and index.
ISBN 0-8032-2406-0 (cl.: alk. paper)
1. Nativistic movements—Congresses.
2. Nativistic movements—North America—Congresses.
3. Nativistic movements—Pacific Area—Congresses.
I. Harkin, Michael Eugene, 1958–
II. American Anthropological Association.
Meeting (98th: 1999: Chicago, Ill.)
GN472.7.R4   2004
306.6'99—dc22   2003016609

CONTENTS

FOREWORD

Anthony F. C. Wallace

My original article, "Revitalization Movements," appeared in the *American Anthropologist* in 1956. It was an early outgrowth of research for a biographical study of the 19th-century Seneca prophet Handsome Lake. As that project evolved, it became less exclusively a life and times work comparable to my earlier Native American biography, *Teedyuscung: King of the Delawares* (1949), and more a type case for a special kind of social movement. Such events of cultural reform seemed to be extraordinarily widespread, a pancultural phenomenon, recognizable both in small-scale societies on the colonial fringes of great empires and also in the heart of the larger polities themselves. The Handsome Lake study itself, however, did not see print until 1970 with the publication of *The Death and Rebirth of the Seneca*, and unfortunately the original theoretical essay was not printed as an appendix to that volume. Nevertheless, the Handsome Lake book has enjoyed considerable popularity, particularly among historians, who have in recent years entered the field of American Indian ethnohistory in increasing numbers. By now the expression "revitalization movement" has been somewhat routinized and is sometimes used as a generic term without reference to its source, and the concept has been applied in contexts far removed from the situations mentioned as illustrations in the original article.

Perhaps the most flattering of its most recent uses is in a doctoral dissertation by Wesley Peach, submitted to the faculty of theology of the University of Montreal, and published in 2001 in the series Perspectives de theologies pratique, under the title *Itineraires de Conversion* (2001). This work presents pathways to successful conversion to Christianity, illustrated by a dozen case histories from Quebec, analyzed in the light of revitalization theory. My writings on revitalization are accurately described in detail and are considered as a kind of pastoral model for Catholic and Protestant evangelical programs. That the theory is recommended for use by professional practitioners of conversion I take to be an ultimate testimonial to its validity in the world outside academe! But the accolade calls for a certain caution: When does description become prescription? When does prophecy theory become self-fulfilling prophecy itself?

The thoughtful introduction by Michael E. Harkin and the descriptive chapters in the present book provide a welcome comparative perspective on the domain of revitalization as they test its usefulness in a number of empirical studies of Native American and Oceanian movements. These applications raise significant issues with respect to the nature of the theory itself. Rather than comment on these excellent contributions individually, let me mention briefly a few of the larger issues of reassessment raised by the several authors.

Of particular interest to me are the possibilities of modifying the structure of revitalization theory itself that are suggested by some of the chapters in this book. At the time of my original writing, in the 1950s and 1960s, interdisciplinary research was in vogue, and concepts of "stress" and "equilibrium" were being widely applied to unite biological, psychological, and social domains of inquiry under the rubric of "systems theory." The model articulated in the 1956 article makes use of an organismic analogy and proposes revitalization movements as a process of equilibrium restoration that may be applied to any society, whatever the source of the failure of harmony and the rise of anomie. But it is rather abstract and perhaps fails to attend sufficiently to the unique texture of cultural and historical circumstances of the kind that fills the pages of the Seneca book. The suggestion of using chaos theory as an enrichment of the model in order to take account of the uniqueness of original events and conditions as determining the timing of revitalization events, the content of the prophetic code, the course of the movement and its impact on the surrounding society, and so on strikes me as promising. One of the virtues of postmodern ethnography (and ethnohistory) is its appreciation of the singularities of human experience. Generality and singularity are a dialectic that inevitably generates art—and anthropology. As Blake has observed, it is the task not only of the scientist but also of the poet to discern the universal in the particular:

To see the world in a grain of sand
And a Heaven in a wild flower,
   Hold Infinity in the palm of your hand,
And eternity in a hour.

Another question that these chapters raise, or imply, is whether the revitalization model is applicable only to those situations of colonialism in which a subordinate group is impelled to reform its way of life in reaction to pressures imposed by a dominant power. Such reforms may, as several chapters suggest, not go in the direction of nativism or withdrawal and may take the form of conversion to the religion of the oppressor. This model is congenial to a postmodern scholarly environment, invoking hegemonic Power and the oppressed Other. Classic examples of revitalization, such as the Ghost Dance, the Vailala Madness, and the New Religion of Handsome Lake, fit easily into the imperialist, colonialist mold. And it would seem to be ever more relevant as the tide of globalization washes over the world, producing neocolonial situations in which "emergent nativisms" (to use my colleague Robert Grumet's phrase) flourish in revitalistic response.

But I would like to see an exploration of a supplement to the colonialist hypothesis: that revitalization does not merely occur among the fringe peoples of the world but, in fact, happens in the belly of the beast as well. As Harkin suggests, and as Weston La Barre, in *The Ghost Dance*, and others have shown, the colonialist hypothesis may not be adequate; revitalization may apply to larger, even imperial polities. The model here is the notion, developed by several philosophers of history, particularly by Hegel and his Marxist heirs but also in simpler form by Toynbee, Alfred L. Kroeber, and others, that each "civilization" (or "culture area") follows a life cycle of birth, florescence, and decline as a result of inner dynamics, of potentialities and vulnerabilities inherent in the system itself. In the case of Marxist theory, the inner dynamic is the economic and political struggle between classes in the course of cultural evolution, and in this model revitalization movements may appear as primitive rebellions of the lower classes or counterrevolutionary conspiracies of defeated elites. Thus the Taiping Rebellion in 19th-century China—a massive and bloody revolt against the Manchu regime, led by a semi-Christianized prophet and suppressed with the aid of European mercenaries—can be seen not merely as an acculturationist revitalization movement but also (by Chinese scholars) as a premature peasant revolt, harbinger of later, successful wars not merely against external powers but, more importantly, against internal oppression by the ancient regime.

On the other hand, the present studies of relatively small Native American and Oceanic revitalization movements, which generally conform to a colonialist hypothesis, may still provide a model for the understanding of revitalization processes in larger polities that are profoundly affecting the contemporary world. A prime example is surely the ongoing ferment in Muslim societies to return to what are perceived to be the more healthy values of an original Islam, uncontaminated by Western decadence, perhaps as promulgated by the Wahhabi movement in Saudi Arabia and certainly by Sayyid Qutb in his inspirational writings, such as *Social Justice in Islam*. Although there is a strong nativistic component in the Islamic revitalization process, and Americans tend to be focused on the question "Why do they hate us so much, when we are so good?" ("It is because they are evil"), within Islam the issue is the devising of a just society that takes advantage of Western technology without abandoning the principles of Islam. In Iran, for instance, the revitalization process would seem to center on finding a way to achieve social justice while preserving the power of the clergy to interpret the law of God as revealed to Muhammad, and the institutional device is to combine a democratic Parliament with a Council of Guardians.

Finally, I would suggest, there is a fertile field for exploration of revitalization processes right here at home in the United States. In recent years we have seen the rise of a militant Christian Right, inspired by fundamentalist ideas taken straight out of that fountain of Christian revitalization movements, the Book of Revelation. And in a more secular idiom, we have seen a neoconservative movement, many of whose intellectuals spring from departments of political science, taking command of American foreign policy. Neoconservative politicians wage "culture wars," demanding the replacement of "politically correct" professorial cliques that purvey a foreign, socialist ethos by patriotic instructors committed to the values of Western civilization, the merits of Western literature, and the knowledge of history as seen from the gates of the "City on a Hill." Although Americans are hardly now a fringe people on the edges of someone else's empire, neoconservatism is in the eyes of its adherents a revitalization movement to save America, and the world, from the perils of Marxism, terrorism, and (in its fundamentalist expressions) the forces of Satan. Indeed, this system of belief would seem to grow out of a traditional American faith, shared by many since the founding days of our republic, that America is the "redeemer nation," destined to save the world for democracy, free enterprise, and Christian values. Thus one might argue that the colonialist model may apply to the *mentalité* of contemporary revitalization movements in large polities, even though an objective evaluation of the economic, political, and military situation denies them colonial status. Colonialist fears may be psychologically true for revitalizers, who see social conflict and culture change not as the result of internal contradictions but as the play of malevolent external powers that are subverting the old values.

The editor and contributors to this book are to be thanked for putting together a work that raises issues of such significance for anthropology and for history. But these issues are, of course, relevant to public policy as well. The society needs studies of the United States and other industrial nations in the globalization era by anthropologists, studies of large, hegemonic, imperial systems that disequilibrate not just from the external impact of alien cultural hegemony or natural disaster but from internal social, ideological, and economic conflicts of interest intensifying over time and in due course generating revitalization movements of massive size and, unfortunately, of xenophobic philosophy. Such studies would complement the already successful analyses, as illustrated by essays in this symposium, of the efforts at revitalization by the "others" who are victims of globalization.

ACKNOWLEDGMENTS

This book came out of an invited session at the 98th Annual Meeting of the American Anthropological Association in Chicago. Our ability to hold such a large session in "prime time" was entirely due to the sponsorship of the American Ethnological Society and the Society for the Anthropology of Consciousness, for which we are very grateful. The discussants for that session, Raymond Fogelson and Paul Roscoe, were very much appreciated. My colleague Lin Poyer was instrumental in lining up the Oceanists who contributed to the session and this book. Lamont Lindstrom and the University of Nebraska Press's anonymous reviewer provided extremely helpful close readings of the manuscript and gave valuable advice that made this a stronger book. Finally, speaking for all the chapter authors, I would like to thank Anthony F. C. Wallace for giving us all a wonderful and inspiring body of work over the course of his remarkable career.

INTRODUCTION

Revitalization as History and Theory

Michael E. Harkin

As the title of this book makes clear, we are examining two classes of cultural phenomena (political-religious movements) within the same basic theoretical framework. The central thesis of this book is indeed that the model of the revitalization movement, associated mainly with the work of the Americanist anthropologist and ethnohistorian Anthony F. C. Wallace, is a useful way to view both sets of phenomena, from North America and the Pacific. This goes against the grain of previous analysis, which has tended to keep the two quite separate and to reserve the term *revitalization movement* for the former. In our view, this confuses the map with the territory, as Gregory Bateson (1972:454–455) used to say, for it mistakes a theoretical lens with the ethnographic object itself. Apart from tradition and bibliographic association, there is no reason to consider the Ghost Dance a more typical version of revitalization than, say, John Frum or other manifestations of the "cargo cult."

It is necessary to address, at the outset, the question of revitalization movements in relation to cargo cult. We must, in the first instance, recognize that descriptions and analyses of the two come from entirely different, and rarely intersecting, traditions of political control and description and ethnography. Postmodernist accounts of cargo cults (Kaplan 1995; Lindstrom 1990, 1993) have stressed the importance of these representational strategies in constituting the phenomena themselves. This is surely an important factor. The British colonial and ethnographic tradition has tended to make great use of the trope of irony (in opposition to the Americanist tradition, which has been far fonder of tragedy); all those novels of the colonial encounter, from Haggard through Forster to Naipul, have been redolent with the irony that derives from what Homi Bhabha has called "the ambivalence of mimicry" (1984, 1994:86). That is, the inability, and, indeed, active unwillingness, on the part of colonial subjects to achieve a culturally valid performance of the norms of the ruling society leads to the sort of overproduction of certain symbolic elements that is found in cargo cults. The readiness of colonial administrators and ethnographers to accept such descriptions, which, viewed from an interactionist perspective, may have conditioned subaltern people to take up such strategies that would attract the most attention, offers a reasonable explanation for the particular characteristics that cultural movements in Oceania and other parts of the British Empire took on.

Lamont Lindstrom (1990, 1993) goes further and states that discourses of cargo and cult participate in a chiasmic structure of power and knowledge. As Westerners (colonial officials, anthropologists) construct a discourse of cult, it is at the same time a structure of power and control. Conversely, Melanesians use *cargo* as the key term in a discourse that attempts to structure relations with the West. Both discursive regimes possess criteria that allow them to establish the truth conditions of individual utterances. Knowing all this, we are in the position of establishing a metadiscourse, which incorporates both discourses as well as our own Foucauldian knowledge of the functioning of such discursive systems. This seems, ultimately, to be self-defeating, for a variety of reasons. Any explanatory or interpretive system is seen a priori to be a form of the exercise of power, rather than a framework for understanding. Surely the important contemporary forms of Western power (economic globalization, military hegemony) are in no way dependent on cultic discourses. Anthropology must cease to exist if we view our own tentative attempts to comprehend cultural practices as ipso facto exercises in discursive and political power.

A second problem with such views is that they tend to dissolve the object of study into the ether of postmodern reflexivity, which is, in the final analysis, not terribly reflexive. As Marshall Sahlins (1993, 1995) has persuasively argued, extreme constructivist arguments deny the very reality of culture, and hence the dignity that goes along with that, to non-Western peoples who provide the context of traditional anthropological research. That is, we assume that all markers of difference are necessarily part of a discourse of exoticism and essentialism, taking as the purported norm a remarkably unreflective hegemony of cultural reason: the ideological essence of bourgeois Occidentalism (Sahlins 1995:148–156; see Obeyesekere 1992:19). Cultures that fail to "live up to" such standards are assumed to be mere ethnographic fictions, in a much stronger sense than Geertz (1973:16) has suggested. On the other hand, Western society itself is hardly free from the sort of antirational millenarian behavior that is characteristic of revitalization. Indeed, parts of the rural United States, especially in the west, are practically hopping with it in the form of New Age, Christian, and quasi-Christian cults and movements (see Trompf 1990). Indeed, because such movements among aboriginal people are seemingly a function of the "contact zone," as Mary Louise Pratt (1992) has called it, then one might argue that they are as much or more a product of Western culture itself: its grounding in its own "negative dialectic" (Adorno 1973).

However, this is surely only part of the picture. Although one hardly wishes to return to the scholarly debates over the aboriginality of Plateau Prophet movements and similar phenomena, plentiful evidence exists that such movements predate European contact (see Aberle 1959; Miller 1985; Spier 1935; Walker 1969). The spread of cannibal dance societies on the Northwest Coast, the tradition of subarctic prophets, and the diffusion of Mississippian "death cult" themes throughout eastern North America all point to the aboriginality of revitalistic religious movements.[1] Perhaps no case could be stronger than that presented by the League of the Iroquois, which Wallace views as a precedent for the Handsome Lake movement he studies (Fenton 1998:104–119; Wallace 1970a).

In Melanesia, recent scholarship on cargo cults (e.g., Lattas 1998) explores the complex uses of mimesis in the context of early postcontact worldviews, which presumably can be "upstreamed" to a recent precontact era (see Fenton 1953). Although the belief that whites were the ghosts of dead ancestors did arise in North America (see Nabokov 1992:10–12), it was much rarer and never so thoroughly systematized. In parts of Melanesia, this view fit neatly into a preexisting structure of mimesis, in which the world of the living reflected the underworld of the dead, which in turn could be seen as a mirror of the external world of the whites (Lattas 1998). Such homologies created a structure within which colonized people could exercise control over forces seemingly beyond their ken.

These ethnographic specificities, and not merely the textual traditions of various colonial regimes, must surely be taken into account. This by no means excludes the applications of external models, particularly revitalization, which has generally been conceived at a fairly high degree of abstraction. Wallace, in particular, has viewed the project as one in which theory (1956c) preceded application (1970a), both logically and temporally. Although such abstract theoretical models have generally fallen out of favor in most quarters of professional anthropology, this is a pity, because without them we lack the ability to address cross-cultural data in a comparative context (see Gingrich and Fox 2002). At a historical juncture when anthropology, through models such as revitalization, has the ability to address a range of issues of central importance, an opportunity on a level that has not existed since the 1960s or possibly even World War II, we run the risk of irrelevance.[2]

Why Revitalization?

On the face of it, revitalization seems a concept whose time has come and gone (see Wallace 1956a, 1956b, 1956c, 1956d, 1958, 1970a). It dates to the 1950s and 1960s, an era when social thought tended toward the creation of formal, rule-driven constructs that attempted to account for the entire range of human behavior with reference to one or two driving principles. It attempts to achieve an explanation, rather than or in addition to an interpretation, of human behavior. Finally, it possesses the once-admired classical virtue of holism, which is often taken today as a kind of intellectual hubris. Such models, including cultural ecology, ethnoscience, structuralism, and the like, have fallen out of favor in anthropology, although they frequently turn up in other disciplines, often in transmuted form.

There are, however, very good reasons for holding onto the revitalization concept, if in some modified version. These reasons are of two sorts: heuristic and political. First, revitalization has proved a very good tool for understanding ethnohistory and contemporary cultural movements. Far from making simplistic assumptions about cultural boundaries, as did most cultural theory of the classical era, revitalization is premised on transcultural exchanges and even a form of transnationalism avant la lettre. As the chapters in this book demonstrate, chains of causality and influence transcend linguistic, regional, and national boundaries. Moreover, revitalization has application beyond the two or three famous cases drawn from American Indian history with which it is most closely associated. Here we examine cases from Oceania and North America. Beyond the scope of this collection, cases from Europe (Cohn 1970; Hobsbawm 1963), Africa (Fernandez 1978), and elsewhere (Adas 1979) may be productively studied as revitalization movements. Although it would be naive to assert that "revitalization movement" unproblematically identifies something in the social world, apart from the concept itself, it is perfectly logical—and indeed the essence of human science—to suggest that revitalization successfully models recurrent bundles of behavior that appear in diverse times and places, under similar historical and cultural conditions. While we need to keep clear the distinction between map and territory, as Bateson phrased the epistemological problem addressed by philosophers such as Whitehead and Wittgenstein, it can be very useful at times to have a map.

The second sort of reason for retaining and indeed promoting the revitalization model, the political, is perhaps less compelling but is worth making nonetheless. The retreat by cultural anthropology, over the past 30 years, from formal and empirical models—something akin to what is traditionally understood by the term *social science*—has left the field open to those with much less respect for culture as collective, symbolic, learned behavior. Most notably, sociobiologists, especially in their more recent incarnation as evolutionary psychologists and cognitive linguists, have attempted to apply neo-Darwinian explanations to questions of human behavior and culture (Pinker 1999; Thornhill and Palmer 1999). Such explanations, although vigorously challenged by those with perhaps better claim to the mantel of Darwin, tend to subsume all of culture under the umbrella of biological evolution and allegedly adaptive patterned behaviors (see Gould 2002). Many of the critiques that Boas mounted against the evolutionism of his day still apply, especially the stark fact of cultural variation, most of which is independent from environmental factors. However, this is not the place to refight old battles. The point is that the culturally and institutionally powerful role of explaining human behavior has largely been ceded to nonanthropologists, who often have a professional interest in discounting culture as a real force in shaping human existence.

The revitalization model is especially useful in this context, as it does embody the classical virtues of anthropology as social science. It is holistic; it considers material reality, for example, nutrition and ecology, alongside ideology and psychology but without privileging any particular level. It embraces both the individual and the collective, such as Handsome Lake's illness and dreams, as well as the larger cultural context of the Seneca at the turn of the century (Wallace 1970a). It is inherently comparative; we see connections across time and cultural boundaries.[3]

To embrace revitalization is not, however, to embrace all the assumptions of 1950s and 1960s positivism, which have been justly subject to devastating criticism over the past 30 years. The position of the observer, gender bias, and the politics of textual inscription are all valid issues to examine most critically. At the same time, such healthy skepticism need not devolve into the epistemological cynicism of Feyerabend (1975) regarding the ability to say anything at all about the outside world. Indeed this danger, solipsism, has been richly illustrated in the past 20 years (see Clifford 1997). Simply because it is impossible to achieve the sort of antiseptic value neutrality envisioned by Max Weber does not mean that we need either give up the enterprise entirely or foreground this dilemma itself to the near exclusion of other matters (see Geertz 1988:73–101). What this means in the context of revitalization is that we examine the concept critically, including its intellectual genealogy, which is in fact rooted in folk culture and religious beliefs, but not abandon it.

Revitalization: Pre-Theoretical Models

The concept of revitalization, for all its value as a theoretical construct, did not come simply from Anthony Wallace or from his immediate intellectual ancestors. In fact, much of the resonance it seems to have (at least for Western readers) derives from its pre-theoretical antecedents. One of the places it came from is the experience of political-religious movements, experienced and imagined in European folk culture. Numerous religiously inspired social movements have defined European and American history of the Middle Ages through the modern era—including followers of Jan Huss, the Lollards, various Puritan sects—and down to the 19th century when rural New York State was known as the "burned-over district" for spawning a variety of charismatic, revitalistic cult movements. In addition to such seemingly straightforward "religious" movements (which were all utopian and often involved the radical overturning of dominant cultural values relating to private property, sexuality, marriage, and gender roles), we find some movements, such as the Luddites, that had more obvious economic and political import (Thompson 1980:598–659). In addition, numerous nationalist movements, even predating the 19th-century heyday of nationalism, draw on an implicit revitalization teleology. The national histories of Germany, Poland, Lithuania, and Ireland, in particular, are redolent with revitalization themes (see Schama 1995). For Wallace these include "an awareness of ancient glories, of a sense of wrong and deprivation, and a dream of a golden age returned" (1965:vi). This "Arthurian" formulation is, for

Wallace, the archetype that James Mooney—an Irish American active in Fenian politics—applied, although never explicitly, to the first scholarly study of a revitalization movement, the Ghost Dance (Mooney 1965; see Moses 1984).

The Christian tradition of chiliastic prophecy, especially as it appeared in medieval Europe, provided a conceptual basis for this essential trajectory of history, moving from an imperfect present to an ideal future (or, more accurately, an ideal period out of historical time itself) that is in some way a reprise of an earlier golden age. Marx embraces this theme in his revolutionary writings (which are less frequently studied by scholars than his critical and philosophical works) and popularized it among leftist political groups in Europe and elsewhere (at the same time giving this traditional leitmotiv a nightmarish quality for the bourgeoisie).[4] In other modalities, the millennial theme persisted: both in traditional Christian discourse (largely in the guises of evangelical and Pentecostalist Protestantism, Seventh Day Adventism, and Marian Catholicism) and in the cultural transformation analyzed by Max Weber as the very "spirit" of capitalism. It contributed significantly to the sense of American exceptionalism and destiny (manifest and otherwise) that has driven modern American history.

The interconnection between folk and formal theoretical concepts has been examined in other contexts, primarily cognitive anthropology (e.g., Kay 1987; Linde 1987). It demonstrates clearly one tenet of the current postmodernist orthodoxy: there is no Archimedean point from which to stand and observe the social world. Any concepts we bring to the act of observing are already immanent in that which we observe. "Kinship" (a formal study) is a particular way of viewing kinship (a cultural practice, accompanied by a powerful ideology consisting of "folk theories") (Schneider 1980). The situation is even more complicated with respect to revitalization movements, for they are specific historical sets of events with a determinate trajectory. That is to say, the fact that such concepts exist in the colonizing culture has an undeniable effect on real historical events and their interpretations. Thus, in the case of the "cargo cult" that advertises more clearly its medial role as both explanation and the thing to be explained, as both folk culture ("cargo") and academic discourse ("cult"), the assumptions of the empowered observers (missionaries and government agents) clearly affected the outcome of whatever was going on among the natives. This is, of course, true in other cases as well, in North America, Africa, and elsewhere. In certain cases, missionaries seemed to define the movement to a large degree, such as the case of Tswana Zionism (Comaroff 1985). However, as Jean Comaroff is quick to point out, this movement, although deriving some of its symbols and ideology from abroad—indeed, it was a true transnational phenomenon among oppressed peoples—was constituted by conflicts arising out of Tswana society and its relation to the colonial enterprise. The issue here is not the degree of manifest content that derives from exogenous sources but, rather, the ends to which symbols are put in the local context.

What I am arguing here is that revitalization as a generic concept was part of a colonial worldview that was by definition shared to a certain extent by colonizer and colonized. It may be usefully described as a "cultural model" (a concept not that far from Wallace's own idea of the "mazeway"), which is actuated under certain circumstances (see Holland and Quinn 1987). It contains a prototype (e.g., the Ghost Dance, John Frum), a script, and recurrent metaphors, all of which is, of course, inflected regionally and locally and on different sides of the contact zone. This helps us to understand why the actors in these dramas seem to the remote observer really to be following a predetermined script, much more so than in nonrevitalistic encounters between colonizers and colonized.

The Aporia of Time

The particular affinity between European thought and the concept of revitalization does not necessarily undermine its value as a theoretical concept, nor does it mean that non-Western cultures could not have arrived at some form of revitalization as an indigenous solution to transcultural problems of human existence. In fact, they quite certainly did so. The assumption made here, and which, I think, underlies any cross-cultural examination of religion, is that Western theoretical discourse is but a particular modality of interpreting existential issues, which are themselves common to humankind. We must indeed be wary of simply applying Western constructs to non-Western cultures, and we must further be aware of the interpretive and pragmatic power such constructs have by virtue of their alliance with powerful institutions; but we must not make the error of assuming that any observation of similarities between Western and non-Western movements is simply an artifact of unexamined assumptions. The existence of St. Vitus Dance does not preclude the possibility of Vailaila Madness.

The common human problem of time is at the heart of revitalization movements. In all cases, they are predicated on the possibility of a transformation of mundane time and history into a return to a "Myth Time" in which key variables (demographics, ecology, organic health, morality, economics, etc.) will be restored to a desired state. This possibility reflects, most obviously, a desire to make things better, but as well it addresses the problems of temporality rooted in the human experience. On a superficial level, humans perceive a contradiction between time as a linear, irreversible process, modeled on the human life span, and cyclic processes evident in diurnal, seasonal, and annual cycles. At the same time, the human life, viewed from a broad perspective (social or cosmic), is also cyclical, for the process is repeated endlessly, and birth and death can be seen as parallel and balancing events (see Gell 1992:91–92; Munn 1992:110). Most religions resolve this contradiction by weighing in on the side of cyclicity, promising reincarnation or participation in cosmic cyclicity. Frequently, American Indian religions simply assert that individuals are "recycled" within the relevant kin group (see Mills and Slobodin 1994).

However, the aporia of time, as described first by Saint Augustine of Hippo (1961), undermines the common perception of time as either linear or cyclical. Episodic time is insufficient to comprehend temporal crises, where a "past" becomes clearly distinct from a present (Jebens 2000:187). This "epistemic break," as Foucault calls it, highlights the incompatibility of linear and cyclical temporalities and relativizes the concept of time itself. If the life world appears as unalterably and irreversibly different from a remembered past, then the possibility of cyclicity to balance linearity is called into question. In the most extreme cases, such as the postcontact era in, say, highland New Guinea or the Northwest Coast of North America, an existence that had been fairly stable for 100 generations or more was suddenly overturned.

Indeed, in the end pure time is simply unanalyzable—a conundrum that Augustine demonstrates by attempting to divide time into a series of instantaneous moments—and is fraught with both danger and possibility. What the Greeks called *chronos*, or normal time, is contrasted with *kairos*, a temporal singularity, pregnant with possibility. The possibility of what the Christian tradition terms *gnosis*, which appears in many other religious traditions as well, "presents" itself. One achieves the revelation of a transcendent temporal perspective, which relativizes the sense of time as an endless series of "nows." For the Christian gnostic, this includes the revelation of salvation; for other cultures, it likewise involves the consciousness of an "everywhen" (Eliade 1959; Puech 1957).

Certain intellectual traditions, such as Tantric Buddhism, yoga, and Australian Dreamtime, have developed such ideas more fully than others (Eliade 1957). However, it remains that this aporia of time is, at base, panhuman. Revitalization movements possess a natural appeal because of this fact. Indeed, in traditions in which temporal speculations are relatively undeveloped, one of the primary attractions of Christianity, Islam, Buddhism, or other exogenous ideologies may be that they seemingly provide solutions to this problem at the very moment that it becomes foregrounded by exogenous disruptions in the historical flow. Such ideologies may be inflected with specific technologies that appear to be useful in coping with disruptions: ghost shirts, means of obtaining cargo, or, indeed missionary-brought literacy and numeracy as a means to societal reform.

When missionaries have appeared on the scene offering these new ideologies and technologies, indigenous cosmological systems were frequently—indeed, in many cases, necessarily—under stress. The very existence of Europeans may have undermined native cosmology, as in highland New Guinea, although at the same time providing a stimulus for creative reformulation (Brutti 2000:104). In other cases, such as among the 19th-century Heiltsuks, missionaries have used sophisticated means to expose weaknesses in traditional practices and ideologies, which are increasingly seen as ineffective and outmoded. One of the main sources of missionary power is their presence at a critical juncture when indigenous theories of temporality seemed no longer to be valid. Time is embodied in both practice and narrative. As traditional Heiltsuk "seasonal rounds" were curtailed in favor of more lucrative forms of wage labor and as, simultaneously, cosmological and genealogical narratives were relativized by missionary-inspired accounts of the past, one could say that the traditional Heiltsuk temporality was effectively in a state of crisis (Harkin 1997a).

There are thus two poles to the concept of revitalization. On the one hand, it fulfills a human psychic need to cope with the basic temporal aporia common to all people but which becomes foregrounded in times of crisis. On the other, it is inflected by specific cultural and historical forms. To focus solely on the former is to run the risk of ignoring the ethnohistorical specificity. To focus solely on the latter is to ignore the similarities of such movements across time and place and their rooted-

ness in certain recurring human dilemmas, albeit ones that are particularly prone to be felt during historically parlous times.[5] The preferred
interpretive strategy is thus dialogic, as the phenomenology is as well. It
is facile to dismiss the revitalization model because it may be applied to
different sets of events among radically different peoples. At the same
time, there is indeed danger in reification of the model, confusing map
with territory and applying it willy-nilly to an uncontrolled range of
phenomena.

Revitalization as Dialogue

Contemporary scholars differ on whether they choose to employ revitalization explicitly or not. Thus, a recent volume (Stewart and Strathern
2000) examines millenarian movements without reference to revitalization. In the same journal, an American anthropologist has employed the
model to describe a millenarian movement among the Navajo (Schwarz
1998). This is a question of interpretive choice and sociology of knowledge. British- and European-trained anthropologists working outside
North America tend to eschew revitalization, whereas American anthropologists are more likely to employ it; historians, generally, are less likely
than anthropologists to use it. Obviously, the contributors to the current
book are at least comfortable with the concept. The point remains, however, that the social movements in question (e.g., "y2k millenarianism"
in New Guinea) fall within the parameters of the revitalization model
but are not thereby substantively "revitalization movements" (neither
are they "revitalization movements" because they have not been called
that). Rather, they are religiously inspired social movements that share
a "family resemblance," in Wittgenstein's terms, with other such movements in other times and places. I believe that revitalization is the most
sophisticated theoretical lens through which to view such movements.

However, it is difficult, given the constraints of English, with its
prodigious production of substantives, to talk about something without
seeming to confer on it a certain materiality (see arguments over the
status of "culture"). With this caveat in mind, what is interesting is
our ability to talk about "revitalization movements" at all. What is it
that constitutes this family resemblance, which makes such phenomena
recognizable and referable to social scientists and other observers? A
basic condition that allows us to speak comparatively of revitalization
movements is the fact of their transcultural and transhistorical similarity.
A diagnostic list of features is always open to revision, but tentatively we

could say that they do share certain core features: millenarian expectations, prophecy, and crises in key dimensions of social life (e.g., demographics, ecology, core values, autonomy) that make them recognizable.
(Although frequently nativistic, revitalization movements often are not.)
Moreover, they crop up at a similar point in the process of colonial
"articulation," when relations with the colonial power are beginning to
be routinized and bureaucratized. And, obviously, they are recognized as
similar phenomena, the awareness of which seems to reside in the collective unconscious of colonial agents. That is, they are given a quiddity or
"thingness" that allows for correct reference, meaningful propositional
utterances, and so forth. However, colonial authorities, including missionaries, administrators, and informal agents, did not simply replace
indigenous ideologies with foreign ones. Revitalization movements, and
other engagements with colonialism, represent a dynamic attempt to
make sense of the world in new ways not fully present in either donor
tradition.

A truly ethnohistorical approach will examine the dialogic space between the two cultures, their relationality, rather than the internal dynamics of a single culture. I think that cargo cults did exist, although
certainly the descriptions of them by colonial agents or anthropologists
are not to be mistaken for objective accounts. Indeed, an ethnohistorical
Heisenberg effect is integral to understanding such dynamic historical processes. In part, the actions of the cultists were shaped by the
expectations that colonial agents had of them, and these expectations
themselves became self-fulfilling prophecies. As the actions of individual
actors were comprehended and interpreted within a regional, multi-
cultural context, these events would come to conform more closely to
the dominant interpretive paradigm. These interpreted events would
feed back into the arena of action, affecting the key actors' next moves.
This dialogic approach to ethnohistory, which I have developed more
fully elsewhere (Harkin 1997b), overcomes the rather questionable separation between historical fact and interpretation. Rather, it recognizes
that humans are always already making sense of what they see and hear
and that this sense-making activity is inextricably intertwined with the
actions they see and hear.

We should indeed examine the genealogy of the tropes in question
("cargo cult," "rebellion," even "mutiny" but not "revitalization," which
is an ex post facto social science category). Thus, for Kaplan (1995),
"cargo cult" is a powerful trope kept alive by the culture of colonialism.

That is, we must look to interoffice memos and personal correspondence, as well as the formal literature of colonialism in authors such as Haggard and Kipling, to understand the ideological apparatus employed by the colonial officials. However, to examine this line of evidence to the exclusion of other, equally rewarding ones seems to invert and repeat the errors of an earlier anthropology that looked exclusively at the culture of the native while bracketing that of the colonial.

The concept of cargo cult or Ghost Dance thus functions as a medial term between the two cultures, one to which both sides bring their culturally specific expectations and through which they reach a common, if often tragic, understanding of an evolving social practice. The semiotic process is essentially that described by C. S. Peirce (1998) in which a sign is first perceived as a singularity and then in comparison to other similar events and is finally conceived of and agreed to be a token of a type. The typification of a series of events as "cargo cult" or "Ghost Dance" may misrepresent the reality of the social practice, but over time, through manipulation of expectations and self-fulfilling prophecy, praxis tends to become deformed by the typification. For example, the Lakota version of the Ghost Dance, which famously became much more militant than the Numu prototype, became such largely in response to the expectations that whites on the northern Plains had for a "pagan" religiously inspired rebellion. Images of massacres (which were always in large part projections onto the Other of the violence of the frontier imagination) defined the movement in advance as a violent uprising. This ensured a substantial and aggressive military presence, which in turn empowered the more militant Lakota, which further provoked the military. Such interactions need not proceed in purely schismogenic fashion, but they are always the product of encounters between culturally defined sets of expectations. This, indeed, seems to be the sine qua non of revitalization movements, that they are defined in the dialogic space between cultures. Although they may very well draw on indigenous prophetic traditions, they are given their characteristic form only in the interplay between cultures, usually colonial and indigenous ones, and meanings.

To borrow from an example I have already cited, the Heiltsuks underwent a period of rapid demographic and cultural change during the last quarter of the 19th century (Harkin 1997a). Among the consequences of this change is an inevitable shift in their mythico-historical praxis in the wake of certain irrevocable breaks with the past. A temporality, in which the Myth Time appeared as always at the same remove from a present that recycled personages and forces from more recent history, was shattered by events that suggested irreversible transformations. These events were accompanied by exogenous theories of temporality embodied in evangelical Methodism and petit bourgeois ideologies of commerce and labor. These new theories seemed to be borne out in real events and to provide the key to understanding and mastering new social arrangements, and so they gained credibility among the Heiltsuks. At the same time, Heiltsuks found it possible to incorporate such ideological novelties within traditional mythico-historical frameworks. Thus, the encounter with Europeans was seen as a type of mythological encounter, and the new forms of knowledge acquired from them were glossed as equivalent to modalities of "supernatural" power acquired from nonhuman beings. Although it may stretch the revitalization model almost to the breaking point to suggest this, it is not unreasonable to see the Heiltsuk adoption of a rather orthodox Methodism as a form of revitalization, for it was clearly treated as a form of supernatural power. Moreover, it was, like previous intervention of the sacred into human affairs, timed to address current needs and problems of human beings.

Although lacking certain characteristic features of revitalization, such as nativism and even, on the level of explicit ideology, syncretism, the Heiltsuk experience in postcontact British Columbia is instructive to those who wish to extend the revitalization model. The experience of the Heiltsuks, while unique, is more similar to a broad spectrum of aboriginal cultures encountering Europeans and forging a "vernacular Christianity" than were the more famous and spectacular instances of indigenous religious movements that we have tended exclusively to view as "revitalization" (see Barker 1998). As even among the latter there are both external and internal influences, the difference between Ghost Dance and conversion to vernacular Christianity may be one of degree rather than kind. Both arise from a sense of temporal and historical crisis; something utterly new is happening in the world, and traditional means of dealing with gradual change (e.g., mortuary rites) are no longer adequate. What ensues arises out of a dialogical context in which the world is fundamentally re-horizoned.

Beyond Deprivation

As several contributors to this book (Lepowsky [ch. 1], Martin [ch. 2], McMullen [ch. 12]) argue, the revitalization paradigm has become almost exclusively associated with "deprivation," as Aberle (1959, 1982) has called it. That is, the typical case involves a group declining in political power, wealth, well-being, population, or, usually, a combination of these that develops a movement out of a bricolage of its own cultural materials, with the explicit purpose being to eliminate or at least exclude the threatening dominant group. The archetype is the militant Lakota version of the Ghost Dance of 1890. And yet even this was derived from Wovoka's message, which was accommodationist and almost Gandhian in its nonviolence (Hittman 1997). Wallace himself (1970a) emphasizes syncretism and accommodation in his treatment of Handsome Lake, which remains the single best study of a revitalization movement. Similarly, the Navajo, who rejected the Ghost Dance, developed the syncretistic religious form in peyotism, which was, according to Aberle (1982) at least, caused by the deprivation of the 19th and early 20th centuries, from Kit Carson to stock reduction.

Certainly, most of the examples in this book involve some degree of relative deprivation. Part of the problem with using this as a diagnostic category is that it is subject to ethnocentric interpretation. It is not enough to assume that aboriginal groups faced with European material culture suffered a "crisis of rising expectations" (although clearly some did); rather, it is necessary to examine, as does Aberle, core cultural values (the size and well-being of livestock herds) and their trajectory within a given historical period.

Beyond the question of exactly what variables should constitute the basis for an analysis of deprivation, there is the question of the limiting nature of a focus on deprivation itself. As the historian Robin Fisher (1977) has provocatively declared, the Northwest Coast in the 19th century is better seen through the lens of an "enrichment thesis." At the time of intense European colonization, aboriginal tribes were drawing on new wealth and technology to create a finer, more monumental, and more extensive art. However, one must point out that at the same time they suffered decimation of population and increasing impotence vis-à-vis Euro-Canadian society. Perhaps such a topsy-turvy world was ripe for revitalization movements. However, few of the classic variety arose, and there were none with the regional presence of the Ghost Dance (but see Spier 1935). Indeed, this paucity of classic revitalization movements is itself a good reason to view indigenized Christianity as a type of revitalization, for we know that historical conditions were favorable (Barnett 1957; Harkin 1993; Miller 1984; Usher 1974).

Several chapters in this book apply revitalization to such nonclassic social phenomena (Lepowsky [ch. 1], Poyer [ch. 5], Carucci [ch. 9], Henry [ch. 11], McMullen [ch. 12]). Should we accept these interpretations, despite the fact that deprivation is not always clearly present? Joel Martin (ch. 2) offers us a way to interpret revitalization more broadly. For him, deprivation is only one possible state of relations between aboriginal groups and colonial societies. Others include parity and ascendancy. What is significant for our purposes is the dynamic that defines the relation between the two. It is movement between one state and another, rather than the absolute state, that will stimulate revitalization. Thus, a movement from deprivation to parity or ascendancy may provoke a revitalization, just as the reverse trajectory did. This conception allows us to include contemporary phenomena, such as Mashentucket Pequot gaming and invention of tradition (McMullen [ch. 12]) and Samoan massage and ethnomedicine (Henry [ch. 11]). It seems very much the state of things at the beginning of the 21st century that aboriginal groups are rising to positions of equality and in a few cases superiority through land claims, gaming, and political and constitutional processes, just as it was the case at the end of the 19th century that such groups were in decline. Thus, while deprivation works for most historic cases of revitalization, we would expect it to be less and less relevant in the present. That is not to say that deprivation, especially economic deprivation, does not continue to exist in many aboriginal communities or, indeed, that classic revitalization movements are entirely a thing of the past. The Seneca longhouse religion, peyotism, and even the Ghost Dance persist to the present in some form, while neoclassic forms such as the sweat lodge have arisen recently (Bucko 1998). However, a more catholic conception of revitalization, with an awareness that it marks not necessarily deprivation but simply change in the social matrix, will allow anthropologists and historians to continue to find it a meaningful and useful concept.

Revitalization and Complexity

One possible weakness of traditional revitalization theory is its reliance on a linear, stochastic model of social process. As the historian Randolph Roth (1992) points out, Wallace, in his analysis of the Handsome Lake movement and the Second Great Awakening, presents a simplified model that lacks adequate feedback mechanisms and reflexivity. Wallace's model, like most social science models, draws from outmoded classical mechanical and scientific theory. Roth proposes, instead, to employ a reflexive model based on nonlinear mathematics, "chaos theory," and advanced studies of phenomena such as magnetism and autocatalytic chemical processes. The essential advantage gained by employing such a model is that it disaggregates elements that undoubtedly interact in ways that are crucial to the outcome of the process. Thus, rather than looking at societies or cultures as organic wholes, systems in steady states of equilibrium and disequilibrium that strive to attain new states of equilibrium, we might examine the "butterfly effect" of microsociological events in determining outcomes of the process as a whole. Thus, in Roth's example, the deterioration of a marriage leading to the suicide of the wife in early-19th-century Vermont led to the rejection of a revival movement by an entire community. Similarly, some of the contingencies in the life of Wovoka as described by Hittman (1997) can be seen as crucial to the "success" of the Ghost Dance movement in the Plains.

A further point made by Roth is that such systems may exist in several different states of equilibrium, as well as chaotic states of "excitability." Systems reach threshold levels that propel them into new states. Just as the beating of a butterfly's wing in China may produce a hurricane in the Caribbean, the addition or subtraction of a single element may alter the state of the system. In more commonsense terms, we speak of "ripple effects," although this fails to capture the "cross-catalytic" effects of the system, as Roth calls them—that is, the potentially endless series of reactions that may be produced by the presence of a certain element. In Lin Poyer's study of failed revitalization (ch. 5), we can see, by contrast, how the removal of certain features shut down a fairly widespread movement.

Because the essential elements in the system are individual persons, Roth sees demography as the key variable in understanding systemic transformations. Just as pumping an element through a self-contained vessel may trigger chemical catalysis, so the "processing" of persons through society constitutes the background conditions of the cultural system. If the rate of throughput increases, through either excessive mortality or excessive fertility, new states of equilibrium and excitement can be produced. This coincides with Russell Thornton's (1986) conclusion that demographic renewal is the object of the Ghost Dance. According to Thornton, the 1890 Ghost Dance occurred at the demographic nadir for almost all the participating tribes. That is, populations rebounded soon after the revitalization movement.

Roth's critiques are quite reasonable, although they have the dis-advantage of being rather arcane to the nonscientist. However, one is forced to ask how they may be operationalized. It seems extremely un-likely that any social process could be recorded with such precision as to have a complete enough picture to meet Roth's criteria. If potentially any social interaction, be it a chance encounter or casual comment, could set the system off in a new state of equilibrium or excitement, then it is quite likely that we would miss the precise datum we need to understand the process. This is doubly true in the case of ethnohistory, where we are at several removes from the events themselves. Moreover, even in the cases Roth cites—the Vermont suicide and a sex scandal in New Hampshire that seemingly had the opposite effect on the community's adoptions of the religious revival—we cannot escape the question of interpretation. What makes a microevent the sociological equivalent of a beating butterfly wing can only be approached retrospectively, by which time it has been embedded in the consciousness of the community in a deterministic fashion. Is it not equally possible that the events Roth cites are in fact "epitomizing events," as Fogelson (1984) calls them? That is, rather that actually being the trigger for the changes in the system, they become symbolic of it. Indeed, if we asked members of the New Hampshire community where the sordid case of incest and forced prostitution occurred why they had participated in the revival, most 1830s informants would tell us that they did so because of this case of extravagant moral corruption. However, this probably constituted at best a single factor in individual decisions to become "born again." At the same time it became a convenient symbolic vehicle to address the issue, especially to outsiders. Moreover, the entire work of narrative creation did not occur within the community but, rather, in the regional mass media, which surely knew a good story when it saw one. The com-munity in this case is as much the imagined one as the experienced one (see Anderson 1983). Thus, it is rather naive to assume that we can put a finger on a specific determinate cause of a systemic change, even (or perhaps especially) if we are told that it is the cause. While introducing complexity at the level of analysis, Roth embraces simplicity at the level of causation.

This applies especially to the demographic argument that Roth and Thornton make. I think it is clear that sharp demographic trends, either positive or negative, can have transformative effects on the sociocultural system. Indeed, classic structural-functionalist anthropologists viewed demographic changes as the major threat to a presumed equilibrium state. However, to view demographics as a necessary or even sufficient condition for revitalization is clearly mistaken. In addition to the inherent weakness of monocausal explanatory models in social science, we can point to at least some cases of revitalization movements in the absence of demographic crisis. In Melanesia, for instance, most such movements occurred without population decimation. Rather, the crisis existed in the cosmological realm, especially with regard to ancestral spirits. This extension of the social world into the cosmos was shaken by the presence of European and Australian whites who resembled ancestral spirits. Moreover, the increase in the flow of goods, not persons, was destabilizing. Thornton is undoubtedly correct when he says that revitalization represents a reasonable attempt, within the context of specific cultures, to address crisis situations; that is, they are not "hysterical" reactions, as he believes Kehoe (1989) views them, but they need not be "about" demographics primarily or even at all. That said, the issue of demographics is not innocent; rather, it lies at the heart of differing interpretations on different sides of the contact zone. What was taken to be a "death knell" of traditional Plains Indian society and culture by whites was recast as a turning point by native people. But, again, this is a question of interpretation, not causation.

Roth's scientistic model, while introducing greater complexity into revitalization theory, seems to get us past only some of the problems of reflexivity. For surely the most important form of reflexivity in social process is interpretive, not causal. Especially when we are dealing with questions of religious belief, which are subject to endless degrees of hermeneutic activity, and especially as most religious beliefs, having a strong counterfactual element, are in constant need of apologia, it seems almost superfluous to talk about exogenous causal factors at all. That is, the relevant dynamic process is largely an ideological one, in which interpretations and reinterpretations of doctrine are both the stimulus and the response for systemic changes.

Interpretation and Explanation in Revitalization Theory
Attempts to apply scientific concepts such as nonlinearity to human culture are valuable, especially for their critiques of existing models. Ultimately, however, any description of revitalization movements or any other patterned behavior is dependent on good empirical data and a methodology that does not allow a preexisting model simply to be im-

posed on a particular situation. This is contrary to the critical spirit of anthropology and history. Although caricatured as the "not in my village" syndrome, it is integral to the ethnographic perspective that theoretical models are subject to stringent criticism before they are applied to a specific set of data. It is a tribute to the value of the revitalization model that many distinguished anthropologists and historians, such as the contributors to the present book, are willing to use it, at least as a departure point, for their examinations of ethnohistorical data.

In the end I—and, I believe, most of my colleagues contributing to this collection—would opt for a type of critical interpretation augmented by a loose sort of explanation. Most of the present would follow Geertz's (1973) dictum that the most scientific (although not scientistic) approach to the study of human society is interpretation based on an immersion in the culture (or cultures, as well as times) under consideration: what he calls "thick description." At the same time, one must be ever aware of the transcultural and transnational processes operating, to appreciate the more-than-local quality to the encounter between, say, a Moroccan Jew and French colonial authorities (Geertz 1973:7–10). Moreover, we must be open to seeing certain regularities and commonalities across time and place. As James Peacock has aphoristically put it, anthropologists must "think relationally, act uniquely" (Strathern 2002:xv). The events, behaviors, and processes we observe in local contexts are always conditioned by transcultural and transnational factors. There is really no such thing as the cultural isolate, and where it appears that there is, this apparent isolation is itself a cultural project.

Revitalization movements, which may apparently isolate (in the case of nativistic movements) or connect cultures and groups, are simply one of the most obvious and obviously transcultural mechanisms by which groups attempt to articulate with the outside world. At the same time, such articulations have profound resonance on the individual, who feels threatened and insecure in a changing world and who may fall back into a contemplation of the nature of history and time, to the temporal aporia. This is particularly the case of the prophets, such as Wovoka or Handsome Lake, who experience ecstatic religious states outside the normal flow of time. Revitalization, by virtue of its ability to model characteristic responses to such situations, becomes, in a loose sense, an explanation for them.

What we can finally say about revitalization is that it has undergone transformations and accretions and that it will certainly undergo more in the future. Anthropologists have been, in my opinion, too quick to discard theories that have certain remediable problems, rather than to experiment with, play with, and "riff off" them. I hope that the present book will demonstrate the value of such an exercise.

Notes

1. One could argue, alternatively, that these revitalistic phenomena, although predating European contact, are nevertheless products of contact zones involving different aboriginal peoples and cultures.

2. I am very much in agreement with the spirit, if not entirely with the letter, of the recent book *Anthropology, by Comparison* edited by Andre Gingrich and Richard Fox (2002). They, like me, call for a "revitalization" of past theoretical paradigms and more attention to macro- and comparative perspectives. They also place this call within the framework of a politically aware public anthropology.

3. One example of the applicability of the revitalization concept to an issue familiar to most American readers would be the political, cultural, and economic synthesis achieved in the mid- to late 1990s. The "new Democrat" policies of Bill Clinton—curtailing welfare, fighting crime, balancing the budget—combined with the new economy of the Internet and high technology gave the modal American voter the sense of combining an idealized past and future, the crime rates and unemployment figures of the early 1960s and the boundless optimism of an approaching millennium. This came in the wake of a period of prolonged "malaise," as Jimmy Carter called it, characterized by steadily increasing crime rates and other indicators of social ill. The political dynamic of this period is familiar to students of revitalization. Opposed by both conservative and radical forces (which categories crosscut accepted ideological lines), the movement achieved a stable consensus that seemingly eclipsed previously sharp debates. Whether we view this movement, from the postelection and post–September 11 perspective, as a death knell of liberalism or as its rebirth is, obviously, a matter of interpretation, not to mention political inclination.

4. Karl Popper (1966) speaks confusingly of "historicism" in Western philosophy, by which he means the belief in a telos determining historical events. Although I share Popper's view of Marx (in his prophetic guise, at least) as being tied to an ancient millennial tradition, I disagree rather strongly with his assessment of such beliefs as antithetical to an "open society," as he calls it. Indeed, if we take the United States to be a model of such an open society (which is, in an ethnographically informed view, a rather meaningless concept), then it is quite clear that the prevalence of "historicist" ideology is quite pronounced and probably greater here than in totalitarian and formerly totalitarian societies (see

Bloom 1992). As with any great "us versus them" dualism, Popper's is guilty of great distortions.

5. It should be remembered that St. Augustine himself was the product of a period of turmoil and decline in the late Roman Empire. His awareness of the problematic nature of time was certainly conditioned by these historical forces (see Wills 1999).

1. INDIAN REVOLTS AND CARGO CULTS

Ritual Violence and Revitalization in California
and New Guinea

Maria Lepowsky

Resistance is a word that has been overused in recent years. But it properly describes the militantly anticolonial and sometimes violent aspects of North American prophetic movements, Pacific Island cargo cults, and revitalization movements in other parts of the world. For almost five decades, anthropologists, historians, and religious scholars have deployed Anthony F. C. Wallace's term *revitalization* to categorize a diverse array of past and current movements in non-Western societies undergoing catastrophic social change, including "nativistic" political and religious movements, millenarian cults, and cultural revivals.

Ritual violence—symbolic or corporeal, religiously validated by gods or spirits, old or newly recognized—is often a key element in revitalization and oppositional politico-religious movements. But it has received less analytic attention than it deserves. Anthropologists studying Pacific Island cargo cults, for example, have long been preoccupied instead by what Ralph Linton (1943) calls magical nativism: the supernatural motifs, syncretic inspirations, and ritual strategies outlined in these prophetic movements. Like members of the public in colonial and postcolonial metropoles, we have been fascinated by cargo cults' explicit emphases on appropriation of European technologies and wealth by magical means and their prophecies of events such as return voyages of ancestor spirits to the land of the living. The most important element of cargo cults, though, is their prophecy of a utopian, millennial future in which the living and returned dead share both indigenous abundance and European power—without the Europeans.

Anthropologists have often underemphasized the overtly revolutionary means and goals of cargo cults, their close connection not just to revitalization movements but to other oppositional political movements, uprisings, and revolutions, failed or otherwise. Cargoistic and other prophetic movements are strategies of cultural transformation, a range of oppositional and potentially violent forms of what Marshall Sahlins calls "the indigenization of modernity" (1993:21). The classic articles by Linton (1943) on nativistic movements and Wallace (1956c) on revitalization, for example, make no explicit mention of violence against the dominant society or colonial power or of its forcible expulsion. But these were often prominent strategies—prophesied and implied if not actualized—in the Pacific, North America, and elsewhere. Colonial administrators in New Guinea made no such oversight, imprisoning and even executing cultists, whom they explicitly recognized as a danger to colonial order.

Cargo cults emphasize magical violence and ritualized attack. This is no surprise, for Melanesian warfare is founded on magical potency and prayers to ancestors, place spirits, and other supernatural beings, by either warrior or ritual specialist. The cargo cult prophet assumes and then transforms preexisting cultural roles: war magician and ritual expert. Comparable traditions of prophecy and ritual violence have long existed in North America, the most famous being the Ghost Dance (Mooney 1965; see also Harkin [ch. 6]). In fact, millennial prophetic movements inspiring ritual violence have erupted around the world for several centuries among ethnic minorities and conquered peoples, as I show later.

There is a continuum of what I am labeling ritual violence. It ranges from magical attack intended to subvert the will of another to rituals enjoined by prophecy to usher in the apocalypse, magical attacks that practitioner and victim think lead to death, and sorcery attacks that include the use of poison. It continues with the corporeal assaults of warfare when warrior and weapon are ritually blessed or decorated to invoke divine power and convey invulnerability. Prophecies predicting the departure of European colonials or settlers may advocate or foretell any of these forms of ritual violence; many Europeans, perceiving the world differently, acknowledge only physical attacks as forms of violence.

In the Southwest Pacific, Islanders, by contrast, explicitly recognize magic, sorcery, and witchcraft as ritual attacks, the subversion of another's autonomous will and bodily integrity, whether by love or by war magic. Indigenous Californians have similarly recognized the potentially destructive powers of shamanic and other ritual attacks. In Alta California, Spanish military and religious authorities occasionally identified indigenous prophecies and related ceremonies as threats to colonial hegemony. In other cases they ignored or were oblivious to them until they sparked armed insurrection. Still other times they were unaware of the religious inspirations that triggered uprisings. In colonial New Guinea, British and Australian officers recognized prophecies and magical attacks—those they learned of—as subversion. They invoked indigenous spirits, objects, and rituals to sow fear in enemies, potentially unifying indigenous groups and threatening colonial social order and control. Classifying sorcery as a crime, colonial officers, for example, imprisoned its most notorious practitioners from the islands of southeastern New Guinea, and they hanged the leaders of cargoistic uprisings that led to ritual attacks on Europeans.

In this chapter I explore ritual violence, anticolonial resistance, and their implications for rethinking revitalization by comparing and contextualizing two little-known cases, one from North America and one from the Pacific. The first is an Indian uprising over two hundred years ago near the Pueblo of Los Angeles, and the second is a series of cargoistic revelations and revolts unfolding in the islands of southeastern New Guinea over the course of the 20th century. As an ethnographer of Pacific islands long roiled by cargoistic prophecies, more recently beginning research on California, when I encountered stories of the revolt at Mission San Gabriel I found its key motifs, events, and historical contexts strangely familiar.

The Toypurina Uprising: Mission San Gabriel, Province of the Californias, New Spain, 1785

When Spanish interrogators at Mission San Gabriel asked Toypurina, a 24-year-old woman and a shaman, "Didn't you come here armed to kill the Padres and the soldiers?" she answered instead, her interpreter said, with the grievance that generated the revolt of 1785: "She states that it is true that she sent chief Tomasajaquichi to persuade the Christians not to believe the Padres, but only her and that she advised him that it was because she was angry with the Padres and with everyone at the Mission because we are living here in their land" (Archivo General de la Nación 1785–87). Mission San Gabriel Arcangel was founded in 1771. Its original location (Misión Viejo, Old Mission) was a few miles farther south, where the San Gabriel River and the Rio Hondo wind near each other in the marshlands between two hills, a spot now known as Whittier Narrows. The mission complex was relocated in 1774 or 1775 to the fertile, oak-dotted uplands above the rivers, which were far less flood prone; better for growing corn, beans, and wheat; and closer to indigenous communities, sources of potential converts and labor for the Spanish (Bancroft 1886, vol. 1:179–181; Johnston 1962:129–131). Two Franciscan friars, guarded by a contingent of soldiers commanded from the presidio at San Diego 100 miles down the coast, controlled the adobe-walled compound.

Most of the people whose land they were on kept their distance in the early years. A man who in 1774 was given the Christian name of Nicolas José, later a leader of the 1785 revolt, was only the 87th to accept baptism. The people at first thought that the Spanish might be spirits. Still, they largely rejected the radical change in belief, autonomy, and subsistence that they were offered, for some years compelling women who gave birth to light-skinned offspring to kill them and go through a lengthy purification ceremony. But by October 1785, more than 1,270 Indians had been baptized, double the number just two years earlier. The majority—those who had neither fled nor died of European diseases—lived at or near the mission, spending their days working for the padres and soldiers (Bancroft 1886, vol. 1:459; Heizer 1968; Mission San Gabriel 1774–85).

A small pueblo (town), its name later shortened to Los Angeles, was founded in 1781 by Spanish-speaking mestizos from what is now northern Mexico, who walked from Mission San Gabriel a final nine miles toward the ocean to settle on the west bank of the Los Angeles River. Mission and pueblo lay in the center of the territory of the most culturally influential ethnolinguistic group in Southern California. They later became known as the Gabrielino or Gabrieleno—from the Spanish Gabrieleño—after the mission (Bancroft 1886, vol. 1:333; Bean and Smith 1978; Kroeber 1925; McCawley 1996). Many of their descendants now call themselves Tongva.[1]

Lieutenant Pedro Fages, the governor of Alta California, reported from the provincial capital at Monterey on December 5, 1785, to his commanding officer, Comandante General Jose Antonio Rengel in Arispe, Chihuahua: "Since on last November 5, I was advised by the Comandante of the Presidio of San Diego that the Christian and pagan Indians of the Mission of San Gabriel, having been deceived by a superstitious pagan woman, went on the night of October 25 to the home of the missionary Padres inspired to kill them, believing that the soldiers were already dead because of the said instigator; but upon the corporal of the guard learning this prepared a defense, and taking advantage of the situation, gathered his men to frighten them, such that neither side used arms, and then the Indians, seeing they had been deceived, fled in fear." Busy with the "regular ship from the Philippines," which had first called at San Diego and from there brought reports of the affray to Monterey, Governor Fages did not depart on the 13-day overland ride to San Gabriel until December 14. He stopped en route at the presidio of Santa Barbara to pick up Sergeant Jose Ignacio Olivera, who later interrogated the four accused ringleaders. Meanwhile, at San Gabriel a few days after the revolt soldiers rounded up 16 Indian men near the mission. They were held in chains in the soldiers' barracks, part of the mission compound. One of them was Toypurina's brother.

Toypurina came from a nearby *ranchería*, written as Jachivit (Japcha-vit, Jaichivit) by the Spanish, which lay in a lower canyon of the steep San Gabriel Mountains north of the mission. Her brother and father were chiefs (*capitanes*).[2] Toypurina was "accused of having been the instigator [*inductadora*]" of the revolt, wrote Fages. One of the other alleged leaders was Tomajasaquichi (also written by the Spanish as Temesajaquichi), chief of Juyuvit, possibly meaning Tujubit—from Tuhunga (Tujunga in Spanish)—some 15 miles northwest of the mission, where Big Tujunga Wash, a tributary of the Los Angeles River, leaves the San Gabriel front range (cf. Johnston 1962:126). Ajiyivi (also written as Ajillivit) was the third alleged leader and chief of Jajamovit (from Hahamongna), "three leagues" from the mission, northwest at the base of the San Gabriel Mountains by the gorge of the Arroyo Seco, the Los Angeles River's most important tributary.

The fourth of the accused "heads" of the insurrection, Nicolas José, a 33-year-old married man from Sibapet (Sibangna or Shevaanga, just southeast of Mission San Gabriel), was the only neophyte—or baptized Indian. He lived at the mission itself, and his indigenous name is un-known. He had, he admitted, instigated an earlier, failed uprising at San Gabriel in 1779 and had been imprisoned and warned. Nicolas José and the other three told the Spanish in 1785 that he had helped spread Toypurina's message, inciting Christian Indians to revolt, and that he was responsible for coordinating the armed attack. He testified, his soldier/translator said, that "he was angry with the Padres and the corporal since they would not allow them to have their dances and pagan abuses [*bailes y abusos gentiles*]." And he said that "he himself went to help the pagan Toypurina and gave her beads in order that she call the other pagans, and that he gathered the Christians."

Temejasaquichi "stated that he came in a fighting spirit . . . the pagan Indian woman deceived him into coming, and that the Christian Nicolas urged him to act." Sergeant Olivera writes, "Nicolas added that the others were there out of fear of Toypurina, whom they held to be very wise, and who could kill them by will alone." The shaman Toypurina, unarmed, accompanied the warriors, she testified, "because the Indian Nicolas José persuaded her, she came with the rest because they gave her beads, and she came to inspire them that they might have the heart to fight."

The Spanish *asesor* (legal counsel) in Chihuahua, Pedro Galindo Navarro, reviewing the charges and recommending sentences for the *comandante general* in 1787, notes that Toypurina was "known among her people as one of the most learned and wise [*la mas instruida y Sabia*]" and that she was given "beads and other trifles [*Abalorios y otras bagatelas*]" by Nicolas José. It was Tongva custom to give strings of marine Olivella shells, or Olivella shell disc beads, to shamans when requesting their help in healing or divination. Shell necklaces were also presented to allies before commencing a joint attack. They were a major item of exchange by coastal peoples in trading networks that archaeological evidence shows had extended as far inland as New Mexico for at least 1,000 years and linked most of Southern California for 5,000 years or more (e.g., Bean and Smith 1978; Boscana 1978:69; Kroeber 1925; McCawley 1996). It is likely, then, that Olivella shell disc necklaces and related ritual wealth items were the "beads" presented to Toypurina. Among Tongva and their neighbors, shamans had great influence through their powers to communicate with spirits, divine the future, heal the sick, kill enemies by magical attack, and transform themselves into grizzly bears and other potent beings. Along with chiefly families with whom they overlapped, shamans constituted a political and ritual elite in coastal Southern California (Bean and Smith 1978; Heizer 1968; Kroeber 1925).

Inspired by Toypurina's prophecies, warriors from more than eight rancherías joined the attack on the mission. Five bands came from the mountains ("Sierras"), three from the valleys, and various others from elsewhere, Nicolas José testified. Toypurina said that six rancherías came with their capitanes (chiefs) and that others came alone. They carried bows and arrows. Were these newly made in accordance with prophecy? The warriors and their weapons were likely consecrated by shamans, according to custom—perhaps some or all by Toypurina herself.

This was a regional uprising, involving at least two dialect areas of Tongva. It may also have included other ethnolinguistic groups: Maringayam (Morongo), Kitanemuk, Tataviam (Alliklik), or Vanyume, collectively known locally since the late 18th century as "Serranos" (mountain dwellers). Speakers of four other Takic languages, they came from the north, northwest, and east of the Los Angeles Basin: the eastern San Gabriel Mountains, the San Bernardino Mountains still farther east, the transverse mountain ranges north of the San Fernando Valley, and adjacent desert canyons over the mountains (King and Blackburn 1978; Kroeber 1925:611–619). Nicolas José's reference to mountain rancherías is ambiguous. There were Kitanemuk neophytes at Mission San Gabriel (the Franciscans later recorded their language as "Guiguitamcar") (Engelhardt 1927:97; Kroeber 1925:621). Tongva mission runaways and unconverted Tongva whose valleys had been taken over by the Spanish for wheat growing and cattle grazing fled in the 1780s and later to remote mountain canyons and desert oases to live among Serranos, outside the effective zone of mission control. They and their hosts could well have heard the 1785 Toypurina prophecy and joined the attack.

Settlements whose names appear in the Spanish interrogation of 1785–86 as sending warriors to attack Mission San Gabriel are Jaichivit (home to Toypurina and her brother), Jajamovit (Hahamongna), and Juvit or Juyubit, all at the base of the mountains or in their lower canyons, as well as Sibapet and Azucsavit on the alluvial plain. Other places go unnamed. The homes of the warriors, thus, at minimum covered a territory stretching more than 40 miles, from present-day Tujunga, against the mountains north of the San Fernando Valley, to Azusa in the eastern San Gabriel Valley. Inhabitants from each ranchería show up in mission baptismal records—and burial records—of the period. Some of the combatants' relatives and former neighbors were living at Mission San Gabriel under Spanish control.

As Governor Fages confirms, Toypurina's prophecy was, in part, that the warriors, slipping over the mission walls, would find the soldiers already dead from her shamanic power to kill at a distance. Then the Franciscan padres, undefended by the soldiers' guns and the mission cannon, could easily be killed by the warriors; the Christian neophytes could return to their rancherías; and the old way of life would resume—though perhaps transformed in some now unknown way by the moral guidance of Toypurina's prophetic revelations. The full details of her prophecies were likely never known to the Spanish, as I discuss below.

The uprising was foiled when the corporal of the guard, José Maria Verdugo, somehow hearing of the upcoming attack, informed the two padres, Miguel Sanchez and Antonio Cruzado, and ordered his soldiers to lie in wait for the invaders (Archivo General de la Nación 1785–87). If the plot had not been discovered, the revolt might have succeeded and driven off the Spanish—for a while. Toypurina and the Tongva had surely heard that their trading partners, the Yuma, had successfully destroyed two Spanish settlements on the Colorado River, some 150 miles east, seven years earlier. And they would have known of the bloody revolt in 1775 at Mission San Diego, when the resident priest was killed (Bancroft 1886, vol. 1; Bolton 1930; Mason 1975). This common knowledge was part of the rational calculus of Tongva ritual violence.

Governor Pedro Fages was an experienced Indian fighter, a veteran of actions against the Seri of Sonora, the Apache, and three campaigns following the Yuma revolt of 1778, when he rescued 63 Spanish captives and buried the corpses of 91 dead, including two padres (Bancroft 1886, vol. 1). Fages drew up an *Ynterrogatorio*, a list of ten questions to be put to Toypurina and the captive warriors by Sergeant Olivera. The questions, and the prisoners' answers, were translated by a 21-year-old soldier stationed at the mission, José Maria Pico.[3]

Fages's third question—"What moved you to try your luck, knowing that it was impossible to kill the soldiers, since they could have killed so many of you by firing their cannon?"—is oddly evocative of white responses, a century later, to Ghost Dancers who believed themselves impervious to bullets when wearing their sacred ghost shirts (Mooney 1965:115–118). What induced the Tongva, and later the Ghost Dancers, was religious prophecy, supernatural aid invoked through ritual and shamanic intercession, and belief in the moral rightness of their cause: ridding the land of Europeans and returning to old, harmonious relations with the land and indigenous, though reenvisioned, spirits.

One of the accused, Ajiyivi, chief of Jajamovit (Hahamongna), had with his nephew killed "two cows belonging to a soldier from this company" a few days earlier, implying that he was acting in coordination with Nicolas José and perhaps with Toypurina's prophecy. The other three principals testified that, as Toypurina puts it, "Nicolas sent others to take the sheep and he offered to share them with her . . . and that Nicolas also sent for three cows, but they did not take them." The shepherds, mission neophytes, willingly gave up the sheep. Ajiyivi states that "no one invited him" to the attack: "He came because he ran into the rioters, and knowing that they came to fight, and seeing them so excited, he wanted to come and see if their courage was real." This seems to be a reference to Toypurina's prophecy of magical death for the soldiers.

Governor Fages, after hearing the interrogations of the four principal prisoners, on January 4, 1786, wrote to Comandante General Rengel in Chihuahua, "The pagan Indian named Tomasajaquichi, in addition to being an accomplice, is also charged with having been sent by said Toypurina to corrupt the Christians with her sorceries [*su Echiserias*]." Fages ordered Nicolas José, Tomasajaquichi, and Ajiyivi imprisoned in the presidio in San Diego and Toypurina imprisoned at Mission San Gabriel until he received further orders. He also commanded that the other 16 or so prisoners, alleged major figures in the revolt, including Toypurina's brother, receive 20 lashes (25 for those who were involved in the 1779 revolt) and then be set free: "The sentence will be carried out before all in order that the punishment be for all. And on my behalf, they will be given the most severe warnings about their ingratitude, condemning their perversities, and showing them the deception with which the said woman dominated them, and that their pagan abuses have no power against those of us who are Catholics."

The interrogatories, and Fages's correspondence, make it clear that the Spanish saw Toypurina, her prophecies (her "deception"), and the "pagan abuses" of her followers as powerful threats to their own political and religious control and that Toypurina saw the priests and soldiers as rivals for the moral, spiritual, and political leadership of her people. By the night of the uprising, Father Antonio Cruzado had, just two days earlier, performed the mission's 1,278th baptism, of a man from Aluibit who took the name Juan Capistrano. As in other times and places in the Spanish borderlands, an Indian woman or mestiza was called witch or sorcerer for resisting—subverting through devilish and magical means in Spanish eyes—the moral order of colonial social hierarchies: male over female; Christian over pagan; Spanish over Indian or mestizo; and, as colonial domination intensified on the frontier, landowner versus landless (cf. Behar 1989; Castañeda 1998; Erickson n.d.). But Fages, by his own standards, added a plea for mercy for Toypurina: "Since the Padres of this Mission have informed me that the pagan Indian woman prisoner Toypurina pretends to be a Christian, and since it is known positively that the pagan Indians who participated in the disturbance because of her persuasions, respect and fear of her and her superstitions threaten her with death if she goes free, because she deceived them and

they have been punished, I, the Governor, therefore ask the Comandante General if he will consider that if the said woman is baptized, she
might be sent to another Mission, far from this one, where she might
marry and remain free from said danger?"

In Arispe, Comandante General Ugarte consulted Asesor Navarro,
who agreed with Fages, submitting to Ugarte on December 14, 1787,
his recommendations for sentencing the four remaining prisoners. The
way Navarro reports the event, based on the investigation and interrogations at San Gabriel (and possibly in consultation with Fages, who
was in Arispe at that point), is that Nicolas José persuaded Toypurina
"to seduce those from six Rancherías to participate in the event, making
them believe that when they got to the Mission they would kill the
Padres with their crafty superstitions, and that they only had to capture
the Corporal and soldiers whom they would find unprepared." Thomas
Temple (1958) also tells the story this way (see note 2). The original
testimony as translated and recorded by the Spanish in 1785–86 is that
Toypurina and her followers would find the soldiers already dead from
magical attack and needed to kill only the (unarmed) padres.

In either case, Navarro states that because the rebels were "seduced
and deceived" by Toypurina into attempting murder, Temesajaquichi
and Ajillivit should be released after two years' imprisonment. Nicolas
José should be further imprisoned, and both he and Toypurina should
be perpetually exiled because of the risk that they would return to San
Gabriel to incite another rebellion. Comandante General Ugarte ordered, "Do as the Asesor advises."

Nicolas José was sentenced to six more years of hard labor in leg
shackles, Governor Fages wrote on December 14, 1787, "in the Presidio
furthest from said Mission, and to perpetual exile therefrom, and after
completion of the six years he shall be sent to one of the furthest missions
where there will be no chance that he will return to live among his
people."

Three years later, during the provincial census of 1790, "Nicolás,
indio, prisoner at this Presidio from San Gabriel" aged 40 was the 38th
of 41 persons enumerated at San Fancisco, and the only prisoner to be
counted. He was one of only 26 Indians listed in the Alta California census, most of them women married to Spanish soldiers (Mason 1998:2,
104). The ultimate fate of Nicolas José is unknown.

Toypurina was baptized at Mission San Gabriel on March 8, 1787, by
Padre Miguel Sanchez, whose death by ritual violence she had prophe-

sied in 1785. She had been a prisoner for a year and a half, awaiting a heavy sentence. The possibility that she was coerced is strong, especially in light of Fages's letter suggesting that she be baptized and married off (to a Christian) in her exile. She could also have "pretended to be a Christian" as a pragmatic course of action in her desperate circumstances, which allegedly included death threats by her fellow prisoners. Or this could have been a sincere profession of faith in the new religion by an indigenous leader and philosopher facing a world transformed. Her baptism, in a group of eight adults, was the 1,408th since the mission's founding in 1771. She was renamed Regina (Queen) Josefa Toypurina.

Toypurina was sentenced by Governor Fages "to perpetual exile from the Mission San Gabriel, and [to] be taken to one of the furthest missions where she [would] have no chance to return to her relatives nor cause further rebellions through her influence and deceit" (Archivo General de la Nación 1787). Comandante General Ugarte's December 12 "Decree Punishing Certain Indians" uses nearly identical language, permanently exiling "the Indian woman named Toypurina . . . that she be taken to another mission where she will have no hope or rejoining her relatives, nor of causing new revolts ith her influence and deceptions" (Mission Santa Barbara 1787).

Governor Fages wrote Father Fermin de Lasuén, who had succeeded Junípero Serra as president of the Franciscans in Alta California, to ask which distant mission would be the best place of exile for "Maria Regina, alias Toypurina of San Gabriel." Lasuén responded on June 14 with strong reluctance to have the missions host any prisoners, especially "such decidedly pernicious persions" known for fomenting revolt. In letters dated June 10 and June 15, 1788, Fages—who notes Toypurina's sex, her unmarried state, and her status as a convert to Christianity—first proposed sending her to Mission San Antonio, which lies in a remote valley in the Coast Range southeast of Monterey. In his second letter he offers Lasuén two options: San Antonio or Mission Santa Clara on San Francisco Bay. Lasuén bowed to secular authority, writing on June 15 that "[s]he will be welcomed enthusiastically at which ever mission Your Excellency desires to send her" (Mission Santa Barbara 1788).

The first stage of her journey into exile remains a mystery, but one year later, on July 26, 1789, in the mission chapel at Carmel, Toypurina married Manuel Montero, a Spanish soldier stationed at nearby Monterey. Again there is no way of knowing whether her marriage to the soldier Montero—in a frontier society where there was a drastic shortage of marriageable Catholic women—was by her own free will or by the will of Governor Fages himself, laid out in his 1787 letter. She may have met Montero at San Gabriel while she was a prisoner and he was stationed there or at the nearby pueblo of Los Angeles. Toypurina evidently lived among the Spanish-speaking townspeople, at least after her marriage. Manuel Montero was enumerated in 1790 in the Alta California provincial census as living at Monterey—his "caste," or racial designation, noted as *español*—with his wife Regina—caste *india*—and a child, whom parish records show was a one-year-old son named Cesario. Toypurina and her husband had four children in all. None of her descendants ever returned to live in her homeland. Toypurina's sentence by the Spanish authorities of perpetual exile turned out to be devastatingly effective. It has in a sense already lasted more than two centuries.[4]

Toypurina died at the early age of 38. She was buried on May 22, 1799, in an unmarked grave at Mission San Juan Bautista, founded only two years earlier, a day's march south of San Francisco Bay. She probably lies in the shade of the old olive grove just east of the mission church, whose still lumpy and uneven ground, right on the San Andreas Fault, pungent from a carpet of fallen uncured olives, is the site of a mass grave of several thousand baptized Indians.

Prophetic Movements and Ritual Violence on the California Frontier

Prophetic movements that generate ritual violence are likely, I suggest, to cross ethnolinguistic boundaries, linking indigenous people from a wide region under conditions of colonial domination. The 1785 Toypurina uprising, an 1810–11 rebellion at San Gabriel, and a series of outbreaks in Chumash country culminating in revolts at three missions in 1824 were all regional in scope.

These eruptions of ritual violence were, I believe, connected not only to one another but also to the prophecies and revelations of a new religious movement. Based on veneration of the deity Chinigchinich and adherence to his ritual and moral codes, it spread up to 300 miles along the coast and well inland, especially in the first three generations after the Spanish arrival. The Tongva were the originators of the new religion. It was first described in writing in the 1820s by Father Geronimo Boscana of Mission San Juan Capistrano, nine miles south of Tongva territory.

Chinigchinch was born, or first appeared, either at San Clemente or Santa Catalina Island or on the coast at Puvungna, near the estuary formed by the mouths of the San Gabriel and Los Angeles Rivers, now the twin ports of Long Beach and Los Angeles. From his origin in the Tongva homeland, descendants and scholars agree, his prophecies, moral codes, myths, and ceremonies reached north and east to Kitanemuk, mountain Cahuilla, and Southern Yokuts and east and south to Acjachemem (Juaneños), Quechnajuichom (Luiseños), Cupeños, and the northern Yuman (Hokan)-speaking Diegueños (Ipai, Tipai). Steatite carvings from Catalina Island of whale dorsal fins and the dolphins that guard the world, rock paintings of men in bird costumes, and the ritual use of hallucinogenic datura may mean that the new religion reached Chumash country, the northern Channel Islands and the mainland around Santa Barbara and San Luis Obispo. Pimu, Catalina Island, is one of the sacred places represented in sand paintings central to initiation and mourning rituals honoring Chinigchinich. A golden eagle chief deity, prayers to sun and moon, and a puberty rite for boys using datura are signs that the religion spread even further north to the Hokan-speaking Salinans of the Salinas Valley and southern Big Sur coast. Diffusion of the new religion to the southeast of Tongva country took several generations, from the mid-1780s to 1850 and beyond. Ceremonies related to it have continued up to the present in a few remote communities southeast of the Tongva homeland.

Spreading around the time, or just before, the first missions were established in Alta California in 1769, the new prophecies gave an explanation—moral disorder—for the great epidemic waves of infectious European diseases that ravaged the people and caused their catastrophic death rates compared with that of Spanish speakers, epidemics that struck even before the Spanish invasion. The new religion synergized earlier beliefs and ceremonies with prophecies catalyzed by and in opposition to the new revelations of Catholic religious philosophy.[5]

The Christian influences and parallels of the Chinigchinich religion may be drawn too sharply in the written record from the 1820s to the 1920s. First filtered through the sensibilities of the Franciscan Boscana, they are amplified by testimonies of baptized, often forcibly missionized Tongva, Acjachemem, and Quechnajuichom (Luiseño) adherents to recorders such as Hugo Reid, Constance DuBois, and J. P. Harrington. The religion's original prophecies and inspirations, like Toypurina's, were never written down, and like all enduring religious movements, it changed and evolved to meet new circumstances. But it had deep roots in indigenous rituals and continuities with beliefs that predated the Franciscans' arrival in Alta California. There is clear evidence of related practices in Tongva territory in 1602. On the sacred island of Pimu (Catalina), home to prosperous communities of maritime traders, Islanders had constructed a ceremonial enclosure, decorated with feathers, possibly encircling a sand painting, and a sacred figure flanked by representations of the sun and moon. They also venerated huge crows or ravens that frequented the ceremonial grounds.[6] The Chinigchinich religion did not arise, an entirely new entity, from inspired prophecies of the early mission period. We cannot now know just what the pre-mission-era rituals and moral philosophies were, if or how they spread from Pimu to the mainland and across the region, and how they were transformed during the period of religious ferment and existential doubt that followed the Spanish soldiers and friars into the Tongva homelands.

Archaeological evidence from coastal Southern California shows that ritual objects associated in the last 200 years with the veneration of Chinigchinich, such as long quartz crystals, charm stones, and ceremonial bundles, were in use many centuries earlier (e.g., Bean and Smith 1978; Kroeber 1925). Linguistic evidence suggests that Southern California Takic terms for ranked shamanic and chiefly elites predated the advent of the Spanish in Alta California by many centuries (Kroeber 1907). The ritual use of datura was central to the new religion. *Datura meteloides*, a shrub with dramatically large, bell-shaped white flowers, grows prolifically across much of Southern California. Its hallucinogenic, medicinal, and potentially poisonous properties, of its seeds especially, would have been known since people first tried to make a salad of it, suggesting that it has been in some kind of ritual use for millennia. Rituals using datura, particularly by shamans and at male puberty ceremonies but also by individuals seeking contact with spirits, extended as far north as the Costanoans of San Francisco Bay; inland to the Miwok, Valley and Foothill Yokuts, and Kawaiisu; and into the deserts of the California border among the Chemehuevi, Quechan, Mohave, and Cocopa (Bean and Vane 1978:668–669; Levy 1978:489–490; Spier 1978:482; Wallace 1978:456–459). It is also used in northern Mexico, as among the Yaqui.

The inspirations of the Chinigchinich religion, as they spread across the region from the 1780s to the 1850s, and its sacred objects, laws, prophecies, and shamanic and social orders must have been creatively reconfigured, through prophecies and other communications with spirit beings, from an ancient matrix of religious philosophy and practice. What 18th-century Tongva prophets incorporated from Catholic theology, if anything, will never be clear. What is clear is that prophecies and rituals associated with Chinigchinich intensified and spread just as the Franciscans came to the homelands to proselytize, backed by soldiers with cannons and harquebuses to guard the missions, round up potential converts, and hunt down runaways. The Chinigchinich religion reached many thousands of people, spreading 300 miles across ethnolinguistic boundaries in the Franciscan era and beyond, as an indigenous, secret moral philosophy and alternative to Catholicism. Its shamanic prophets grew in influence in opposition to the missionaries and soldiers and to the miasma of violence, environmental destruction, and epidemic disease that the Spanish brought with them. The Chinigchinich religion took hold across Southern California as a ritual of resistance to the theological, moral, and political crises of the Spanish and Mexican occupations.

Chinigchinich was born (or appeared) after the death by poison of Wiyot, who was reborn as the moon. In some origin accounts Wiyot was born at Puvungna, to Sirout ("Handful of Tobacco," who is also a comet) and his wife Ikaiut ("Above"; possibly Ukat in Tongva). He was the ruler of the first beings—including certain named stars, mountains, minerals, plants, animals, and human ancestors—born of, or descended from, the primordial sister and brother, earth and sky (night), who were wife and husband. Wiyot became a tyrant in some accounts, but his murder brought death into the cosmos. Wiyot also lives on an island to the west, *tolmul*, land of the dead. After Wiyot's death and rebirth, the male creator night divided the first beings, including the ancestors of humans, and assigned them their languages and places (Boscana 1978:31–32; DuBois 1908; Harrington 1933:117, 147–148; Kroeber 1925:623, 637, 677–678).

Chinigchinich is also known as Ouiamot, which is similar to Wiyot (Ouiot) and may be his name in childhood before initiation (Harrington 1933:128). His other names, linguistically Tongva, are Saor, before he was initiated; Tobet, which refers to his dancing and is the word for the feathered dancing costume he taught people to make; and Quaguar, after he had ascended to the stars (Boscana 1978:30; Quaguar also appears as Qua-o-ar, as collected in 1852 by Hugo Reid from Tongva elders [Heizer 1968]; Kwawar [Kroeber 1925:638]; or K(w)á'uwar [Harrington 1933:139]). His parents were Tacu and Auzar, in the Tongva language.

In other accounts he was born of Tamáayawut, earth, "he had neither father nor mother," or he came from the stars (Boscana 1978:29, 33; Harrington 1933:127, 153, 227; Kroeber 1925:637). There has been debate for over two centuries on whether Chinigchinich was always a deity or, rather, was a great prophet of religious renewal who became deified. There are parallels between him and Jesus, each born on earth in unsettled times and risen into heaven, a newer god than the original creator, and a promulgator of a new moral code. In the early 20th century, consultants volunteered to Harrington that Chinigchinich was the "Indian Christ" and Wiyot, the "Indian God" (1933:127). Boscana reported in the 1820s that it was Chinigchinich who changed many first beings into animal and plant spirits and heavenly bodies.

Using language reminiscent of the Book of Genesis, Boscana writes that Chinigchinich "created man, forming him of clay found upon the borders of a lake" (1978:29; (this is likely Lake Elsinore, east of San Juan Capistrano [cf. Kroeber 1925:678]). He continues, "Both male and female he created" (1978:29; Harrington 1933:129). Chinigchinich was, he told the first beings, "a captain of greater power" than Wiyot. Boscana says, "From this time they looked upon Chinigchinich as God"; his name means "all-powerful or almighty. . . . [H]e was ever present and in all places. He saw everything, although it might be in the darkest night, but no one could see him. He was a friend to the good, but the wicked he chastised" (1978:29–30).

It was Chinigchinich who created the high-ranking ritual caste of the *puplem*, shamans (also *puula*; *puur* in Tongva), Boscana writes, teaching people how to initiate boys and girls. His first commandment was the building of a temple or ceremonial enclosure, the *wamkish* or *wankech* (Boscana's *vanquech*, from Acjachemem *wamkitc*; *yuvaar* or *yoba* in Tongva; Hugo Reid's "Yobagnar"). The puplem, and those of chiefly rank, were initiated into his mysteries during puberty ceremonies and enjoined to keep them secret. Male initiations, certain mourning ceremonies, and other rituals involved the use of the sacred hallucinogen datura (*toloache* in Mexican and California Spanish), sometimes mixed with a native species of tobacco or saltwater. Sun and moon, highly sacred beings, were venerated with Chinigchinich, represented on the wamkish and in sand paintings used at initiations. So were icons of crow, raven, owl, eagle, bear, mountain lion, coyote, rattlesnake, and beings such as the Milky Way, night (sky), Pleiades, Orion, Altair, Mount San Gorgonio, Catalina Island (Pimu), the toloache mortar and pestle, and winnowing basket, representing offerings and Chinigchinich himself. The wamkish and its sacred pole were decorated with feathers of eagles, red-shafted flickers, and other offered birds (Boscana 1978:28–29; DuBois 1908; Harrington 1933:153, 195; Kroeber 1925:628, 637–638, 662–664; cf. Bean and Smith 1978; Bean and Vane 1978; Johnston 1962).

It was a stern religion for chaotic and troubling times. The raven, or large crow, was Chinigchinich's primary messenger and oracle, reporting to Chinigchinich and his most adept shamans any secret transgressions of his moral code. His sacred animals, plants, and rock forms avenged the insult of disobedience with suffering and death. California's fiercest animals—including grizzly bears, mountain lions, rattlesnakes, black widow spiders, tarantulas, and stingrays and especially golden or white-headed eagles and condors—were among his sacred beings. In addition, stinging nettles, thorny wild rose, and long quartz crystals—his arrows, shot by ravens—were sacred to him. These were all among the first beings created (Boscana 1978:29, 43, 72; DuBois 1908:99, 130–142; Harrington 1933:130–134). His father Tacu (Takwish or Tacué, sometimes called Sirout, like Wiyot's father) also appears as a comet or meteor, a messenger from spirit beings, including high chiefs and shamans, who have ascended to the stars, one of Chinigchinich's abodes. Tacu is a harbinger of death who takes people's spirits; in many accounts he is a cannibal, with a home on Mount San Jacinto at the desert's edge (Boscana 1978:77; DuBois 1908:126; Harrington 1933:147, 153, 184; Kroeber 1925:679–680, 713).

In what Boscana sees as a kind of purgatory, Chinigchinich "doomed" the spirits of those "not of noble rank" to "the borders of the sea, or to the hills, mountains, valleys, or forests. There they remained an indefinite time while Chinigchinich made them do penance for the faults they had committed in not obeying his precepts" (1978:77). Boscana does not give many details of these precepts besides the ceremonies that the new deity ordained. Other laws of Chinigchinich, given at initiations, are to keep the rituals secret, to observe ritual fasting, to bathe daily at dawn, for the young not to eat before the elderly or finish the last of the harvest of acorns and seeds, to eat sparingly, to be kind to the elderly and generous to strangers, and to never whip children, whose spirits would be stolen by other lingering spirits, causing them to die (DuBois 1908:82–83, 96; this child-rearing philosophy is in stark contrast to that of the 18th-century colonial Spanish, visible in the missions' appalling record of floggings and deaths of young people, and it no doubt helped the people explain the deaths).

Chinigchinich also lives with other beings in *tolmec* (*tolmal*; probably *tolmar* in Tongva), an "earthly paradise," Boscana writes, inside the earth, where people other than high chiefs and shamans go after death. This is the navel of the universe, home of the dead. (The same term was applied to Wiyot's western island of the dead, perhaps an earlier religious belief.) Boscana was told that in tolmec " 'there was plenty to eat and drink and to wear, that there was constant dancing and festivity, that no one labored, no one was sorrowful, but on the contrary, all were contented and happy, every-one did as he pleased, and selected the number of wives he wished.' The reader will compare this belief with the doctrine of the immortality of the soul. It was taught by the moderns undoubtedly, and since their conversion to Christianity, for the old men at the time of their gentilism had no such idea" (1978:76; cf. Harrington 1933:139, 199; Heizer 1968: Letters 4, 15; Kroeber 1925:637–638, 662–664).

A new style of ritual dancing on Chinigchinich's ceremonial grounds was central to his worship. By dancing, "their wants could be relieved. The sick would be cured, and the hungry receive food" (Boscana 1978:34). "This new manner is full of gestures and violent motions," Constance DuBois says, "while the old style of dancing, still to be seen among the Diegueños of Manzanita, was performed in a quiet and restrained manner" (1908:75). The style associated with Chinigchinich was "a continued and very rapid whirling," reports Kroeber (1925:660). (Both ethnologists were eyewitnesses in Luiseño country, in 1906 and 1904, respectively.) Chinigchinich's name, Tobet, refers to his initiation dance and the ceremonial costume he taught people to wear. Painted black and red, in his skirt of golden eagle or condor feathers and his eagle feather headdress, dancing as Tobet, he ascends to the stars, becoming Quagoar (Boscana 1978:30, 57–60; Harrington 1933:139–140, 175–177).

The reason given by Nicolas José for the 1785 revolt at Mission San Gabriel, the soldier-interpreter Pico said, was that the padres had forbidden "their dances and pagan abuses." Because honoring Chinigchinich, supplicating him for health and prosperity, meant long nights of dancing in the style sacred to him, the anger of the Tongva at having their dances prohibited, and the opposition of the Franciscans, may become clearer. Did Toypurina receive prophetic revelations from Chinigchinich? Was she a key figure in the elaboration and spread of the new religion, with its moral codes, explanations of disease and death, and hopes for relief from suffering? Did she receive new revelations that to live in harmony according to Chinigchinich's moral laws the Spanish must be killed and that the mission must be driven out of the homeland? Or was she the prophet of revelations from other beings, related or unrelated to him?

The timing and setting of her prophecies are exactly right to place Toypurina at the center of the evolving Chinigchinich religion. The year 1785 was a likely peak of religious intensification related to Chinigchinich in Tongva country, and San Gabriel was the primary mission to which Tongva from across the homelands, including Puvungna, were being forcibly removed in the early 1780s. Constance DuBois, on the basis of detailed oral histories collected from elderly Luiseños in 1906, has calculated that the Chinigchinich religion first reached their country 120 years earlier, meaning around 1786. This suggests either an initial or an intensified wave of Chinigchinich prophecies and ritual elaboration just beforehand in Tongva territory, their universally acknowledged place of origin.[7]

In most existing accounts, up to the recent past, the veneration of Chinigchinich was led by a secret society of male shamans (e.g., for Luiseños, DuBois 1908; Kroeber 1925). Would Toypurina, a woman, likely have participated in his rituals or have received prophecies from him? Whether her shamanic powers came through toloache or other avenues of communication with spirits can never be known. During the 19th and 20th centuries, the toloache ritual, central to the initiation of males, was not normally part of female initiation. But Toypurina was an acknowledged shaman and a chief's daughter, a *maniisar*, a title indicating a melding of political and religious power. The term comes from the word *manit*, which means both datura and the toloache ritual (Kroeber 1925:623, 640). This suggests a close tie between the politico-religious office she held, use of the sacred hallucinogen, and Chinigchinich, who in contemporary religious thought instructed people to use it. Similarly, although toloache and the ceremonial grounds were restricted mainly to shamans and male initiates (but also to girls at initiation and mourners of both sexes), elderly Tongva told Hugo Reid at San Gabriel in 1852 that "female singers"—ritual practitioners—were allowed on the Yobagnar (Harrington 1933:138; Heizer 1968). There are other accounts from the mission era of indigenous women taking datura and receiving messages from spirits. Toypurina's revelations could have come, of course, from communication with other spirit beings. If so, in light of later prophetic movements in Southern California, discussed below, another possibility is that they came from Tamáayawut, or earth, mother to Chinigchinich in some accounts and ultimately of almost all beings. Both deities held powers over health and illness in this time of great sickness and dying. And Toypurina is the one who said that "she was angry with the Padres and with everyone at the Mission" because "estamos viviendo aqui en su Tierra" [we are living here in their land, their soil, their earth].

The Chinigchinich religion, as reflected in early written accounts, did not direct ritual attacks against Europeans. Its ritual violence was internal. Violators of Chinigchinich's moral laws would be killed by grizzly bears, mountain lions, rattlesnakes, black widow spiders, or other of his sacred animals, sent to attack by the deity or his high shamans, or executed by the people themselves. Offenders could seek shelter in Chinigchinich's sacred enclosure until their cases were heard by a council of chiefs and shamans. But if the guilty were not killed and offered to him, then Chinigchinich would send plagues and early death to all (Boscana 1978:43; DuBois 1908; Kroeber 1925:639).

There is evidence that throughout the mission era underlying and evolving indigenous religious beliefs—the Chinigchinich religion, the veneration of earth (Tamáayawut in Tongva, Chupu in the Chumash language)—were periodically catalyzed by new prophetic revelations, like Toypurina's, into divinely inspired acts of external ritual violence: attacks against the Spanish and Mexicans. After these were suppressed, the religions again went underground; ritual dances and initiations were held largely in secret; and shamans, chiefs, and the people awaited the aid and blessings of the deities and further revelations. A review of rebellions against Spanish missions and presidios in Southern California shows—in spite of the pervasive element of secrecy and the sparse written and oral historical evidence that survives—clear manifestations of ritual violence and inspired prophecies in many. The sheer number of uprisings belies the stereotype long held in anglophone California histories and taught in public schools of docile "mission Indians" gratefully accepting Spanish political, economic, and religious rule.

The Toypurina revolt, the first that came to Spanish attention as involving indigenous beliefs and prophecy, was neither the first nor the last at Mission San Gabriel. The Tongva opposed the founding of the mission from the beginning. According to the Spanish, even their initial confrontation contained mystical elements. In an often retold story—recorded later by Father Palóu (who was not present) and repeated in Bancroft's *History of California*—on August 6, 1771, a party of two Franciscans and 18 Spanish soldiers and muleteers set out from San Diego to establish the new mission, two days' hard march to the north. As Bancroft recounts, closely paraphrasing Palóu, "At first a large force of natives presented themselves under two chieftains and attempted by hostile demonstrations to prevent the purpose of the Spaniards; but when one of the padres held up a painting of the virgin, the savages instantly threw down their arms and their two captains ran up to lay their necklaces at the feet of the beautiful queen, thus signifying their desire for peace" (1886, vol. 1:179–180).

The Indians continued to make "offerings of pine-nuts and acorns to the image of Our Lady" in the weeks following the raising of the cross on September 8 and during the construction of the first *tule* (marsh reed thatch)-roofed, wooden mission building (Bancroft 1886, vol. 1:179–180). Father Junipero Serra, who was not present either, recorded in 1773 that it was the Indian women who offered "seeds and eatables" to the "holy image" (Engelhardt 1927:3–6, 10). An oil painting of a long-faced, pallid Virgin Mary, in three-quarters view, dark eyes gazing heavenward—described in a pamphlet for visitors as the very painting that accompanied the first Franciscan missionaries—still stands in the Mission San Gabriel chapel on an ornate eight-foot stand of iron and beaten copper just to the left of the altar.[8]

By October 9, 1771, the beatific interlude of intercultural harmony and Indian ritual offerings to the Virgin, as remembered by mission commentators for two centuries, had ended. The chief of a nearby hamlet led an attack on the soldiers guarding the rough stockade at the Misión Viejo, seeking revenge for his wife, lassoed and raped by a Spanish soldier. The chief shot an arrow at the rapist, who deflected it with his shield and fired his musket. The chief fell dead. His corpse was beheaded by the soldiers, who left his head to decay on a pole stuck in the stockade. The Franciscans a few days later learned the attack's provocation and, appalled by the rape, returned the head to relatives who pleaded for it. Rapes and abductions of Indian women (boys too, Father Serra says) by soldiers at Mission San Gabriel continued for years to precipitate anger and insurrection according to both Franciscans and military officers, but there were no more officially recorded deaths (Bancroft 1886, vol. 1:180–182, 202, 314–315; Engelhardt 1927:6–15).

At San Diego and San Juan Capistrano, armed uprisings continued. A regional revolt by 800 warriors from nine villages destroyed Mission San Diego in 1775. The corporal of the guard, Antonio Briones, was killed in battle near San Diego two years later (Cook 1943:66). That same year, Corporal Guillermo Carrillo led a party from San Diego on a punitive raid against Alocuachomi, near Mission San Juan Capistrano (founded a year earlier), whose people allegedly threatened mission neophytes. The Spanish killed three men and wounded others. Bancroft records their grievance as "disorders among the soldiers," a euphemism for sexual assault and revenge on a "native chieftain" who furnished soldiers with women—the chief received 15 lashes, and the soldiers were merely transferred to the presidio at San Diego (1886, vol. 1:314–315). At San Diego in 1778, Carrillo's forces captured men from several bands (Ipai, Tipai, Kumeyaay—the so-called Diegueños), seizing "eighty bows, 1500 arrows, and a large number of clubs"; the men received 30–40 lashes apiece. Aachil, Aalcuinn, Aaaran, and Taguagui, alleged leaders, were sentenced to death by two volleys of musket shots in front of the assembled Spanish troops and the "Christian rancherías" (Bancroft 1886, vol. 1:315–316).

As the interrogatory of the 1785 Toypurina uprising at Mission San Gabriel shows, Nicolas José himself helped lead a 1779 revolt and was imprisoned. The Spanish claimed that a Tongva chief threatened revolt in 1786, while Toypurina was still a prisoner at Mission San Gabriel (and Nicolas José, Temejasaquichi, and Ajiyivi were imprisoned at San Diego), but the Spanish for some reason allowed the matter to drop (Bancroft 1886, vol. 1:460). The last major Indian uprising against Mission San Gabriel took place a generation later, from 1810 to 1811. It involved some eight hundred neophytes and non-Christians, desert- and mountain-dwelling Cahuillas and Serranos as well as Tongva, an alliance reaching across 100 miles. It ended months later, after Spanish reinforcements were sent from Northern California, in defeat and capture, the forcible baptism and removal of children to the mission, mass whippings, and the imprisonment, lashing, and forced labor at the presidio of Santa Barbara of some 33 alleged leaders (Heizer 1968; Mason 1984). This was no placid acceptance of Spanish control and the Catholic faith.

The Spanish colonists had planted the fertile uplands around San Gabriel with corn and wheat; turned sheep and cattle out to graze driving out deer and antelope; and cut down prolific, acorn-bearing coast live oaks and deciduous Engelmann oaks half a thousand years old to use for firewood. European wild oats and other exotic grasses quickly spread from cattle forage, outcompeting indigenous bunch grasses and forbs, from which the people gathered seeds, and suppressing the resprouting of oaks. So it is logical that just before the 1785 attack, the mission shepherds—Tongva neophytes—were giving away mission sheep for slaughter and distribution by the rebels. Similarly, in 1778, after a chief's wife "eloped"—or was abducted—to Antigua California, Acjachemem from three rancherías assembled and threatened to attack Mission San Juan Capistrano "to avenge the death of their comrades slain the year before [in the earlier uprising]; also claiming that the Spaniards were really devils come to destroy the crops by drought" (Bancroft 1886, vol. 1:314–315). Here contemporary Spanish documents, used by Bancroft, confirm a grievance against environmental degradation and destruction of the (wild) food supply. These accounts also implicitly testify to anger at the destruction of sacred places where powerful supernatural beings control the fertility and health of land and people. The reference to the Spanish as devils (as the Spanish understood it), or beings with malevolent supernatural powers to be combated, suggests elements of ritual violence and religious prophecy.

Restoration of the land and of religious practices likely were closely linked goals of all uprisings against the Spanish missions. The religious philosophies of Tongva, Acjachemem, and their neighbors stressed harmonious relations with supernatural beings—many appearing in animal form—dwelling in sacred mountain peaks, rock outcroppings, lakes, and trees (e.g., Boscana 1978; Heizer 1968; Johnston 1962; McCawley 1996). The land was occupied, its flora and fauna were displaced, and contemporary Spanish documents record that mission neophytes and residents of nearby rancherías alike periodically suffered from hunger. In the year before the Toypurina uprising, the inhabitants of Los Angeles alone produced 4,500 bushels of grain, mostly corn and wheat, primarily using unpaid or poorly paid Indian labor. Vast nearby fields were planted in grain under the control of Mission San Gabriel, one of the most productive missions in the Californias. Townspeople complained that Indian labor was in short supply, as people in adjacent rancherías—not restricted in their movements and obliged to work, as in the missions— were busy with their own seasonal gathering (this would be the autumn acorn crops, piñon nuts, and annual grass seeds [Bancroft 1886, vol. 1]). Environmental destruction by oppressive outsiders is a key grievance underlying the efflorescence of prophetic movements, including, notably, the Ghost Dance, which found its most famous adherents among peoples of the northern Great Plains suffering the catastrophic collapse of the great buffalo herds.[9]

Seizure of lands, loss of food supply, desecration of sacred sites, imprisonment, forced labor, murder, rape, abduction, and assault are more than sufficient precipitating causes for uprisings against the Spanish invaders. But the Spanish, locked in what the padres saw as a holy war against the devil for the souls of the Indians, were highly unlikely to learn of secret prophecies of religious renewal and ritual attack that accompanied, or precipitated, the acts of resistance that continued against the California missions through the 1820s.

Toypurina was not the only female prophet on the early California frontier. In Santa Barbara, 100 miles northwest of Mission San Gabriel and 16 years later, another young woman, inspired by a powerful deity, prescribed new forms of ritual violence against the mission. This time, more details of the prophecy were recorded, and possible links to the Chinigchinich religion can be discerned. In 1941 Robert Heizer, prospecting in Berkeley's Bancroft Library, found a letter dated 1805 from Father Estevan Tapis (president of the Franciscans in Alta California) to Governor Arillaga describing what Heizer calls "a messianic movement . . . the earliest historical record of such a movement in California. Although much has been written on the Ghost Dance in California [in 1870], we have little or no knowledge of defeatist cults which originated in the state. It is possible that this type of reaction, explainable as a desperate expedient to seek relief from oppression, was fairly common in the mission district of California in the late eighteenth and early nineteenth century. There are certain indications that the major revolt, in 1824, of the Santa Barbara Channel missions is explainable in these terms" (1941:128).

Heizer, who suggests combing mission archives for corroborating evidence, is quite correct, I think, that similar prophecies were "fairly common" in the mission zone of influence from the 1770s to well beyond the 1820s. The Toypurina revolt of 1785, of which he was unaware, may have been part of the first major "messianic movement" in California, inspired by prophecies related to the ascended Chinigchinich or another sacred being. As Father Tapis writes:

In the year 1801 when an epidemic of pneumonia and a waist ailment (pleurisy? [Heizer queries]) caused the deaths of many pagans and Christians, a single female neophyte succeeded in deceiving the Christian Indians of Santa Barbara. It happened that after a pretended trance she said that Chupu (an idol worshipped in the Channel region), appeared to her and told her that the pagan Indians were to die if they were not baptized, and that the same fate was to befall the Christian Indians who would not give alms [offerings] to Chupu, and who would refuse to wash their heads with a certain water . . . the news spread immediately through all the houses of the Mission; almost all the neophytes, the alcaldes included, went to the house of the visionary to present beads and seeds, and to go through the rite of renouncing Christianity . . . the fashion extended to all the Indian settlements of the Channel [coast and islands] and of the Sierra [Mountains], and . . . the missionaries did not know about it. Chupu had revealed at the same time that all those who would report the affair to the missionaries would die immediately. For three days we remained ignorant of this event until a neophyte, overcoming his fears, told us what was happening. If the Indian woman had added, that in order to stop the epidemics, it was necessary to kill the missionaries and the soldiers of the guard, the alcaldes and the rest of the natives would have believed it too. . . . Who would have escaped death . . . ? [S]uch a thing might have happened . . . the neophytes know how to scheme their plots at night with such a secrecy and reserve so that the custody of the missions with a thousand neophytes altogether should not be entrusted to two, three, or a few more soldiers who compose their guard. [Heizer 1941:128–129]

Chupu in Chumash religious thought was the earth, a female being with three aspects: wind, rain, and fire. She was venerated along with sun, a male deity, in ceremonies involving ritual use of toloache, presided over by the secret society of shamans, ?antap. [10] Father Tapis immediately sees and comments on the potential for overt violence implicit in prophecies of counterbaptisms to Chupu and ritual renunciation of a Christianity linked to deadly epidemics. He rightly emphasizes the secrecy with which the movement spread to more than one thousand Chumash. Common themes in the 1801 outbreak and the 1785 revolt thus include a young woman prophet, the prescriptions of secrecy (probably supernaturally sanctioned in both cases), rapid regional diffusion of the prophecy, and the gifting of "beads and seeds" (similar to presents of "beads and other trifles" to Toypurina).

Tongva and Chumash religious philosophies and shamanic practices had much in common. Shamans from both ethnolinguistic groups— more often males, who came from shamanic or chiefly families—were part of an interethnic political association of shamans, ?*antap* among the Chumash and *yovaarekam* among the Tongva (e.g., Bean and Vane 1978; McCawley 1996:95–96). Like Toypurina, the young woman prophet of Santa Barbara may have been a recognized shaman, her communications with spirits thus given immediate credence. Some accounts say that a healer gave her datura—associated with shamanic trances, initiations, ceremonies, and healing and with Chinigchinich—before she had her vision (cf. Sandos 1985:119). In any case, she was both participating in and transforming shamanic traditions in receiving and communicating her revelations from Chupu. The much later Chumash prophecies may differ from Toypurina's in their syncretic incorporation of Christian elements, such as pouring sacred water on the head in dedication to Chupu. But details of Toypurina's prophecies, and ritual acts she prescribed besides the attack on the mission, are barely known from the Spanish interrogations and may also have had syncretic elements.

The largest uprising in the California missions was the Chumash revolt of 1824. A classic example of ritual violence and the clandestine and oppositional nature of religious prophecies under conditions of colonial hegemony, it was a coordinated revolt across a wide region, with attacks at three different missions, each a day's journey from the next: Santa Barbara, Santa Ynés, and La Purísima. Documents from official investigations were lost, and most chroniclers seem unaware of indigenous prophecies as precipitating causes, though Bancroft says that "some local event" triggered it (1886, vol. 2:527–537; Osio 1996:55–69). But Heizer (1941:128) suggests that the 1824 revolt was tied to a messianic movement and that prophecies that the unnamed Chumash woman received from Chupu in 1801 circulated clandestinely among her people for a generation. Kroeber notes, "The god *Achup* or *Chupu*, whose 'worship' a missionary report of 1810 mentions as being uprooted among the Purisima natives, may or may not have had connection with the toloache cult," closely associated with Chinigchinich (1925:567). Offerings at shrines to Chupu persisted into the 1820s among the Chumash (Grant 1978:513).

Father Boscana's contemporary account, from 1825 at San Juan Capistrano, 150 miles to the southeast, suggests that revelations associated with Chinigchinich and the return of powerful spirits underlay the 1824 Santa Barbara revolt and continued to circulate in the region afterward:

About the middle of December, 1823, a comet appeared in the north which was visible until the latter part of January of the ensuing year. In September, 1825, another was seen. . . . The Indians, who had observed them, believing they were their deceased chiefs, consulted together as to the cause of their appearance and were all of the opinion that they denoted some important change in their destiny; but how or in what manner it would be, they were ignorant. Some thought that they would return to their primitive mode of life; that it was Sirout, whom they had seen, he, who was the father of their grand captain, Ouiot; and when he came he ever brought good things, for their profit and happiness. Others believed that it denoted that they were to live free and do whatever they pleased, without being under subjection to any-one; although they would still remain occupants of the mission.

The elder ones said Sirout foretold that another people would come who would treat them as slaves and abuse them; that they would suffer much hunger and misery; and that the chief thus appeared to call them away from the impending calamity. Still others said that the comet was Tacu, the father of Ouiamot or Chinigchinich, which was generally assented to. [1978:89]

In Southern California religious beliefs, a comet generally signifies a chief or shaman returning to earth, bearing a message. Stars are the hearts, or spirits, of powerful beings, including high chiefs and shamans. The term for comet in Acjachemem (better documented than the related Tongva language) means star with a headband tied around its head. Another term for comet means "his life's spirit is making a (medicinal) smudge" (Boscana 1978:77, 89; Harrington 1933:200–201, 226). Headband can also mean Milky Way (Harrington 1933:201). It is a symbol of the spirits, and it is the sacred net personified in the male initiation ritual of *wanawut*, also represented in the outer ring of sand paintings used in male and female initiations and mourning ceremonies. All of this is associated with Chinigchinich.

Headbands have further ritual connotations. A pad of human hair, bound by a special cord (sometimes also of hair), held the eagle feathers of the ceremonial headdress worn by human and spirit dancers on the wamkish and the ritual emblem of rank used at the installation of a new Tongva chief. They were used in shamanic divination and were blessed by shamans for use in battle (DuBois 1908:85–88; Kroeber 1925:640, 645, 662–664, 671–672). By the end of January, a month after its apparition, the bright comet of 1823–24, also recorded by European astronomers, had developed two tails, one pointing toward the sun and the other, away (Harrington 1933:226). The 1824 Chumash uprising began in February, days later.[11]

In 1914 John Peabody Harrington collected oral historical accounts of the revolt from Maria Solares, a descendant of Chumash participants from Mission Santa Ynés. The story is laced with elements of ritual violence and religious prophecy. According to Maria Solares, before the attack the Indians used *pespibata*, an indigenous tobacco (*Nicotiana* sp., used ceremonially and by shamans in much of Southern California, often with datura). At Mission Santa Ynés, upon hearing that the soldiers planned to attack them, "some of the Indians said, 'The priest cannot hurt me—I am a medicine man.' Many Indians said thus." Several captured Chumash at Mission La Purísima were bound, blindfolded, and shot by the soldiers. One man survived. The soldiers "examined him and found that he had an ʔatiswin [amulet] of woven human hair about his neck, and that was the reason he did not die. They broke this and all shot at him again and then the man died. . . . The Ineseños were all saying something like this: 'If they shoot at me, water will come out of the cannon; if they shoot at me, the bullet will not enter my flesh'" (Blackburn 1975:123–126).

Human hair symbolizes the spirit in the theology of the Chinigchinich religion. Hair ropes were used in ritual sand paintings at each of the four cardinal directions to represent the world and as the "sacred rope" of initiation. Male initiation in the toloache ritual itself conveyed "impenetrability to arrows" (Kroeber 1925:626, 658).

The immediate trigger of the uprising was the flogging of a neophyte at Mission Santa Ynéz, which was then burned nearly to the ground (e.g., Castillo 1978:103). A Chumash messenger from La Purísima, en route to the revolt at Santa Ynés, killed a Spaniard and took his clothes and horse. When a suspicious Spanish soldier named Valentín tried to capture him, the messenger "disappeared when he jumped on the horse, giving a cry as he did so. Horse and rider had disappeared, and Valentín was holding pure air." There are also stories by Chumash descendants that, at Santa Ynés, two armed Indians were able to slip into the mission guardhouse through the keyhole. Chumash men several times used a "magic string"—a headband, the *takulsoxsinas*, "a woven band such as Coyote used" worn around the head in battle—in divination ceremonies to find out if they would live or die in the 1824 revolt. One man cut the band in half and placed it on the ground in the form of a cross, to the consternation of others present (Blackburn 1975:123–126; Sandos 1985:125, 128).

There is a paradox here. The ritual violence and prophecies of re-vitalization of the 1824 Chumash uprising were also part of an intel-lectual synergy on the California frontier that included quintessentially rationalist, Enlightenment ideals of individual liberty. In 1821 Mexico declared independence from the Spanish Crown. A short-lived empire was proclaimed in May 1822, but the distant province of Alta Califor-nia seven months later became part of the new republic of Mexico. A minority of provincial officials and Hispanic landowners had long held the liberal, republican, and anticlerical views, directly influenced by the French Enlightenment and French Revolution, that galvanized Mexican revolutionary leaders. In Alta California this included the conviction that Christian Indians, too, had individual rights as citizens and should be liberated from the tyranny of the missions and given property as individuals (e.g., Monroy 1990:117–123; Osio 1996). More cynically, of course, expelling the mission would also free huge, fertile tracts of land for ownership by Californios—Spanish-speaking settlers—and provide a large, additional pool of cheap or free Indian labor. The order to sec-ularize the missions, and dispossess the Franciscans, finally came from Mexico City in 1833. The official goal of the Franciscan missions, since the 1770s, had been to civilize the Indians and hold mission lands in trust for them, presumably for ten years. As decades passed, the padres and provincial governors, justifying continuation of the mission system, blamed Indians for refusing to give up their savage ways (e.g., Bancroft 1886, vol. 1; Monroy 1990:117–123). Father Boscana, describing Ac-jachemem and Tongva interpretations of the 1823–24 comet as portend-ing the advent of a new people come to enslave them, from whom they should escape, says, "These ideas undoubtedly have arisen from the fact that when the declaration of independence was proclaimed in Mexico, the Indians were made to believe that they would no longer be subject to the regulation of the missions; and that each family, or person would live separately as colonists. But the government considering them unfit for such a condition has not made any innovation up to the present time of November, 1825" (1978:89–90).

Boscana states that at San Diego, when the Mexican Empire was proclaimed in 1822, "there were many Indians present who listened attentively to the declaration that Mexico no longer acknowledged the Spanish authority" (1978:88–89). He alleges that in a related incident of internally directed ritual violence a few months later, at a regional eight-day "grand feast," San Diego area Indians burned alive a tyrannical chief and put another in his place. When censured by pueblo authorities, they cited the Mexican revolution and the execution of the Spanish viceroy (Boscana 1978:88–89). Ideas of liberty, tyranny, citizenship, and the rights of man were much discussed among Californios and apparently indigenous Californians as well in the revolutionary years of the early 1820s, including at the presidios of Santa Barbara and San Diego. The Chumash uprising was led by fluent Spanish speakers, many second-generation Catholics, who would have heard and likely participated in some of these conversations, heated debates, and proclamations.

From at least the time of the 1785 uprising at Mission San Gabriel, inspired by the prophecies of Toypurina, through the 1820s, politico-religious movements swept the California frontier and occasionally erupted into armed resistance. They combined a rational calculus and politically revolutionary goals with revelations from ancient and newly revealed sacred beings and creative reinterpretations of European philosophies of religion and society. They occasionally reached the attention of Spanish and Mexican authorities in their corporeal manifestations of ritual violence. The transformative insights and revelations that underlay these movements have evolved and continued, almost unnoticed by outsiders, in secret and sacred ceremonies on dancing grounds in remote Southern California valleys, inspired by prophecies of moral renewal and social harmony related to those that moved Toypurina and the Tongva of Mission San Gabriel in 1785. Prophetic movements arising under extreme conditions of colonial oppression have been similarly and surprisingly long-lived in other parts of the world as well.

Cargo Cults and Ritual Violence: Milne Bay and the Louisiade Archipelago, New Guinea, 1880s–1990s

Hearing Lily Burfitt's story on the beach at the Grass Island feast some 20 years ago is what made me grasp the realities of the violent core of many prophetic movements. A barefoot woman in her sixties in a blue-flowered cotton dress with smooth, light brown skin, long gray hair, gray eyes, and a powerful gaze, she was what in Papuan pidgin is called a *hapkas*, a half-caste, or mixed-race person. Daughter of an English gold miner and a woman from Vanatinai (or Sudest, the largest island in the Louisiade Archipelago, 200 miles southeast of mainland New

Guinea), she was one of the few half-castes in the region. I later read other versions of the events that transformed her life in the distancing prose of yellowed, typed reports at the government station on Misima Island.

Lily married George Burfitt, who like her had an English miner and trader for a father. His mother was from Misima Island. George and Lily took up the lease on a coconut plantation at Panawina Island, in the Calvados Chain of small islands running between Misima and Vanatinai, and also ran a "canteen," a small trade store. In early 1942 the Australian colonial government and white civilians made a panicked and disorderly withdrawal from the islands ahead of the Japanese naval advance; then came the Battle of the Coral Sea, fought over the Louisiade Archipelago, which marked and ended this southernmost advance of the Japanese in the Pacific during World War II. About ten months after the colonial government withdrawal, the Australian Lieutenant Mader and his party, including six Papuan police, sailed to the Louisiade to establish a military government. Until that point, Islanders told me years later, they had thought that the Europeans were gone for good.

About one hundred fifty island men, followers of the prophet Buriga (or Bulega) of Misima Island, planned to carry out the bloodiest part of his prophecy: kill all the white and mixed-race people in the islands, the world as we know it will end, and the spirits of the dead will come sailing back with all the cargo, or material wealth, that the Europeans have unfairly diverted from the Islanders. Lieutenant Mader and his party, hearing of the planned revolt, set out to capture Buriga's men. Just as the small government boat was anchoring in the shallows off Motorina Island, in the Calvados Chain, Lieutenant Mader was stabbed in the back—with a black palm spear, the traditional weapon of war. A key symbol of ritual violence, its use was part of the prophecy. (Accounts of non-cult-related warfare from the 1890s to the 1920s mostly describe Islanders attacking with captured or illegally obtained Snider rifles or with steel bush knives, machetes.)

George Burfitt, who had joined the Australian military party as a local pilot through the treacherous coral reefs, was the next man speared by the cultists, his body shoved overboard into the lagoon. He was followed in death by six Papuan members of the military party. An elderly half-Filipino, half-Papuan pearl trader was murdered on his boat a few days later. In another incident a "native policeman" who came to recruit men to labor for the Allies at Milne Bay (at the tip of the New Guinea mainland) was speared to death on the beach. Eyewitnesses told me that right before this last attack, one man from the Calvados Chain said, "Why should we go and die for the *lumolumo* [Europeans]?"

Buriga and his men were eventually rounded up, and the ringleaders were hanged before the entire, forcibly assembled populace of Misima Island—one man, a child at the time, told me that he still sees this scene in his nightmares. Buriga managed to hang himself in his cell the night before. Most of the raiders were sentenced to long jail terms, further impoverishing and embittering their home communities. The ancestors never returned with the cargo. Lily Burfitt spent the rest of her life as a childless widow, managing a remote plantation by herself.

By the time I met Lily Burfitt I already knew of several interwoven strands of cargoistic belief, prophecy, and action that had swept the archipelago since the 1930s, when Buriga first began to proselytize. The Vanatinai people had not joined the World War II–era revolt, which found its largest number of adherents among the small, infertile Calvados Chain islands to the northwest. Speakers of a different language, they intermittently traded with and (until the 1920s) raided Vanatinai. At least one Vanatinai man was speared by the cultists in 1942, in revenge for his alleged sorcery murders. My Vanatinai neighbors, regionally notorious for the power of their sorcery, spent much of the period of the uprising hiding in the upland forests, avoiding further attacks— and the suddenly increased chances of unwanted contact with *gavamani*, the colonial government, now personified by officers of the Australian military administration.

It was not that Vanatinai people disbelieved in the return of the ancestors with cargo. They just did not believe Buriga. One of their most often told myths continues to be that of Alagh, who lived at the summit of Mt. Rio, home of the ancestor spirits, with his two wives. A carpenter, he disturbed the sleep of Rodyo (the spirit "owner" of the mountain and of the dead) with his constant hammering and sawing. Rodyo ordered Alagh to leave. Alagh took one of his wives and his assistant and sailed away on his European-style boat, *Buliliti*, to the "land of Europeans." He took the noisy things (*bigibigi*; in pidgin, *cargo*) that offended Rodyo: engines, hammers, nails, saws, chickens, cattle, and gold (extracted with powerful machinery in European-owned island mines). This is why Europeans are so rich, and Papuans have only shell valuables. The corollary, of course, is that one day Alagh and the other spirits might sail back with the cargo.

Prophecy and Ritual Violence in New Guinea

According to Lieutenant Sidney Smith, who investigated the World War II cargoistic murders in the Louisiade Archipelago, one man involved "in the murder of Lt. Mader and his party . . . returned to his village [where] he boasted of his deeds and hoisted a flag made out of scraps of calico, saying that the Government had now been killed and they would fly their own flag. After these latest murders it seems quite definite that every native in the Calvados Chain . . . had decided that Government control had more or less ceased to exist and they could return to their old fashions and kill with impunity" (Misima Station 1943b; I was once this man's houseguest at a Panawina Island mortuary feast). Another wartime officer, sentencing a Vanatinai sorcerer to six months of hard labor, writes, "This native said he did not give two pins for the Government and that he would kill anyone by sorcery if he so wished. Apparently thought he had seen the last of the Government in this district" (Misima Station 1943a).

The Louisiade Archipelago cargo cult uprising's anticolonial message was explicit. So was its targeted violence, inspired by prophecies of a new moral and social order revealed by communications with spirits. Similar themes had appeared in the former British New Guinea (after 1906 the Australian-ruled Territory of Papua) since at least the 1880s. In the earliest manifestations recognized by the British (who first declared southeastern New Guinea a "Possession" in 1884), the theme of antiwhite violence, embedded in inspired prophecies, was implicit. But colonial administrators and missionaries immediately perceived the threat that these prophecies posed to colonial social order and their potential for eruptions of armed attack.

These politico-religious movements, including the 20th-century efflorescences that came to be known as cargo cults, have characterized the entire swath of Melanesia from Fiji to Dutch New Guinea. There are striking similarities among these phenomena, from the 1880s Tuka movement of Fiji to the cargoistic prophecies of the late-20th-century Louisiade Archipelago.[12] The similarities of these Pacific prophetic movements are quite unlikely to be the result of diffusion, over 4,000 miles, from a single point of origin. Clearly, some of their diagnostic features must result from similar situations of colonial domination: political, economic, and religious. These overlay analogous Melanesian cultural substrates, particularly Melanesian magico-religious philosophies and worldviews as they relate to, and explain, the careers and fortunes of people and objects. Nevertheless, the degree to which earlier waves of prophecy and ritual violence have been remembered and periodically transformed over decades and generations has, I believe, been underestimated by European colonial authorities and some anthropologists.

The coasts, hinterlands, and islands of southeastern New Guinea, for example, have been linked for centuries by overlapping (though continually shifting and reforming) webs of trade and ceremonial exchange that cross ethnolinguistic boundaries. These routinely bring "foreigners" and new ideas and customs to local communities. This is one way in which prophecies, cults, and details of cargoistic outbreaks in distant places spread across wide regions. I can personally attest to this from having heard about contemporary movements partly from visitors arriving by outrigger sailing canoe at Vanatinai, one of the most out-of-the-way islands in the Pacific.

Colonial situations in British New Guinea and Papua intensified interethnic contacts. The increasingly effective suppression of warfare allowed more freedom of movement and more trade in some areas and for some groups, including new markets for foodstuffs and tropical commodities exchanged for cash or credit at European-owned trade stores. The system of indenture, whereby young men signed two-year contracts to labor for Europeans in distant coconut plantations or goldmines or to be personal servants, moved people from their home communities and, while restricting their freedoms, put them in close contact with men from ethnic groups in other parts of the colony. As Keesing (1978) notes, workforces of colonial plantations and mines throughout Melanesia effectively amplified and diffused cargoistic prophecies and practices.

As on the California frontier and elsewhere in the world, Melanesian religious movements or armed attacks that involve more than one ethnolinguistic group and sweep across larger regions are more likely to involve politico-religious prophecies and elements of ritual violence. Secrecy is usually a key element of the prophecies, just as in California. This is consistent with Melanesian magico-religious beliefs more generally, whether of love, exchange, or warfare. They lose their potency for the owner when revealed to others, particularly their targets—lovers, exchange partners, enemies. So, again as in California, many movements and their prophetic origins and details have remained unknown, or poorly known, to colonial or postcolonial authorities.

The prophecies of Buriga, who in the 1930s began to preach about the expulsion of Europeans by ritual violence and the return of spirits with cargo, did not arise from nowhere. Misima and the rest of the Louisiade Archipelago were linked by traditional maritime exchange network to the New Guinea mainland and to islands stretching as far as the Trobriands, through the *kula* trading system made famous by Bronislaw Malinowski (1922) and related networks of exchange (Lepowsky 1993). And beginning in 1888, Europeans have mined gold at Misima: by the 1930s there were hundreds of indentured laborers, from most parts of the Territory of Papua, at work in the mines. Detailed reports, transformed by repetition and the passage of time, of earlier cargoistic prophecies and events became, I suspect, common knowledge on Misima and other islands courtesy of exchange visitors, indentured laborers, and, during World War II, conscripted laborers for the Allies on the mainland. So it is fruitful to compare the cargoistic prophecies and ritual violence of the Louisiade Archipelago during World War II with two better known cases, one and two generations earlier, the Milne Bay Prophet movement of 1893 and the Vailala Madness of 1919. Both involved people from the British New Guinea/Papuan coast with whom Louisiade Islanders had long been in contact, through exchange links in the first case and through indentured laborers at island gold mines in the second case.

The Milne Bay Prophet movement of 1893 was not the first such movement to arise in what became British New Guinea. Colonial and mission accounts (e.g., Abel 1902:111–112) mention Domu, the prophet of Mita, a hamlet somewhere in the Milne Bay region, probably active in the 1870s or early 1880s, whose prophecies were not recorded by the British. But the 1893 movement that originated on the north shore of Milne Bay—at the eastern tip of the great island of New Guinea—is the first well-documented New Guinea prophetic movement. Its details are noted in colonial reports and by a young English missionary, Charles Abel, based at Kwato Island some 30 miles away. Nearly contemporaneous with the second wave of the Ghost Dance in North America, the Milne Bay Prophet movement had an explicit anticolonial theme.

A young man named Tokeriu, from the village of Gabugabuna, one night received a vision from a tree spirit. Based on his vision, Tokeriu prophesied that a cataclysmic earthquake, volcanic eruption, and tidal wave would wash away every coastal village on both shores of the bay. In order to avoid destruction, people must cast away all European goods, such as tin matchboxes and pocketknives, and return to the use of stone implements. As a sign of adherence, they should tuck into their woven armlets a long *bisare* (this is a narrow, soft, flexible leaf used in beauty and exchange magic, still an item of adornment for dancing at regional mortuary feasts, connoting contact with ancestor spirits). The tree spirit said that people should kill, distribute, and eat all their pigs and consume all their garden food. And they should move away from the coasts, founding new villages inland "where the tidal wave and the white man cannot come near thee," in Abel's translation. After the cataclysm, a new island, covered in ripe yams and taro, would rise in the middle of Milne Bay. The wind would always stay to the southeast (the direction of the reliable trade winds, as opposed to the northwest monsoon or the cyclonic storms that come from the southwest). A huge vessel would anchor off the island. On it would be all the spirits of the dead. Tokeriu would then form a government (Abel 1902:107–109, 122–123; Worsley 1968:52).

One notable element of this prophecy is that it is, in some ways, an anti–cargo cult: the people are instructed by the tree spirit, via the prophet, to renounce all European material possessions in order to usher in the new world of Papuan plenty, social harmony, and the return of the dead. The major exception to the anti–cargo cult theme is, of course, the great European-style boat. The prophecy reveals it to be owned by the spirits of the ancestral dead, rather than by the government, the missionaries, or the white traders. And this boat would be larger than the *Merrie England*, the government steamer and visible manifestation of white power. The 1893 movement is thus preoccupied with cargo and its symbolic meanings in contexts of then-increasing colonial control. In ritual and material acts of resistance, Islanders should return to using only precolonial forms of wealth and technology. The dead will then sail back. They will bring not the generalized wealth of the white man's trade store, symbols of inequity and growing economic dependency in the early stages of a plantation economy, but, rather, the most powerful of all European cargo, the government boat, symbol and reality of armed British colonial domination. After the apocalypse, the prophecy makes clear, indigenous people will have their own formal government, replacing not only the British colonial regime, then only a few years old, but also the small-scale, unstable, big man–dominated polities and alliances that characterized the region before the British arrived. There will be a new moral and social order.

Tokeriu's home district was not yet under direct missionary influence, but Charles Abel received word of the movement and set off with another missionary, a Mr. Walker, to Wagawaga, on the south shore of Milne Bay (whose people speak a different language), where they found only the "native teacher" (missionary) Biga. Everyone else had moved inland in accordance with the prophecy. After a lengthy harangue, Abel and Walker got up a party of Wagawaga men, unarmed, to confront the prophet at Gabugabuna, across the bay. It too was deserted. At the new, inland cult village, they met a hostile crowd of men. Waiting, uninvited, on a long veranda that linked the row of houses (an architectural innovation that was part of the prophecy), Abel threw a stick of twisted, molasses-cured trade tobacco to some of the men. It was immediately "hurled back," he reports, "and struck me on the ear" (1902:116–119). This was a violent act in Papuan terms. The European wealth item, a gift, was rejected by throwing it like a spear at the head of the giver, a deadly insult in local custom.

Abel tried to preach but met only hostility. Tokeriu himself finally appeared, "showing all the symptoms of a man under the strain of a great emotion. The muscles of his face twitched nervously, and all the movements of his body showed he was trying to hold himself under control" (Abel 1902:120). These are startlingly like the spirit possession symptoms that came to be known, 400 miles down the coast and a generation later, as the Vailala Madness. As Abel watched, Tokeriu became possessed again by the tree spirit and began to prophesy, the atmosphere grew more threatening, and Abel's party decided to leave, in fear of their lives. They were pursued to the beach by an "infuriated mob" of "armed shouting natives" brandishing weapons who allowed the outnumbered visitors to escape in their boats. Tokeriu was later arrested by British colonial authorities. Abel (1902:121–127) took a photograph of the prophet, young, lean, and handsome, looking up warily, squatting in leg irons in the yard of Samarai Island Gaol, where he was imprisoned for two years.

Dissident Methodist Charles Abel himself undoubtedly contributed to the cultural matrix that shaped Tokeriu's prophecies. In Milne Bay and on nearby islands, apocalyptic Christian preaching evoked indigenous awareness of the power of the dead—ancestor spirits—and their close relations with the living, implying new revelations for new times. The tensions between old technologies and religious idioms and new, and the intensifying threat of European control of land and spirit forces, produced a creative synthesis: one that could lead the way to a golden age of Papuan abundance, without the Europeans. By the implications of the prophecy, Europeans would all be washed away by the tidal wave that brings back the spirits of the dead. This is a classic revitalization movement, containing elements of three of Wallace's (1956c:275–276) "varieties"—he notes that many movements have aspects of more than one type. Both revivalistic and utopian, in Wallace's terms, it contains one key element of an importation movement, the great ship. The Milne Bay Prophet movement's followers also showed hostility to Europeans. The movement and its prophecies were characterized by ritual, though not corporeal, violence.

Half a century later, in 1943, about seven hundred men from Vanatinai and Misima Islands were sent to the northern shore of Milne Bay to build a new wharf at the old Lever Brothers coconut plantation, extend the airstrip, and unload military ships. Americans and Australians continued to use Milne Bay as a staging area for the New Guinea campaign, and a huge number of Allied troops and enormous quantities of war matériel and supplies passed through. I suspect that the cargoistic beliefs of the Milne Bay Prophet movement of 1893 had gone underground but not vanished and that their embers were fanned in this wartime context of cataclysmic social change, material evidence of enormous European wealth and power, armed violence (by Americans, Australians, Japanese, and Papuans), and unprecedented interracial contacts.[13]

The Vailala Madness of 1919 is a classic example of what Wallace calls an importation movement, and it is the first well-documented prophetic movement in New Guinea where the cargo element is a major motif. Another and closely related theme is what Wallace (1956c:276), borrowing from Bruno Bettelheim, calls identification with the aggressor. Its antecedents are illustrated by the Milne Bay prediction that the Papuan ancestral dead will control the great European ship. The Territory of Papua's government anthropologist, F. E. Williams, who wrote a valuable and lengthy report on the movement (see 1923), rather condescendingly describes the politico-religious philosophy of the Vailala Madness as "vague ideas of Papua for the Papuans." Its key elements include a belief that Papuans will turn white and that the ancestors, who will be white, will sail back with the cargo that the Europeans on the scene have diverted from Papuan hands through their trickery. In other words, then, the colonial specimens are the false Europeans, and the Papuan dead are the true ones. The movement was thus both imitative and expulsive, as in the later cargoistic movements in the Louisiade Archipelago I have already described, prophesying control of European wealth and power but without the currently dominant Europeans. There were several principal Vailala prophets, one of whom early on received spirit messages from a Lifebuoy Soap ad showing a hospital scene. He also received inspiration from one of his prized possessions, a novel called *Love and the Aeroplane*—likely the left-behind reading material of some colonial officer—whose cover art, Williams surmises, evoked local memories of the first plane ever to fly over Papua, a recent and supernaturally portentous event.

The movement spread along the coast and up and down several major rivers. Adherents became possessed by spirits; they were called, in pidgin, head-he-go-round men (a close translation of one of the indigenous terms for the movement's participants). They showed physical evidence of spirit possession, shouted out "English" or "German" phrases—some recognizably of plantation origin—built cult houses with wooden tables and benches and beer bottle vases, and flew village flags. The flagpoles were also for wireless communication with the steamer of the dead. Early on, men performed military-style drills with rifles, which of course greatly alarmed the few whites in the region. Traditional mortuary and male cult ceremonies were discarded, traditional objects were burned, and adherents to the new cult held feasts to honor the spirits. Notably, men and women sat and ate together for the first time. Spirit messages proclaimed the equality of women, intriguingly, the morality of cleanliness, and prohibitions on adultery and theft—the latter prescriptions reminiscent of the Ten Commandments. Elements of Christian theology surfaced not only in the apocalyptic vision of the returning dead but also in transformed concepts of Hedi (Heaven), Yesu (the place of the dead), and Jehova, the younger brother of Jesus, identified with a portrait of King George V. The movement lasted, sporadically, at least a decade, though in more clandestine and less public forms (Williams 1923, 1934). Simultaneously incorporating and opposing Europeans, their ideologies, and their material possessions, it contained strong elements of ritual violence. Adherence to its prophecies was the way to bring on the end of the world and the disappearance of the current run of Europeans—government officers, missionaries, and traders—and usher in a new world of happiness, prosperity, and autonomy. This would be signaled by the return of the ancestral dead with all the European material possessions of which Papuans were deprived by colonial whites.

The Vailala Madness of 1919—erupting at the close of the Great War, a time of disruption of the colonial order even in the distant Territory of

Papua—was particularly widespread among plantation laborers, village constables, interpreters, and former indentured laborers in European-owned gold mines. Many of these men were migrants from rural hinterlands, and they had more direct and sustained contact than most Papuans with European power and wealth. I suspect that information about the Vailala prophecies, and other, more subterranean cargoistic beliefs, reached Misima Island, site of Papua's most productive gold mine of the 1920s and 1930s. Large numbers of indentured laborers from around the territory were employed at the Misima mine, particularly men of the Vailala region, known generically in Papua's eastern islands as "Kiwai." The prophet Buriga's home village of Siagara is just a few miles from the Misima mine.

The motif of the spirits of the dead returning by ship is found in the 1893 Milne Bay Prophet movement, in the 1919 Vailala Madness, in Buriga's prophecies, and in other cargoistic beliefs held by Islanders of the Louisiade Archipelago up to the present. The Vailala prophecy stated that a steamer would return the ancestral dead with cargo that includes a shipment of rifles, as well as more standard European trade store goods such as rice and tobacco. But by the 1940s, and the stunning event of the Australian civilian withdrawal under threat of Japanese invasion, Buriga's prophecies explicitly stated that the dead would not return with the cargo until all the European and mixed-race people had been killed.

Returning home at the close of World War II, the young men from Vanatinai who had labored for the Allies at Milne Bay reported that American soldiers and sailors (temporary sojourners who were not their colonial masters) contrasted sharply with Australians in being immensely rich and generous, giving them food, clothing, tobacco, and money. Black Americans dressed like and worked with whites, and black and white Americans sat down and ate together. Vanatinai Islanders, young and old, concluded from these reports that the spirits of their own dead travel not only to Mt. Rio, the highest mountain on the island, but turn white and go to America, land of the dead. They decided that this must be the land of Europeans described in the Vanatinai myth of Alagh, recounted earlier.

This resembles Buriga's prophecy—but without the homicidal theme. One day the spirits of the dead will sail back from America bringing all the cargo revealed during the war. And this is why Vanatinai people born in the years before World War II firmly believed that I, an American, was an ancestor spirit, returning to live among them and bringing cargo to share among my neighbors. They eventually decided that I was the spirit of an important and recently deceased woman named Taineghubwa, whose hamlet I was living in with a local family. Although I have always denied all spirit identities, I was never able to change the minds of any of the elders. The people most active in proclaiming my spirit nature on Vanatinai and nearby islands were the men who in their youth had labored for the Americans at Milne Bay. The elders saw me as a portent of a more general return of the spirits, predicted in the myth of Alagh as reconfigured and reinterpreted by wartime insights and prophecies (Lepowsky 1989, 1993).

The "Americanist" theme of many other better-known postwar Melanesian cargo cults is obvious (Guiart 1951, 1952; Keesing 1978; Lindstrom 1989; Worsley 1968). Here the postwar Americanist variant of cargoistic prophecy replaces European enemies (Australian colonials) with Americans (GIs, sailors, and myself) who are really Papuan ancestors, supernatural exchange partners of the coming golden age when Islanders and spirits will live together in harmony and prosperity. Again the cult is simultaneously imitative and expulsive, differentiating between good and bad, true and false, Europeans and supernatural sources of power and wealth. Myths of the origins of European wealth are found from Dobu (Fortune 1963:136) to the Wissel Lakes in former Dutch New Guinea (Worsley 1968:134). They often feature, as in the myth of Alagh, what Michael Young (1983) calls "the theme of the resentful hero," who is treated badly and leaves, taking the valuables with him or her and impoverishing the region. Similarly, the most important myth on Vanatinai tells of a female snake spirit that produces from its excrement the first shell currency but is chased away to neighboring Rossel Island by foolish young men (Lepowsky 1993). The parallels of this myth to the departure of Alagh with European wealth are striking.

Some Australian government reports on Buriga's prophecies testify that he openly proclaimed that the dead turn white (cf. Nelson 1976:46–48). The Vailala Madness was preceded by a report that a missionary pastor, around 1912, had been greeted by "highly excited . . . natives" as a returned ancestor spirit (Worsley 1968:80). Such beliefs have a history in parts of New Guinea as long as contact with Europeans (cf. Sahlins 1995). My own conviction is that beliefs in ancestor-European connections and their millennial connotations—the end of the known world and a coming inversion of existing situations of frontier, colonial, and postcolonial inequality—are far more pervasive in time and space in the Southwest Pacific than has currently been documented. The believers are, or were, nonliterate; cult practices and philosophies are often secret; and in New Guinea, for example, British, Australian, and Papua New Guinean governments have all punished even verbal expression of such beliefs with jail terms—for the crime of "spreading false rumors."

Ritual Violence and Revitalization

Rarely, with the exception of officially atheist countries such as the Soviet Union, have armies, or bands of warriors, gone into battle without attempting to secure the blessings of gods, spirits, or divine kings. But revolutionary millenarian movements, to adapt Stern's (1982) useful phrase, invoke supernatural power in new ways during periods of moral crisis, to aid politico-religious campaigns of social transformation.

Movements or armed revolts involving people from a wide region and multiple ethnolinguistic groups are, I propose, the most likely to be generated by prophecies of resistance, ritual attack, and religious renewal in colonial situations. This is so for frontier and colonial California, New Guinea, and around the world. Existing religious philosophies and the political arrangements that they once validated are severely challenged by interlopers' newly revealed religious and material powers. This creates a period of existential doubt and religious ferment, generating inspired and syncretic prophecies, which travel through kinship, ceremonial, and trading relationships. They spread with newly possible rapidity across the region. New forced or voluntary contacts across indigenous ethnic boundaries are created by colonial institutions, as in California's missions, presidios, and ranchos and in New Guinea's plantations and gold mines. The result is widespread oppositional movements advocating ritual violence to expel the oppressors and return to a revitalized and renewed indigenous moral and political order.

Prophetic movements are generated initially by the symbolic and corporeal violence of colonial encounters, developing across the colonial world synergistically with, or in opposition to, Christian proselytizing. They sometimes continue, under conditions of marked inequality and oppression, as largely underground movements in postcolonial states, coming to the notice of authorities when there are visible, corporeal eruptions of ritual violence.

There have been outbreaks in Africa, for example, from the time of the Mahdi of the Anglo-Egyptian Sudan, whose followers believed that British bullets would turn to water. Among the Tshidi, forms and symbols of mission-derived Protestantism were indigenized by "inspired leaders." In apartheid-era South Africa, adherents, "Soldiers of Zion," wore uniforms and followed prescribed dietary rules and healing rituals, collective forms of "ritualized resistance" to South African neo-colonial hegemony (Comaroff 1985:12, 166–167, 247–248; Comaroff and Comaroff 1997:96–118). The present-day Holy Spirit movement of millenarian, self-described Christians continues to precipitate corporal forms of ritual violence, waging war on Ugandan government troops to usher in a new order of pan-tribal peace and prosperity, following the prophecies of Alice Lukoya, the Lakwena, or "Messenger," a young Acholi woman from northern Uganda. When believers draw crosses of ash on their bodies, rub themselves with shea nut oil, and go into battle singing and chanting, the Holy Spirit protects them from enemy bullets, which are turned on the troops that fire them. The stones that believers hurl will explode like grenades. Followers who die in battle are sinners, the Lakwena tells journalists, or possessed of insufficient faith (Vanderwood 1994:99–100, 112–119).

In the mountains of Indochina from 1919 to 1921, in what French colonial authorities called the Madman's War, the Hmong, revolting against colonial taxation policies, followed a messianic prophet who climbed trees to receive messages from heaven, staging guerrilla attacks against the French with cannons fashioned from tree trunks (e.g., Fadiman 1997:17; Quincy 1988). And in the Burma of the new millennium, Karen followers of the 12-year-old Htoo twins, Luther and Johnny, who call themselves God's Army, believe Luther's prophecy that the world will soon explode, that he has given them magic bullets, that the twins command 400,000 invisible soldiers, and that bullets and land mines will bounce harmlessly off the child leaders, who are reincarnations of ancient heroes. The God's Army movement, a synthesis of Buddhism, animism, and fundamentalist Christianity, came to international attention in January 2000 when one faction took 800 patients and staff members hostage in a disastrous raid on a hospital in a Thai border town in which ten people died (Mydans 2000).

Prophetic movements that catalyze episodes of symbolic or corporeal ritual violence have flowered in Latin America among Indians and mestizos from 17th-century colonial Peru (Stern 1982) to the 19th-century Rio Negro and Amazonia (Hill 1996); 20th-century Colombia, Peru, Guyana, and Venezuela (Brown 1991; Staats 1996; Taussig 1987;

Vidal and Whitehead in press); and 21st-century Guyana (Whitehead 2001). Well-documented revolutionary movements from Sonora and Sinaloa in northwestern Mexico in the 1880s and 1890s were triggered by the prophecies of Teresa Urrea, the illegitimate mestiza daughter of a rancher and his young servant. She fell into a prolonged trance at age 16 and received a vision from the Virgin Mary empowering her to heal the sick and foretell the future. Mestizos, and Mayo and Yaqui Indians, made pilgrimages to "Santa Teresa de Cabora," who preached about the world's three greatest evils—priests, money, and doctors—and called on the people to repent or face God's punishment. Her mestizo followers in the mountains of Chihuahua rose up against the federal troops of Porfirio Diaz; Mayo Indians attacked the Sonoran town of Navojoa in reprisal for the expropriation of their lands, using Santa Teresa de Cabora as their battle cry; and a party of Yaquis attacked the Mexican customs station on the Sonora-Arizona border at Nogales, killing several officials. Yaquis found dead after the battle carried "powder and ointments" to "shield the attackers from the bullets of their adversaries"; over the heart of each was a photograph of Teresa Urrea (Vanderwood 1989:229). She was forcibly deported to Arizona in 1892, where she continued a career as a healer and died young of tuberculosis (Erickson n.d.; Vanderwood 1989, 1994, 1998). Her memory continues. Her aid was invoked by striking Mexican American copper mine workers in southern Arizona in the late 20th century (Sharyn Yeoman, personal communication, 2000; cf. Vanderwood 1998).

Other prophetic movements continue in postcolonial, multiethnic states with great disparities of wealth and power. In parts of South America, the ascribed supernatural power of dispossessed or distant indigenes, "the magic of the Indian," fuses with that of the African slave and the Christian cultist and becomes, for an ethnically diverse range of citizens, a new kind of "Third World modernism, a neocolonial reworking of primitivism" (Taussig 1987:171–172). Ritual violence, with its symbols and practices of supernaturally charged "indigeneity" and the invoked power of the despoiled land, arises in the oppositional politico-religious movements of ethnic minorities. But it can become a tool of the powerful, "the magic of the [postcolonial] state" (Taussig 1997), when charismatic leaders harness supernatural powers to turn the minds of voters, terrorize the populace, and control enemies, as in Duvalier's Haiti or Forbes Burnham's Guyana (Vidal and Whitehead in press).

Anthony Wallace's classic article on revitalization explicitly compares

North America, especially the Handsome Lake movement and the Ghost Dance, with the Pacific Islands, particularly Melanesian cargo cults. In thinking about California revolts and New Guinea cargo cults, the concept of revitalization remains analytically valuable. But Wallace underemphasizes the continuum of ritual violence that underlies many revitalization movements and, thus, their explicitly revolutionary, oppositional nature.

Wallace makes the key point that revitalization movements often embody an ambivalence regarding "traditional and imported cultural material" and that "both the traditional and the foreign model are regarded both positively and negatively. Culture areas seem to have characteristic ways of handling the identification [with the foreign] problem" (1956c:276). North America, he suggests, is a "revival" area, and Melanesia is an "importation area," for "Melanesians were often subjected to a more direct coercion by foreign police power" and thus identify with the aggressor, whereas "American Indians north of Mexico were never enslaved on a large scale, forced to work on plantations, or levied for labor in lieu of taxes" (1956c:276). Just the reverse is true for the subjugated peoples of the Alta California missions versus the Islanders of the Louisiade Archipelago, where (except on Misima) Islanders could, and can, go for months or even years without seeing a white face. The two principal cases I present here suggest, then, that areal similarities of prophetic movements characteristic of Melanesia and North America must be caused by something else. They more likely, I think, result from regionally similar indigenous cosmologies and religious philosophies, with oppositional revitalization movements often varying according to the stage of European control then current.

The Toypurina uprising fits what Wallace calls a revival movement. It likely was a utopian movement as well, in his scheme, just as the Chinigchinich religion is both. But details of Toypurina's prophecies are largely lost. In the islands of southeastern New Guinea, Buriga's prophecies were a violent form of a classic cargo cult or, in Wallace's terms, an importation movement. It too was utopian in its vision of a prosperous and harmonious future shared by the living and the dead. The 1893 Milne Bay Prophet movement was a revival and a utopian movement. I think that this is because it was a response to an earlier and less pervasively established phase of colonial domination. But all these movements had common themes: expel Europeans through ritual or corporeal violence; regain control of land, wealth, and personal autonomy; and live harmoniously with spirits, although in new ways, as they are newly revealed by prophecy. The incorporative, or imitative, aspects of the cargoistic prophecies and movements I have described are only one side of them. They are also expulsive and oppositional: case studies of ritual violence, implicit and explicit. Buriga and others may have identified with the aggressors, in psychoanalytic terms, and wanted to become them symbolically. But they also wanted to kill them, replace them, possess their powers and goods, and, fundamentally, reclaim their own.

In California, enough elements of Toypurina's prophecies survive to show clear parallels with later phenomena such as the Ghost Dance: supernatural forces affect enemies and make one impervious to European weapons, ridding the land of despoiling European invaders. They also show clear parallels with Melanesian cargo cults of the Louisiade Archipelago and elsewhere: ritual attacks that use supernatural power and indigenous weapons that ritually protect indigenous warriors against soldiers armed with guns or cannons and, again, ridding the land of European invaders. Ghost Dance prophecies, like cargoistic ones, foretell the return of the spirits of the dead bringing social harmony and prosperity to the living. Toypurina's prophecies, the Chupu revelations, and the advent of the two-tailed comet said to be Tacu, father of Chinigchinich, may well have also.

The Chinigchinich religion and related philosophies and ceremonies of moral and social renewal have outlasted the 20th century among some indigenous Southern Californians less devastated than the Tongva by the disease, violence, and expropriations of white conquest. In addition, a California Indian Renaissance—overlapping, newer revitalization movements—has reached Tongva and neighboring people. Many of these movements explicitly seek to honor and renew indigenous religions and to emphasize both the sacredness of relations with the natural world and the connection between religious practice and political autonomy. The Gabrieleno-Tongva Tribal Council, with over three hundred enrolled members, has petitioned for federal recognition. At its request, and backed by research conducted through the University of California–Los Angeles American Indian Studies Program, Representative Hilda Solis of the San Gabriel Valley (herself a Californiana) in 2001 introduced a bill in Congress "to reaffirm the status of the Gabrieleno/Tongva Nation." Other groups of Tongva descendants have also organized themselves, as have descendants of the closely related

Fernandeños, who seek federal recognition as well. Tongva descendants speak out through regional media to protect sacred sites, prehistoric villages, and endangered mountain lions. One of these endangered places is Puvungna, home of Chinigchinich, which has been threatened by a proposed strip mall. Ancestral dead whose remains have been disturbed by development and construction are now being repatriated to descendants and ceremonially reburied. A traditional planked canoe was constructed by the Ti'at Voyaging Society, and in 1995 it was ritually dedicated and paddled 25 miles from Catalina Island to the mainland. A Tongva dance troupe performs at Los Angeles area public events, sometimes introduced by speeches in the Tongva language. Other Tongva have dedicated themselves to cultural education—visiting schools, museums, botanical gardens, and other institutions to share their knowledge of indigenous life and history with other Southern Californians and emphasize that the Tongva are still here. Tongva activists have established Harakmongna, an American Indian cultural center, in an old ranger station high in the San Gabriel Mountains. A model Tongva village was dedicated in October 1999 in a park near the San Gabriel River, just below the site of the first Mission San Gabriel, in the Hispanic-majority City of Santa Fe Springs. In San Gabriel itself, a small city park a few hundred yards from the former hamlet of Sibanga reopened in June 2002 dedicated to commemorating the Tongva, its new playground equipment shaped like dolphins, whales, and other sacred animals and Tongva mythology–inspired pavement mosaics much admired by a multiethnic array of local adults and children.

Among the Acjachemem and Quechnajuichom, with whom Tongva have intermarried for more than two hundred years, activists are working to restore indigenous languages (the last speaker from infancy of Quechnajuichom died in the 1990s; the last Tongva speaker from infancy died in the 1970s) (e.g., Hinton 1994; Locklear and Elliott 2002). Acjachemem and Tongva activists lead a yearly "Ancestor Walk" of descendants and supporters to village sites and burial places to commemorate ancestors and protest encroaching, massive development and desecration (e.g., Robles 2002). The Juaneño Band of Mission Indians Acjachemem Nation has some one thousand four hundred enrolled members. Its petition for federal recognition advances at a glacial pace through the bureaucracy of the Branch of Acknowledgment and Research of the Bureau of Indian Affairs, achieving "Ready Status" in 1995. The growing number of heavily advertised casinos, the band-sponsored intertribal powwows, and the recent casino-based wealth and political influence of federally recognized bands of Serranos, Cahuillas, and Luiseños, a short distance away to the east and south, have led to unprecedented regional visibility for indigenous Californians and helped to fund renewed drives toward cultural and religious revitalization.

In the contemporary Pacific Islands, cultural transformation movements range from cargoistic movements like those documented in classic anthropological accounts; to the Clean and Green movement of environmental renewal and economic self-sufficiency among Mortlock Islanders on Pohnpei, in Micronesia; to the overlapping Hawaiian Renaissance, Kanaka Maoli, Hawaiian Sovereignty, and Hawaiian Independence movements, which make sophisticated use of print and electronic media and have powerful, oppositional influences on Hawaiian politics.[14]

Back in the Louisiade Archipelago, yet another variant of millennial, cargoistic prophecy has arisen, on Misima Island, in the last 25 years. The prophet is none other than the wartime prophet Buriga's sister's son—this is a matrilineal area—and prophetic rituals are heavily inflected with a syncretic blend of Methodism and ancestor veneration. The wartime theme of violence has been muted into ritual practices that will banish Europeans and current forms of national and local government and will bring back ancestors and cargo. Like his uncle, the most recent prophet has found adherents in the impoverished Calvados Chain islands and among Misima Islanders angry at the stark disparities of wealth made visible by the opening, in the 1980s by a multinational corporation, of one of the world's largest gold mines near Misima's government station.

Disparities of wealth and power, and the continuing loss of autonomy in a neocolonial periphery, still provide fruitful ground for prophetic movements. The Islanders of the Louisiade Archipelago, who unlike the Tongva retain their languages, voyaging canoes, and webs of social relations largely intact, continue to consider cargoistic prophecies and new ritual approaches to the power of spirits and the regeneration of social order. Several times so far, though, the world has failed to end as predicted.

All revitalization movements are oppositional, arising among cultural minorities, catalyzed by the moral and political crises of colonial and postcolonial hegemony. Some are separatist or retreatist, while others are explicitly confrontational. Not all revitalization movements generate ritual violence. But many do, whether they are separatist or confrontational. Ritual violence predates the rise of a revitalization movement as part of indigenous politico-religious practice. It is then transformed and incorporated into the new movement. Prophetic movements generating ritual violence tend to spread across ethnic boundaries, redefining the borders of social groupings into nascent, religiously linked polities opposed to colonial institutions or the colonial state.

Ritual violence follows a continuum from magic and prayer to the corporeal violence of divinely inspired warriors. The objects of ritual violence follow an intersecting continuum that runs from the most internal to the most external. Ritual attacks, from magical to corporeal, can be directed internally within the kin network, the settlement, or the ethnic group, as in witchcraft, sorcery, shamanic attack, feuding, or raiding. They can cross ethnic boundaries to target members of other indigenous groups through sorcery, raiding, and warfare. They can be directed to internal transgressors of a prophetic or proselytizing religion that has itself crossed ethnic boundaries. Or they can target external enemies, whether by dancing to bring on the end of the world and the disappearance of whites or by ritual attacks, magical or corporeal, on colonial overlords. The targets of ritual violence of a particular ethnic group or religious movement may be fluid, moving over time from internal to external and back again in response to perceived moral transgressions, new prophetic revelations, or further colonial repression. The internally directed destructive powers of witchcraft, sorcery, shamanism, and war magic, which can be turned outward against traditional enemies, may, in response to prophecies like Buriga's, be reconfigured and used against the colonials. After the revolt is suppressed, the movement may return to secret rituals intended to bring on the return of the ancestors with their wealth and power and the disappearance of the colonial or postcolonial state. The ritual violence of the revitalizing Chinigchinich religion was internally directed by divine commands to sacred animals and high shamans to kill initiates who disobeyed his moral code or betrayed his secrets, on pain of mass death in his terrible plagues. It may have erupted periodically into armed, ritualized revolt as new epidemics struck, new acts of violence were perpetrated against the people in missions and towns, or inspired prophecies such as those of Toypurina revealed new insights from him or related spirit beings such as earth. After the uprisings failed, the prophecies and rituals, sacred and secret, went back underground.

Colonial and postcolonial states reserve to themselves the right to commit violence, internally in punishing violators of their laws and codes and externally in making war. This means that all acts of ritual violence by minority peoples are inherently subversive or revolutionary, dangerous both to the institutions and to the very survival of the state in its current form.

Notes

Portions of earlier drafts of this chapter were presented at the session "Reassessing Revitalization: Perspectives from North America and the Pacific" at the American Anthropological Association Annual Meeting in Chicago in November 1999; and at the Henry E. Huntington Library in December 2000. I thank Michael E. Harkin, Lin Poyer, Jim Roscoe, Ray Fogelson, Tim Buckley, Mac Marshall, John Jeffredo, Lowell Bean, Cecilia O'Leary, Tony Platt, Lisbeth Haas, David Weber, Harry Kelsey, Peter Nabokov, Heather Singleton, Anthony Forster, Steven Hackel, Michael Engh, Margaret Hunt, Roger Knight, Sharyn Yeoman, Kirstin Erickson, Alice Oleson, and Robert Brightman for their comments on aspects of this research. Special thanks go to Craig Torres, Cindi Alvitre, and William M. Williams for sharing their knowledge and perspectives. I am grateful to Robert C. Ritchie, David Zeidberg, and the librarians and entire staff of the Huntington Library for their professional and practical support and assistance and for providing me with an ideal setting for scholarly research and writing. Jerry Sulliger kindly translated the 18th-century Spanish documents on the Toypurina revolt for me. Thanks also go to Lisbeth Haas for Spanish transcriptions of letters from the Mission Santa Barbara Archives and especially for sharing her insights into 18th- and early-19th-century California. All quotations in this chapter from Spanish documents related to the investigation of the 1785 San Gabriel revolt come from new translations of the original manuscripts (Archivo General de la Nación 1785–87; Mission Santa Barbara 1787–88).

My ethnographic and archival research on New Guinea has been supported by the National Science Foundation; the University of California–Berkeley Chancellor's Patent Fund, Department of Anthropology, and Lowie (now Hearst) Museum; the National Institute of Child Health and Human Development, National Institutes of Health; the Wenner-Gren Foundation for Anthropological Research; the National Endowment for the Humanities; the American Philosophical Society; the American Council of Learned Societies; and the Graduate School and the William F. Vilas Trust of the University of Wisconsin–Madison. My research on California has been supported by the Graduate School and the William F. Vilas Trust of the University of Wisconsin–Madison, the Dora and John Randolph Haynes Foundation and the Historical Society of

Southern California, and Andrew W. Mellon Research Fellowships from the Henry E. Huntington Library, San Marino CA. I am deeply grateful for all this financial support.

1. The term *Tongva* has been increasingly preferred by descendants over the last decade or so. The elderly Mrs. James Rosemyre (Narcisa Higuera), 100 years ago near Fort Tejon, told ethnologist C. Hart Merriam that the term *Tongva* was used to describe the inhabitants of the vicinity of Mission San Gabriel (cf. McCawley 1996). There is no presently known collective term that was used by the entire ethnolinguistic group to describe itself in pre-mission times, which is characteristic of most California groups. Speakers of a Takic (California Shoshonean) language, the Tongva/Gabrielino occupied all of what is now the Los Angeles Basin, from the San Gabriel Mountains to the ocean (up the coast as far as Topanga Canyon; Chumash territory begins at Malibu, and the two place-names are derived from the Tongva and Chumash languages, respectively). Tongva territory includes the San Gabriel Valley to the east, the drainage of the Santa Ana River to the southeast and as far southeast as Aliso Creek in what is now Southern Orange County, plus the three southernmost Channel Islands of Santa Catalina, San Clemente, and tiny San Nicolas. Speakers of a closely related dialect, known for two centuries as the Fernandeños (after Mission San Fernando, founded in 1797), occupied the San Fernando Valley, north of central Los Angeles. Kroeber (1925:620) suggests that there may actually have been as many as "half a dozen" mainland dialects of this language but that they were later standardized into two dialects because of the two missions. This seems likely. A separate dialect was spoken on Santa Catalina and San Clemente Islands, and yet another was spoken on San Nicolas Island. The Franciscans in 1812 discerned four languages (*idiomas*) among Mission San Gabriel neophytes, "Kokomcar" (location uncertain—coastal Comicranga at Santa Monica Canyon in West Los Angeles?), "Siba" (from Sheevanga, the inland hamlet adjacent to the mission), Carbonanga or Corbonamga (location uncertain—Kawenga, whose name continues at Cahuenga Pass in the Hollywood Hills?), and Guiguitamcar (Kitanemuk), a separate Takic language once spoken in the mountains north and east of the mission (Engelhardt 1927:97; Kroeber 1925:621; the guesses are mine). The population just before the Spanish mission era was probably 5,000–10,000 (Bean and Smith 1978; Kroeber 1925). Island and related coastal people were sometimes in hostile relations with inland ones, partially disrupting their food supply, particularly fish. Mission neophytes, drawn at first from inland communities, went hungry in early years because of hostilities and crop failures and were turned loose for weeks by the Franciscans to hunt and forage. South of Aliso Creek was the territory of the Acjachemem or Juaneños— after Mission San Juan Capistrano, founded in 1776—speakers of the northernmost Luiseño dialect. Luiseños (Quechnajuichom, Khecham, or Que-esh, from the name of the coastal area near Mission San Luis Rey, founded in 1798) speak a

separate Takic language (Bancroft 1886, vol. 1:202; Bean and Shipek 1978; Bean and Smith 1978; Kroeber 1925; McCawley 1996).

Unconverted Indians were called gentiles (pagans) by the Spanish. Their settlements, many made up of several extended families though others were larger, were known in California Spanish as *rancherías*—still used in California today to refer to rural Indian communities, most not on officially recognized reservations. Neophytes, baptized Indians, presumably subject to Christian instruction, were compelled to live within, or just outside, the mission walls. If they fled to their home communities or the mountains, Spanish soldiers would track them and bring them in chains back to the mission, where they were whipped, shackled, and sentenced to a term of hard labor. Unknown numbers of Tongva/Gabrielino escaped the missions or moved away from their home territory to join neighboring ethnolinguistic groups to the north, east, and southeast, in the deserts, mountains, and San Joaquin Valley, that remained free of mission control.

2. The suffix *-vit* means "person from a given place"; *-nga* or *-ngna* indicates place. A chief's firstborn daughter held a title, *maniisar*, indicating her high rank. His oldest son, called *tomyaar* (chief), normally succeeded him. The 1785 uprising at Mission San Gabriel is briefly mentioned in the history by Bancroft, based on Spanish documents. Bancroft does not name Toypurina but relates: "The neophytes and gentiles were tempted by a woman, so at least said the men, into a plan to attack the mission and kill the friars" (1886, vol. 1:460). Similarly, A. J. West's *A History of Los Angeles County* (1889) refers, without attribution, to an "aboriginal eve" who tempted the Indians at San Gabriel into revolt. Father Zephyrin Engelhardt's history of Mission San Gabriel closely paraphrases Bancroft on "neophytes and gentiles tempted by a woman" (1927:60–61).

Thomas Workman Temple II, a lawyer, self-taught genealogist, and amateur historian whose Hispanic ancestors arrived at Mission San Gabriel in the 1770s (and Anglo forebears at Los Angeles in the 1830s and 1840s), says that he heard the story of an Indian revolt at the mission led by a woman from his mother, descended from Mission San Gabriel soldiers born in what is now Mexico. Years later, he says, finding mention of the incident in Bancroft's history (1886, vol. 1) and remembering the story, he located a microfilm copy of the Spanish *Expediente* (*Proceedings*) at the Bancroft Library and traces of Toypurina's later life in mission records. Temple's reconstruction of the Toypurina revolt, published in *The Masterkey*, the Southwest Museum of Los Angeles periodical, is a mixture of fabrication and historically accurate detail traceable to Spanish colonial documents. Temple presents it as historical fact, based on his archival search for documentation of his mother's story, using phrases such as "these are her [Toypurina's] exact words," followed by quotations (e.g., 1958:148). But many of his quotations do not match the Spanish archival texts he cites. Temple does not specify what elements of his tale—replete with individually named soldiers dressing up as priests, feigning death in a mock wake, and lying in wait for the attackers—he received from his mother's *cuento* (story). If he had, then this would be historically and ethnographically valuable testimony from one Californio family's oral traditions, with the reader's understanding that, as Temple puts it, the cuentos were "interpolated with what flourishes succeeding generations had added or subtracted from the storied past of our San Gabriel Valley." But Temple attributes only general remarks to his mother on "wild Indios in war paint," "apprehensive padres praying for deliverance," and "brave soldados." Absent his testimony on what details of the event he heard through family oral traditions, his account might best be described as historical fiction and should be cited only with caution. Temple (1958:141) also writes that a failed uprising at Mission San Gabriel in 1779 was led by neophyte Nicolas José (a leader of the 1785 revolt), motivated by his "jealous rage" over the "advances" made to his intended bride by a "Baja California neophyte" (a Christianized Indian accompanying the Spanish to Alta California). "The padres and soldiers were also to be killed," Temple writes. There is no documentary evidence to back up Temple's account of the grievances behind the 1779 revolt. In spite of its failings, Temple's 1958 article has remained the principal source for most later discussions of the 1785 revolt, such as those by Phillips (1975) and Castillo (1991), who cite it in overviews of Indian resistance movements in Southern California, and by Monroy (1990:40) and McCawley (1996:199), who discuss Indian-Spanish relations in 18th-century California. Tongva descendant Louisa Jeffredo-Warden (1999), like Temple (a distant relation through a great-grandmother), heard family stories of Toypurina in childhood. She uses (though with skepticism) Temple's account but adds brief excerpts from a new translation of Spanish documents. Mason (1975) uses the original Spanish documents in an article on Governor Fages's relations with Indians mentioning the 1785 revolt, as does Castañeda (1998) in a broader gender analysis of pre–gold rush California's multiethnic history. Hackel (n.d.) uses his own translation in analyzing Spanish colonial legal culture, critiquing Temple (1958) and emphasizing the leadership of neophyte Nicolas José in the 1785 uprising. He shows that in summer 1784, hundreds of neophytes were moved to the mission vicinity from coastal communities, then in hostilities with inland people, arguing that this further strained the subsistence economy (already threatened by Spanish farming and grazing) and helped precipitate the 1785 revolt.

As comments in works by Castillo, Castañeda, and Jeffredo-Warden reflect, in the last decade or so Toypurina has, fittingly, begun to be recovered in Southern California as a heroic icon of indigenous resistance to Spanish colonial domination. Castañeda interviewed Vera Rocha, a Tongva elder and activist, who "received the story of Toypurina and the Gabrielinos as a very young girl from her great-grandmother, who received it from her mother" (1998:238). Rocha recently worked with UCLA professor and sculptor Judith Baca to create "a prayer mound dedicated to Toypurina," public art that is now part of a commuter rail station in the San Gabriel Valley. Toypurina will be a central figure in a major exhibition on the Tongva planned for the UCLA Fowler Museum of Cultural History (Cindi Alvitre and Craig Torres, personal communications, 2001). And in a recent storybook for school-age children, called *Great Indians of California*, a final page touting forthcoming titles in the series advises its young readers, "Soon you can read all about the amazing adventures of Toypurina, The Remarkable Indian Woman Leader" (Knill 1999:47). These books for California children represent a dramatic cultural and philosophical shift since the days when my fourth grade class in Los Angeles read a little book on early local history that our teacher contextualized with derogatory remarks on "Digger Indians."

3. Future father of Pio Pico, a governor of Mexican California, and Andrés Pico, who in 1846 defeated the invading Americans at the Battle of San Pascuál, José Maria Pico came to Alta California with his soldier father in 1775 at the age of about 11. José Maria, the investigation of the 1785 revolt testifies, "understands well the language of the natives." This is itself an intriguing piece of evidence about life on the early California frontier. The Pico family, from Sinaloa and Sonora, now northwestern Mexico, was primarily of Indian (possibly Yaqui or Mayo) and African ancestry (e.g., Gray 1998; Mason 1998). A Mission San Gabriel Franciscan father says similarly in1812 that "the settlers in the town [Los Angeles] commonly speak the Indian idiom also, and even better and more fluently than their own language which is the Spanish" (Engelhardt 1927:97). This may have referred to "settlers" (*pobladores*; townspeople) from families living in the pueblo whose fathers were Spanish mestizos and mothers were Tongva, Acjachemem, or Serrano and whose descendants were later counted as Californios, California Hispanics. Tongva was the lingua franca between Spanish speakers and Indians in Los Angeles until around the 1840s (Kroeber 1925).

4. See Mission San Gabriel 1784–85; cf. Mason 1998:96. There is a continuing oral tradition among some Tongva descendants (which Temple [1958] also notes without documentary evidence) that Toypurina was married at the time of the 1785 revolt, that her marriage was put aside when she accepted Christian baptism. There is no evidence of any previous marriage in mission records of her 1787 baptism or of her 1789 marriage. Correspondence in 1787–88 between Governor Fages and the Franciscans regarding Toypurina's exile calls her a single woman (*soltera*; see Mission Santa Barbara 1787–88). Jesuit priest and California historian Michael Engh (personal communication, 2001) has informed me that 18th-century Franciscans in Alta California would have recognized the Pauline Exception, an early church doctrine in which a formerly pagan, newly baptized Christian spouse whose partner refuses to convert can have an existing marriage annulled and then marry a Christian. An existing marriage for Toypurina is thus theoretically possible, although the Pauline Ex-

ception was rarely used in Spanish California. If such a marriage indeed existed, then there would be no way of confirming if it was annulled with Toypurina's consent or by coercion.

Manuel Montero's birthplace in the 1790 provincial census is given as Puebla, indicating the colonial city in the Valley of Mexico (Mason 1998:96). But in 1807, at the marriage of his 15-year-old daughter, Juana, to Josef Maria Benavidez at Mission Santa Clara, Manuel is listed as a "native of the Town of Los Angeles" (*natl. de la Puebla de los Angeles*). Los Angeles was founded in 1781, and none of the original settlers had the surname Montero. Because he was married in 1789, Manuel was almost surely born in Mexico but may have been posted to Los Angeles, recorded erroneously as his native town in 1807. Juana's mother is described, eight years after her death, as "Maria Regina (Toypurina) Yndia dela Misn. De Sn. Gabriel [Indian of the Mission of San Gabriel]" (April 18, 1807; marriage record number 722). Her baptismal name is clearly and simply written at Mission San Gabriel in 1787 as "Regina [Queen] Josefa." Later documents, such as the baptismal and matrimonial records of her children, usually give her name as Maria Regina, Maria Queen, a reference to the Virgin Mary in her aspect as Our Lady Queen of Angels—from which the city of Los Angeles, in Toypurina's homeland, takes its name as well. Other times she is called Maria Regina Teipurina. The name Maria Regina is a subtle but symbolically important transformation. Inscribed by later Spanish authorities, it celebrates her Christian piety rather than her political leadership.

Regina Josefa—Toypurina—and Manuel Montero's children were Cesario Antonio (baptized at Mission San Luis Obispo, August 27, 1790; baptism number 906), Juana de Dios (baptized at Mission San Luis Obispo, March 7, 1792; baptism number 1095), Josefa (baptized in 1793), and Maria Clementina (baptized at Mission San Carlos [Borromeo] de Monterey, November 24, 1794). Toypurina thus became grandmother to numerous well-known families of Californios resident in the San Francisco Bay Area, whose surnames include Alviso, Archuleta, Benavidez, Castro, Mesa, Vasquez, Smith, and Vioget (through a granddaughter's marriage to Jean Jacques Vioget, a noted Swiss French gold rush–era San Francisco painter). A daughter, granddaughter, and great-granddaughter each bore her baptismal name of Josefa. I am most grateful to William M. Williams, lineal descendant of Toypurina, for sharing and discussing the fruits of his years of genealogical research with me.

5. See Boscana 1978; DuBois 1908; Sparkman 1908; Kroeber 1925:567–568, 621–630, 636–641, 662–664, 707–708, 712–716; Harrington 1933; Bean and Smith 1978; Bean and Vane 1978; Wallace 1978:456–459; Hester 1978:502–503; and McCawley 1996. Associated religious practices may have been present in northern Baja California in the 1700s, when the sacred raven and the ritual feather headband were recorded by Venegas (DuBois 1908:75). The new Chinigchinich religion may have first arisen in the Tongva homeland "as a result

of contact with Christian deserters or castaways, since many of its features are reminiscent of Christian themes" (Bean and Vane 1978:699; cf. White 1963). The incorporation of Christian-inspired elements in prophecies related to the Chinigchinich religion could have begun before the presidios and missions of Alta California were founded. Word of new and powerful religious mysteries may have spread northward, reaching the maritime trading hubs of San Clemente and Santa Catalina Islands, as indigenous people traveled north and south of the present-day Mexican border to visit relatives, trade steatite and Olivella shell beads, and attend healing, initiation, and mourning ceremonies. These kinds of social ties first introduced deadly European diseases to Alta California in the years before the missions. Pablo Tac (1952), a Quechnajuichom seminarian who died in Rome, wrote in 1835 that there were great waves of disease and death near San Luis Rey, his birthplace, just before Spanish settlement (cf. Bean and Smith 1978:540). The first Jesuit missions in Antigua (Baja) California were established in 1697, almost a century earlier. After the Jesuits were expelled by royal decree from all of New Spain, the missions were taken over, in 1768, by Franciscans, who immediately expanded the reach of their missions northward (Crosby 1994; Robertson 1978).

The original spelling, Chinigchinich, is Father Geronimo Boscana's, recorded in 1825. Native peoples of Southern California, and anthropologists and linguists of the last century, agree that the name contains only three syllables, not Boscana's four. Other renderings are Chingichngich, Chingichnich, Chungichnish, Chengiichngech, and Harrington's "English spelling Chee-ngich-ngich." The accent is on the second syllable, and the approximate pronunciation is "Chi-ngyich-ngyich." I use the orthographically inaccurate but common Boscana rendering for historical purposes here. One Tongva tradition, which says that Chinigchinich and his prophecies and rituals originated on San Clemente and Santa Catalina Islands, reaching the mainland at Puvungna and then spreading throughout Southern California (John Jeffredo, personal communication, 1995), matches Kroeber's note that "all southern [Luiseño] accounts mention Santa Catalina and San Clemente Islands as the seat of the source of this cult" (1925:621). He refers to the toloache ritual, in which hallucinogenic datura is ceremonially ingested, particularly at initiations. This is, as he says, "intimately associated with beliefs in a deity called Chingichnich or Chungichnish" (1925:622). Other Tongva, Acjachemem, and Quechnajuichom—and Boscana in 1825 (see 1978:127), relying on three aged consultants—describe Puvungna (Pubu, in Boscana) as his birthplace.

Kroeber gives linguistic evidence that key Juaneño and Luiseño religious terms and place-names in myths—recorded by Boscana in the 1820s and by Kroeber himself from Luiseños in the early 20th century—were borrowed from the Gabrielino (Tongva) language, as were many sacred songs. He concludes of Boscana's Chinigchinich, "A large part, possibly the bulk, of the information conveyed by the assiduous and sympathetic priest is certainly of Gabrielino origin" (1925:636). This may have been, he notes (1925:636–637, 644, 659–660), either cultural borrowing in pre-mission times or information from Gabrielinos, a significant minority of the neophytes at Mission San Juan Capistrano. The name Chinigchinich was never, in the 1820s to 1920s, collected from explicitly identified Tongva speakers (although Boscana does not identify his consultants or their natal communities). It may be the deity's name in Acjachemem and Quechnajuichom dialects.

6. Dramatic evidence comes from the 1602 voyage of exploration of Sebastián Vizcaino along the California coast, when the Spanish came ashore at the island they named Santa Catalina. Father Antonio de la Ascensión of the Barefoot Order of Nuestra Señora del Carmen, who accompanied Vizcaino, describes the encounter of Spanish soldiers on the narrow isthmus dividing the island:

> The soldiers ran all over the island and in one part of it fell in with a place of worship or temple where the natives perform their sacrifices and adorations. This was a large flat patio, and in one part of it, where they had what we would call an altar, there was a great circle all surrounded with feathers of various colors and shapes, which must come from the birds they sacrifice. Inside the circle there was a figure like a devil painted in various colors, in the way the Indians of New Spain are accustomed to paint them. At the sides of this were the sun and the moon. When the soldiers reached this place, inside the circle there were two large crows larger than ordinary ones, which flew away when they saw strangers, and alighted on some near-by rocks. One of the soldiers, seeing their size, aimed at them with his harquebus, and discharging it, killed them both. When the Indians saw this they began to weep and display great emotion. In my opinion, the Devil talked to them through these crows, because all the men and women hold them in great respect and fear. I saw with my own eyes some Indian women cleaning some fish on the beach for food for themselves and their husbands and children. Some crows came up to them and took this out of their hands with their bills, while they remained quiet without speaking a word or frightening them away, and were astonished to see the Spaniards throw stones at them. [Wagner 1929:237]

Venegas writes that the painted sacred figure was "holding in its hand a figure of the sun and moon" (DuBois 1908:98–99). In another contemporary account, Vizcaino himself "put the name 'Jesus' over the head of the devil and told the Indians that it was good and from heaven, but that the idol was the Devil" (Wagner 1928:402 n. 137). The response of Vizcaino's men to the island's sacred grounds and its crow oracles, slaughtering them with crude but powerful guns, is iconic of the intercultural encounters that became the Spanish conquest in North America.

This was not the first European contact in Tongva country. Searching for the fabled Straits of Anian, or Northwest Passage, Juan Rodríguez Cabrillo and his men attempted to winter over on Catalina Island in 1542–43. They called it San

Salvador or Isla Capitana but recorded its indigenous name fairly accurately as
Limu or Limun (for Pimu, Pimungna, or Pipimar) (Kroeber 1925:634; McCawley 1996:79). The Islanders tried to drive the Spanish away; and, coming to the
relief of a watering party under attack, Cabrillo himself, jumping ashore, broke
his leg. It turned gangrenous, and he died a few weeks later. He lies buried at an
unknown and unmarked spot on Pimu, Catalina Island (Kelsey 1986:157–159,
230).

7. DuBois calls the spread of the Chinigchinich religion, with its prescription
to "give toloache" in initiations and new styles of ceremonial songs and dancing,
a "genuine missionary movement" that "had every requisite of a conquering
faith. It had a distinct and difficult rule of life requiring obedience, fasting, and
self-sacrifice. It had the sanction of fear . . . and imposing and picturesque ritual.
And above all it had the seal of an inviolable secrecy" (1908:76). Conversion to
it "occurred comparatively late in time, and was carried on under the very eyes
of the Spanish and Mexican priests by their Christian converts, whose zeal for
their ancient religion may have been increased by the example of missionary
effort shown on their behalf by white men" (DuBois 1908:74). It "came to the
mountains from the coast," spread at first by visitors from the (Acjachemem)
village near Mission San Juan Capistrano south to the region of San Luis Rey.
From there each community in turn converted its neighbor to the eastward:
Pala, Pauma, Potrero, and La Jolla (DuBois 1908:75). Lucario Cuevish, born at
Mission San Luis Rey, told DuBois that Chinigchinich's "religious dances" were
performed by Indians living at the mission in the 1830s and 1840s: "The padres
never objected to this. The Indians who could not talk Spanish were allowed to
pray in Indian in the church; but they kept up the old dances outside." DuBois
notes that "it is not likely that any of the fathers except Boscana fully realized
the significance of the Indian dances" (1908:74–75). Apparently, at Mission San
Gabriel in 1785, with the mission in an early and precarious stage, the Franciscans and soldiers did recognize the threat that Tongva "dances and pagan abuses"
posed to Spanish religious and political control.

8. This is the third mission building. Its cornerstone was laid in 1791, but it
was not finished until 1805. Designed by Father Antonio Cruzado, born in the
Córdoba region of Andalusía (who baptized a convert the week of the 1785 revolt), it is Moorish in design, built of stone and mortar (cf. Engelhardt 1927:71,
286–287). The church is still used for special masses and weddings. The 1785
revolt took place in the second mission structure, the first built of stone at the
new location.

9. Conflicts over land and subsistence between Indians and settlers, and their
potential to generate unrest and armed rebellion, were noted ten years after the
Toypurina uprising by an astute governor of Alta California, Diego de Borica.
He warned the viceroy in 1795 that settlers' numerous cattle were despoiling the
wild fruit, seeds, water supply, and forests, causing anger among the Indians that

might lead them to revolt, as with the Comanches and Navajos who threw out the settlers and soldiers in New Mexico. Therefore, he advised, facing numerous petitions from soldiers finishing military service in Alta California, it would be unwise to grant additional ranchos to would-be settlers unless the grants respected the preexisting rights of the pueblos, missions, and settlements of gentile (pagan) Indians (Mason 1984:125–128). Wallace (1956c:269) astutely lists "floral and faunal change" as a type of "systemic stress" that may generate revitalization movements. Harkin (ch. 6) points out that this was clearly so in the Smohalla movement, whose adherents saw farming as violence against the earth. For comparable examples from lowland South America, see Vidal and Whitehead in press.

10. See Kroeber 1925:567; Blackburn 1974; Grant 1978:513; Bean and Vane 1978:669; Hudson and Underhay 1978:20–23, 72; and Sandos 1985:119. Chinigchinich was born of Tamáayawut, the Tongva name for earth, in some accounts of the origin myth.

11. James Sandos (1985), using newly located Spanish and Mexican documents and Harrington's unpublished field notes, has also proposed that the 1824 uprising was linked to the comet's apparition. He calls it a "cultural revitalization," particularly based on eyewitness reports of its aftermath and the socially reconfigured lives of rebels who fled inland to the San Joaquin Valley. The southern end of the great Central Valley and its surrounding mountains had for five decades already been a refuge area for Tongva and other people from the south fleeing mission control, who undoubtedly contributed religious practices and customs to their hosts. Two generations after the Santa Barbara uprisings, this homeland of the Southern Valley Yokuts was swept by the 1870 Ghost Dance, with its prophecies of the return of the dead—and the destruction of whites—relief from sickness, peace, and prosperity (DuBois 1939; Gayton 1930; Wallace 1978:460). The involvement of this ethnically mixed group of resisters and survivors in the southern San Joaquin Valley in successive waves of prophetic movements and ritual violence—the Chinigchinich religion (among Tongva, Chumash, and Southern Yokuts), the 1824 Chumash revolt, and the 1870 Ghost Dance—suggests that these movements have cultural connections over time of belief, ritual, prophecy, and receptivity to new revelations. These connections have not previously been noted. I suggest similar interethnic cultural continuities and receptivity over several generations in the New Guinea prophetic movements I describe later.

12. For an overview, see Worsley 1968. Astute anthropological commentators have stressed the incipiently or overtly revolutionary nature of cargoistic movements. Martha Kaplan (1995), writing about the Tuka movement of 1880s colonial Fiji, coins the useful phrase "ritual politics." With its prophet Ndugumoi, who foresaw a return of the ancestors, sailing back led by twin sons of the banished carpenter god, after which whites will serve natives and

chiefs will serve commoners, and finally whites will be driven into the sea—the Tuka movement is an early Pacific example of ritual violence and resistance in an era of intensifying colonial control. Jean Guiart (1951) half a century ago aptly called World War II and postwar cargo cults "forerunners of Melanesian nationalism." Roger Keesing similarly describes the postwar Maasina (Marching) Rule "politico-religious movement" of Malaita in the Solomon Islands as a "continuation and expansion" of 50 years of related movements lying between "the pole of millenarianism (the classic cargo cults) and the pole of anticolonial politics" (1978:241–242).

13. Keesing (1978, 1982a, 1982b, 1992) analyzes comparable wartime examples from the Solomon Islands.

14. For Hawaii, see Linnekin 1983 and Trask 1999; for New Zealand Maori, see Hanson 1989; and for Pohnpei, Alice Oleson, personal communication, 1999. Haunani-Kay Trask, in a preface to essays on Hawaiian cultural nationalism, American colonialism, and Hawaiian sovereignty, invokes her ancestors "from the Pi'ilani and Kamehameha lines especially, who believed the dignity and inheritance of my Hawaiian people could only be taken in war" (1999). Labeling cultural nationalist or revitalization movements as the invention of tradition (after Hobsbawm and Ranger 1983) infuriates indigenous activists and intellectuals for good reason. Compare, for example, the nationwide controversy in New Zealand that greeted the publication of Hanson's (1989) anthropological article on the Maori renaissance and Trask's (1999:123–135) scathing repudiation of an array of anthropologists' analyses of Native Hawaiian movements. When anthropologists or historians label elements of indigenous cultural practices as creations or inventions, no amount of appeals to history or cultural relativism—"All traditions/customs are created/invented"—will soften the reality that such labels attack the authenticity, and thus challenge the validity and political potency, of the movements of historically or contemporaneously oppressed minorities. Persisting makes us into political enemies. The culture business, which anthropologists are in, can be an uncomfortable one, putting us, if we are not careful, in opposition to those we study and seemingly allied with their historical oppressors or present-day opponents. The strength of their anger becomes clearer when we acknowledge that they are trying to make a cultural, and thus a political, revolution.

2. VISIONS OF REVITALIZATION IN THE EASTERN WOODLANDS

Can a Middle-Aged Theory Stretch to Embrace the First Cherokee Converts?

Joel W. Martin

In those days [that is, before the 1830s], our people must have believed that being considered civilized would save us from the forced exile to Indian Territory which many other Eastern nations had already suffered. – Cynthia Kasee (Cherokee), "Homecoming"

On July 10, 1817, a young Cherokee woman named Catharine Brown requested permission to enroll at Brainerd, a new mission school in southeastern Tennessee. Cyrus Kingsbury, the missionary who interviewed her, responded with skepticism. Her wealth, beauty, and confidence unsettled him: "With all her gentleness and apparent modesty, she had a high opinion of herself, and was fond of displaying the clothing and ornaments in which she was arrayed. At our first interview, I was impressed with the idea, that her feelings would not easily yield to the discipline of our schools, especially to that part of it, which requires manual labor of the scholars" (Anderson 1825:18). Kingsbury told Brown to think it over, but he could not dissuade her. She had traveled 100 miles from her home region of Creek Path and Will's Valley, Alabama, to join the school, and join she did. Although initially received "with some reluctance" (Hall 1824), in the end she proved to be a sincere and dedicated student, a favorite of the missionaries, and something of a celebrity in their circles.

Indeed, Catharine Brown the pupil became Catharine Brown the teacher and Christian missionary. In 1820 she helped found a school for the Cherokee women of her home valley in northeastern Alabama. This made her the very first female Cherokee schoolteacher (Brainerd Mission 1820; Phillips and Phillips 1998:176). Through these and other efforts Brown helped bring Christianity to many Cherokees, including her siblings and parents, to African Americans, and to other American

Indians. Her work was cut short by tuberculosis—Brown died on July 18, 1823—but "this lovely saint" was not soon forgotten (Anderson 1825:120; Phillips and Phillips 1998:539). The Brainerd missionaries provided material about her life to the American Board of Commissioners for Foreign Missions (ABCFM), and within months the board published the *Memoir of Catharine Brown, a Christian Indian of the Cherokee Nation*, a volume it republished nine times in the next decade (see Anderson 1825).

Although the memoir has long since fallen into obscurity, its reading of the Cherokee convert's story endures in at least one important regard: Catharine Brown continues to be viewed as an exceptional Cherokee who left her natal culture to join that of whites and never looked back (Horton 1992:192; Perdue 1998:169–170). Once considered the exemplary individual from a model native nation, Brown is now viewed by most historians and literary scholars as the idiosyncratic aberration, an isolated, deracinated figure, one who will not teach us, except by contrast, about the Cherokees' lifeways (Krupat 1994:115). Almost no one considers how Brown played a leading role in a Cherokee revitalization movement. And yet such a role is confirmed in historical records and oral traditions. We need to reinterpret her story and, indeed, the whole story of Cherokees' adoption of Christianity. To do this, however, we need to rethink revitalization. Specifically, we need to restore to this concept some of its original range and flexibility.

If scholars continue to mismeasure Catharine Brown and others like her, larger discourses and theoretical conventions are surely to blame. These include a "chronopolitical" discourse directed against modern Indians, widespread scholarly disdain of native converts, and theoretical overlinkage of revitalization with experiences of deprivation. Critiquing these discourses and conventions, we can expand the typology of what counts as revitalization and widen the range of whom we recognize as revitalization leaders.

As Johannes Fabian (1983) has shown in his analysis of how anthropology makes its object, leading discourses steadfastly relocate the "native" in the past, yoking authenticity to that which is marked as pre- or antimodern, primitive and natural. "Chronopolitics" help legitimate colonial projects, including those still unfolding in the states built on settler societies. In Australia, for example, a current celebration of the "folkloric and primitivized culture" of Aborigines "denigrates and marginalizes urbanized or apparently acculturated members of these populations who speak English, lack ethnic dress, do not obviously conduct ceremonies and do not count as real natives to the same extent as those who continue to live in the bush and practice something closer to traditional subsistence" (Thomas 1994:30). As Nicholas Thomas argues, this "primitivism" renovates "white identity" (1994:190), injecting new color, style, and aesthetics into consumer culture even as it holds knowledge of current colonialist practices at bay. Thomas notes parallels in America's ongoing colonial project, calling attention to the popularity of the Oscar-winning film *Dances with Wolves* (1991), a film set in the Plains Indian buffalo culture of the mid–19th century. In the United States, it seems that real Indians are not modern.

White Americans made this assumption long ago, and generations of nonnative Americans have found it extremely useful (P. Deloria 1998). The dominant culture can give Indians' putative nonmodernity a positive or negative valence, depending on the particular needs of the moment. In the age of Removal, U.S. government officials assumed that eastern woodland Indians could only survive as Indians in a distant diaspora beyond the zone of white settlement and commercial agriculture. They rationalized the forced relocation of many eastern peoples from their homelands to Indian Territory, saying that removal would protect them from the corrupting influences of white civilization and enable Indians to preserve their "ancient" ways of life, that is, "hunting," until they could achieve a more "civilized" status (Satz 1991). Chronopolitics, ascribing a separate time to the other, justified dispossession and apartheid, segregating the other in a separate territory. Two generations after Removal, when American settlement had spread west, Gilded Age reformers argued that traditional tribal identities were no longer salvageable. Considering "Indianness" to be toxic to assimilation, reformers created boarding schools, imposed allotment, and forced detribalization to erase Indian cultures, languages, and sovereignty (Niezen 2000). Such was the theory that caused great suffering among modern native peoples. More recently, in the latter part of the 20th century, nonnative New Agers have celebrated Indians as natural ecologists and superspiritual primitive people. New Age romantics, frustrated with urban life in a late capitalist society, enjoy "playing Indian" but turn angry when actual Indians do not conform to their stereotypes or confirm their anachronistic expectations. Chronopolitics continues.

In May 1999, for example, when Makah people of the Olympic Peninsula of Washington State killed a gray whale, many non-Indians reacted negatively (Erikson 1999; Sullivan 2000). Although Makah people saw this act as a resumption of an important practice central to their oral and material culture, critics suggested that the whalers' use of motorboats, modern harpoons, and a .50-caliber antitank gun violated tradition. However, as religious studies scholar Sean Connors explains, "there is an elaborate knowledge among the Makah elders about how to kill a whale as quickly and humanely as possible. . . . The special gun allows them to perfect this part of their culture. . . . In fact, because the gun has been specially designed for this particular Makah application, it can hardly not be called Makah technology" (1999:7). In sum, Makah people, in spite of nonnative assumptions about Indians, have determined that one of the best ways to be Makah is to be modern.

Anishinaabe writer and humorist Jim Northrup makes the same point: "Some people opposed to spearing [walleye] say we should do it like it was done in treaty signing times. Go back to the birch bark canoe and flaming torch. Why should we be stuck in the last century, I wondered? Yah, right. I'll go back to a birch bark canoe when you go back to a horse and buggy" (1997:141). Hammering home his point, Northrup concludes, "Anishinaabe are alive today because we have changed and evolved" (1997:141). Finally, Northrup stresses the value of formal education, quoting Plenty Coups's words: "With education, you are the white man's equal, without it, you are the white man's victim" (1997:238).

By analogy, in this chapter I argue that Catharine Brown and other elite Cherokees thought that formal education of male and female Cherokees would benefit their communities and people. Cherokees who shared Brown's conviction rallied to realize it. Participating in an emerging, multifaceted, and exhilarating movement of Cherokee-initiated renascence, Brown helped lead an important form of Cherokee revitalization.

Unfortunately, historians have had trouble recognizing this. Just as native peoples' creative adaptations of modern technology prove a stumbling block to nonnatives who would fix them in an ethnographic oral past, so native peoples' adoption of Christianity and formal education scandalizes those who think that Indians cannot be native *and* Christian, Indian *and* educated. This zero-sum assumption has produced contradictory reactions among historians of missions and mission schools (Thomson 2000). An earlier generation of church historians provided hagiographic depictions of missionaries as bearers of a superior civilization. They celebrated individual converts like Catharine Brown as transcendent exemplars who abandoned native traditions. More recently, revisionist historians have tended to vilify missionaries as cultural imperialists. They accent the corrosive power of Christianity: the alien religion's power to sunder tribal bonds, undermine traditional authority, and effect what George Tinker (1993) terms "cultural genocide." Correlatively, they view converts negatively. These scholars use the word *convert* reductionistically to identify native men and women as "assimilated Christian 'mouthpiece[s],'" as if the Christian Indian must be "thoroughly absorbed into dominant cultural structures" (Weaver 1997:59). Thus, for the very reason earlier scholars revered converts, revisionist scholars dismiss them. Both use a simplistic binary form of analysis as if a person were either a "one" or a "zero." Clearly, if we are to argue that Brown acted as a kind of revitalizer, we will need to forge an alternative interpretation of her conversion and her education. It can be done, but this will require close review of the historical details.

Before doing so, it is important to deal with the third "strike" mitigating against Catharine Brown as revitalizer, namely, her background as a privileged member of the slave-owning, propertied, politically powerful Cherokee elite. She does not seem to fit the pattern of the classic (male) revitalizer whose powerful vision restores hope to a beleaguered people in their time of urgent crisis (viz., Neolin, Handsome Lake, Tenskwatawa, Hillis Hadjo, Wovoka). Or does she? Brown, too, suffered deprivation, experienced a powerful life-changing dream, and acted charismatically to inspire her community to build something new at a critical time in its history.

As a child and teenager, Brown experienced angst and agony aplenty. Her father married unhappily and struggled with alcoholism. Tension and uncertainty also colored Brown's community of Creek Path. Because it was located in the heart of Chickamauga country, it was filled with memories of not just resistance but also defeat. By 1800, the year of Brown's birth, the Cherokee people had been politically subordinated to the United States and faced serious "social deprivation" (Champagne 1992:756). Some Cherokees sought escape by voluntarily removing to the west, making those who remained behind worry if they had made the right decision. Removal crises shook Cherokee communities during Brown's youth, took relatives away, and divided clans and communities. She experienced this firsthand and repeatedly; her father periodically threatened to remove west as well, introducing yet another type of uncertainty into his daughter's life. For Brown, the political was personal.

The Creek War of 1811–14, itself born of a revitalization movement led by prophets, involved Brown's relatives in combat against the Redstick Creeks and brought unprecedented levels of violence, disruption, and change to the region (Martin 1991). During the Redstick War, Andrew Jackson's invasionary army camped at Ft. Deposit "near her father's residence" in Creek Path (Anderson 1825:14). John Melish's 1818 "Map of Alabama" traces the route of the army on its way from Tennessee to war with the Creeks of central Alabama. That army passed directly by the area where the Browns lived. The best account of Jackson's route places him at "Camp Deposit at Thompson's Creek," later called Brown's Creek (Reid and Eaton 1817:40; Smith 1989:167 n. 17). And a map based on the Melish atlas and housed in the State of Alabama Department of Archives and History, "For General Jackson's Campaign against the Creek Indians, 1813 & 1814" (n.d.), traces two major streams of soldiers converging within a mile of "John Brown's" property, passing directly by the inn John Brown operated. In short, there is no question that hundreds of young soldiers came very close to the home of this 14-year-old Cherokee woman in October 1813. This army would later slaughter Muskogee men, women, and children at the Battle of Horseshoe Bend. Even before that event, as Davy Crockett's narrative and other more reliable sources verify, the army inflicted pain on many native peoples who encountered it, including some allies of the United States (Martin 1991:158–159).

Soldiers disrupted the Browns' home and threatened their safety. In a letter of protest to Andrew Jackson, John Brown described a series of thefts involving "white people" taking livestock, corn, farm tools, rails, boards, whiskey, and money. On one occasion, "they burnt down the chimney" (Brown 1813). The *Memoir of Catharine Brown* suggests that one or more of the soldiers may have tried to rape Catharine. The memoir, however, reports this assault euphemistically. It states that she "fled into the wild forest, to preserve her character unsullied" (Anderson 1825:14). The memoir further notes that General Jackson, who "had a high opinion of Catharine," "remarked, 'she was a woman of Roman virtue, and above suspicion'" (Anderson 1825:14). More concerned with her chastity than her humanity, the memoir does not probe how her encounter with sexual violence may have disrupted her life. In addition to traumatizing her, it most likely led her family to send her north during the Creek War to the Ross's Landing. There she would reside in a safer place with relatives and friends. In this way, she became familiar with the region even before the ABCFM missionaries arrived to build Brainerd.

If the profile of the revitalizer must reflect experiences with "deprivation," Brown qualifies. Her class did not protect her from stress. And her gender exposed her to a particularly horrible form of colonial terror. At the risk of taking a detour from the historical narrative, an important theoretical question needs to be raised. In speaking of revitalization and revitalizers, why do scholars always feel compelled to find proof of deprivation? For the sake of argument, let us propose that exposure to deprivation, actual or perceived, absolute or relative, is not always a precondition for revitalization or an attribute of its leaders. Doing so, we can begin to reintroduce flexibility to an aging theory.

Anthony F. C. Wallace, it seems, offered a less restrictive theory, one not focused on deprivation per se. In his classic article "Revitalization Movements," Wallace states that almost everyone who has lived has probably been involved in "an instance of the revitalization process" (1956c:267). Wallace could make this bold claim because he defined revitalization in an expansive manner. His catholic vision included a very wide variety of movements. "Revivalistic" ones defend traditional ways, "vitalistic" ones emphasize "the importation of alien elements into the mazeway" (Wallace 1956c:267), and so on. Regardless of type, these movements have helped people deal with widespread social "stress" by providing new visions of reality and codes for behavior. Most important, Wallace's theory embraces a wide spectrum of movements including, but also exceeding, those associated with increases in deprivation.

"Stress" is not the same as "deprivation." Moreover, not all "stress" correlates with a loss of power, territory, autonomy, wealth, and so forth. Stress also occurs when horizons of possibility expand, when increases in power, territory, autonomy, wealth, and so on cause communities and individuals to desire new visions, to crave change, and to rethink codes. Colonizers as well as the colonized needed revitalization movements. New Worlds demanded new religions, reformations, and great awakenings. In the 19th century and others, in the United States and elsewhere, revitalization movements arose in response not just to diminished communal opportunities but to enlarged ones as well. This theoretical point shifts our attention away from fixation on deprivation per se and toward any profound structural historic shift in power relations affecting the nations and peoples in question (McMullen [ch. 12] influences my thought here with her emphasis on shifts in power, not culture).

Another way to put this is to say that deprivation theory represents only half of all possible power shifts. It describes only those situations characterized by a decline in power. In practice, because of historical factors, this has worked very well in describing historic Native American revitalization movements. Given the colonial dynamics shaping their history, most of these movements have indeed contended with declines in power. So the scholarly fixation on deprivation did not seem misplaced. Historical study seemed to confirm the theories that guided its research. Being nearsighted, after all, is not a problem if one only looks at objects that fall within the prescribed range of focus. Even a myopic sees some things clearly, though one has lost the capacity to recognize a much wider range of phenomena. Similarly, our fixation on deprivation might prevent us from recognizing a deeper range of revitalization movements in the past, present, or future. As historians have shown, Native American responses to contact and colonialism were far more complicated and creative than earlier scholars represented and much more complicated than popular myths assumed (Calloway 1997; Kupperman 2000; Merrell 1989; R. White 1991). To recognize this complexity, revitalization theory needs to expand its vision of what counts as revitalization and what causes it. Like many 40 year olds, the theory needs some good bifocals, complementary "lenses" that enable it to recognize different types of power shifts. These include some of power shifts that were not negative and, thus, fall outside the ordinary range prescribed by deprivation theory.

Six ideal types of power shifts suggest themselves: the shift may be (1) from superordinate power to parity of power, (2) from a context of parity to one of subordination, (3) from a context of subordination to one of parity, (4) from a context of parity to superordinate power, (5) from a context of superordinate power straight to subordinate status, or (6) from a context of subordinate status straight to superordinate power. Types 5 and 6 involve such extreme changes that each overlaps with two of the other types, which respond to less apocalyptical reversals. Thus, a given revitalization movement may enable people to respond to a loss of well-being, territory, autonomy, and so on (types 1 and 5); another may help them deal with the experience of deprivation (2, 5); another might allow them to celebrate the cessation of deprivation (3, 6); and another may herald the arrival of flush times (4, 6). Not to put too nice a point on it, we may want to speak of "seasons" of revitalization: fall (descending from plenitude), winter (descending into deprivation), spring (ascending from deprivation), and summer (ascending into plenitude). (Here I am adapting Wesley Kort's [1975] analysis of basic plot types in fiction.) Again, because some movements must respond to apocalyptic reversals, they may actually encompass two "seasons" virtually simultaneously. In the past, to grossly generalize, the "seasons" of fall and winter prevailed in many stretches of Indian Country, so in many instances deprivation theory does not seem misapplied; as stated above, its assumptions fit. Many historic native revitalization movements sought to restore lost power or help people cope with dreadful situations (Pueblo revolt; Handsome Lake movement; Lakota Ghost Dance; early peyotism among the Lipan Apaches, Comanches, and Kiowas).

In contrast, in the present, to again generalize, springtime movements seem to be spreading. The nadir of the late 19th century has passed. The Sun Dance and other banned practices have reemerged from the underground. The "postcolonial" moment encourages native men and women to reinvent institutions, reimagine identities, reinvigorate languages and ceremonies, and regain communal capital in a context of lessening domination (Connors 1999; see also McMullen [ch. 12] and Nesper [ch. 10]). "Summer," an enduring experience of plenty, may follow for some. Perhaps one day we may witness a Native American revitalization movement that begins in a context of secure social and political power and helps native men and women adjust to widely expanded possibilities of action. If this seasonal synopsis oversimplifies—making the past too universally dark, the present too naively light, and history too coherent—it does underscore the theoretical point of severing revitalization and its leaders from deprivation per se. We can now revisit the pre-Removal Cherokee elite and resume a study of the career of one of its daughters, Catharine Brown.

With the British defeat of the French in 1763 and even more so with the American triumph in the Revolution in 1783, power relations in the eastern woodlands shifted decisively toward a new order, negative for many interior Indians, an order of domination in which nonnatives began to define unilaterally the terms of coexistence of themselves and native peoples. In the Southeast, the shift in power relations brought forced land cessions, intrusive cultural imperialism, the decline of traditional modes of intercultural diplomacy, the rise of internal class divisions, profound gender system changes, and grave and novel degrees of economic dependency (Braund 1993; Martin 1995; McLoughlin 1984). Not surprisingly, classic revitalization movements emerged in the Southeast. Among the Creeks, for example, the "wintertime" shift from parity to subordination helped evoke a massive anticolonial revitalization movement that aimed to restore native power and land, erase class divisions, and destroy internal collaborators (Martin 1991). Although defeated by the U.S. military, Creek Redstick leaders, influenced by Tecumseh and Tenskwatawa, anticipated contemporary Indian efforts to define a distinct identity in a world of market capitalism (see Nesper [ch. 10]) and to develop traditions that can serve subordinate communities eager to resist dominant narratives (see McMullen [ch. 12]).

The Redstick War and its aftermath changed southeastern history (Usner 1992:89) and directly affected the Cherokees, next-door neighbors to the Creeks. Well before the war erupted, Cherokees had learned of Tecumseh's call for a pan-Indian resistance movement. They heard the Redstick leaders' anticolonial teachings, but several factors convinced them to not join the Redstick movement (Dowd 1992:157–181). Remembering recent defeats in wars against the British and the United States, they realized that the odds against them had only worsened. With American forts in their midst and hostile white populations on three sides of their territory, courting war seemed suicidal. Meanwhile, a removal crisis in 1808–09 had already led a thousand Cherokees upset with white incursions to move west (Dowd 1992:158). Many of these people came from the Chickamauga area (northeastern Alabama, southeastern Tennessee), which had been home to a militant anticolonial movement from the 1770s to the early 1790s (Pate 1969). Thus, their departure had preemptively deprived the Redsticks and the larger pan-Indian movement of their most likely allies among the Cherokees. Also militating against revolt was the unique character of the Cherokee polity. The Cherokees, to an extent greater than other southeastern peoples, had developed a structure of leadership and governance differentiated from religious ideology and capable of uniting various classes in defense of broad Cherokee interests (Champagne 1992:86). Instead of being drawn into a prophetic movement led by charismatic leaders and shaped by eschatological rhetoric, the Cherokees allied with the United States and the non-Redstick Creeks.

Many Cherokee men, including several male friends and relatives of Catharine Brown, fought at the Battle of Tohopeka (Horseshoe Bend). Witnessing the devastating defeat of the Alabama Redsticks, they saw firsthand the wisdom of not fighting the United States directly. Shortly after the war ended, in 1817, a ferocious debate divided the Cherokees. Under intense pressure from surrounding whites to cede additional lands, some felt that they should voluntarily remove westward, following the lead of earlier Chickamauga emigrants. Indeed, more than one thousand decided to move. Ten times more Cherokees, however, determined to stay put in their ancestral lands (Champagne 1992:129–134). This larger objective helped them to overcome the major internal tensions and class divisions that divided them and to unite behind the leadership of a transcultural elite (Peyer 1997:17).

Not surprisingly, members of this elite, which included planters and slave owners with significant European ancestry, were not above using their position to their own benefit. They wrote laws that protected their interests. They reaped private profits from their involvement in slavery, trade, and diplomacy, as any inventory of their property will confirm. But the overall distribution of power and position may also have benefited the Cherokee nonelite as well. Among other things, they seem to have used the elite to shield themselves from the intrusive and domineering gaze of American authorities and missionaries. By delegating diplomacy and intercultural negotiations to the elite, the nonelite protected a Cherokee cultural "underground" where traditional dances and religious practices could continue and where some counterhegemonic discourses, humor, alliances, and activities could emerge (Martin 1995). In other words, the nonelite may have wanted the transcultural elite out there, visible, doing business, speaking and writing English, and listening to missionaries talk about Christ, sin, and salvation. The overall distribution of power was something they helped authorize. Tellingly, during this period the elite did not rule by coercion—it led by consensus (Champagne 1992:142).

To better protect Cherokee sovereignty, Cherokee leaders, after the Redstick War, further centralized their government and aggressively appropriated the forms of the dominant society in a "process of conscious acculturation." These efforts produced "the remarkable renascence of the Cherokees under new forms of government and a new social order which was largely the result of their own determined effort" (McLoughlin 1984:6). To put it another way, Cherokees, already involved in an impressive and systemic revitalization movement at the time of the Redstick War and probably since 1794, recommitted themselves to it with new zeal. As external pressures mounted, their internal resolve increased. They would develop a state in order to resist colonialism (Conser 1978). Sensing "winter," they would force "spring."

A preeminent leader of this movement was John Ross, the son of a Scottish trader and a Cherokee woman who also had European ancestry (Conser 1978). A wealthy slave owner literate in English, he ran the river landing, store, and warehouse that would become the nucleus of the town of Chattanooga. Ross was not a typical Cherokee or even a typical member of the Cherokee elite. Indeed, he might have failed a Cherokee vocabulary test. But, when judged by nonracialist, nonfundamentalist measures for who counts as a Cherokee, Ross easily qualifies. His "communitism" or activism in behalf of the Cherokee community was large even if his blood quantum was small (Weaver 1997:xiii, 6). No wooden figure, Ross helped his people negotiate extraordinary changes, from invasion to diaspora. Not for nothing did Ross lead anti-Removal Cherokees from 1819 to 1839 and post-Removal Cherokees until 1866.

Ross, like other members of the elite, promoted literacy, finding it an essential tool for commerce, government, and the defense of Cherokee lands. By no means the first American Indian to value education and certainly not the last, Ross had long lobbied for schools for Cherokee youth. In 1816, Ross, other leaders, and the Cherokee Council approved a plan by the ABCFM to bring a school to Cherokee country. As in earlier negotiations with missionary organizations, the Cherokees made it clear that it was the missionaries' school, not the missionaries' religion, that made them desire their presence. In October 1816, the ABCFM purchased the improvements of the 25-acre plantation of John McDonald, an elderly Scottish trader living on Chickamauga Creek in Tennessee (two miles north of present-day Georgia's state line). McDonald left his plantation and went to live with his daughter Mollie's son, John Ross. Within a few months the first missionaries arrived at the plantation, which they initially called "Chickamauga" (also spelled "Chickamaugah") and later renamed "Brainerd" (Evarts 1821:4; Malone 1956:99; McLoughlin 1984:104, 110). According to a leading missionary, the site placed the mission near "the children of half breeds and of the leading men in the nation" (Phillips and Phillips 1998:4).

Not coincidentally, Ross had a strong connection to Catharine Brown. Brown was the granddaughter of European and Cherokee forebears and the daughter of a slave-owning leader of the Creek Path community in northeastern Alabama. Ross had spent part of his childhood in Willstown, near Brown's home area, and had later run a merchandising concern there (McLoughlin 1984:110; Moulton 1978:5). Later one of Brown's relatives moved to the area near Ross's Landing. Brown herself, fleeing the chaos and violence associated with the Creek War, "spent a few of her juvenile years in Mr. Ross's and Mr. Coodey's family" at Ross's trading post on the Chattanooga River (Hall 1824). Given her strong connections to Ross and other leaders in the area, Brown was probably among the very first Cherokee youths to learn about the mission school. Indeed, it does not seem too much of a stretch to assume that Ross encouraged his protégé Catharine Brown to enroll in the new ABCFM school built on his grandfather's farm. If *conversion* means an abandonment of a preexisting life, then "conversion" was not her goal, and *convert* does not adequately describe her subsequent identity.

When she came to the mission and first appears in its written records, Brown was already familiar with the area, with a half brother living nearby in addition to her friends in the Ross family. She was at home, not cut off from family or kin. Moreover, because of her social position and intimacy with Cherokee leaders, she had full knowledge of the Cherokee elite's "progressive" social program. This conditioned her approach to the missionaries and their religion. Brown approached the missionaries with the kind of pragmatism and public purpose characteristic of John Ross, who at that time showed no interest in converting. Arriving in the midst of the second Removal crisis, Brown came to Brainerd to acquire literacy, not explore faith.

Brown's common sense told her that Christianity was not for her. She came equipped with several by-then-standard Cherokee arguments against the religion. Because "the Cherokees were a different race from the whites," some Cherokees concluded that they could have "no concern in the white people's religion." Other Cherokee critics of Christianity developed an epistemological argument holding that the Christians' stories were "mere legendary tales." And still others pushed an ethical argument; after observing how Christians acted, they concluded that Christians were hypocrites (see Martin 1995:132). Brown held the ontological view tying a religion to race. But she also developed an epicurean argument that reflected her own joy in sensual life: She rejected conversion because she thought that it was incompatible with happiness; Christians seemed to take "no pleasure in this world" (Anderson 1825:19).

One can understand how Brown reached this grim conclusion. The missionaries viewed life as a cosmic drama, if not a melodrama, in which sensuality distracts human beings from heavenly matters. Consider Brainerd missionary Daniel Sabin Butrick's journals (n.d.:18.3.3., v. 4):

A richly dreary collection of self-berating comments by a young Massachusetts Puritan introspect ("I am a wretched, hateful creature, and grow worse and worse"), the diary chronicles his struggles with sensual indulgence ("I give loose to my corrupt propensities"). The diary condemns Butrick's increasing "vileness" and reveals his unending and unsuccessful effort to crush his lust for Catharine Brown, of whom it was said by another male missionary, "Nature has done much for her" (Hall 1824, quoting his own July 10, 1817, diary entry). Butrick is a fascinating character in his own right, who, among other things, wrote a 500-page work comparing "Jews and Indians," which he thought proved that native peoples are a lost tribe of Israel and their religion is a derivative distortion of ancient Hebraic practices (n.d.:18.3.3, v. 3, pt. 2). Although he later worked closely with Brown, Butrick, ordained at age 28 as "a minister to the heathen" (n.d., January 1, 1822, entry), did not convince her to reappraise Christianity.

Less visible actors played a more direct role. Other Cherokees had helped Brown learn to read before she arrived at Brainerd. It is even possible that one of her father's African slaves played a role in her education (ABCFM papers record that an African slave taught another Cherokee woman how to read). This again emphasizes that Brown did not enter the space of "civilization" cold. Hidden transcripts had already shaped how she read and believed (Scott 1990). In short, it is important to consider her own initiative and agenda, to ask whether she did not come to Brainerd prepared to engage in "colonial politics at the local level" (Thomas 1994:63). The story of the Cherokee convert may resonate with the stories of other native men and women who found ways to assimilate assimilation, to convert conversion.

Recently, scholars writing on missionized Indians have stressed Indian agency in the process of acquiring literacy and Christian theology (McNally 2000; Peyer 1997; Treat 1996; Weaver 1997; Wyss 2000:16). This corrects the older "binary" either/or models that saw converts as "pacified, angelized Christians" to be celebrated or condemned. Jace Weaver, for his part, challenges the negative characterizations of famous converts such as William Apess among the Pequot and Peter Jones among the Anishinaabe. He advances a less polemical, less pejorative approach, what might be termed an "analog" form of analysis. It is more finely tuned to the specificity of unique persons, historical actors reimagining their complicated communities in ever changing contexts. Instead of celebrating or damning converts a priori for becoming Christian, Weaver would have us consider how particular converts used Christianity to promote the well-being of their often imperiled communities. Apess, for example, used early Methodism's egalitarianism to call into question racist practices of white New Englanders, whom he said would have discriminated against Jesus himself (O'Connell 1992:160). Similar reinterpretations of converts have appeared in works on nonelite whites in the Chesapeake region, African Americans in the South, and "natives" in South Africa, the Solomon Islands, and elsewhere (Raboteau 1980; Schneider 1993; Thomas 1994; R. White 1991). As this new scholarship argues, the site of mission and evangelicalization is far more complex than is often depicted. Not just a space for assimilation, it is also "the space of practical resistance, acceptance, and appropriation" (Thomas 1994:63), a space that native people entered to engage colonialism and its agents. In this space, native people often found and exploited fissures and contradictions in the colonial project, including those gendered ones so prevalent in missions.

At Brainerd, Catharine Brown reappraised Christianity as she grew close to female teachers, missionaries, and mission family members such as Matilda Loomis Williams, Isabella Murray Hall, Esther Booth Hoyt, Flora Hoyt Chamberlin, and later Laura Weld Potter. While she maintained close ties to her local kin and friends, she subjected herself to these women's surveillance. The tight and charged domestic scene generated intense psychological pressures and emotional tensions. These women saw Brown not just in school but in their homes. They taught European domestic arts to the young Cherokee woman, showed her proper dress and behavior, inquired about her spiritual state, monitored her behavior closely, corrected her manner of expression, supervised her morals, taught her to seek God, and listened to her nightly prayers. They witnessed her transformation and, most important, recorded details that the memoir and all subsequent histories have overlooked.

For 90 days, Brown had been reading the Bible, saying her evening prayers, and discussing Christianity with her host family, the Halls. Then she had a powerful dream. Indeed, it seems fair to describe this as a life-changing dream, a pivotal vision that changed or at least cemented Brown's path. As important as this dream was, however, the memoir does not mention it; nor have any historians who have written about her noted it. We know about the dream only because she related it to Isabella Hall, who relayed it to her husband Moody, who recorded it in his journal and then later, after Brown's death, included it in a profile of her that he drafted for Boston officials (1824). Notice how the written voice slips from the first person to the third:

> In my sleep I tho't I was traveling and came to a hill that was almost perpendicular. I was much troubled about it, for I had to go to its top. I knew not how to get up. She said [she] saw the steps which others had gone and tried to put her feet in their steps, but found she could not ascend in this way, because her feet slipped. Having made several unsuccessful attempts to ascend, she became very weary, but although she succeeded in getting near the top, [she] felt in great danger of falling. While in this distress in doubt whether to try to go forward or return, she saw a bush just above her of which she tho't, if she could get hold it she could get up, and as she reached out her hand to the bush, she saw a little boy standing at the top, who reached out his hand; She grasped his thumb, and at this moment she was on top and someone told her it was the Saviour. [Hall 1824]

Before analyzing the dream's content, it is important to consider what any powerful dream could have meant to her. Like most Cherokees, indeed most native people, Catharine Brown considered dreams important, authoritative gateways to fuller knowledge of ontological reality. Anthony F. C. Wallace's description of the importance of dreams among the Iroquois applies here as well and deserves to be quoted at length: A major class of dreams

> showed powerful supernatural beings who, in the dream, usually spoke personally to the dreamer, giving him a message of importance for himself and often for the whole community. Sometimes these were personality-transformation dreams, in which the longings, doubts, and conflicts of the dreamers were suddenly and radically resolved, the dreamer emerging from his vision with a new sense of dignity, a new capacity for playing a hitherto difficult role, and a new feeling of health and well-being. Such experiences were particularly common among boys at puberty. Retiring to the woods, fasting, and meditating in solitude, the youth after a week or two experienced a vision in which a supernatural being came to him, promised his aid and protection, and gave him a talisman. The guardian spirit, in a sense, took the place of the parents upon whom the boy had hitherto depended, and from whom he had now to emancipate himself if he were to become a whole man. [Wallace 1970a:72–73]

Elsewhere Wallace emphasizes that such dreams came to women as well: "In the winter of 1669–70 a woman at Oneida was visited in a dream by

Tarachiawagon, who told her the Andaste (southern enemies of the Five Nations) would attack and besiege the Oneida village in the spring. . . . The woman became for a time a prophet" (1970a:69). In the mid–18th century, a female prophet appeared among the Delawares.

Similarly, Cherokees of Catharine Brown's day took their dreams and visions seriously. Their contents revealed important future shifts in the life of the dreamer. If, for example, the dreamer saw a person going west, holding eagle feathers, going down a stream of high water, or wearing very clean clothes, the dreamer or a loved one was sure to die. A house burning or flooding meant the same, as did a low-flying eagle or heron or someone singing or dancing. Signs of sickness included dreaming of a person dead, of people marrying, of clothes on fire, and of snakes. But dreams also communicated good things—success in hunting and plenty in crops. Hunters who dreamed of "having bread" or "peaches or any kind of fruit" would have success in killing deer. As Daniel Butrick recorded, they "used to pray for such a dream" (Payne-Butrick Papers n.d.:81).

Inevitably, visions and dreams guided how the Cherokees assimilated Christianity and the civilizing mission. The first Cherokee hymn, for example, resulted from a vision experienced by Lydia Lowery (Foster 1899:37–40). Also a student at Brainerd and a friend of Catharine Brown's, Lowery heard missionary William Chamberlin recite the Lord's Prayer at a morning lesson. Later that day, she fell asleep by Little Chickamauga Creek to the sound of water coursing over rocks: "She dreamed of a grove of wonderful beauty, in which had gathered a vast concourse of Cherokee people. They were seated around in a semi-circle, and in their midst stood a wonderful being, giving praise to the Great Spirit, the whole congregation repeating again and again the words after him, in joyful Cherokee song" (Foster 1899:39). After she woke up, "the song of her dreams still filled her mind, and she went and told Missionary Chamberlain" (Foster 1899:39). This hymn opened the way for many more. They continue to be sung to this very day in Cherokee in churches in Oklahoma (Smith 2000).

Among the Cherokees, any striking dream deserved attention. Brown deemed hers "a singular one" (Hall 1824). Needing to tell it to someone she trusted, Brown selected a female missionary, Isabella Hall. Brown had formed a very intimate bond with Hall. Later, she would address her as "sister." In a letter written in 1820, she confessed to Hall that she feared that she may have loved her more than the Heavenly Father

Himself (Catherine Brown, letter to Isabella Hall, March 8, 1820, in Anderson 1825:59).

Hall listened closely and respectfully to Brown's narrative of her dream. Friendship may have motivated her, but additional reasons likely played a role as well. Missionaries, by the 18th century, had learned that native respect for dreams could sometimes help connect them to Christianity (Sobel 2000:42). When Brown asked Hall "if she believed any thing in dreams—She was told that something might be learned fr. Them. she then asked if it was right to tell dreams. She said she had a singular one and if there was no harm in it she would tell it"; "being encouraged," she related her vision (Hall 1824). Together it seems that these women improvised an oneiric contact zone, a temporary fusion of religious consciousnesses, something truly novel, irreducible to Chero-kee or Christian tradition. Maybe that is why the missionaries, when they recorded Brown's dream, began in the first person and ended in the third; writing, they moved away from a fragile vernacular empathy to a more distanced metropolitan reporting.

Turning now to the dream's content, the fact that the protagonist saves herself by gripping a male's extended "thumb" must draw the at-tention of post-Freudians. The dream might reflect Brown's experience with sexual violence during the Redstick War. In any case, the fact that the dreamer herself is present in the dream and that she confronts a direct threat to her existence underscores this dream's significance. A "self-state" dream (Kohut 1977) showing a high level of self-perception and reflection (Rossi 1972), this dream helped the dreamer imagine and start to make a future. Here Sobel's analysis of revolutionary-era dreams fits well. Natives and nonnatives before the 1830s and 1840s invested great power and meaning in dreams and changed their lives in response to powerful dreams. Individuals found in dreams support to "reconstruct their selves" (Sobel 2000:229, 236). Dreams provided an important "technique of the self" (Sobel 2000:241). Narrating one's dream to another, one fashioned oneself as an actor in a narrative. In a sense, by dreaming and taking one's dreams seriously, one authored oneself.

As Sobel shows, revolutionary-era dreams often refracted the racial, religious, and gender tensions shaping political and social life and pro-leptically revealed possible resolutions. Sobel's theory warrants fuller quotation: "Change in the self was often worked out on the dream-screen, and this change was played out in the narrative report of the waking life. In crucial dream . . . an alien other was targeted and a dream-screen commitment was made. Many people awoke determined to act on this recognition and commitment. As introjection occurred in these dreams as well, dreams both targeted enemy others and helped bring about a more inclusive reconstruction of the self" (2000:12). In other words, crucial or "singular" dreams were to the transculturating individual what "vitalistic" revitalization movements were to colonized communities, a way to import the other into the self in a way that empowers action and identity.

Charged with psychological meaning and historical resonance, the content of Catharine Brown's "singular dream" fit the hybrid social space in which it was dreamt. Brown's dream seems to have blended Christian and Cherokee religious symbols. If the savior figure reflects devotional stories of Christ's infancy and youth, he also resembles the "diminutive deities" prominent in the visions of earlier Delaware, Shawnee, and Cherokee prophets and dreamers (Dowd 1992:179). Most particularly, he partially fits the profile of the Cherokee "Little People." Had a Little Person helped Brown in her ascent to Christ?

According to a Cherokee story, "The Little People (yunwi' djunsti) are about two and one-half feet tall, are dressed in white, and have long hair. They live in rock slides in the cliffs where one can see 'floors' that they have made—flat places that they keep swept perfectly clean. They can hear whatever you say about them" (Lankford 1986:135). According to Molly Sequoyah, a Cherokee woman interviewed in 1945, "It is a bad omen to see them and death may follow" (Witthoft and Hadlock 1949:415). Yet some traditions hold that the Little People help children and healers. They "take care of children who wander from their homes, feeding them and teaching them how to use herb remedies before returning them to their parents" (Gill and Sullivan 1992:170–171).

Near contemporaries of Catharine Brown told many stories regarding the Little People and other mountain-dwelling spirits. One story describes men climbing a rocky mountain on a quest to gain the spiritual advantage "against their enemies" (Payne-Butrick Papers n.d.:3:16). While climbing on the first two days, they "see no person, but could hear a voice from above speaking to them." The third day they understand that the voice relays a message from God. On the fourth, fifth, and sixth days the voice continues to encourage them. Finally, on the seventh day they reached "the top of the Mountain, heard a rushing noise above them, and saw a strange people."

Other stories describe the "Na ne hi," beings "living, some under water, some under the ground, and others in rocks on the mountains" (Payne-Butrick Papers n.d.:4:572–573). To see a "little na ye hi [spirit living in bluffs]" at the start of a journey was a sure sign of death (Payne-Butrick Papers n.d.:4:199 or 131). A similar class of spirit beings terrified a man who survived to tell the story to Daniel Butrick: "He and another Indian were on a high mountain hunting. Night came on, and they lay down to sleep by a high rock. Just as the day broke they heard chickens crow in the rocks, and various other noise. At length they heard a door turning on its hinges in the rock, and being now too much frightened to remain any longer they fled" (Payne-Butrick Papers n.d.:4:572–573). Still another story circulating among Cherokees describes how a "little boy" (not a Little Person but more likely one of the Little Thunders) defeated the Gambler, the wicked man who always defrauded Indians. Although the identity of the "little boy" in Catharine Brown's dream is impossible to determine and may well reflect some Christian influence as well, ample evidence suggests that his presence in her dream, his mountainside location, and his association with a spiritual quest would have resonated strongly with Cherokees of her day. They would have understood it as a strong sign of some portentous change to come and would not have been surprised that it marked a turning point in her life.

The missionaries who watched Brown in subsequent days noted that "after this she became more free in conversing on religious subjects and would constantly read her Bible" (Hall 1824). Not much later she confessed her sin and became baptized as the ABCFM's first convert: At her baptismal service, a leading ABCFM official, Cyrus Kingsbury, preached on the New Testament passage from Galatians 3:28—the traditional text Christians have used to embrace cultural others in communion: "There is neither Jew nor Greek, there is neither slave nor free, there is neither male nor female; for you are all one in Christ Jesus." The memoir reports this detail (Anderson 1825:23), but nowhere does it entertain the idea that a traditional Cherokee spirit protector had convinced a young Cherokee woman that she could make a safe approach to Christ.

Once converted, Brown did not abandon her family or community but, rather, returned frequently to visit them and live with them, caring for her parents even as she suffered from her own illness, which she initially misdiagnosed as a bad cold. Catharine was emotionally closest to her brother David, who converted soon after she did, attended

Cornwall Academy in Connecticut and Andover Theological in Massachusetts, lectured in the east on behalf of missions, and later helped Daniel Butrick translate the Bible into Sequoyan. In their letters to one another, Catharine and David spoke often of desiring to be of service to their people. They believed that Christianity held universal promise. Nonnative Christians tested their confidence. In 1823, when one of David's friends, John Ridge, married Sarah Northrup, the daughter of a trustee of Cornwall, newspaper editorials in Connecticut condemned the union (Andrew 1992:133). Such racism alarmed David. Closer to home, Catharine felt acutely the stigma that whites imposed on native peoples. When missionaries and others, eager to demonstrate the success of the civilizing project, published batches of her letters without her permission, she said that she supposed they had done so "at *first*" because they wanted "to show that an Indian could improve" (Anderson 1825:128). She used the word *Indian* here as fellow convert John Ridge used it in his letter to the *Missionary Herald* published in July 1822: "If an Indian is educated in the sciences, has a good knowledge of the classics, astronomy, mathematics, moral and natural philosophy, and his conduct equally modest and polite, yet he is an Indian, and the most stupid and illiterate white man will disdain and triumph over this worthy individual" (Peyer 1997:182). Similarly, Catherine used the "I-word" to express her outrage. She wanted the missionaries to know that she resented being treated like a walking anomaly, an exotic freak, the writing savage. Unfortunately, what she said to her kin about this unwelcome exposure remains part of a hidden transcript long lost.

In spite of all the mixed messages of acceptance and rejection, cultural chauvinism, and white racism, Catharine and David Brown did not give up on Christianity or Euro-American civilization. They maintained a strong sense of mission: They wanted to master "civilization" and bring it home to their people and, at the same time, mirror a "civilized" image of their people back to an increasingly hostile and overwhelmingly powerful white society, goals they shared with the anti-Removal ABCFM missionaries.

Their efforts did not go unnoticed, within and beyond the Cherokee Nation. In 1820, "the people [of Brown's home region heard] that Sister Catharine was willing to teach girls as soon as a [school]house could be prepared. . . . [The people] immediately resolved to build a house, the same size" as the school Butrick ran for Cherokee boys (Brainerd Mission 1820). They raised it in a day, a feat that reflected the status of Brown's father but also reflected the strength of her own charisma. There Brown taught her pupils the alphabet, scripture lessons, and Cherokee hymns but also provided religious guidance and disciplined pupils. She formed a female missionary society to promote missions to other Indian nations. She gained official recognition from Butrick (1820), who named her the spiritual leader for women at the station. Brown's rise to authority stands out even more when it is compared with the declining public status of her Cherokee sisters in the Cherokee republic. As Theda Perdue argues, Cherokee women were losing political power at this precise moment, as local council houses waned in influence and a "new male structure virtually eliminated women from any role in choosing representatives, arbitrating disputes, or meting out official justice" (1998:145). This contrast underscores the importance of reconsidering Catharine Brown from multiple vantages. From the perspective of the missionaries, to be sure, she was the exemplary convert. But from the perspective of the Cherokee elite and perhaps an even broader set of Cherokees, she was a leading participant in their "deliberate, conscious, organized effort . . . to create a more satisfying culture" (Wallace 1956c:265) by pursuing formal education, building schools, and teaching other Cherokees to read and write.

At Creek Path, Butrick and Brown were alone together often, and for the first nine months there were no other missionaries on the scene to supervise them or restrain Butrick. Butrick's sexual desire and love for Brown intensified. One day in spring 1820 something happened that troubled him deeply. It is important to clarify that Brown, although she was in his thoughts on that particular day, was out of town, so there is no question of any erotic exchange occurring at that time. In his diary, Butrick wrote: "I am foolish and vile. . . . I am so sinful I can't keep near [the Redeemer]. I grieve him from me. . . . I am vile, sold under sin." Continuing, he speaks in the plural and suggests that something threatening to his faith had occurred: "O Thou dear Jesus do keep us. O don't leave us again." The fact that this formulation is plural does not mean very much. Butrick often used this construction in prayer. He was not saying that he and Catharine had sinned together. However, the very next words in his diary refer to Brown: "O do be with Sister Catharine, and her to glorify thee as long as she lives, and never let go of her to fall into sin and distress" (n.d., March–June 1820 entries). This syntagmatic proximity suggests that the missionary felt some kind of intimate connection between his confession of sin and his plea to Jesus, on the one hand, and his attraction to the beautiful Cherokee convert, on the other, as if the latter necessitated the former.

Had they actually become lovers? This is doubtful. Brown left no writings indicating that she reciprocated Butrick's feelings. No one else seemed to perceive the frisson between them. Unless further evidence is forthcoming, it seems reasonable to conclude that their intimacy had not become sexual and that Butrick simply had a hard time dealing with his own desire (study of his subsequent awkward love life suggests that this was the case). Butrick expressed his problem with Protestant dualistic precision, sublating passion into piety, in an entry from fall 1820: "My love to her is all spiritual. When my mind is carnal, her loveliness disappears. It is only as a lamb—a tender lamb that I would lay her in thy sacred bosom, and pour out floods of tears in her behalf" (n.d.). Attempting to follow the path proscribed by St. Paul, who said that it is best to remain single and chaste, Butrick, in spite of his very strong desire, sought to spiritualize the relationship, to repress the body. For her part, Brown never seems to have expressed desire for him or any other man; she turned down marriage proposals and remained celibate her entire life. (I do think, however, that she was aware of Butrick's desire, but that is an argument for another day.) The missionary and the convert had not become lovers in spring 1820, and they never would.

Brown's sickness worsened, and a married non-Cherokee missionary couple soon took over the school she had started. When she was only a few years into her teaching career tuberculosis killed Catharine Brown, but not before she sought help from two doctors: one, an Indian practitioner selected by her parents, and the other, a white physician in Huntsville, Alabama, who was friends with the missionaries. This final episode from her life reveals the complex multilateral character of her position: her simultaneous commitment to at least two communities and two changing, complex traditions and the ways they claimed her and contested for her loyalty. That she served them well is perhaps verified by how her two primary communities remembered her. Considering her life exemplary, the missionaries published the memoir and wrote other texts about her (Chamberlins 1830). Even earlier, in 1819, a missionary couple, the Chamberlains, had named their daughter Catharine Brown, and Christians in New Haven had scripted an eponymous play glorifying her character.

Cherokees also memorialized Brown in rich ways. In 1939, a journalist in Tulsa, Oklahoma, consulted David Brown's great-granddaughter,

Mrs. Clover Brown Barrowman, about her ancestors. Barrowman, the Brown family's historian, possessed a cane that David Brown had brought west on the Trail of Tears. Moreover, she provided an invaluable insight into how Cherokees understood and remembered Catharine Brown. Catharine, she said, "seemed to possess such spiritual qualities that she was called 'The Priestess' by the Indians" (1937). Such a title indicates spiritual power and authority within a community, something that we do not normally associate with the label "convert" or with cultural sellouts but which we might link readily to the role of a revitalizer. Long after her death, Cherokees participated in "Catharine Brown Sunday Schools" and still spoke of "her beautiful character" (Barrowman 1937). And, honoring the pathbreaking role she played as the first female Cherokee educator, they formed Catharine Brown Literary Societies. Surely the Cherokees' interpretations of her impact should carry some weight? Why, then, have scholars ventriloquized the words of missionaries and accepted their judgments uncritically?

A less rigid, totalistic, or binary understanding of "conversion" will help us avoid mismeasuring Catharine Brown. Although she did not speak as prophetically regarding the evils of white domination as more famous Indian converts Apess and Jones, her public life signified something other than capitulation to an alien culture. Her work in behalf of Cherokee women expressed Cherokee "communitism," a word that Jace Weaver coins to express activism in behalf of community (1997:xiii). Her emphasis on formal education and literacy signaled Cherokee dynamism, a willingness to adapt and change that contradicts chronopolitical assumptions regarding Indians. And her involvement in the larger Cherokee effort to domesticate "civilization" helped enable survival in perilous times, times better suited to a priestess than a prophet, a teacher than a warrior. For this reason, Cherokees long remembered and celebrated her life in ways that mission hagiographers and revisionist historians have yet to note.

My contention—that Brown's "conversion" did not connote total capitulation but, in fact, contributed to Cherokee revitalization—conforms to interpretations developed by scholars such as William G. McLoughlin, Kenneth Morrison, William Taylor, Nancy Shoemaker, James Treat, Rebecca Kugel, and others. Thanks to their efforts, we now know better than to depict Christianity as solely acidic or to identify all converts as compradors. Instead of endorsing essentialist conclusions, these scholars, like the new Indian historians, highlight cultural exchange and transformation. With their work, it looks as though scholarship has moved beyond the modernist search for the pure, authentic tradition and has given up on finding the exterior Other who can provide the vital antidote to urban ennui (P. Deloria 1998). We have moved from Neihardt's Black Elk, whose story stops tragically at Wounded Knee, to Raymond DeMallie's Nicholas Black Elk, whose story continues for half a century afterward and involves two marriages and conversion to Catholicism. Comfortable with ambiguity and drawn to hybridity, these scholars emphasize the creative ways native men and women appropriated, used, reinterpreted, modified, and reinvented Christianity, the multiple ways they connected and continue to connect pluralistic Christianities to their own manifold, changing traditions to create complex positions suited to their multifaceted lives. Conversion, these interpreters argue, can connote survival, not surrender—not erasure but, rather, renewal. This vantage opens up new ways of thinking and writing about Native American revitalization because it allows us to take seriously the lives of native leaders, including those who were female, affluent, literate, and Christian.

As contemporary historians have finally come to realize, the older analytic vocabulary, replete with binaries such as *assimilation* and *resistance*, *traditionalist* and *progressive*, now seems stiff and stale (White 1998:44). It smells residually of the Manichaean ethos of the Cold War era that privileges dualistic thinking in all domains. Of course, there is no guarantee that the latest terms—*liminality, ambivalence, border crossing, transversal politics, creolization, metissage, mestisaje,hybridity, ethnicity,* and *plurality* (Eagleton 2000:85; Werbner and Modood 1997)—are any less shaped by a mushier but nonetheless dominant "episteme" that we are still struggling to name and critique. Even so, promising theoretical developments exist that may invigorate revitalization studies. Robert Allen Warrior, for example, has developed a postessentialist discourse to describe native movements and traditions. Warrior, an Osage intellectual, formulates his thought in dialogue with other native intellectuals such as Vine Deloria Jr. (Standing Rock Sioux) and John Joseph Mathews (Osage). Indianness, Warrior proposes, is highly fluid, relational, improvisational, and continually re-created in community and in relation to land and orients people toward survival in the face of colonialism. That kind of language holds promise because it can embrace and comprehend the communalistic efforts of Powhatan, Delaware, Shawnee, and Creek prophets and Pequot, Anishinaabe, and Cherokee converts.

It recognizes the innovative religious movements of people who seem initially most radical and those who appear at first most compliant. It does not carry forward a shallow secularization thesis that assumes that religiously shaped movements must be retrograde, fatally compromised, or "nativistic." It defines movements as much in terms of the ends sought as in terms of the means used. Further, it does not elide the political dimension.

Guided by such thoughts, historians and anthropologists may return to the archives and reinterpret historical Native American movements in surprising ways. My directing figure here is that of the chiasmus. When confronted with a binary, the best way to critique it may be to invert its two terms. In order to break the old discursive system, to expose more fully its inadequacies, I would urge that we pay more attention to the modernity of prophetic movements. One can, for example, interpret prophetic movements quite well without using the word *nativism* by showing how these movements responded to nascent class divisions and religious tensions produced by economic developments and political shifts (Martin 1991). Paying attention to power shifts, we can avoid older ways of dismissing these movements' significance. This will position us to recognize that they were not allergic reactions to contact or psychologically generated phenomena (cf. Wallace 1956c). Focusing on the full range of types of power shifts, we can also correct the current tendency of historians to overextend the metaphor of the "middle ground," as if it could explain everything or describe every form of contact and exchange. Clearly, we need a richer range of metaphors to describe shifts in power relations (Richter 1993). We require stronger and nimbler theories to do justice to the wide array of power relations where parity never existed or flickered all too briefly.

Correlatively, I would urge scholars to also reappraise those movements that look most "accommodative." Reexamine the stories of converts. Reconsider those who have been written off as sellouts. Look behind the writings of missionaries and historians who depended too heavily on the missionaries' versions of events and ventriloquize their assumptions. As the biography of Catharine Brown suggests, if we seek, then we may find neglected facets of her story, for example, a horrible experience with attempted sexual assault, a singular dream with intriguingly hybrid elements, a deep intimacy with a white female friend, and the assumption of an innovative and authoritative social role in her hometown at a time when Cherokee women were losing power.

Stitching these neglected facts together, we can create more complete, more complicated, and more compelling portraits of individual converts and their communities. Once that is done, we will probably discern additional creative movements of strategic importation and domestication in response to shifts of power in the eastern woodlands and elsewhere. While complicating our view of Native American revitalization, such results will support Wallace's theory's universalism. Stretching our middle-aged theory a little, we may yet revitalize it in significant ways.

Note

For materials that provide important background to the case of Catharine Brown, see Brereton 1991; Brown 1819; Buff 1995; Fogelson 1982; Halbert n.d.; Hoole 1986; L. Smith 1989; Wright 1940.

3. PRIESTS AND PROPHETS

The Politics of Voice in the Pacific

Jukka Siikala

The Problem

The problem of revitalization or similar collective phenomena has been the focus of anthropological analysis for more than half a century. The time span of the discussion itself guarantees that a lot has happened, not only in the world but in anthropological theorizing during that time. Instead of following a dictionary definition of the term, "giving new life or vigor to" the lives of some social wholes or totalities, we have witnessed the death and disappearance of the kinds of life or "cultures" giving birth to the revitalization movements. Michael E. Harkin (ch. 6) emphasizes how revitalization has actually seldom worked; instead of revitalism, the movements actually celebrate death in a cathartic way. The evidence provided by time is convincing in this respect. There are, however, other aspects of the early discussions about revitalization that lead to ambiguous interpretations or even more ambiguous realities. Here I discuss some aspects of the theories of revitalization and base my views on ethnographic cases from Polynesia.

To begin with, I summarize the relevant main points of Anthony F. C. Wallace's influential theory of revitalization inspired by his study of the Seneca. Wallace's interpretation is, before all, an equilibrium theory; his ideal typical description of revitalization begins and ends with a *steady state* of the society, which is characterized by the fact that "for the *vast majority* of the population, culturally recognized techniques for satisfying needs operate with such efficiency that chronic stress within the system varies within tolerable limits" (1956c:267, emphasis added). This simple formulation has some drawbacks. Wallace does not say what a society is, and neither does he define the needs or the nature of culture. Society consists only of numbers (a vast majority), and the rest of the conceptualization is a simple means-ends formula: individuals aim at satisfying their needs with better or worse luck. And when the luck turns out to be worse, things begin to happen and events leading to a revitalization movement begin to unfold. Stress increases, and stress-reducing techniques multiply and differentiate. As a consequence the culture is internally distorted; the elements are not harmoniously related but, rather, are mutually inconsistent and interfering, leading to an increase of stress. The maelstrom is ready.

Based on a means-ends conceptualization, the satisfactory functioning of Wallace's society as a system presupposes harmony among its elements and thus a high degree of orchestration of individual actions. The coordination is achieved not directly through techniques to satisfy needs; on the contrary, Wallace limits the possible variety of the techniques to those accepted by the culture in question. The classical formulation for this coordination got its expression in culture and personality interpretations of the standardizing influences of primary institutions, the mother's milk with which people internalize the conceptual and cognitive system of their culture. Thus, for Wallace the collective coherence of individual incoherences is attained though culture. In his general discussion about culture and personality he reminds us that "in marital relationships, entry into an age grade, the giving of a feast—in all such contracts, the motives may be diverse, but the cognitive expectations are standardized" (1961:41). Although the social actors' motives are not in harmony, their expectations are. And Wallace goes on, "From this standpoint, then, it is *culture* which is shared (in the special sense of institutional contract) rather than personality, and culture may be conceived as an invention, which makes possible the maximal organization of motivational diversity. This it is able to accomplish because of the human . . . cognitive capacity for the perception of systems of behavioral equivalence" (1961:41). Here we, in fact, have the classical Hobbesian notion of social contract in the form of culture. The diverse individual motivations, obviously conflicting ones, are maximally organized toward a common goal of survival with the help of a social contract, which for Hobbes required the existence of a higher power, a sovereign. In fact, for Hobbes "men have no pleasure, (but on the contrary, a great deale of griefe) in keeping company, where there is no power able to overawe them all" (1987:64). This disdain of sociality has for him two kinds of consequences: "warre of every man against every man" in the competition for resources or the social contract and giving the power to the sovereign with it. Likewise in Wallace's theory of revitalization the period of cultural distortion is characterized by antisocial behavior, intragroup violence, and desperate attempts of individual, personal adjustments, which do not lead to the necessary orchestration of the whole back into an integrated society. Revitalization is a pendulum between contractual and noncontractual situations, between individualism and society.

Why do people, then, have to reach the "maximal organization of motivational diversity" with the help of culture or a sovereign or otherwise engage in war with everybody? Hobbes expresses this in the simplest terms: "From this equality of ability, ariseth equality of hope in the attaining our Ends. And therefore if any two men desire the same thing, which nevertheless they cannot both enjoy, they become enemies" (1987:63). The scarcity of resources is an essential element in all means-ends conceptualizations, and it is the common denominator of Hobbes's and Wallace's notions of society. For Wallace the world we are living with is a "mazeway" through which we have to make our way with social coordination. The constant decision making at all corners and crossings does not require a uniformity of motivations but, rather, a perception of a system of behavioral equivalence. The world appears as a congested system of highways through which the population has to move toward a common destination without major traffic jams or disorganization, which might lead to road rage or other versions of stress-related wars of everybody against everybody. Culture becomes the institutional contract of the rules of the road, enabling everyone to move smoothly in the same direction.

This mazeway/highway image of human behavior and the role of culture in it is appealing. That is how our society seems to work. To interpret cultural systems and social behavior everywhere on the basis of the same logic is dubious, though. The sovereign, the culture, and the mazeway are all collectivizing images, and so is revitalization when it is applied to whole societies or cultures. The attempt to look for a unifying motivational organization corresponds to the way Spengler identified civilizations with their Ur symbol or Benedict, with leitmotiv. Populations, or vast majorities of them, were assumed to be organized by these collectivizing symbols as types of civilizations or different cultures. Accordingly, cultures or societies died and emerged with the collective reformulation of these symbols. Death and possible rebirth are then experienced collectively, enacted through mass movements, which are totalizing and holistic. Culture as an institutional contract that is never made but still agreed on seems to be the principal generator of Wallace's thinking. He takes that assumed contractual culture as the justification and foundation for the ways of instrumental action. Agreed meanings become instrumental devices for detached individuals.

Social Movement as Society-Generating Action

Because of the collective nature of the action connected with the revitalization movements, the problems arising out of their interpretation have a history that is helpful in analyzing the enigma of revitalization. The classical formulation of a mass movement with completely contrasting overtones can be found in Gustave Le Bon's *The Crowd: A Study of the Popular Mind* (1960), originally published in 1895. Le Bon's psychology of the masses emphasizes in detail some behavioral aspects of revitalization movements as described by Wallace. First Le Bon connects the lack of emotional restraint and an incapacity for moderation with the resulting diminishing of the role of intellect in determining social action. The result is well known: "We see then the disappearance of the conscious personality, the predominance of the unconscious personality, the turning by means of suggestion and contagion of feelings and ideas in identical direction, and the tendency immediately to transform the suggested ideas into acts" (Le Bon 1960:32). With the lowering of intellect and the disappearance of conscious personality, the actions of the massed crowd begin, according to Le Bon, to be based on images that are "hallucinatory" in nature but collectively experienced, so that they thus have the aura of authenticity (1960:42).

The connecting point to Wallace's notions is clear here. The collectively experienced authenticity of the "hallucinations" creating images publicly open to the senses is clearly culture. The "institutional contract" is not in the hands of just any "institution" but, in fact, is made by the collection of people participating in the mass movement. The immediacy of interagreement about culture is not a result of contract as a third ground between action and shared meanings; rather, it is intertwined in the action itself.

The impossibility of the externalization of a meaning-standardizing contract is clearly highlighted in the classic interpretation by Émile Durkheim of the rituals witnessed by Baldwin Spencer and Frank Gillen in Alice Springs in November 1896. According to the description of Spencer and Gillen, "The smoke, the blazing torches, the showers of sparks falling in all directions and the masses of dancing, yelling men, formed altogether a genuinely wild and savage scene of which it is impossible to convey any adequate idea in words" (1904:237). Although Durkheim's (1965:249 n. 31) interpretation is not based on this meager description alone, he could deduce his famous distinction between sacred and profane out of the impossibility of creating images conveyable by words:

> One can readily conceive how, when arrived at this state of exaltation, a man does not recognize himself any longer. Feeling himself dominated and carried away by some sort of an external power which makes him think and act differently than in normal times, he naturally has the impression of being himself no longer. It seems to him that he has become a new being: the decorations he puts on and the masks that cover his face and figure materially in this interior transformation, and to a still greater extent, they aid in determining its nature. And as at the same time all his companions feel themselves transformed in the same way and express this sentiment by their cries, their gestures and their general attitude, everything is just as though he really were transported into a special world, entirely different from the one where he ordinarily lives, and into an environment filled with exceptionally intense forces that take hold of him and metamorphose him. [1965:249–250]

The metamorphosis of the individual in Durkheim's interpretation occurs only accompanied and aided by participation in a collective action that creates the institutional agreement about the new state and distributes it through mutual participation to all members of the society.

The "external power" that the individual feels and which "carries him away" is for Durkheim not only the sacred but also the sacred as the basis of society as a collective, which creates the categories of thought, logic, and morality for the maintenance of that collectivity. After the creation and reinforcement of these in the seasonal ritual, the people can disperse again into their individual activities for the rest of the year and come together again to celebrate their unity in the next ritual of "eternal return" (Eliade 1971:388). They do not necessarily do so, but, as Durkheim himself has to admit, the exaltation itself is a double-edged sword; it can turn the most mediocre and inoffensive bourgeois into a hero or a butcher through following the moral authority of the imagined collective of the ritual. Despite this fact, the experience of collectivity subordinates the individuals to work in harmony with the collective effort by defining the general aims of the social organization in question.

The moral collective constructed by Durkheim seems very much a whole, which is presupposed before any manifestations of it are analyzed. Even in his description of the ritual he takes the dancing and shouting men to be the whole society and does not pay any attention to what the women and children are doing and does not even mention if all the men are taking part in the general exaltation (see Carucci [ch. 9]). Thus, he is imposing a unifying totality over disparate observations and creates out of these the image of a rule-governed society that ultimately finds its legitimating power in the powerful bureaucratic world of the European nation-state (Grimshaw and Hart 1993:26–27). If we look carefully into the phenomena described as revitalization movements, it is possible to find instances where the whole revitalized is not the creation and institutional contract of culture or the organizational totality, which both suppress individuality with their collective telos. What is revitalized or emerging can be the forms, which enable individuals to express their own intentionalities through orchestrated social action instead of suppressing themselves under the totality.

Orchestration through Differentiation

In my early research into the so-called revitalization movements in the Pacific I found that the movements did not result in new totalities; in fact, the opposite seemed to be the case (Siikala 1982). Religious-political movements, which in their dramatic outlook puzzled the European observers, were witnessed all around the Pacific Islands during the early days of colonial intrusion and the beginning of missionary activities. Although the movements seemed to be totalizing and holistic and affected whole villages, islands, districts, and even islands and island groups, they were at the same time inventing differentiations. They did not create bureaucratic-rational social organizations or make institutional contracts about the emerging culture. Island-wide revivals resulting from missionary activities and tensions inside the islands' political systems facing absolutely new challenges surely forced the "vast majority of the population" to reformulate their worldview, even reshape their social structure, but it occurred under conditions in which the people were very much in charge of the overall social situation. They had not been deprived of the conditions of the reproduction of their way of life. On the contrary, the maintenance of that system was very much the precondition for the survival of the happenstance missionaries and traders, whose own lives were very much dependent on the functioning local system they tried to change.

The classic example is provided by the conversion to Christianity on Rennell and Bellona, vividly described by the oral traditions collected by Elbert and Monberg (1965). These Polynesian outliers in the Solomon Islands were brought into European consciousness in 1790 by Captain Wilkinson, and the islands were first visited by Europeans in 1856. The Rennellese killed the first missionary in 1910, and the missionary activities were put to a halt (Elbert and Monberg 1965:392). More detailed knowledge of Christianity reached the islands in the 1930s through the Islanders visiting missionary stations elsewhere. The rumor-like information about the new and powerful god led the people to syncretistic experiments attempting to maintain good relationships with both the old and the new supranormal powers. The culturally accepted means to satisfy needs were working as before, but the Islanders had to find a way to conventionalize the innovations constantly flowing into their world with people returning from outside and telling about their experiences. We can thus identify this historical phase as containing some of the basic features of the stage of cultural disintegration as described by Wallace (1956c:269) and characterized by initial considerations of a substitute way of life.

This syncretistic experimentation came, however, to an unexpected end at a great ritual harvest arranged by the chief-priest Tegheta of Rennell Island in 1938. The dramatic events were narrated by a Rennellese informant and are published in their entirety by Elbert and Monberg (1965). The following is based on their ethnographic material. As the possessor of the most sacred knowledge, Tegheta was the person responsible for the rituals, and ultimately he was thus also responsible for deciding whether any new gods should be added to the ones already worshiped. According to the legend the chief called the people together to "discuss the religion and that we should decide whether to worship both God and Semoana (Tehainga'atua) [God of Christianity or the traditional religion]" (Elbert and Monberg 1965:397). The situation was charged with tension. Tegheta organized an experiment, divided the people, and ordered three to pray to the Christian God and four to pray to Semoana. The people waited for some sign by which they could make their decision. And their wishes were fulfilled. Tegheta was possessed by a god, but his behavior in possession was highly contradictory. First he scolded Taupongi, who was his own father, a chief, and also senior in the ritual duties. Something more unexpected and inventive was to follow: "Arrangements were made to bring an end to the taboos concerning brother and sister [avoidance], and then there were many marriages, as the lying mediums said to get ready to go to heaven, and God was going to set fire to this earth. Thereupon marriages were made, all the adults, teenagers, and children, and even suckling infants did [this], and people lame in their feet did [this]" (Elbert and Monberg 1965:397).

The complete breakdown of conventional social morality continued. The population gathered in one house, where each couple had a sleeping shelf. It was expected that the house would go to heaven: "The people were ready, and some wept and trembled, because [they] might fall out when the house would be taken away, and some people wept for their children who had not come and who were outside the house, and the lying mediums offered consolation, and [asked them] to stop [weeping], as [it] made no difference, for the [children] would be exchanged in heaven. . . . Mostly we called on God in heaven, and after about two hours nothing had happened, and [we] went back outside again and built ovens" (Elbert and Monberg 1965:398). After destroying the sexual morality and even social reciprocal relationships, people began to destroy property and burn their mats and houses, cut down the coconut trees, and kill the pigs, chickens, and even each other. The night was a time of exaltation, and "many were beaten that night, and it was very short, about two hours, and then daylight brightened" (Elbert and Monberg 1965:399). In broad daylight, after the night's events of killing and beating, people bathed in a single place, "the men and women were naked, [it] made no difference, and the men looked at the women and the women also looked and were unashamed" (Elbert and Monberg 1965:400). The general commotion continued for several days, alternating between beatings and prayers, and then the events ended in an interesting way:

> One night we were all at prayer to God. . . . And our high chief Taupongi stood up in the centre of the group and he took out the picture of Jesus and held [it] and stood [it] on its head, and turned his back to us. . . . But he turned the picture to face us . . . and the mouth of the picture spoke. . . .
>
> Our high chief suggested that we arrange ourselves in three groups, his, Moa's and Tegheta's. Saying: You Moa, take that group and go south. You Tegheta. Take that group and go east, and we will go back west. So I took some people and went to Hutuna, and Tegheta took others and went to Tigoa, and we did the worship of the SDA [Seventh Day Adventists], and Taupongi went back to Niupani and did the worship of the SSEM [South Seas

Evangelical Mission], and another small group went to Tabaitahe and they took the name of the Church of England. [Elbert and Monberg 1965:401]

The dramatic events that emerged out of pressures toward accultura-tion, as defined by Wallace (1956c:269), led to a principal change in the outward appearance of the culture. The objectified form, as manifested in the picture of Jesus, changed. This upside-down form with all its novelty created an upside-down result. Though the image was a novelty, it was just a reformulation of the old one without any structural change. The appearance changed, but the appearing remained the same.

There is a parallel in the mythical narratives about the population of the island. These tell how the canoes sailed in search of new land to live on, carrying two black stones from the temple of their homeland. However, these black stones were lost in the sea during the journey, and the people had to replace them with a stalactite. The stalactite image of the stones led the people to decide which gods they would call for protection. The narrative telling about these events, long before the conversion to Christianity, has a form and thus also a structure identical to the above legend: "And Kaituu said: 'My deity is Tehu'aingabenga, and [my] heavenly deity is Tehainga'atua.' . . . And Taupongi said: 'Mine is Singano and [my] heavenly deity is also Tehainga'atua.' Tongo said: 'Mine is Singano, and [my] heavenly deity is also Tehainga'atua.' Ngoha said: 'Mine is Tepou, and [my] heavenly deities are Ngutupu'a and Te-poutu'uingangi'" (Elbert and Monberg 1965:174–175). After all the groups had selected their gods, they divided the land accordingly, and "all the seven lived in these settlements" (Elbert and Monberg 1965:177). The major revitalization of November 1938 replicated the image the Islanders had about the original sociologic of their island. The upside-down image of Jesus just replaced the black stones as the unsaturated forms of similarities waiting to be filled with the contradictions of social life. The institutional contract leading to agreement seems to be com-pletely missing, and instead we find a form that allows for disagreement or nonagreement.

The Nonpolitics of Incorporation

The differentiating instead of collectivizing cultural logic clearly runs opposite to what both Durkheim and Wallace would presume. In a more recent example it is also clearly visible in the way the different segments of the Cook Islands society related to two female prophets whose activities I was able to observe in the 1980s and 1990s. Both prophets are female, and both are socially ambiguous, but the social reaction to their activities and preaching was equally enigmatic.

One of the female prophets is of a chiefly family from one of the outer islands in the Southern Cooks. Her biography reveals the general sociological indicators that make her suitable for a prophetic role. She was living in a marriage of convenience with a local man of considerable social significance who had a Western education and a professional job, thus combining traditional and modern high statuses. When she was pregnant with their fourth child she had a dream. In the dream she had a crown on her head and saw her mother dead. Afterward she inquired about the state of her mother, but she could not get confirmation for the death news, which meant that the mother was still alive. The dreams continued, however, and as a result of those she wanted to legalize her marriage with the father of her children. With the help of the police, a chief administration officer, and the Protestant minister, she finally succeeded in this.

After two more children were born, she became seriously ill. She visited both the doctors and the traditional healers, *ta'unga*s. Finally one ta'unga told her that she was not sick at all but that she was a prophet. As a result of this she turned to Catholicism despite the resistance of the Catholic priest. The children's father left her, her mother died, and in the end she was left alone with 11 children. With her new prophetic status she changed her name and combined the chiefly title of her family with a name derived from the Bible. Besides these revivalistic features she also promoted clear perpetuative or nativistic programs, to use Ralph Linton's classic 1943 terminology. The perpetuative tendency was demonstrated in her way of stressing the importance and necessity of selected aspects of the traditional way of life. Thus, she made herself a cloth of tapa and gave up some of the innovations brought to the islands by outside contacts. After clothing herself in the tapa cloth she killed a large pig, divided it, and gave portions of it to all the ministers, fathers, and chiefs of the island and began to follow these portions of the pig herself. The division and distribution of the sacrificial pig are of utmost importance in Polynesian sacrificial practice, and they replicate in tangible form the structure of the social differentiation (Valeri 1985:56–59). Thus, she frequents the meetings and services of all the denominations and congregations on the small island—and there are a lot of them. Besides the Cook Islands Christian Church, the successor to the London Missionary Society, there are Catholics, Seventh Day Adventists, Mormons, and Baha'i, and all of these have two congregations in the two villages of the island. The population fluctuates between 570 and 650.

In the meetings she stands up, is very outspoken, and delivers long speeches filled with quotations from the Bible, which she seems to know by heart. She also resists most of the *papa'aa*, European customs, and though she has now given up her tapa cloth, she dresses herself only in white. She has forced the same dress code on all her children and has also forbidden the children to attend the school. As a consequence of the severe limitations she has imposed on the lifestyle of her children, one after another of them has deserted her and run away. This generally known fact does not prevent the island families from giving their children to this prophet as "feeding children" or even offering them for adoption. The circulation of children through the different kinds of adoption practices forms one of the principal modes of reciprocity and forms another iconography of the culture of nature (Levy 1973:482–484). Since 1983 three of the prophet's children have run away, but she has adopted three younger ones to replace them. Though the children desert her and the teachers of the local school are critical of the neglect of the children's education, the general attitude is that of tolerance toward her lifestyle and message. Even the ministers and priests of different denominations demonstrate an enigmatic understanding toward her. She is not prevented from attending the religious meetings, and she is not interrupted and is allowed to preach. She is even an expected speaker in the Sunday afternoon religious meetings, and her speeches are listened to intensively. She herself also faithfully follows the precedence of the portions of her first sacrificial pig and continues to give monetary contributions to all the churches alike. The limited monetary resources available for her are mainly from the contributions of her runaway children. The domestic reciprocity thus continues, despite the desertion. On my inquiry about the religious tolerance, one of the ministers just explained that one never knows, "it might be God speaking through her."

In this apostle's life we have an example of revitalization on the individual scale. Using the language of Wallace's times we can say that this woman was of a high status. She was a chief's daughter and a notable man's wife. Through her mother's death and her husband's desertion her world began to collapse. The stress began to increase to intolerable levels, and she fell sick. After this typical "shaman's sickness" she was reborn and found out that she was a prophet.

The new combination of cultural imagery resulting in this redefinition of self did not create any better means to satisfy her needs, nor did it redefine them. She does not live as an ascetic withdrawn from the society; indeed, quite the contrary is true. The revitalization occurred on an individual level as a reorganization of existing images, and the society contextualized her in a conventional way according to the Polynesian cultural logic (similar to that of the previous case). In this logic the difference is highlighted against the similarity, and thus even a universalistic religion like Christianity can be turned to serve individualizing intentions and tolerated as such. This same cultural logic can be found behind the nonpolitics of tolerance in the community and the multiplicity of audiences she addresses.

The other prominent prophet and faith healer, Apii Piho, arrived from New Zealand in March 1988. She told that she had been elected to be the mouthpiece of God already in her mother's womb. However, she did not know anything about that before she fell sick and suffered amnesia. With her recovery she was also "reborn" to her actual role as a prophet. Her special ability is to bless the water so that "a total of 35522 people whose illnesses have varied from cancer, diabetes and curses have received her attention," as was reported in the local newspaper, the *Cook Islands News* (1988a:6). She began her activities on the home islands surrounded by great fervor. During the first four days of her stay in Rarotonga more than five hundred people visited her for treatment (*Cook Islands News* 1988b). The government had to step in and help her to organize larger and larger houses to accommodate all her patients. Immediately upon her arrival she "blessed the water supply of Government House No. 67 at Arorangi. Jug after jug of blessed water were filled from the kitchen tap and patients given a glass each to drink. . . . Some had come with their own containers to fill with the blessed water and presumably take home to assist in curing their various complaints" (*Cook Islands News* 1988a:6). The blessed water was in high demand, and so was the Johnson's baby oil. To meet this demand she blessed the whole supply of oil in Rarotonga Pharmacy, and the oil was quickly sold out.

Within a few days more than half the population had visited her on the main island, Rarotonga, and the outer islands sent requests for her to visit them also. Upon her arrival on Atiu she was met by the chairman of the Island Council, Teiotu Tangatapoto, and the chief administration officer, and she blessed the water supply of the island. Practically every person on the island attended her meetings. The same kind of enthusiasm met her on Aitutaki and Mauke. On Mauke I observed the power of the water at the local rugby match. The rough game, which is played barefoot in a field filled with fist-sized coral rocks, inevitably leads to injuries. The bleeding players were sprinkled with the blessed water from a bucket hurried to the site of the accident. The injured players continued their play immediately after feeling the soothing effects.

On Aitutaki Apii Piho again blessed the water supply, and island officials quickly calculated that there would be enough blessed water for only two days with the hugely increased water consumption (*Cook Islands News* 1988c). Day and night people were filling every possible container with this miraculous water.

The life history of Apii Piho again can be cast into a scheme of revitalization, even a successful one. As a female migrant in relative deprivation she was able to reformulate her personal mazeway and "die" through amnesia, experience rebirth as a healer, and return to her home islands as a celebrity. And this celebrity status is interesting. The whole society seemed to circle around Apii Piho for a few weeks until her departure. The news in the local newspaper again makes interesting and illuminating reading:

> Cook Islands faith healer Apii Piho will return to the Cook Islands from New Zealand in May on a permanent basis. She left Rarotonga on Sunday for New Zealand after being hosted as a guest of honour in the island's airport VIP Lounge. . . . Four tables were laden with island food for the faith healer and the people who came along. Hymns sung by those present lifted the night's of celebration to high levels. . . . After being notified by government that the house in Arorangi will remain her residence when she returns, Ms Piho finalised the decision to come back and live among her own people. Ms Piho intends to remove the 17 months old power of blessing over the water at her South Auckland residence. When she left the Cook Islands with the blessed sanction on the water at Arorangi residence remaining so that the people can obtain it anytime for their needs. [*Cook Islands News* 1988d:7]

Apii Piho's individual revitalization was thus immediately incorporated in the conventional context of island councils, chiefly administration officers, government ministries, and VIP lounges. So we have to ask, where is the collective nature of this revitalization, in which the majority of the population clearly took part? In the previous prophetic case, the activities of the prophet were mainly tolerated, not celebrated. The collective celebration of Apii Piho's miraculous gifts seemed to lead to social turmoil, which turned out be temporary, without any major changes in the tolerating structures.

Conventions and Inventions of Revitalization

Revitalization movements fold out in a regular way on the surface. There is something that we might call stress; there is something that we might call the death or disintegration of the old—either on an individual or a collective level; and there is also the emergence of something new. The dialectics of collective and individual, convention and invention, are obviously extremely complicated though. We cannot explain the activities of these prophets, and even less those of the people of Rennell, on the basis of a means-ends conceptualization. Needs do not have a role to play in them; all seem to be completely based on symbolization and its social organization. The instrumental role of symbolization in Wallace's theory might reveal an ethnocentric wisdom about the nature of our own culture. He postulates "that events or happenings of various types have genotypical structures independent of local cultural differences. . . . Their uniformity is based on generic human attributes, both physiological and psychological" (1956c:268). He supposes a transcendental unity behind human behavioral diversity and thus creates out of his supposed steady state a model of high modern society with its "straitjacketing" effect of demanded uniformity (Scott 1998:345–347). The singularity of the collective social intention necessarily creates "deviants" out of real, not abstract, citizens.

Deviation is, however, a phenomenon connected with modern society's tendency for "bracketing contingency but also standardizing the subjects" (Scott 1998:345) in its belief in genotypical behavior. In Western society, which gave birth to the theory of revitalization, this is the case. But an extension of those societal conditions to other societies can be questioned.

If we look at culture as images instead of institutional agreement, then we have to pay attention to variation more than to the process of creating uniformity. Images as collective devices can perform amazing tricks in social life. Because of their metaphorical nature (as in the case of the black rock, the upside-down Jesus, the white clothing, Johnson's baby oil, water), they create differences out of similarities. The same image is brought into different uses, meanings, and practices. This is a logic completely in opposition to modern society's modus operandi, which supposes unity despite the differences. Thus, the female prophets were not deviants, and the image of Jesus created a replication of the tribal divisions already expressed in the mythical accounts of the origin of the population. Some of the principal structures of the cultures were really revitalized, but attention to these very differences or cultural specificities is a prerequisite for understanding the process.

Roy Wagner has stressed that "we live our lives by ordering and rationalizing, and re-create our conventional controls in creative swoops of compulsive invention, tribal and religious peoples live by invention in this sense, and revitalize their differentiating controls from time to time in bursts of hysterical conventionalizing" (1981:59). The Rennellese conversion to Christianity can be seen as a "burst of hysterical conventionalizing." The same can be said about the general fervor surrounding the activities of Apii Piho. The same interpretation is valid also for the preaching of the anonymous female apostle from the outer island. The images conventionalized did not have to be old ones: Johnson's baby oil was a completely suitable image for that purpose. There was less need for maximal coordination of motivational diversity than for maximal differentiation of inventive activities.

The politics of voice follows more the guidelines dictated by the poetics of life than the manual for production. All kinds of individualities can be tolerated—and not only tolerated but accommodated in the social praxis. The reason for this is in the ethnographically obvious dialectic, which "operates by exploiting contradictions against a common ground of similarity, rather than appealing to consistency against a common ground of differences" (Wagner 1981:32).

The problematic nature of the culture concept behind the classical formulation of revitalization theories becomes even more clear if we compare revitalization to scientific revolutions, as Thomas Kuhn (1964) has used the term. The puzzle solving in science proceeds well as long as everybody agrees what the puzzle is and follows the rules of logic to accomplish the task. If (when) the puzzle is not solved, then stress increases and other rules are attempted, until the whole paradigm changes and a new puzzle is constructed. Paradigms are controlling devices attempting to collectivize the individual efforts in problem solving, coordinating the creative swoops of compulsive invention into the service of a collective project. But scientific paradigms are scientific, and we make a major mistake in putting culture on a par with them. The incorporation of invention instead of the reformulation of the mazeway seems to be the logic of Polynesian cultures, at least as long as the straitjacket of Western rationality does not strangle that principal cultural process.

4. THE WASITAY RELIGION

Prophecy, Oral Literacy, and Belief on Hudson Bay

Jennifer S. H. Brown

Ever since Anthony F. C. Wallace's seminal work on revitalization movements in the 1960s, the concept of revitalization has served to frame discussions of religious innovations and renewals in postcontact indigenous
societies. Yet, like Richard White's "middle ground" more recently (Joel
Martin [ch. 2]), the phrase may become a substitute for more developed
descriptions and explanations. The analysis of any religious movement,
however framed, presents challenges, especially when the subject matter
leads us across cultural borders and into historical situations beyond our
range of observation. For one thing, the writers of the documentary
sources we must use were usually outsiders (fur traders and missionaries,
in the events studied here). Their cultural and religious views shaped
what they thought they saw and how they wrote about and perceived
what was going on among the people they observed. We who later try
to analyze what these old sources tell us are doubly removed from the
events and actors in question.

Another problem is that in searching for effective ways to formu-
late and conceptualize prophetic movements in terms considered effective and intelligible within our academic disciplines, we risk exoticizing
them, distancing ourselves from the people involved, and neglecting the
historical and cultural perspectives that their descendants could offer.
There is also a risk of idealizing these movements. Their themes of energy and hope, rebirth, revival, and innovation in the face of deprivation
or cultural loss may win our favor but may obscure their negative aspects. Their success may have served some community members' needs
and interests well but could be hurtful to others. Leaders may fail or
become self-serving, leaving a mixed legacy that celebratory traditions
about them may not capture.

Recently, I have had opportunities to review a Hudson Bay Cree prophetic movement of 1842–43 with an Omushkego (Swampy Cree) scholar and storyteller, Louis Bird, who has thoughtfully reflected on some questions of language and narrative bearing on this topic. His commentaries have enriched this study, encouraging me to return to a topic I last examined in the 1980s. The invoking of Omushkego memories and views of these events and of narratives about them provides a reminder that the concept of "revitalization movement" is itself emic to social science and is not readily translatable into Cree or other indigenous languages. To illuminate 19th-century spiritual and religious experience on the west coast of Hudson Bay, we need to turn not only to outsiders' documents and anthropological models but also to insights that the Cree language and Omushkego stories and scholarship can provide.[1]

This chapter begins by reconstructing the Hudson Bay prophetic movement of 1842–43, building on earlier, shorter studies to outline its main events (Brown 1982, 1988; Long 1989). Exploring the generative role played in it by a Cree syllabic writing system that had just been introduced in the region by a Methodist missionary, I then look at some intellectual and symbolic aspects of the movement as they were recorded at the time, taking particular interest in Omushkego concepts of worship, writing, and books. Finally, I discuss some 20th-century Omushkego oral narratives and perspectives that provide a range of indigenous assessments of the subject and some fresh contexts in which to view it.

The Events of 1842–43: Context

As pieced together from European writings, the story of the rise of the prophets Abishabis ("Small Eyes") and Wasitek or Wasitay ("The Light"), and of their heavenly visit and the novel ideas and practices that resulted, begins in the summer of 1842. By that time, the Hudson's Bay Company (HBC) had been trading for furs at several major posts on Hudson Bay for more than a century and a half. Numerous Omushkegowak, known to the HBC men as Home guard or Home Indians, were living at least seasonally around the posts, supplying them with fish, game, geese, and other waterfowl and with labor of various sorts as well as furs. These people had long acquaintance with the English and Scottish sojourners. Over several generations, their kinship ties with the traders had proliferated through marital unions that more or less followed native custom, as Christian churches and European women were absent until the early 1800s in Rupert's Land (the Hudson Bay watershed that had been granted by royal charter to the HBC in 1670). These ties did not mean that HBC men "went native" or that the Omushkegowak became Europeanized; they both maintained their own communities, contrasting values and forms of governance, and distinct lifestyles. Even if the trade brought them into a shared social sphere with mutually understood exchange rituals and overlapping aims, the two parties did not live in the same society (cf. Brown 1980:xvi–xvii).

In 1842, the first Christian missions to become established in the Hudson Bay watershed north and east of Lake Winnipeg were only two years old, although they were already moving quickly to build their own webs of association with Northern Algonquian communities. In the summer of 1840, the HBC had allowed several Methodist missionaries to travel from Upper Canada (Ontario) or Britain to build missions at selected fur trade posts in Rupert's Land. One of those missions was at Norway House near the north end of Lake Winnipeg on the main water route to the Hudson Bay post of York Factory (Manitoba), and another was at Moose Factory (Ontario), just upriver from the southwest corner of James Bay. They were headed, respectively, by two English ministers: James Evans, who had already spent several years in Indian mission work in Ontario, and George Barnley, who had come straight from England. Evans at Norway House in 1840–41 quickly began work on translating scriptures and hymns into Cree. Improvising a printing press, the first in the region, he devised a Cree syllabary, a writing system that, although unintelligible to the fur traders and even to his fellow missionaries until they could be taught it, was easily and eagerly learned and passed on among Cree speakers themselves. The use of Cree syllabics spread rapidly, paralleling in some respects the rise of the Cherokee syllabary developed by Sequoyah in the 1820s, far to the south (Fogelson 1996). Mission influence and the rise of a distinctive Cree literacy were important elements in the synthesis of ideas and practices that stimulated this prophetic movement.

Economic and environmental conditions also doubtless supplied some tinder for prophetic fervor. In 1842–43, game animals and fur returns were in a state of decline in the long-exploited fur trade regions all around Hudson Bay. HBC officer George Barnston wrote from Albany Factory to his colleague at York Factory, James Hargrave, on November 23, 1842, that the northern and southern departments seemed "to be in a dead heat—who shall decline fastest. The Albany District from one end of it to the other scarcely exhibited half a trade" (1842:2440). Climatic conditions appeared more severe than usual; on May 25, 1843, John Cromartie, a clerk at the Severn post on the Hudson Bay coast north of Albany, recorded that he was experiencing the "most Backward Spring that I have Ever Seen for this Thirty years back" (Hudson's Bay Company Archives [HBCA] n.d.: HBCA B.198/a/84, f. 31).

Subarctic cold cycles and resource shortages in themselves, however, do not suffice to explain the rise of this movement or its nature. For one thing, these particular severe conditions were probably no worse than other similar crisis points in the boreal forest lowlands along Hudson Bay during the "Little Ice Age," a cold climatic episode that extended across the northern hemisphere from approximately 1550 to the 1850s (Fossett 2001:29). David Aberle has aptly noted the risks of assuming that deprivation in itself causes such movements and then reading the evidence accordingly: "It is always possible after the fact to find deprivations." He draws attention, however, to "relative deprivation" as a useful concept. People facing situations of change or blockage of their expectations, and experiencing "the insufficiency of ordinary action," may turn to extraordinary actions and innovations and to withdrawal from the existing social order if they feel that it has failed them and "cannot be reconstituted" (Aberle 1965:538–541). They would surely be more likely to do so if, as on Hudson Bay, plausible leaders emerged in their midst, bringing a blend of old and new ideas and practices and a new sign system (here, the Cree syllabary), that seemed empowering and likely to fulfill hopes and needs.

The Rise of Abishabis and Wasitek

In the fall and winter of 1842, HBC traders from York Factory southward to the Severn River on Hudson Bay and later at Albany Factory (Fort Albany, Ontario, on James Bay) became concerned about some new practices among their native trading partners and provisioners. Hunters and trappers were neglecting their usual pursuits for other activities that the HBC men saw as harmful both for the fur trade and for survival. At the Severn post, John Cromartie wrote on September 4, 1842, that the local Omushkegowak were being "a pest" to him, "with their psalm Singing and painting Books that has been all there occupation this three weeks back." The numbers of people gathered there increased during the next weeks, and on October 23 Cromartie wrote that they were "making the woods to Ring today with music and at the same time they have empty stomacks and I am afraid it will be the case with them after this if they Continue as they have done all the Fall" (HBCA n.d.: HBCA B.198/a/84, f. 13).

Cromartie's comments offer fascinating clues that the Omushkego-wak involved in the movement were not only creating documents of some sort (on which, more later) but also adopting what was for them a new style of worship ("psalm singing"). Being Christian himself, how-ever, he doubtless failed to grasp the extent to which psalm singing in particular was an innovation for the people involved. Such a col-lective performance stood in radical contrast to traditional Northern Algonquian songs and rituals, which were highly individualized and per-sonal.[2] Omushkego observers of the Europeans, as Louis Bird explains, found that one of the most striking things about the newcomers' mode of spiritual communication (whether of clergymen or, in earlier years, of HBC officers holding Sunday services at the forts) was how people would speak (pray) aloud or sing together under a leader, all saying the same words in unison. In Cree, worship of this new sort came to be called *uyumeha'win*, a word related to *uyumew*, "to speak," and by extension, "to pray" (Faries 1938:152, 179).[3] A standard (and not very illuminating) English translation of this term is "religion." Cromartie, then, was wit-nessing, in a sense, the arrival of "religion" among the Omushkegowak.

The movement spread widely during the fall and winter. In October 1842, the Rev. George Barnley at Moose Factory was approached by two men from Severn who had learned about the syllabics from their friends at York Factory. They asked him to help "decypher a piece of writing the work of an Indian who has not seen a Missionary till his interview with me. . . . The subject was a hymn and the characters employed those of the Rev. J[ames] Evans' invention" (Brown 1982:58). Barnley was unacquainted at the time with Evans's syllabics, and after a day's labor, he failed the test, doubtless elevating the standing of those Omushkegowak who could read them.

The following spring, HBC officer George Barnston, in charge at Albany Factory on James Bay, became concerned about what he saw as the prophets' misleading influence and false claims. He decided that it was necessary to lecture the local native hunters "on the subject of the new superstitions, that have spread so generally among them concerning the two York [Factory] natives [Abishabis ('Small Eyes') and Wasitek ('The Light')] who they believe have been in heaven and returned to bring blessings and Knowledge to their Brethern. . . . A few observations regarding the wrath of God and the wiles of the Devil excited their alarm. . . . I then saw a paper whereon there were lines drawn, some straight and many Crooked or waved, which they had conceived to be the 'Track to Heaven,' and thereupon I explained that the Road to Heaven was—to love God and each other: I observed also, that if it were my property, I should burn that paper. It was then handed to me for burning, by the priestess, an elderly woman who walked from York last fall" (HBCA n.d.: HBCA B.3/a/148 [June 8, 1843]).

It is quite likely that the markings on the paper included Cree syllabics, and indeed James Evans had preached at York Factory where the "priestess" came from (and whence came the syllabic text presented to Barnley at Moose). Barnston at Albany, several hundred miles to the south, would probably not have seen this scribal innovation before; it was the Omushkegowak traveling and communicating along the inland and coastal waterways who rapidly transmitted the syllabics far and wide before the fur traders in their posts realized what they were. All Barnston could do, within his frame of reference, was to reject this writing intuitively, as some form of heresy to be destroyed, in good Christian fashion, by fire.

At a deeper level, the idea of "heaven" itself presented challenges for mutual understanding, as Barnston's account indicates. As a Christian who held Sunday prayers for everyone at the factory, Barnston probably tried to teach about heaven as a destination for good believers after death. In his frame of reference, the prophets could not have traveled to heaven; their claims represented "the wiles of the Devil." A central translation problem was that the Christian *heaven* lacked an equivalent in Cree cosmology. Its elaborate English-language significance as a final destination for moral Christians was brought by outsiders, both devout British fur traders such as Barnston and missionaries. In traditional Omushkego belief, however, the dead journeyed to a land and afterlife in the remote west, not in the sky, and to judge by limited evidence, they were buried facing west (Brownlee and Syms 1999:40).

Where, then, had the prophets journeyed, in Omushkego terms, to learn "the Track to Heaven"? The English-language word for heaven was simply translated into Cree as *kicheke'sik*, "big sky," or *ispimik*, "above" (Faries 1938:95). In Cree, they would have stated that they had gone up into the sky to a place where they were given blessings and knowledge. This would have struck their listeners as plausible; Northern Algonquians were quite familiar with dream experiences and narratives that featured the travels of persons or their souls through the air to visit spirit helpers. A Rock Cree of northern Manitoba, Jean-Baptiste Merasty, in the 1970s told Robert Brightman a story about how his ancestors initially interpreted some of the teachings of the first Roman Catholic priests to reach that area in the late 1800s. At first, because the priests said that they should pray for what they wanted, "they thought they could get food and trade goods just by praying for them and without doing any work." When this failed, they selected "one man who would travel to Heaven in the sky and get all this food and all these trade goods from God." Brightman observed about this story: "The expedient of 'flying to Heaven' appears as an additional empowerment associated with Catholicism, although the ability to fly through the air with the aid of spirit guardians figures in other narratives [and notably in the shaking tent ritual] without Catholic associations" (1989:165–166). In this sense, the sky above, as the home of a powerful new potential guardian possessed of untold resources, could readily be accommodated in the Northern Algonquian cosmos, along with the worlds and beings associated with the four horizontal cardinal directions (see, e.g., Brown 1977).

The Prophets' Fall

George Barnston and other HBC men, concerned about how these leaders and the "new superstitions" distracted hunters from trapping furs and fostered "laziness" as well as heresy, increasingly pressed their followers not to support them. But the actions of Abishabis himself began to diminish his support in the York Factory area when he required that his followers give him "tithes of clothing, arms, and ammunition" in large amounts and even demanded some of their daughters and wives (Brown 1982:54). Such hoarding and the making of excessive demands on others violated Omushkego values and alienated Abishabis from the community. As some followers went hungry and even starved to death, the prophets' claims of impending benefits also began to seem empty by the empirical standards that Northern Algonquians applied to their spiritual leaders' claims and activities (Hallowell 1934).

Reduced to a state of "beggary" by July 1843, Abishabis completed his downfall when he murdered a family of four near York Factory (HBCA n.d.: HBCA B.239/a/157, f. 50 [July 31, 1843]). Their supplies gave him the means to make his way to his home base of Severn, where on August 9 the HBC post master, John Cromartie, reported, "None of the Indians appear to Doo him any honor." Three days later, Cromartie wrote, "I was obliged to take the men & go Down Below and take that villan of murdrer in Custody as all the Indians was Cumming heare making Complaints that he was threatning them if they Did not Comply with his requests in Giving him food &c and in fact they was afraid to leave Place while he was hear." Cromartie then "put him in Irons mearly to frighten him So as he might Leave the Quarter when Liberatted." The next day he escaped or was allowed to escape; but as he still made trouble, Cromartie took him prisoner again with a view to sending him to York Factory. On August 30, however, three local men took the matter into their own hands: "[They] draged him out off the house and marched him down to the River Sid[e] and Knocked his Brains out with one of the mens large axes & then tumbled him in the River and fixed a Rop[e] to his feet and Toeded [towed] him across to an Island and Burnt him to ashes & that is the End of that wicked man" (HBCA n.d.: HBCA B.198/a/85, fs. 5–6, 8). They followed this procedure, as James Hargrave later wrote at York Factory, "to secure themselves against being haunted by a 'windigo'" (HBCA n.d.: HBCA D.5/9, f. 308 [December 1, 1843]). In Cree/Ojibwa belief, human beings could occasionally become monstrous, antisocial beings with cannibalistic tendencies who posed great dangers to others. The execution of a *windigo* required the use of an axe and the burning of the remains, so that the heart (which had turned to ice) would be entirely destroyed (Brown and Brightman 1988:168–169).

The dramatic end of Abishabis had quite an effect, so far as the HBC traders could see. The movement seemed to fade, at least in the York Factory and Severn area; numbers of its adherents began giving up or destroying their "books" and other materials. Mission and HBC sources seem not, however, to answer the question of what happened to Wasitek, the second prophet. But in 1934 Simon Smallboy at Moose Factory told anthropologist John Cooper that Wasitek was killed at Moose: "Wasetek got killed here and they cut him all up in pieces. Wasetek got silly over his religion" (Long 1989:7). His fate, then, paralleled that of Abishabis. One might ask if Smallboy was confusing Wasitek's fate with that of Abishabis, but it seems unlikely that he was conflating two executions into one. He was quite positive about the name and place, just as the HBC clerk at Severn was clear about the identity of the prophet who was killed at his post.

Prophets, Books, and Signs

The fur traders and missionaries, although they had different reasons for their concerns, drew similar conclusions about the movement, reading it as a debased borrowing of Christianity. On June 8, 1843, for example, when trader George Barnston spoke to the hunters at Albany about Abishabis (who was calling himself "Jesus Christ") and Wasitek, he tried to explain to them "the Manner in which the Imposters were assuming characters which were known to the Indians at first only by the preaching of the Missionaries, and how they were allowing themselves to be misled." Similarly, Methodist missionary George Barnley, upon returning to Moose Factory in September 1843 after a short trip, "was grieved to learn that Satan had transformed himself into an angel of light [a reference to Wasitek/Wasitay, who seemed better known in the Moose/Albany area], and propagated . . . errors of a ruinous tendency. . . . the credit of the false prophets was firmly established" (Barnley 1843).

The Judeo-Christian tropes of Barnston and Barnley resonate with those still used by anthropologists (cf. Wogan 1994:422) and with terms familiar in our discussions of revitalization movements. When the fur traders and missionaries spoke of false prophets, Satan as an angel of light, and arcane writings, they drew on powerful constructs embedded in their own religious traditions. A prophet was a person who spoke for the gods, telling their will, for example, as an interpreter at a Greek oracle. Millenarian prophecy dominates certain parts of the New Testament, as do accompanying caveats about imposters. Matthew and the author of Revelation warn, for example, that besides true prophets, there are false ones who come "in sheep's clothing, but inwardly they are ravening wolves" (Matthew 7.15; see also the false prophet in Revelation 19.20). Prophecy begins as oral communication; the word is formed from the Greek verb "to speak." But in Christian tradition, it is also written in books; see, for example, Revelation 20.15 and 21.27, on the book of life, and 22.7: "Blessed is he that keepeth the sayings of the prophecy of this book." For both the traders and the clergy who wrote about these events, the power and symbolism of writing and of books were at the core of this story.

This statement, however, could also be made about the Omushkegowak. For the followers of Abishabis and Wasitek, both written texts and the "painting" of books were at the core of their activities. As the word of Abishabis's death spread in 1843–44, Thomas Corcoran, an HBC clerk at Albany, placed on record a number of observations concerning their "Great Books." Wahshellekum, for example, had been "one of the followers of the false Christ, but he tells me that he is no longer . . . he has burned the Great Book of the imposter." Corcoran then commissioned him "to inform the Coast Indians that he may see, of the fate of the Severn false prophet: and also to burn their great Books or Charts which he tells me that they all have" (HBCA n.d.: HBCA B.3/a/149 [December 11 and 13, 1843]). On January 3, 1844, another follower reported that he had "made no effort to hunt this Winter, as his time was altogether engrossed with the new Creed. He has however given me up his Great Book in which he believed as firmly as any Christian does in his Bible." On May 3, 1844, Corcoran received word of another hunter who did not survive the winter, having "depended on the Charts that he had in his possession . . . for all his wants. On these unmeaning scratches—traced on wood or paper—and that are called by Indians the Great Book he did not cease to look from the moment he pitched his tent in the fall to the hour of his death" (HBCA n.d.: HBCA B.3/a/149). On June 19 two hunters and their families arrived at Albany "in a terrible state." Corcoran wrote, "They candidly own that, they in some degree, have deserved it for instead of looking out for their livelihood & furs, they spent their time looking at their Great or Sacred Books, which was the cause of their misery. These Books they gave up today to be burned, and were accordingly committed to the flames" (HBCA n.d.: HBCA B.3/a/150).

What precisely were these "Great Books"? The Swampy Cree term for the Bible is *kichemussinuhikun*, literally, "great book" or "great writing." Wasitek, Abishabis as Jesus Christ, and a number of their followers were equipped with what they may have seen as their own counterparts to bibles, as well as with syllabic writings based on James Evans's system. Methodist missionary George Barnley provided the best clues about some of these writings in a summary report he sent to the Wesleyan Missionary Society from Moose Factory on September 23, 1843. The two men who visited him the previous fall "had a paper which they said was a copy of one of Mr. Evan's books." Further, "two hymns (printed probably by Mr Evans but certainly by some person familiar with evangelical truth, and poetic numbers) were in circulation among the Indians at York Factory, and thence found their way to Severn." As Barnley put it, while "the natives there labored earnestly to obtain a knowledge of them," one of the prophets "conceived the idea of amalgamating those portions of revelation which had come to his knowledge with the crafty fabrications of his own mind, aided by an efficient confederate." According-ing to this conspiracy version, the two withdrew from the others and then returned to present "an extraordinary message from Heaven." As the first of the two hymns alluded to light, and the second to Jesus, they took those names for themselves (Barnley 1843).

Barnley and Thomas Corcoran also reported that the prophets pro-duced a chart with a path branching in two directions, one to heaven and the other to hell (Barnley 1843; HBCA n.d.: HBCA B.3/b/70, 9 [January 15, 1844]), whereas George Barnston earlier had referred only to papers showing the "Track to Heaven." These references to paths to heaven and hell call to mind the Roman Catholic "ladder" widely used in 19th-century Catholic mission teaching and elaborated in the 1860s by Father Albert Lacombe on the Plains (Huel 1996:94–95). Barnley and Corco-ran may have been mistaken on this point, however. Corcoran, from whom Barnley derived some of his information, was Roman Catholic and may have simply equated the prophets' charts with Catholic two-road ladder charts familiar to him. Other writers did not mention the topic of hell (which also was not a Cree concept) or describe so literal a road map, and no Catholic priests had yet visited the region. Another possibility is that Corcoran himself had an image of the Catholic ladder and that local followers of the movement might have seen and borrowed from it, but this is speculation.

The prophets also foretold a replenishing of resources to be easily secured: "a sensual Paradise" provided with deer (caribou) that were "innumerable, amazingly fat, gigantic, and delicious beyond concep-tion" and other benefits. In his journal of January 20, 1844, Barnley described boards on which the outlines of human figures, animals, and various other markings were carved. One board "had the outline of a male figure . . . & surrounded by various animals as a cow, a goat, a buffalo, a sheep &c. [Adherents] were taught that if they worshipped [this] figure the animals they needed would be supplied without further trouble" (Barnley 1844). Barnley gave no explanation of why four an-imals scarcely known in the Hudson Bay lowlands were represented; perhaps he was guessing what they were. In any case, he was told that the possessors of these pictographs "lay down in their tents gazing on the figure & of course almost starving in the midst of an unusually bountiful supply of game, expecting to find deer &c so accomodating as to bring their throats to the knife" (1844).

Books, Writing, and Oral Literacy

As the Cree word for "book," *mussinuhikun*, also simply means "writing," the term that Corcoran and others translated as "Great Books" may have comprised an expanded Omushkego definition of the English term for books. The category, it seems, freely and ambiguously included charts, maps, pages of hymnals, boards with writing and pictographs on them, and probably books themselves, bound in deerskin, from Evans's printing press (Brown 1982). These accoutrements challenge our commonsense stereotypes not only of books but of North American aboriginal cultures as functioning solely by oral communication. The Omushkego integration of written media, notably syllabics, into the new movement might be read as enthusiasm for a powerful and magical novelty, in line with James Axtell's (1988) thesis about the strong impact of the Jesuits' introduction of the printed word among the native people of the Northeast. But Axtell may have overstated the novelty of literacy, according to Peter Wogan (1994). Building partly on Wogan's work, Germaine Warkentin has explored these issues further and finds that native North Americans have been "too easily classified as 'oral' cultures" (1999:4). As she points out, historians of writing "divide sign systems into semasiographic (i.e., pictography) and phonographic (language-based)." Yet closer study shows that "native sign systems . . . elude such categorizations, problematizing the boundary between semasiographic and phonographic as Europeans have conceptualized it" (Warkentin 1999:3). One difficulty with European sources is that Europeans in their exoticizing of native peoples expected them to view writing as magical. This representational problem "has obscured for us evidence suggesting that Native peoples took writing in their stride" (Warkentin 1999:12). Warkentin urges an expanded functional definition of books to encompass such things as Cree pictographs on wood or birch bark: *"marks made upon a material base for the purpose of recording, storing, and communicating information"* (1999:3). This definition works cross-culturally and in calling attention to the uses of books leads to her point that "the development of a written culture may not be the production of a specific kind of object, but something like a form of behavior" (1999:3).

Certainly the Omushkegowak, by all reports, took writing in their stride; they also had a perfectly good Cree word for it. The syllabic system of James Evans was new to them, but it was equally new and strange to the HBC fur traders and to other clergy such as George Barnley who lacked the keys to unlock this code. Compared with these outsiders, fluent Cree speakers had a great advantage when learning to read these signs; they knew the syllables (sound clusters) and could simply sound out the words that were formed by these curious hooks and triangles, without the pitfalls of spelling that beset users of the English alphabet. Further, what might be called their oral literacy allowed for learning informally and socially, in settings such as "psalm singing" or collective prayer where oral and visual cues were mutually reinforcing. As John Murdoch has noted, "If a person were ever expected to read fluently and aloud from these texts, it would most often be in unison with others where one who knew a piece by heart could easily disguise any difficulty he might have in reading" (1982:26).

Murdoch and Suzanne McCarthy have both claimed that Crees attained high rates of literacy in the syllabic writing system in the next decade, and McCarthy adds that "there was a higher incidence of literacy among the Cree than among the English and French communities in Canada at that time" (1995:59; see also Murdoch 1982:23). The claims are hard to test, but McCarthy (1995:61) makes the point that achieving literacy is easier with syllabics than with an alphabet and that Omushkego learners, reading aloud (as they usually did) in a language with a relatively simple syllable structure, could move easily from sign to sound to meaning. From there, it was only a small step for the Omushkegowak to take up reading (or singing) together, that is, using the Cree syllabics to appropriate the worship practices that they saw among the fur traders and missionaries, performing powerful borrowed texts in their own oral and written language. And it was their own; if few outsiders could speak Cree, even fewer could read it using the syllabics. There was, of course, another reason why the Omushkegowak were at home with writing. HBC traders had been coming to their shores since 1670, and their clerks all kept accounts. The Cree root word for "writing" or "book," *mussinuhik-*, also formed, in the context of the fur trade, the base for verbs signifying "he takes debt," "he gives out debt," and "he engages to work" and for nouns such as *clerk* or *writer*, *debt*, *ink*, and *paper*. Native people rarely joined in this writing universe, but they had observed it and had experienced its consequences for action and livelihood for a long time.[4] The followers of Abishabis and Wasitek, perhaps with that model also in the back of their minds, now took up writing and gazing upon books of their own making.

To complete the picture of what was happening on the "book" front in western Hudson Bay in the 1840s, one further innovation needs mention. I have already mentioned the Rev. George Barnley's report of meeting with two men who had a paper from one of James Evans's books and his observation that two hymns printed by Evans were evidently in circulation at York Factory and Severn. Evans by 1841–42 had built his own printing press at Norway House and thereby became the first to introduce printing into the scribal culture of the Hudson Bay region and perhaps into the whole of Rupert's Land. Printing presses came late, in fact, to every region of what was to become Canada; Warkentin (1999:4) notes that there were no presses in eastern Canada until 1751. The sight of printed books and papers was not new, as many were regularly brought from Europe. But the availability of textual materials actually printed in the region was novel—and not just to the Omushkegowak.

Retrospectives: Outsiders' and Omushkego Texts and Exegeses

The prophetic movement arose in a time of climate and resource stress but also among Hudson Bay lowland people who firmly retained their own language and spiritual practices and lived in communities that were strongly interconnected, able to rapidly communicate and spread information and new ideas, and blessed with powerful oral memories. During the 20th century, and into the 21st, it has remained a topic of unfinished and sometimes disconnected conversations and monologues, both outside and within the Omushkego community. This section reopens some of those conversations. No single version or interpretation of the events of the 1840s emerges from this analysis. It is possible, however, to situate some retrospective accounts of them and to see what each one contributes to our understandings and perspectives and what new questions emerge.

The first scholar to mention the prophetic movement of 1842–43 in print was anthropologist John Cooper, who did fieldwork at Moose Factory in 1932–34. He pieced together the story from several oral sources that he then found to correspond closely with details recorded by the Methodist George Barnley—an indication, he wrote, "of the reliability of the aboriginal memory" (1933:48). In the 1980s John S. Long reviewed both Wesleyan Methodist sources and Cooper's publications and field notes. He found much added information in Cooper's notes, including an important narrative written in Cree syllabics by John Fletcher about his grandfather, William Apistapesh. In 1986 Long also recorded a narrative about the prophets from Sister Catherine Tekakwitha, a Roman Catholic nun at Fort Albany.[5] His study of these oral accounts from the 1930s and 1980s and his research in Methodist missionary sources led him to a synthesis that drew the available stories together and integrated, too, the work of other scholars to date (Long 1989). John Long and I have gathered much information and have shared ideas on these topics over the last 20 years (Brown 1982, 1988; Long 1986, 1989).[6] We have shared a natural tendency, in looking at stories about the prophets and about the coming of "religion," to seek common elements in the oral traditions and other sources, assuming that they overlapped and that, taken together, they could be woven into a single whole. As Long concluded in 1989, "The documentary and oral accounts of a syncretic Cree religious movement have been compared and found to be complementary. Each provides information which is omitted in the other" (1989:11). We also both observed that Omushkego oral traditions not only preserved memories of the prophetic movement in detail but attributed the arrival of Christianity ("religion") itself to the prophets, Wasitek in particular, and not to the first missionaries (Brown 1988:4).

Louis Bird, however, points out that the Omushkego traditions and their interpretations are in fact internally diverse. While some credit the prophets as the harbingers of Christianity, as did the Roman Catholic nun, Sister Catherine Tekakwitha (Long 1989:9–10), others (such as James Wesley and Louis Bird himself) have taken other views. Sister Catherine dramatized the story of the prophets as presaging the arrival of the priests (Bird, personal communication, February 2001). Casting the story into a visionary mode, she told of the prophets as bright lights and messengers, angels who sang and prepared the way for the coming of the Roman Catholic Church:

"Two Cree Prophets" (Fort Albany, 1986)

This story was told by our ancestors who lived away back about eight generations. . . . Joseph Chookomolin heard his great great great grandfather tell the story to his grandfather and father. . . . The story is a long time ago there was a group of Indians living at a place up north of Attawapiskat called Ekwan. . . . Among them was an elder who had dreams of the future. He told them what would happen in the future. . . . At last what he told them came to happen, and now at night they waited and watched as the time drew nigh. . . . At last it happened. One night while they were outside watching, they saw a bright light shining up in the sky. They said there were two bright lights. They heard someone talk. . . . So the people said they were told, and everyone heard what was said, that religion would come to them shining bright. . . . So they called it wasitek, religion. . . . Now these messengers started to sing. They heard them sing. One of them called himself wasitek, which means light, and the other one . . . they didn't know who he was. He called him Jesus. . . . They started to sing, and the song they sang was, "Now listen you who are living. There will be a light come to you." . . . They remembered what they were told would happen in the future. They were amazed when he called himself wasitek and also when he talked about Jesus.

So that is when religion started. . . . It was said that later on that winter, a priest came to them, and they thought that the two shining lights they had seen were angels. When the priest told them about Jesus and the angels and also taught them about religion, they began to think back about the story told by the grandfathers. . . . They thought of that right away, when they saw the priest. [And the song that was sung will be written, so it will be easy to understand.] [Long 1989:9–10; the bracketed sentence is from Long's fuller handwritten transcript (1986)][7]

The story as Sister Catherine learned it had been passed down among Catholic Crees; the Chookomolin family was also Catholic. But Louis Bird, while himself a Catholic, sees the prophets quite differently from Sister Catherine and in a more negative light. He views them as *mitewuk*, shamans or conjurors, who used their powers to mislead and harm other people under the guise of the new religion from which they borrowed. It may seem surprising that as an Omushkego elder, he agrees with, for example, the Rev. George Barnley, who saw them as conjurors in 1843 (Cooper 1933:47). Bird is not, however, condemning *mitewin*, the practice of shamanism, in itself; he emphasizes that it can be powerfully used for good purposes. The problem with Abishabis and Wasitek was that in borrowing the new religious ideas and practices and the syllabics and taking on a veneer of Christianity, they blended them with their mitewin powers for their own ends—a recipe for trouble. They took gifts from others in exchange for false promises, and they brought starvation and suffering. Abishabis himself became a murderer who deserved his fate, and Wasitek, too, ultimately came to a bad end, although some versions of the story feature him in a more positive light.[8]

Sister Catherine's account, Bird suggests, was grounded in a devout Catholicism that led her to an uncritical acceptance of the prophets' claims. However, other stories tell of older Omushkego traditions that reach back to earlier times and could also serve as harbingers of Christianity. Bird cites, for example, James Wesley's narrative, "What the People Used to Do before the Coming of the White Man," learned from his grandfather, which John Long (1986:25–29) has also quoted at length. Long (1986:25) noted that Wesley omitted any reference to conjuring and drumming (mitewin) in his account of traditional life and attributed his silence to Wesley being a third-generation Anglican. Bird agrees on Wesley's strong Anglicanism (and adds that it was accompanied by a strong aversion to Catholicism). But he also suggests that Wesley may be making a somewhat different point: that even before Christianity most people did not practice mitewin; they did not need it, and its activities were under the purview of certain specialists who might or might not abuse their powers. As Wesley described it, the Indians in general learned all the practical things they needed to know to survive, and "fending for themselves in this way, [they] did not credit themselves with this achievement; they believed they were helped and guided by manitu, or the Great Spirit. . . . The manitu or Great Spirit was the great provider for the Indians' needs in these early times; the people were thankful for this, and seriously kept it in mind" (in Long 1986:27).

It is a complex matter to trace the changing nuances of meaning surrounding *manitu*, *Great Spirit*, and *Creator*, the terms most often used in anglophone discourse to speak of a higher aboriginal deity. Louis Bird (personal communication, February 2001) heard Wesley and others say that the people long ago sometimes heard a voice from above that spoke about the right way to live and from whom they got blessings and moral guidance, and this voice was from manitu or *kitchi-imanitu* (Great Spirit), the term that later came to be "the Bible word for God" (Anderson Jolly, in Flannery 1984:3). John Long cites from Cooper three older terms used in the Moose Factory Cree dialect to address this being (for whom the simpler gloss, *manitu*, appears to have been elected in Christian and English usage): "Master of Food (kati-belitaman miitchim), Master of the Means to Life (katibelitaman pimatisiiwin), and Master of Death (katibelitaman nipiiwin)" (1987:5). The concept parallels the Ojibwe concept of "Gaa-dibenjiged or Gaa-dibendang, which means something like 'the all-encompassing power of life'" (Matthews and Roulette 1996:354). A. Irving Hallowell understood from the Berens River Ojibwe in northwestern Ontario that this being "is the Boss of Bosses, the Owner of the Owners," and thought that the best English translation was "Lord" (1934:403). Louis Bird provides in his western Hudson Bay dialect (which differs from that spoken at Moose Factory) the term *ka ti pay nee ji ket*, which appears related to both the Moose Factory term and the Ojibwe *Gaa-dibenjiged*, and independently volunteered in February 2001 that it is best translated as "Lord." In sum, the Omushkegowak had a concept of a superior being located somewhere up above, who was a master or boss, not a maker (see also Flannery 1984:6; Preston, in Long 1987:5). This was not monotheism; the being was simply more remote than the numerous spirit helpers who made themselves known to human beings. But when Christianity came, people could find parallels and foreshadowings in their own traditions without invoking the two prophets whose behavior and credibility proved so problematic. Or, on the other hand, the prophet story, powerful in itself, could serve as a foundation story at least for Catholicism, if, as in Sister Catherine's version, its spiritual and visionary messages were highlighted and the all-too-human downfalls of the two mitewuk were forgotten or set aside.

The writing of this chapter has allowed a closer look at the Hudson Bay prophetic movement than was possible when I last examined it in the 1980s. Some new sources and recent writings have helped; so too has the opportunity to work with Omushkego elder and scholar Louis Bird, who helped to situate the stories and their tellers, explained in depth the meanings of key terms and concepts, and contributed his own views and reflections. There is no such thing as a definitive analysis of subject matter such as this; rather, we arrive at partial and contingent truths that reflect our knowledge, outlooks, and the questions we ask at given times and places. Louis Bird himself continues to talk with others of his generation, gathering further stories about the prophetic movement, and his perspectives shift somewhat after every conversation.

The most important questions that have helped enhance my understanding of the Hudson Bay prophets are historiographic and ethnohistorical. They involve delving more deeply into the topic and texts at hand; looking at the tellers of stories, both Omushkegowak and European; comparing what they contribute to the larger picture; and trying to grasp their concepts and vocabularies in Cree and in English while also reviewing the documents and searching out points of interest that were overlooked in my earlier studies. In this context, the question of whether the movement was a revitalization movement or not has become less interesting and, in fact, a distraction from deeper issues of documentation and meaning. To be sure, models are heuristically useful; they pose and frame larger questions. The revitalization model provided a starting point, an opening gambit for the study. But it does not seem particularly relevant, and its application in this instance would obscure more than it would reveal. Cree culture and language in the 1840s were not in need of revival. New ideas and modes of writing and expression were arriving, and certain prophets or mitewuk adapted these to their interests and purposes, creating also a residuum of stories that helped to explain Christianity (Catholicism in particular) when it arrived. But this dynamic was not new; the stories Louis Bird has collected are full of foreshadowings and foretellings of change and of individuals who manifest or claim mysterious powers and knowledge and attain temporary dominance over others.

In sum, to subsume the Hudson Bay movement under the rubric of revitalization risks divorcing it from context and exoticizing it as something different, apart from the dynamic historical and cultural processes ongoing in Hudson Bay before, during, and after its rise. We would do better to understand it as embedded in Omushkego culture and history and as continuing a storied existence among the descendants of those who knew it best. The stories will not all agree, and as Louis Bird says, some of them seem to get mixed up. But they also express a range of Omushkego perspectives that will survive and evolve as long as the stories are told.

Notes

1. My thanks go to Louis Bird of Peawanuck, Ontario, on Hudson Bay for his patient and thoughtful explanations. Our work was funded in part by the Social Sciences and Humanities Research Council of Canada through a major research grant (1999–2002; George Fulford, principal investigator) at the University of Winnipeg, for research on and transcription of Bird's collection of about two hundred fifty audiotapes of legends and histories. As he notes, "Cree" is a generic English-language name introduced by outsiders; his own people's term for themselves is "Omushkegowak," people of the muskeg (describing the most notable feature of Hudson Bay lowland topography). David Pentland traces the term *Cree* to *Kiristinon*, a name that the French first recorded from the Ojibwa in 1640; it referred to a little known band of Indians south of James Bay. The term was soon often shortened in French to *Cris* and applied to all who spoke the language now known as Cree. Later fur traders sometimes misspelled

Kiristinon as *Cristeen* or *Christianaux* and so on, leading to the more recent idea that the term referred to a band of Christianized Indians (Pentland 1981:227). This chapter uses *Omushkego* (pl. *Omushkegowak*) to refer to Louis Bird's people and *Cree* in reference to the language, for example, "Cree syllabics."

2. Lynn Whidden, an ethnomusicologist who worked some years ago with Cree hunters on the east side of James Bay (where mission influences arrived much later), learned that the hunters sang individually: "In fact each had a very distinctive vocal timbre and style." An Anglican priest with whom she talked said that it was difficult to create a choir: "People just didn't sing in unison and certainly not in harmony" (Lynn Whidden, personal communication, March 25, 2001).

3. Compare these terms to the Plains Cree *ayamihawin*, the term for saying prayers, church service, religion, and "the Roman Catholic Church" (Wolfart and Ahenakew 1998:348).

4. In 1724, in an oft-noted passage, the HBC censured the officer in charge at Albany Fort for evidently fostering native literacy, expressing its displeasure "that any Indian is taught to Write & Read" (see, e.g., Dickason 1992:145; Francis and Morantz 1983:91, in Long 1987:8). It is unclear to what extent this complaint reflected a broad policy regularly enforced; the fact that such teaching actually occurred is perhaps the most interesting point.

5. As a nun, Catherine received the name of Kateri (Catherine) Tekakwitha, a Catholic Mohawk convert of the 1600s who was known for her exceeding piety. Louis Bird states that her family name was Nee-shwa-bit ("Two Teeth" or "Buck Teeth").

6. In 1980 two other scholars published articles on the prophetic movement in the same issue of *Studies in Religion* (Grant 1980; Williamson 1980). Neither used oral sources besides those quoted in Cooper 1933 or appears to have worked further on the topic, and Williamson's interpretation is idiosyncratic in several respects.

7. The first Catholic priest in the area was an Oblate, Nicholas Laverlochere; John Long notes that he "baptised or rebaptised half of the Fort Albany Indians between 1847 and 1851, causing a division which remains today" (1987:12).

8. In July 2001 Louis Bird noted (personal communication) that Toby and John Michel Hunter, brothers living at his hometown of Peawanuck on the Winisk River near Hudson Bay, agreed that Abishabis was a *miteo* trying to imitate Christianity. They thought, however, that Wasitek was more benign, bringing news of a new religion associated with light and with a song or hymn (partially remembered by their mother, Sarah Carpenter Hunter) that spoke, as Sister Catherine did, of the coming of a Light. Sarah Hunter never mentioned Abishabis. This could be on account of his downfall or because he came from the Severn region, a long way to the north.

5. REVITALIZATION IN WARTIME MICRONESIA

Lin Poyer

During World War II the people of Micronesia suffered physical destruction, social dislocation, and psychological stress. The end of the war in Micronesia was accompanied by a momentous transition from Japanese to American rule. As we might predict from the research on revitalization movements, one response to these events was indigenous revival. In several regions, wartime pressures and the social vacuum characterizing the worst years of war encouraged the renewal of traditional social, religious, and political activities. These renewals in some ways followed the expected trajectory of revitalization movements, which have been described as nativistic religious responses to secular colonial stresses. What is interesting about the Micronesian examples is that the revivals were—with one exception—short-lived and, in the words of one observer, "faded into insignificance after the war" (Fischer 1957:64). Most Micronesians, in other words, found revitalization movements of only temporary practical use.

The movement that survived the war was Modekngei, in Palau, which had originated early in the century. Japanese and American studies of Modekngei see it as a revitalization movement (usually with stress, rather than deprivation, as the motivator). Yet even Modekngei saw its power weaken dramatically after the war. Modekngei "failed" as a revitalization movement, however, only because Palauan culture "revived" without its assistance.

Modekngei's wartime success, its relative postwar decline, and the overall history of war-era revitalization movements in Micronesia reveal the historically contingent nature of the concept. Although it has been useful in analyzing certain phenomena in the era of colonial expansion, I suggest that postwar cultural "revitalizations" be studied as a qualitatively different sort of political activity in the modern global contest for legitimate and empowering political identities.

Prewar Acculturation

Japan took control of Micronesia as a League of Nations mandate in 1914 and soon established a colonial civil service administering regional commerce, transportation, health care, education, and law enforcement. In the late 1920s, Japanese colonial activity intensified, with the goals of increasing the value of Micronesia to Japan and acculturating Micronesians to Japanese ways. The colonial government began—and, in the mid-1930s, dramatically accelerated—a massive immigration and economic development program centered on sugarcane, phosphate mining, copra, and fishing.

By the end of the 1930s Japanese and Okinawan immigrants outnumbered Micronesians on some islands. Micronesians benefited from the economic boom through the increased availability of goods and cash, travel opportunities, and infrastructure such as roads, wharves, and electricity. But Micronesians also experienced increasing pressure to adhere to Japanese law, custom, and socioeconomic expectations (Peattie 1988).

Wartime Experiences

If revitalization movements are most likely at times of stress, it is unsurprising that World War II saw the emergence of a variety of such responses to local conditions throughout Micronesia. Late in the decade Japan began military preparations throughout the region. Although the December 1941 attacks on Pearl Harbor, Wake, the Gilbert Islands, and Guam mark the start of the Pacific War, for Islanders the impact of war began either earlier or later, depending on when Japanese military activities affected local communities.

The first phase of military base construction in the Marshalls, Pohnpei, Chuuk, Yap, Palau, and the Marianas brought in large numbers of military workers. Traumatic changes for local people, including confiscation of land, relocation, and intensified wage labor, soon followed. Even areas not selected for base construction were affected by the first, offensive period of war, through the massive movement of men for conscripted labor, increased nationalist propaganda and tightened security, and in some cases direct military service.

The most severe wartime stresses, though, came after the turning point of the Pacific War, late in 1943, when the Allied advance, starting in the Gilbert Islands, came north through the Marshalls and then took the war westward through the Carolines and the Marianas in the first half of 1944. As Japan shifted perforce from an offensive to a defensive stance, the Micronesian islands became successive defensive walls, each fortified in turn to protect Japan itself from invasion.

Micronesians' wartime experiences depended on where their islands fell in the military planning of the contesting powers. In islands invaded by U.S. forces—Kwajalein, Enewetak, and Majuro in the Marshalls, Ulithi, Saipan, Guam, and Peleliu and Angaur in Palau—people lived through massive bombardment and invasion and then experienced a dizzying shift from Japanese to American rule. But the rest of Micronesia was bypassed by Allied strategy. As American forces leapfrogged across the Pacific, parts of the Marshall Islands, most of the Carolines, most of Palau, and parts of the Marianas were left under Japanese control while the Allies invaded key islands farther west. Bypassed islands were isolated, blockaded, and constantly bombed. Chuuk, for example, was hit by a first major bombing raid in February 1944 and was regularly bombed in large-scale raids for a year and a half, until Japan's surrender in August 1945.

In addition to the fear and destruction of daily (or even twice-daily) American air raids, those on bypassed islands struggled to survive under harsh Japanese military rule, stressed by conditions in which a vastly swollen military and civilian population had to be fed on local resources alone. These conditions led to violence by the Japanese Army, fragmentation of community and family life, and starvation to the point, it is said, of cannibalism in some locales. As the war reached its climax, Micronesians in many places thought that the Japanese planned to annihilate them, either to relieve the burden of feeding civilians or as a violent response to losing the war. The relief of Japanese surrender, then, was great.[1]

Postwar Acculturation

Whether an island was taken by invasion or surrendered in August 1945, the U.S. Navy took control. However, because of the demands on Navy shipping at the end of the war, several areas of Micronesia were left in an administrative vacuum for some time. Although people knew that the Japanese had lost—and in some places Japanese soldiers were quickly removed—no well-organized administration took their place. When the new rulers did come ashore, the American presence was very much smaller, in most places, than the preceding Japanese presence. For example, at the height of war Chuuk's local population of about ten thousand shared the land with about 38 thousand Japanese military men and laborers. At the end of 1946, with most Japanese repatriated, fewer than a hundred Americans were assigned to Chuuk.

Islands where the U.S. military focused postwar interests—such as Kwajalein and Saipan—prospered economically and underwent intensive acculturation to American ways. But most of the region did not have such experiences. Rather, the foreign civilians that had run local businesses were evacuated, and the tiny American staffs that replaced the Japanese colonial administration were unable to restore the level of prewar economic activity. The United States had no long-term plans for governing the islands, in a marked contrast with Japan's colonial order. Wartime destruction, and U.S. disinterest in reestablishing an export economy, dramatically altered the conditions of Micronesian daily life from their prewar state.[2] The combination of wartime stress and postwar neglect set the stage for revitalization movements—and, at the same time, for their eventual failure.

Revitalized Traditions as a Response to Wartime Stress

In describing the stages of revitalization movements, Anthony F. C. Wallace might, in some regards, have been describing a population experiencing the anomalous and traumatic conditions of modern warfare. At first, Wallace has written, "increasingly large numbers of individuals are placed under what is to them intolerable stress" (1966:159). The fact that the stress comes from comprehensible—and usually visible—dangers is perhaps a mitigating factor of war. No one in a war expects anything but stress. But, though Micronesians could see very well that pressure on them came from the Japanese military, on the one side, and American bombs, on the other, they could not make sense of the danger through a confident patriotism or a broad view of geopolitics. They were neither full citizens and loyal subjects of the emperor nor resisters or partisans for the Allies. In fact, for many Islanders, the war seemed to come out of nowhere and to be governed by no predictable rules.

We would expect, then, according to Wallace, to see an increase in what he calls "alienated behaviors," as individuals attempt to deal with societal disequilibrium—not only the obvious disequilibrium of military rule, starvation, forced labor, relocation, and bombing but also the disequilibrium of an experience not readily comprehended within existing frameworks of knowledge. Individuals reach for coping resources, and in Micronesia as in native North America, these resources lie predominantly in the realm of the spiritual, in intensification of Christian practice and renewal of indigenous activities.[3]

Maintaining Christianity

An emphatic, repeated comment of Micronesian survivors of the war is that Christianity was their first line of psychological defense (Poyer et al. 2001). Especially in the Marshalls and the Marianas, where Christianity was most firmly established, survivors recall the importance of maintaining Christian practice, in the face not only of war but of the continual hostility of Japanese officials. At the start of war, foreign missionaries were expelled or imprisoned, and church property was confiscated. During the war, military authorities restricted Islanders' freedom to hold religious services and even to gather informally for prayer. Survivors recall, with anger, being forced to bow toward Japan and pray to the emperor. Yet they persevered in holding secret services and maintained familiar traditions of family and private prayer. The revitalization of non-Christian activity must be seen against this backdrop.

Prophets, Shamans, and Wise Men

While the maintenance of Christian practice was nearly universal across at least central and eastern Micronesia, elderly people also report the revival of non-Christian religious beliefs and practices. Anthropologist John Fischer, who worked in Micronesia after the war, has commented that there was little explicit resistance to the Japanese military but that one form of resistance was "a reversion to certain aspects of the old pagan religion. While there was apparently no outright abandonment of Christianity, on all three high island groups [of the Eastern Carolines: Chuuk, Kosrae, and Pohnpei] certain individuals went into trances and came forth with alleged visions or possession by spirits of the dead. One of the activities of these mediums was to prophesy the outcome of the war and the fate of individuals whom the Japanese had transported to other islands. These activities were directly related to the tension of the war and blockade and later sank into insignificance following the American occupation" (1957:64).

On Kosrae, the Japanese military controlled civilian life, with King John only a nominal chief. Yet King John, as deacon of the island church, and other church leaders worked with remaining missionaries to retain effective control of internal Kosraean affairs, keeping them secret from the Japanese. In the final days of the war, prophets arose establishing new cults, including a woman who predicted that the Japanese would win the war and a man who experienced visions of the struggle between good and evil (Lewis 1967:31–57, 65–68; Ritter 1978:243; Schaefer 1976:54).

On Chuuk, traditional leaders known as *itang*, whose pre-Japanese role of war leaders and wise advisers had been declining for decades, re-gained importance during the period of greatest stress, when Chuukese faced starvation. Itang helped young men plan thefts of food and deceive Japanese authorities. Although they did not form a unified movement, as individuals they led the indigenous moral and social response to the "collapse of the Japanese military and civil administration and the un-certainty as to what was to be expected from the Americans" (Hall and Pelzer 1946:18). Other revivals on Chuuk included the use of traditional medicine, intended for wounds received in battle, applied to wounds from bombs or strafing; and the use of coconut leaf divination to help people decide where to hide during air raids. Chuukese supplemented Christian prayers for protection with prayers to local spirits, as they waited out the daily bombings (Poyer et al. 2001).

In the atolls of the Marshall and Caroline Islands, as well, individuals emerged claiming supernatural visions or links with spirits, which gave them information about faraway relatives or insight into future events, notably the end of the war. On Kutu, for example, a shaman predicted eventual American victory, a prediction concealed from the Japanese military on the island but treasured by the Islanders as a sign that "their time of hardship would soon end" (Reafsnyder 1984:105 n. 40).

In Angaur, the preoccupation of the Japanese during the last year of the war opened the way to a "renaissance" of the indigenous social order (quite separate from Modekngei, which was at the same time growing in strength in the rest of Palau). Traditional leaders resumed their former duties, ceremonies were renewed (including church ceremonies held in secret), and cooperative work ensured survival during the American siege. Unlike Modekngei, as explained below, the Angaur revivals were not an expression of opposition to Japan but, rather, reflected "a grow-ing sense that in their own social order they found comfort" (Useem 1945:579).

All these renewals in some ways followed the expected trajectory of "revitalization" movements, religious responses to secular stresses. In contrast to situations described in several other chapters in this book, the "stress" to which Micronesians were responding was not—or not most immediately—the stress of acculturation. Rather, it was the literal stress of near starvation, forced labor, relocation, and the immediate physical violence of bombing and bombardment. Informants themselves spoke of the desperation of those times as a way to explain why people turned to traditional spiritual and practical resources.

They also explained that, with the end of war, these resources were no longer necessary. In the Marshalls, the Marianas, and most of the Carolines, the end of war and the removal of the Japanese brought these small-scale revivals to an end. People turned eagerly from survival mode to an active effort to construct a new life under the new regime. Christian church activity returned to being a focus of community effort, and trances and the use of traditional medicine became, once again, individual or family, rather than community, activities.

Modekngei

The exception was Modekngei, on Palau, the only long-lasting revitalization movement in Micronesia, which has been described by both Japanese and American researchers (Aoyagi 1987, 2002; Barnett 1949, 1979; Useem 1946; Vidich 1980:228–244). Established in the first years of Japanese colonial rule and reaching its greatest power during the final year of war, Modekngei fits the classic description of a revitalization movement, including a nativistic ideology of resistance, a community order, and political action. It is no coincidence that it emerged on Palau, which hosted the capital of Japanese Micronesia and experienced great acculturative pressure.

Modekngei began with a man named Temedad (or Tamadad, Temudad), who between 1912 and 1916 first experienced visions and claimed supernatural powers. Temedad attended German school and worked for the German constabulary; upon his return home, he experienced a lengthy illness and transformation, in the traditional way, into a medium or priest holding privileged communication with spirits. By performing supernatural deeds, he established a reputation as a spiritual leader.[4]

Temedad and a man named Ongesi (or Ongesii) worked together in establishing Modekngei (from "Ngaramodekne," meaning "it is bound together"). It preached the existence of a single God, one of the local Palauan deities, equated with Jesus. Temedad exorcised other spirits, set out a code of behavior, denounced certain customs (especially payment for traditional healing), and, in a striking departure, abolished totemic food taboos. Modekngei's symbol was the cross, and its meetings were similar to Christian services, but Temedad's most important ceremonies were for healing (Barnett 1949:234–236).

Japanese officials attempted to suppress Modekngei. While the administration may have been alarmed by Temedad's pronouncements and activities, including sanctions against working for Japanese, the incitement to act seems to have come from Palauans favoring colonial policies. Temedad's arrest was also supported by some chiefs and by traditional healers. Temedad (and other Modekngei members) were jailed several times during the 1920s; Temedad died in prison soon after his last arrest.[5]

Temedad's successor, Ongesi, worked quietly after his own release from prison in 1925 to rebuild Modekngei. During this period of intensive acculturation of Palauans to Japanese culture, foreign religious missions (Catholic, Buddhist, Shinto, and evangelical Lutheran) expanded. At the same time, Modekngei was being suppressed, partly because of the urging of Palauans who held positions in the colonial order, who "opposed what they perceived to be a backward and primitive orientation of the *Modekngei* and continued to supply Japanese authorities with intelligence on its activities" (Shuster 1982a:74–75, 79).

Aoyagi (1987:343) identifies six factors that attracted Palauans to Modekngei: healing, prophecy, moneymaking, abolishment of food taboos and banishment of old gods, incorporation of local gods, and the introduction of Christian elements. Barnett identifies Temedad's original philosophy as "progressive" in that it included Christian elements and was not "outwardly opposed to foreign control" (1979:84, see also 1949:237). Under Ongesi, however, Modekngei became explicitly nativistic, banning foreign songs, foods, and cookware: "Ongesi preached that the dark-skinned Palauans were a different kind of men from the light-skinned peoples and that their destinies must be different" (Barnett 1979:84). Modekngei became openly anti-Japanese, opposing colonial schools, health care, labor conscription, and changes in the use of Palauan money, land ownership, and reciprocity customs—changes supported by the "pro-foreign" Palauans (Shuster 1982a:75, 1982b:35; on Modekngei philosophy, see also Aoyagi 2002; Vidich 1980:235–241). This stance achieved some success; indeed, in late 1937, according to Vidich, Modekngei "was in complete control of all native political power in Palau" (1980:233).

It then faced another period of suppression, as pro-foreign Palauans continued to oppose it and as the war in China increased Japanese emphasis on Palau's economic productivity. Pro-Japanese Palauans instigated a 1938 investigation that resulted in a seven-year jail sentence for Ongesi. By late 1940 "*Modekngei* had been thoroughly repressed and Japanese authority was firmly entrenched" (Shuster 1982a:77; see also Aoyagi 2002:198–218; Vidich 1980:243).

Modekngei during the War

It is said that Temedad prophesied, long before the war, "that the Americans would one day displace the Japanese" (Barnett 1949:236–237). He did not apparently predict that the transition would give his movement its next political opportunity. When the United States occupied Angaur and Peleliu in September 1944, Japanese administration of the rest of Palau became ineffective. American bombing raids on Koror and Babeldaob continued until the end of the war. With large numbers of troops and civilians trying to live off the land and with communication disrupted, Japanese authorities become ineffective in governing Palauans. Palauans turned to Modekngei, which offered social organization, reassuring prophecies of future well-being, cures for the wounded, and magical charms to frighten away American bombers and protect individuals from harm. Modekngei leaders made many famous predictions about wartime events, including the outbreak of war, the first bombing of Palau in March 1944, and the end of the war in August 1945. As American military success weakened Japanese effectiveness, Modekngei grew in power, even making efforts to control Palau's traditional chiefs and interfering with Japanese war work. By September 1945 Rnguul (or Runguul, Arangul), who replaced the imprisoned Ongesi, "was acting as the undisputed political leader and policy maker for Palau" (Vidich 1980:246).[6] With the disorganization of war, "those groups which subscribed to the Modekgnie ideology once again had an objective basis for believing that their expectations would be fulfilled. The Collaborators [pro-Japanese Palauans], on the other hand, defined the war-time situation as temporary. They expected that peace would bring a situation similar to that which prevailed in the 1930s" (Vidich 1949:121–122). While pro-colonial Palauans anticipated an American rule similar to that of the Japanese, Modekngei leaders, remembering the German era, thought that they would be able to "develop Palau along the lines of the *ancienne regime*" (Vidich 1949:122). But U.S. policy, as it turned out, resulted in yet another shift in the balance of power within Palau.

Postwar Modekngei

Ongesi, imprisoned in Saipan during the war, died after his release by Americans and was succeeded by Rnguul. Despite uncertainty about the U.S. attitude to Modekngei, over seven hundred Palauans told postwar census takers that they were members (Useem 1946:76). But conditions were soon to prove less favorable to Modekngei.

As the United States distributed administrative resources throughout the former Japanese mandate, Palau's position changed dramatically. As capital of Japanese Micronesia, Palau had been accustomed to a wage economy and a metropole culture, but under American rule it became a backwater. With a minimal U.S. presence and an infrastructure destroyed by the war, Palau saw no effort to rebuild its Japanese-era economy. Life in the immediate postwar years was shaped by the American policy of "restoring" a subsistence economy (Vidich 1980:285–286), a policy that Palauans committed to the Japanese policy of economic development found distressing and incomprehensible.

American policy also supported "restoring" traditional chiefs. U.S. Navy military government's initial goal was indirect rule, but after three decades of aggressive acculturation, Palau's traditional leaders no longer governed. The Japanese had deposed uncooperative chiefs and trained a new generation of leaders (Nero 1989:123). American moves to restore chiefly authority sparked long-lasting dispute. Ambitious men of high rank, Modekngei leaders, and those who had held positions under the Japanese jockeyed for roles in the new administration (Useem 1945:582–583; Vidich 1980:195–197, 273–280).

The U.S. Navy's turn to high-ranking Palauans as a source of legitimate authority "broke the chiefs' link to the *Modekngei* and was the first step in the post-war decline of the movement" (Shuster 1982a:129). Because American policy empowered chiefs, they did not need Modekngei (Vidich 1980:312). The new administration was officially neutral about religion, but in 1947, supported by anti-Modekngei Palauans, it prohibited Modekngei healing practices, bringing a court case against Rnguul and others (Shuster 1982a:130–131).[7] So Modekngei lost power after the war, though it remained a factor in Palauan life and politics.

Why Did Modekngei Persist, While Other Revivals Disappeared?

When John Fischer worked in postwar Micronesia, he commented that Japanese acculturative pressure was a spur to Modekngei and that the similar, smaller-scale wartime movements in Chuuk and Pohnpei "seem to have subsided following the end of the war." He warned American administrators, though, of "the probability of more energetic repetitions in the event of certain kinds of administrative pressure" as "attested to by numerous examples from the history of the administration of dependent peoples in the Pacific and elsewhere" (1957:226). Thus, revitalization theory served as a cautionary tale for the U.S. administration of conquered areas.

It was not likely that Modekngei's success would be repeated elsewhere in Micronesia. Palau experienced three distinctive conditions conducive to the emergence of a revitalization movement. It was a focus of sustained acculturative effort on the part of the colonizing power; Christian ideology and church organization were much slighter in Palau than in many other parts of Micronesia; and Palau experienced a very significant postwar administrative vacuum—certainly, the greatest contrast among prewar, wartime, and postwar levels of colonial control.

This last point also explains why Modekngei eventually faltered. Modekngei might have succeeded in becoming the dominant power in Palau had the United States exercised more assertive rule. But, given the weak postwar administrative presence, traditional Palauan leaders were able to regain control and to extend it through the mechanisms of the new colonial order. During the Japanese era, Modekngei's opponents had been men disadvantaged in the indigenous rank system and eager to succeed through options opened by Japanese rule. Chiefs supported Modekngei, in opposition to these pro-colonialists. After the war, as U.S. policy supported chiefs, it was those disprivileged by customary law who were most likely to support Modekngei. But Modekngei's appeal to tradition carried less weight in a world in which chiefs were rapidly recovering power.

Modekngei remains active in Palau. In 1963 a district publication claimed that a revived Modekngei embraced about one-third of the population. Modekngei members affected elections to the Congress of Micronesia throughout the 1960s by regularly voting in a bloc (Shuster 1982a:132). Modekngei continued to be active throughout the 1970s, establishing businesses and a school and playing a role in the 1974 Constitutional Convention and the 1980 Palauan presidential elections (Aoyagi 1987:343, 2002:223–251; Shuster 1982a:316, 358). By the 1980s factionalism and a decrease in membership had limited its power.

On a current website, Modekngei is called by a Palauan student-researcher "just another religion among the many in the world" and "a combination of all the religion[s] that were introduced to Palau in the early 1900's" (see Adelbai n.d.). But the text also presents Modekngei's claim to cultural authenticity, stating that "the Modekngei religion was continually practiced until foreigners introduced their religions to Palauans, diverting most of the society from its traditional religion" (see Adelbai n.d.).

Analyzing Modekngei as a Revitalization Movement

Scholars have analyzed Modekngei in terms of familiar revitalization theory: as a response to acculturation, as a synthesis of Christian and indigenous theologies, as a sociopsychological response to the wartime "social vacuum," as a nativistic response to stress, and as shaped by internal factionalism exacerbated by external policy. American anthropologist Homer G. Barnett, Japanese anthropologist Sachiko Hatanaka, and American educational historian Donald Shuster agree in explaining Modekngei's origins early in the Japanese era as a case of a common response to acculturative pressures. Barnett and Shuster emphasize missionization, while Hatanaka stresses economic factors.

"As so frequently happens on the frontiers of Christianity," Barnett writes, "in Palau there have been native prophets who have proclaimed messages that reveal an intermingling of native and Christian forms of belief and practice" (1949:230–231). Temedad was among these, and Modekngei "represents an amalgamation of Christian and native beliefs, one of the many such phenomena that have occurred repeatedly in all parts of the world where Christianity has impinged upon native religious systems. Sometimes they are referred to as messianic cults, sometimes as rivivalist [sic] cults, depending upon the particular coloring of the message brought by their leaders and the differing emphasis upon a return to native standards" (Barnett 1949:232).

Shuster explicitly links Modekngei with religious change, identifying its beginnings with the 1915 Japanese expulsion of German officials and Catholic missionaries. Shuster writes that Temedad, Ongesi, and Rnguul had all "been exposed to the basic theological principles of Christianity some of which were incorporated into the indigenous system thereby making it acceptable to others who had been similarly influenced by Catholicism. In the absence of foreign missionaries during the years 1915–21, *Modekngei* leaders had, in a sense, become indigenous missionaries with a new, culturally based message" (1982a:72–73). Shuster adopts the straightforward view of a revitalization movement as acculturative syncretism: "It seems that *Modekngei* was originally an attempt by inspired leaders to respond to foreign cultural pressure by combining old religio-medical beliefs and practices with new Christian ones in order to evolve a viable synthesis that would revitalize and reintegrate Palauan perceptions of the world, a cultural phenomenon more familiar in Melanesia and Polynesia than Micronesia" (1982b:34).

Hatanaka emphasizes economic threats rather than a desire for theological syncretism in explaining Modekngei's origins. Because of large-scale Japanese immigration in 1938, "a type of cult sprang up based on the natives' opposition to the Japanese. . . . The cult also resulted in much agitation among the islanders by starting a rumor that an army sent from Heaven would come to save them from the Japanese (Ishikawa, 1944). An explanation for the occurrence of this phenomenon might be found in their anxiety about the supply of food which was threatened by the increase of the Japanese" (Hatanaka 1967:121).[8]

If Modekngei's origins are plausibly accounted for by the familiar revitalization theme of acculturative stress, its power during the final years of war seems well explained by recourse to the idea of a social vacuum. Sociologist John Useem writes, "*Modekngei* was a relatively small cult during the German and prewar Japanese period. But with the sudden collapse of a nation they deemed imperishable and a way of life that was a model for the acculturated populations, *modekngei* filled the social vacuum. As a result, within a very short time the entire population of Palau became *modekngei*. Following the surrender, and the appearance of a new cultural model, the earlier process of acculturation set in once more and *Modekngei* lost much of its following. The meteoric growth and decline of this movement occurred without any direct actions of the administrations which were preoccupied with war and postwar problems" (1947:6, see also 1948:24). Here we see that Modekngei "filled the social vacuum"; but that vacuum was an interlude in an ongoing process of acculturation that in the end would lose Modekngei its following.

Similarly, Shuster (1982b:35–36) sees Modekngei's wartime growth as a response to the "great crisis" of the latter part of the war as the Japanese order crumbled. Shuster follows American political scientist Arthur Vidich, who argues that the insecurities of this period provided "maximal" conditions for the effectiveness of Modekngei ideology, as its prophesies and protective charms countered the "insecurity of complete uncertainty regarding the future" (1980:244): "Modekngei during the crisis of the actual war period was less a phenomenon of political factionalism than it was a mass psychological response to a confused and unknowable world. All heretofore known conceptions of reality proved to be inadequate for coping with the new situation. Just prior to and during the bombing of Palau, which began in March of 1944, Modekngei again reached a climax in its power" (1980:245). A final common element of analysis is the recognition that Modekngei's trajectory reflects the changing fortunes of the political factions that have shaped Palau over the past century. Japanese ethnologist Machiko Aoyagi writes, "The Modekngei religion, being a blend of Christian and traditional elements, seems to have created an ideal environment for many of those whose attitudes lay somewhere in between those of the reformists and the conservatives. Depending on the circumstances, the leaders presented the Modekngei religion as the indigenous religion of Belau or as identical with Catholicism" (1987:346). Aoyagi (2002:252–272) analyzes the changing fortunes of Modekngei in terms of the sense of deprivation or social advancement of different groups in Palauan society.

Vidich has studied postwar Palauan factionalism in detail, describing how changing colonial orders intersected indigenous political organization to produce shifting tides of allegiance. In fact, Vidich locates Modekngei's origins in the consequences of a colonial transition: "The [early] Modekngei leadership, recruited from among those favored by the Germans and overlooked by the Japanese, had expectations that the Japanese would behave similarly to the Germans. They were not prepared for the drastic innovations introduced by the Japanese. A nativist response resulted from their subsequent disillusionment and resentment" (1980:347). Vidich sees Modekngei's wartime expansion not simply as compensation for the preoccupied Japanese but as a deliberate political strategy on the part of Modekngei's leaders: "During the war, the bombings and general disorganization of the Japanese administration created a near state of anomie. In this situation Modekngei was able to organize rudimentary forms of aid and control, capitalizing on the general upheaval and the Palauans' resentment of the Japanese who allowed them to fall victims to such a fate. Whereas formerly Modekngei members were political outcasts, events during the war allowed them to rise to positions of dominance" (1980:347). He goes so far as to suggest that Rnguul may have intended to set himself up "as the supernatural leader of a religious state" (1980:245). After the war, Vidich traces how American support of traditional chiefs resulted in Modekngei's decline.

Later researchers have followed Vidich in seeing Modekngei's history as the interplay of internal factions with changes in colonial rule (e.g., Shuster 1982a:78–79).

In Vidich's analysis, indigenous political structures meet global strategic policy, and individual agency uses both familiar and new cultural symbols to achieve traditional and novel ends. Although the more common analyses of Modekngei's origins and content in terms of acculturation, syncretism, and resistance seem plausible and useful, Vidich's approach veers from these familiar anthropological themes. In analyzing Modekngei in the same way a political scientist might analyze competing power groups in a U.S. presidential election, Vidich demonstrates the transition to a mode of analysis on which all cultures meet on equal symbolic and practical ground.

Micronesia's short-lived wartime revivals—seen in the work of prophets and shamans throughout the islands during the war—found no takers after the pressures of bombing and blockade were lifted. Modekngei, the most long lasting and successful of these, was eventually slowed by the renewed power of chiefs supported by American policy. Thus, Modekngei as a revitalization movement failed, ironically, because traditional political organization regained sufficient strength to oppose the innovation of cultural revivals. The question of when revitalization movements emerge and under what conditions they persist to become routinized was a focus of interest for students of culture change in the middle decades of the 20th century. The goal of this book is to ask whether and how such questions might interest us as we settle into the 21st.

Wallace's view of revitalization movements has proved useful to anyone studying them. Despite our self-consciousness about functionalism's faults, it remains a powerful lens through which to view cultural novelties. Explanations of Modekngei in these terms bring into focus its origins and transformations under colonial conditions. But is this approach one that can be used forever to study forms of cultural revival? Or is it a scheme peculiarly appropriate to its time and place? Is it most useful to say that Micronesians used revitalization movements (in Wallace's sense) to help them through a hard time and then abandoned them, that within any culture lay the seeds of such a movement, to be stirred into life when enough stress is applied? Or is it more useful to see such movements as characteristic responses to acculturative stress under pre–World War II conditions and to say that, after the war, their time had passed?

While acknowledging Wallace's interest in developing a "general vocabulary" defining revitalization movements "to denote any conscious, organized effort by members of a society to construct a more satisfying culture" (1966:30), I suggest that it is useful to retain a distinction between the "classic" revitalization movements produced by a certain phase of historical change and postwar forms of cultural revival. The innovative philosophies and symbolic forms that anthropologists have studied as revitalization movements were the product of a certain phase of global interaction. As globalization progressed—most dramatically through World War II—conditions changed such that the terms of analysis used to understand these movements are no longer useful in studying modern forms of cultural revival. Modekngei remains a part of Palau's 21st-century political scene, but we would no longer accept an analysis of it in terms of syncretism and acculturation.

The functionalism that our predecessors found effective in the study of cultural innovation can continue to serve if we subordinate it to an acknowledgment of historical time. A classic revitalization movement occurs when a group of people sharing a small-scale social order faces stress created by encounters with industrial society. An important element of their response is the effort to understand what has happened— the intellectual experiment (shaped in ritual, ideology, art, social experimentation) of revising their worldview to include the new people and new modes of social interaction, social structures, ideologies, and technologies of global industrial capitalism. The movements take their distinctive forms—particularly dramatic in messianic cults, cargo cults, and Modekngei's "army sent from Heaven"—from the intense effort to come to grips with the facts of industrial production and the social forms that accompany it.

Revitalization movements, as we know, do not last. This is because they do not, in themselves, give satisfactory answers to the questions of inequities in possessions and power posed by encounters with the industrial world. Global industrial society operates through technological, economic, political, and ideological mechanisms so invisible to normal daily observation that considerable training and abstract information are required to understand where cargo comes from, or how soldiers appear when summoned by radio, or what motivates a global war. But the conditions under which revitalization occurs themselves provide the means to transcend it, as the transactions accompanying prolonged contact have the result of rapidly informing the younger generation, at least, about the unfamiliar order. As learning increases, the aggressive efforts of the original revitalization movement to make sense of experience give way to new understandings. Either the movement fades away, or it is reshaped into a form that more closely mirrors the increasingly familiar social order of industrialized society.

The intellectual requirements of incorporation into global political-economic systems, then, have to be learned. Revitalization movements fill the gap until the learning happens. Once the learning occurs, people and groups then face many questions about their response to this encounter with industrialized society, and we see a plethora of identity-building and -maintaining activities. But at this point analysis of such activities requires a new set of tools.

It is only a slight exaggeration, or generalization, to use World War II as a marker for this historical transition (and for the Pacific it is no exaggeration at all). Colonialism, industrial expansion, the growth of the global market, the expansion of Christianity and Islam (and Shinto and Buddhism as well), and the integration of communities into modernizing processes were, if not anywhere near completed, certainly well under way in most of the world by then. The massive effort entailed by the war, which involved the use of resources from, if not actual combat on, every inhabited continent, brought contact with industrial society to very nearly every part of the world. We can say, then, that the war marked the end of the phase of initial encounters between small- and large-scale societies and that the revitalization movements seen during and immediately after the war were the last wave of this form of social activity.

Small-scale societies today still need creative symbolic and intellectual approaches to manage their interaction with industrial capitalism. What has changed is the large-scale, even global, context in which social action aimed at clarifying, altering, and stabilizing group identity takes place. Postwar cultural revivals occur in a field of intercultural reality, globalization, frank recognition of power differentials, and broader knowledge of cultural and religious diversity. In these "modern" conditions, Wallace's classic revitalization activity would be archaic. We continue to see—as other chapters in this book show—revivals of tradition, inventions of tradition, social action focused on symbols of group identity, and novel religious and secular activities in response to stress, including intensification and innovation in ritual activity. But these are not, and will not be, what we have known as revitalization movements, the category that has proved so useful in understanding such social action in the past 300 years.

Modern—that is, postwar—forms of cultural revival do other things, in other ways, to other ends. We must therefore approach them, in Micronesia as throughout the world, with new terminology and new analytical tools.

Notes

1. Poyer, Falgout, and Carucci (2001) present an overview of World War II in Micronesia and include references to earlier works on the topic. See also Peattie 1988.

2. On wartime and immediate postwar conditions in Micronesia, see Poyer et al. 2001, Hezel 1995, and Peattie 1988.

3. The present chapter continues a tradition of discussing revitalization movements in the Pacific as one of the responses to wartime experiences. Most of this literature deals with Melanesia; see White and Lindstrom 1989, which includes references to earlier sources. An important historical dimension is added by Hiery's (1995) discussion of the impacts of World War I on Pacific Island societies.

Most literature dealing with these responses in Micronesia describes the Modekngei movement of Palau, the largest revivalist movement. A few American reports of the late 1940s and 1950s mention other wartime revivals. Additional information comes from interviews with elderly World War II survivors, conducted throughout Micronesia by Lawrence Carucci, Suzanne Falgout, and myself, under National Endowment for the Humanities Interpretive Research Grant RO-22103-90.

4. For information on Temedad and the origins of Modekngei, and interpretations of the movement, see Aoyagi 1987:342; Barnett 1949:233–234, 1979:83; Hezel 1995:164–166; Shuster 1982a:71–74; and Vidich 1980:228–241. Aoyagi 2002 is a recent, comprehensive study of Modekngei. Hiery (1995:149–150) sets Modekngei in the context of the post–World War I transition from German to Japanese colonial rule.

5. See Shuster 1982a:74–75. Aoyagi (2002:198–218) discusses whether Modekngei was an anti-Japanese resistance movement. Barnett (1949:138–139, 237) dates Temedad's death to 1928; Vidich (1980) gives 1924.

6. In addition to Vidich, information on Modekngei wartime prophesies is in Aoyagi 1987:344, 2002:138–140; Barnett 1949:238; and Shuster 1982b:36.

7. Because healing was such an important element of Modekngei, "the prohibition has amounted to a virtual ban on the cult itself—at least, those who belong

to it make this interpretation" (Barnett 1979:84). Other accusations also affected Modekngei: a public charge of polygamy (illegal under American law) against Rnguul, allegations of a Modekngei member stealing a chalice from a church (Shuster 1982a:131; Vidich 1980:318), and the edict of one of the paramount chiefs forbidding the practice of all native religion (Barnett 1949:232).

8. Hatanaka also writes that the cult spread "throughout Micronesia" in response to local anxieties about Japanese population increases and possible food shortages: "In fact the Japanese settlers were in free competition for all aspects there" (1973–74:14). I am not aware of evidence for the presence of Modekngei beyond Palau.

6. REVITALIZATION AS CATHARSIS

The Warm House Cult of Western Oregon

Michael E. Harkin

Revitalization Movements

The revitalization model has proved productive in the ethnohistorical interpretation of religious cults and nativistic movements. Under this model, revitalization movements are viewed as collective responses to negative conditions ranging from deprivation to severe trauma. The "index case," the Handsome Lake movement among the Seneca described by Anthony F. C. Wallace (1970a), has been seen as a holistic response to exogenous stressors. The movement involved all aspects of Seneca culture and its relation to the physical and social environment and was focused equally on the individual and on collective cultural practices. Such movements establish a micro/macrocosm relation more explicitly than do most religions and attempt to affect the condition of the universe by localized actions. In these points, Wallace extends and sharpens the ethnohistorian's understanding of cultural reactions to extreme stress. However, the model is not without problems. As other contributors to this book have mentioned, one difficulty with Wallace's theory is evident in the name usually attached to such phenomena: "*re-vitalization* movements." This assumes a teleology in which a culture is in a state of decline and is destined to rise again (see Brown [ch. 4] and Martin [ch. 2]).

In the case of the Warm House movement such an assumption of cultural decline is less problematic than the assumption of reinvigoration. This places, a priori, entirely too optimistic a reading on events. Of course, we all know of cases where these have not been successful, and Wallace did too, for he wrote an introduction to a modern edition of *The Ghost Dance* (Wallace 1965). However, on this view we can only see such events as tragically blocked revitalizations.[1] Indeed, ironically, the most famous revitalization movement of all ended in a bloody massacre.

Revitalization, like all universal models in anthropology, such as to-temism or the incest taboo, suffers from the Popperian demands of a generalizing science. It is all too easy to find atypical or even con-tradictory cases that seem to constitute falsification. Since the days of Franz Boas, American anthropologists have rejected generalizing the-ories almost as quickly as they could be invented. Revitalization seems destined to a similar fate. And yet the value of the revitalization concept is such that we simply should not reject it entirely. Indeed, it is one of those productive concepts that spread quickly beyond its origins and ushered in a discourse in the form of "X as revitalization movement." [2] Perhaps it is better to view revitalization not as a scientific theory, sub-ject to endless empirical critiques, but as closer to a literary genre, in which common elements combine to constitute a basic structure, which is then subject to transformations. A useful model here is the formalist study of folklore pioneered by Vladimir Propp (1968), which influenced Levi-Strauss's (see 1978) somewhat more rigid structuralist analysis of American Indian mythology. Such a model allows for, indeed assumes, transformations of basic elements. (However, we need not buy into the more mechanistic assumptions of structuralism itself.) Thus, the opti-mistic teleology of Handsome Lake may be transformed into its op-posite without overthrowing the underlying "mytho-logic." Indeed, as they move through place and through time, revitalization movements, like narrative forms, almost always change in some important ways.

A second important sense in which revitalization movements are like narrative forms involves the centrality of mimesis. Mimetic structures pervade revitalization movements. Participants mime the dead of their own culture, an imagined spirit world, Europeans, or some combination of these. Mimesis is not a simple passive copying but, rather, a creative mirroring of the relevant other, as well as a modeling of connections between self and other (Lattas 1998:xxiv). By such a poetic logic, identity and alterity are symbolically represented in ways that are less problem-atic or more psychologically satisfying than they are in reality.

This would seem to be the case with the Warm House movement. Judging by the similarity of ritual elements to practices of the dead in western Oregon cultures, it is apparent that participants were involved in miming the dead. The optimistic teleology of revitalization ignores the more plausible interpretation that many such movements were not in the end about "revitalization," that they were not centered on the restoration of vitality to a cultural pattern. Indeed, it is not the life drive but the death drive, in Freudian terms, that seems more appropriate to understanding the Warm House cult. Freud's (1961) well-known view of the death instinct, which is that all organisms seek a previous state of being, which ironically is ultimately a state of nonbeing, is singularly appropriate to this case. Much as Freud formulated this theory in the face of the extinction of a way of life embedded in the last days of the Hapsburg Empire and destroyed in the fires of World War I, so the Warm House cult and the related Ghost Dance, in many of its versions, marked the end of a way of life.[3]

In the North American Ghost Dances generally, despite the wide variation in different versions, mimesis of the dead and the destructive elements of ritual practice give us strong clues that it was not something properly termed "revitalization" that was going on (see Spier 1935; Walker 1969). Instead, they were, in the beginning, attempts to recapture lost worlds and, as those attempts failed, increasingly became ritual enactments of cultural dissolution and death. In some cases, such as the one I examine below, they took on almost the character of abreactive utterances, that is, a therapeutic recapitulation of the original trauma.

Richard and Nora Dauenhauer (1995) have remarked that the loss of a language is a cultural death, which causes individual members of the ethnic group to go through predictable Kubler-Rossian stages of emotional reaction (see Kubler-Ross 1970). Similarly, the loss of freedom, territory, knowledge, and personnel entailed in the encounter with colonialism produces collective responses that are oriented toward death. As with the death of an individual, the death of a system of meanings and practices must be ritually marked.

At the same time, such movements in the earliest stages hold out hope that the past may be retrieved. This corresponds to the Kubler-Ross stage of "denial." Just as the mother of a soldier killed in battle may hold onto the hope that the fatal telegram was a bureaucratic mistake, early prophets and practitioners of revitalization may cling to the plainly counterfactual hope that white farmers and missionaries will simply disappear. Indeed, such hopes are common to oppressed people in many historical situations: in the slave rebellions of Nat Turner and Denmark Vesey in the antebellum South, in the Warsaw ghetto denizens of the Holocaust, and in peasant societies of late feudalism. And if the telegram turns out not to be a mistake, it is perhaps possible to rewrite the narrative from one of mere loss to one in which what is lost can be recaptured.

Comparing revitalization movements to both narrative form and psychological syndrome, it seems clear that they contain elements of both. The mimetic representation of the dead through metaphoric and metonymic utterances attempts to restructure the life world along more favorable or less mystifying lines. From one angle this is a narrative structuration; from another, a type of group psychodynamic utterance. However, a further dimension must be considered. That is the ritual modality, which may be viewed as a logical operator that generates positive or negative value. Moreover, this value changes in a predictable way, transforming the overall meaning from positive to negative, much as a sentence or formula may be changed with little change to the constituent elements. In particular, I argue that revitalization movements, at least the ones that involve hopeless projects such as the ejection of whites or the return of the dead, follow a specific trajectory or script, moving from what Gananath Obeyesekere (1990:26–29) calls *dromena*—progressive rites—to cathartic rites. When this shift—triggered by increasing frustration at the failure of dromena—occurs, key symbols and practices become inverted.

The Early 1870s Ghost Dance

I look at the Ghost Dance as it appeared in southwestern Oregon in the 1870s. There it was called the "Warm House" because of its location in the sweat houses that were a prominent part of the culture.[4] It was originally exported from California by Yurok, Karok, and Shasta Indians (Kroeber 1905). By the 1870s the situation in northern California and southern Oregon was even worse, from the Indian perspective, than that on the Plains. In California, Indians were being hunted down with the complicity and support of the state government. In the Oregon borderlands, in a short span of years the Modoc had been placed on the multiethnic Klamath Reservation, defeated in an all-out war, and exiled to Indian Territory (Nash 1955). In Oregon, after the federal treaties of 1853 and 1855, which concluded the Rogue River wars, a disparate assortment of tribes from the Plateau was grouped with several coastal tribes, including the Coos, Alsea, Siletz, Siuslaw, Tillamook, Lower Umpqua, and Tututni, at the Grand Ronde and Siletz Reservations in western Oregon (Beckham 1990:182–183; Jacobs n.d.). The conditions in these two reservations were harsh; during 1857–58, 205 people died of disease and starvation at Siletz alone (Beckham 1990:183). This occurred mainly among the Shasta, or Upper Rogue, a population group numbering

554 prior to this (Beckham 1990:184). Mortality was thus close to 40 percent among the Shasta in this two-year period, although it was closer to 10 percent for the reservation as a whole (Schwartz 1997:166–183). Because of age and gender skewing in the 1857 population figures, we can surmise that population had already declined significantly prior to that point.

An increase in interethnic tension and organic and psychological illness ensued. These further increased as more people and tribes were crowded onto reservations and as expropriation of land by white farmers continued to reduce Indian-held land. The trauma was intense and led to a search for ways to make sense of it and endure it psychologically. Elizabeth Jacobs (n.d.) notes intriguingly that after 1857, when the Coos were first exiled from their land, people in general, and not only shamans, became interested in dreams and their interpretations. Much like the case in the early days of the Handsome Lake movement, the emphasis on dreams and their meanings became integral to an evolving sense of crisis. We do not know precisely what these dreams entailed, but it is quite likely that they were similar to those that were common to all variants of the Ghost Dance: dreams of the dead in an idyllic setting, which perfectly expressed the trauma of cultural disintegration, with their combination of wish fulfillment and traumatic reenactment.

The early California versions were stimulated by the visions of the Numu (Northern Paiute) prophet Wodziwob, whose 1869 prophecy of return of the dead, and by extension the past social and moral order, caught on quickly among groups in the northern Great Basin and adjacent areas of California and the Plateau (Hittman 1973; Kroeber 1905). Although the dance took on specific cultural features as it spread beyond its Great Basin origins, it retained several basic forms and key meanings. Dancing to achieve visions, the restoration of the past, an emphasis on the moral state of the dancers, and, to varying degrees, separation from white society all were stable elements that were retained in the various versions.

The Ghost Dance was originally based on a variation of the Round Dance, the basic ritual form of the Numu and other Great Basin people. In the Round Dance, men and women joined hands and danced in a circle usually around a tree or pole. The tree or pole represented the *axis mundi*, and the ceremony represented world renewal (Hulkrantz 1986). It was associated with the seasonal cycle and, especially, the "first fruits" of key species such as rabbits and piñon nuts. This basic form was well adapted to use in revitalization movements, in the wake of both Wodziwob's and Wovoka's prophecies (see Hittman 1973). Iconically, the unbroken circle is a motivated sign of completeness, one that had special resonance for American Indians, who made extensive use of circular symbolism. Thus, Black Elk's vision involved the key symbol of a sacred hoop that represented the nation in its spiritual form (De-Mallie 1984:122–130). Moreover, the microcosm-macrocosm relationship posited in the Round Dance gave it a great deal of apparent ritual efficacy. The circle of society becomes the vaulted dome of heaven, just as the central pole becomes the axis mundi. The connection with changing seasons and the reappearance of food species, and thus the guarantee of the continuation of society, made the Round Dance an agent of cosmic renewal, not merely stasis. It was entirely logical to extend that renewal to the social world, which was governed by the same structures as the natural world, on which the Round Dance effectively acted.

The moral and spiritual state of the participants was crucial to the success of the Round Dance and subsequent Ghost Dances. To maintain the unbroken circle, dancers had to put selfish and unworthy thoughts out of their minds. In the Ghost Dance, participants took on a more active role. Each person tried to dream and see visions of the dead. Failure to do so resulted not only in the dead not returning but also in the dancer possibly being transformed into an animal, into the bargain (DuBois 1939:27).

Separation from the Euro-American world was a central value of all versions of the 1870s Ghost Dance in Oregon and California. It was thought that living the white man's way deprived Indians of spiritual power. This, of course, often coincided with the material interests of Indian people. In the Great Basin, especially after the discovery of silver in the Comstock Lode in 1859, Euro-American encroachment on Indian lands closed off important resource areas. Given their extensive subsistence patterns, requiring many square miles to support a single person in this arid country, loss of access to such resources was a question of survival. However, there was no clear-cut distinction between material interest and spiritual value. The piñon tree, for instance, was considered sacred as well as constituting a basic staple. The cutting down of piñon trees, an activity in which, ironically, the 1890 prophet Wovoka engaged, was thus threatening on a variety of different levels (see Hittman 1973).

Visions of the Dead

To understand the Ghost Dance as it appeared in western Oregon, it is necessary to take account of aboriginal beliefs about the dead. To a very large degree, Ghost Dances were mimetic performances of the dead (see Lattas 1998:131). Among these groups a variety of beliefs prevailed; this was an area of considerable cultural and linguistic diversity. Indeed, it is almost certainly one function of revitalization movements to synthesize various cultural traditions while establishing identity at a higher, or new, sociological level, such as the regional or reservation community. Where previously local traditions and social identities were adequate, for the new multicultural world created by colonialism, new formulations were needed (see Lattas 1998:304–305). However, much of this precontact ideology is now lost. That which was recorded by the main ethnographers of this region—Edward Sapir and Leo Frachtenberg in the 1900s and 1910s, Melville and Elizabeth Jacobs and John Peabody Harrington in the 1920s–40s—is, despite its high quality, necessarily incomplete and scattershot. Such beliefs that we do have are from only a few groups and, in the case of the latter three ethnographers, from several main consultants, including Coquille (also known as Coquelle) Thompson (Upper Coquille Athabaskan), Victoria Howard (Clackamas Chinook), and Hoxie Simmons (Galice Athabaskan).

With these limitations in mind, we can discuss some of the beliefs that provided a backdrop to the Warm House movement. We should bear in mind that even within groups beliefs were not systematic, and ethnographers frequently found different accounts of these beliefs even from different members of the same linguistic group. Moreover, individual ethnographers' secondary interpretations of these beliefs were not always consistent. Nonetheless, it is possible to sketch an outline of mortuary beliefs and practices. In general terms, the dead continued an existence much like that of the living but in a separate place (Jacobs et al. 1945:73; Jacobs 1959:13). Death originated in the myth age. Coyote and Wolf (in one version he is called Black Man) each lose children. Wolf's (Black Man's) child dies first, and he wants to resurrect it after five days. Coyote refuses, but then his son dies. Inconsolable with grief, he wishes him to be resurrected. However, by then the precedent has been set; to allow him to continue living would threaten the living, in particular their food supply (Harrington n.d.: reel 27:307; Jacobs 1939:26–27; Seaburg and Amoss 2000:282–283). So, instead of returning to the land of the living, after five days the dead move on to the land of the dead.

The land of the dead varies according to different accounts. It is always separated by a body of water from the land of the living. In most cases, it was said to be to the west, across the sea (Harrington n.d.: reel 27:307–329; Jacobs et al. 1945:73). However, it could appear closer to human habitation, such as merely across a river (Harrington n.d.: reel 27:305). There is some association with the western sky as well, for one possible route there is across a path of clouds (Harrington n.d.: reel 28:239). Other celestial phenomena, such as the Milky Way, also had some connection to the land of the dead (Harrington n.d.: reel 28:239). In some contexts, the land of the dead is spoken of as being in the sky (Jacobs et al. 1945:201). In any case, the separation of the land of the dead from that of the living was crucial, for despite the occasional connections between the two in myth, the dead were seen as threatening and of little use to the living (Jacobs 1959:13, 1960:349–351). In the "Myth Age" it was possible to move between the two realms easily, but in human times this was both dangerous to the living and of no real value, for the dead were not seen as having wealth or power but, rather, as being simply pitiable (Jacobs 1959:13). Thus, one essential question that we must ask is why, given the reluctance to have contact with the dead, the Warm House dancers attempted to do so.

The most common route to the land of the dead was a canoe trip. In one myth, it is specified as a half canoe (Harrington n.d.: reel 27:305). The ghostly pilot is aware of the fact that his passenger is living, as indeed all ghosts are aware of the living. As in the Orpheus myth, the ferryman may give specific instructions to his passengers. In one case, a living woman who has retrieved her husband from the land of the dead must not open her eyes during the journey or she will be dropped into the sea; unlike Orpheus, she is successful (Harrington n.d.: reel 27:329). The canoe trip was echoed by burial practices in this region, which often used canoes for burial, either overturned (for the Alsea) on the ground or elevated and right side up, with a drainage hole (Harrington n.d.: reel 27:496–497). In a remarkable inversion of death taboos, during the Rogue River wars of 1854–55, people escaped across the Alsea River using burial canoes in which the holes had been plugged (Harrington n.d.: reel 27:496–497). In addition to a pragmatic action in a military situation, this might be seen as representative of the forced breakdown of death taboos that was characteristic of the early reservation period.

The dead were prolific gatherers of shellfish, as they apparently needed to eat (Harrington n.d.: reel 27:305). Shellfish provided not only food but wealth, as the two main sources of wealth were dentalia shells ("Indian money," as Coquille Thompson called it) and abalone shells. Thus, encounters with the dead proved lucrative. In one case, a living man steals an abalone shell canoe bailer and uses it to pay bridewealth for his warriors, thus becoming a great chief (Harrington n.d.: reel 27:305). Encounters with the dead are dangerous, but, because of the wealth involved, mythical heroes (who lived in the Myth Age, which was both temporally and logically prior to human society) often sought the dead out. As well, Orphic myths, in which a person goes to the land of the dead to seek a loved one, are common. Coyote, for instance, as an inherently transgressive, boundary-crossing character, is frequently involved in such activities (Jacobs et al. 1945:201–203, 227–231; Harrington n.d.: reel 27:307). Such behavior is punished after myth times, however (e.g., Jacobs 1960:350).

One frequently noted characteristic of the dead is that they are often dancing. Indeed, in the story of the man who returns from the land of the dead, the reason he gives for wishing to do so is the excessive dancing. The dead generally dance in the sweat house and prefer it smoky. If living people find themselves there, the smoke may kill them, but this is, in myth, reversible by placing a rock in the fire (Harrington n.d.: reel 27:328). The dead also like the fog, which allows them to approach human villages (Harrington n.d.: reel 28:238). Thus, the dead were fond of miasmas that extinguish social division. This is perhaps related to the egalitarian nature of dead society, in which there were no chiefs or social distinction (Harrington n.d.: reel 27:329). Both of these points were to play a role in the development of the Warm House cult.

The Warm House Cult

In 1873 a Shasta prophet named Bogus Tom brought a version of the Ghost Dance to the multiethnic Siletz and Grand Ronde Reservations of western Oregon (Beckham et al. 1984:96; DuBois 1939; Seaburg and Youst 2002:91; Thompson 1935). It became quite popular and spread rapidly among the native populations both on and off reservations. This dance, called the Earth Lodge by the Shasta and interior Oregon groups that adopted it, became known as the Warm House dance in western Oregon (Nash 1955). It involved several novel features brought from California, such as semisubterranean houses with a central pole and the wearing of feather capes and woodpecker quill headbands (Beckham et al. 1984:96; DuBois 1939:25–27; Kroeber 1905). Dancers danced around a central pole or, in coastal versions, a central fire. In California, dancers would form concentric circles—at outdoor events, as many as ten—whereas in Oregon a single circle was usually formed (Kroeber 1905; Spier 1927:48). Kroeber (1905) reports alternating clockwise and counterclockwise movements, and Spier (1927) says that the Klamath danced counterclockwise. Most likely, this was one of the diacritical markers of the individual lodges as they flourished, especially on the Oregon coast. The Siletz version used split elderberry limb clappers—an innovative use of what had been cooking implements (Seaburg and Youst 2002:92). The rhythm was faster and more syncopated than usual (Seaburg and Youst 2002:92). Dancers shed Euro-American and buckskin clothes and danced either in sagebrush skirts, the dress of the dead (which would barely cover the genitalia), among the Klamath, or completely naked, in some of the later coastal versions (Spier 1927:48). Group bathing was an important practice in most versions. This involved men and women and was said to indicate a lack of bodily shame. In California, taboos on sexual intercourse were strong; Kroeber (1905) reports that an offender's genitalia would turn to stone if the taboo were violated. However, in Oregon, such taboos did not exist. Among the Klamath, there was no restriction on sex; however, those who failed to bathe communally might themselves turn to stone. This was a general punishment for failure to participate in communal Ghost Dance activities (Spier 1927:48–49).

Bogus Tom continued summer visits to Oregon and Washington reservations for four or five years, until the religion began to be suppressed by the authorities. In about 1878 the Warm House dance was taken up by two Siletz Reservation Indians, Coquille Thompson and Chetco Charlie, who spread the word among the coastal groups. Both men were coastal Athabaskans, although Thompson had a Coos mother. They brought the dance to the nonreservation community of Coos, Siuslaw, and Lower Umpqua, who lived at the mouth of the Siuslaw River, near Florence, Oregon (Beckham et al 1984:99; DuBois 1939; Miller and Seaburg 1990; Thompson 1935). Thompson's Coos connection and, reportedly, their oratorical and singing skills made their message popular among this community. Both men married local women and began to proselytize throughout southwestern Oregon. The movement spread to the two main reservations for coastal Indians, Siletz and Grande Ronde.

The Warm House dance took on specifically Oregonian cultural features, particularly eschatological beliefs. Although it entailed a reversal of the normal rules of avoidance of the dead, it assumed the traditional cosmology. For instance, in one (possibly idiosyncratic) version it was believed that the dead could not return to earth because the way was blocked by a great rainbow-like structure (DuBois 1939:33). This re-calls the Coos vision of the afterlife, although normally the dead were striving to reach a second level of heaven rather than to return to earth (Frachtenberg 1913; Jacobs 1939). More generally, as we have seen, the land of the dead is often reached by a sky trail. In the Myth Age and during what Jacobs (1960) calls "transitional times," the path to the land of the dead was a two-way street. The Warm House cult was, among other things, an attempt to reopen that passage in both directions. One consideration was undoubtedly ecological. As it was necessary for the dead to eat, and as death was initially established as a means of control-ling the population of the living, the excess of death experienced in the 30-year period after the arrival of white miners in the early 1850s was clearly a disequilibrium. The excess population of the dead should be returned to the living, in order to reestablish a balance.

The locus of the dancing, the warm house, was significant and rep-resented much more than a borrowing from external sources. In tradi-tional coastal society, the warm house (or "sweat house") was the po-litical and social space par excellence. In its secular dimension, it was a men's house, in which the men and sometimes boys slept (Harrington n.d.: reel 27:296).[5] (Women and children slept in the cookhouse.) It was there that military actions, marriages, fishing and hunting activities, and other aspects of male-dominated social life were planned and discussed. However, it was also the locus of ritual activity in the winter months and in myth was seen as a place of power. John P. Harrington collected sev-eral texts in which the sweat house was the locus of power acquisition. In one such tale, a hunter comes upon a sweat house in which the dead are dancing. He hides from them and finds the next morning a large number of dentalia shells (Harrington n.d.: reel 27:304). In another story, a poor man is ordered by a dead relative to extinguish the sweat house fire by leaving the smoke hole completely open, allowing the rain to come in. His daughters, who are so poor that they wear camas on the skirts rather than dentalia (the two are said to look alike from a distance), are told to sweep the sweat house out. At night Big Snake (probably related to the two-headed serpent of the central Northwest Coast) enters the sweat house and leaves a bounty of dentalia shells, making the man a chief (Harrington n.d.: reel 27:240).[6] Thus, the sweat house was, under special circumstances, a portal to the spirit world and a potential source of wealth and power.

However, it is not a simple path from obtaining power in the sweat house to the Warm House cult. For one thing, the myths stress individual aggrandizement, which is far from the ethos of the Warm House cult. As with other versions of the Ghost Dance, communalism was a normative value. This was said to be in keeping with the values of traditional culture, in which people "were never stingy" (Thompson 1935). Dancers pooled their resources so that those without money or food could continue to dance, sometimes for as long as ten days at a time.[7] Communal ethics thus supported the quest for visions, which came to be seen as essential to the survival of the group. However, this cannot be taken simply as a reflection of traditional culture, for, while helping those in need was indeed part of the ethos, the sponsorship of any ceremonial event was inextricably connected to the sociopolitical hierarchy. In fact, this seems to in part embrace the ethos of the land of the dead, where there are no chiefs and people spend most of their time dancing.

This quest became increasingly desperate, as is evident in the extended periods during which participants would dance—again, like ghosts, dancing to no evident purpose. The repeated lack of success entailed a short-term increase in the intensity and energy invested in it (see Festinger et al. 1959). Eventually, the dance was condemned by authorities, but for a time in the late 1870s it flourished.[8] So great was its dynamism that it produced multiple variants as it spread to different communities. Persons who built warm houses became the "bosses" and used their authority to introduce new practices. These practices were often designed to make the cult more productive of visions, especially in the later phases of the movement. Innovative practices were indeed a sort of last resort for participants who were unable to achieve visions through established practices, even if those practices were taken to extremes, such as dancing for ten days. We do not have any detailed data on the sociology of the warm house lodges, but it is likely that membership and even the existence of lodges were highly unstable, as is the case generally for noninstitutionalized or minimally institutionalized charismatic religions. Variant practices promising better or surer results eclipsed previous manifestations. In such a fluid and charismatic situation, creative variants were likely to crop up quickly. On the macrolevel, this produced a dynamic of innovation and change, which drove the movement toward its denouement as cathartic rite.

One such innovative practice was building up the fire and blocking the smoke hole, creating a miasma of smoke in the house, which made breathing difficult (Thompson 1935). Men were rolled in blankets and then placed upon a fire that had been built up with fir boughs (DuBois 1939:29). Both of these practices were designed to facilitate visions on the part of the male dancers (for it was only men who could have them), but they failed (DuBois 1939:29). The smokiness of the house was modeled on the miasmic conditions favored by ghosts in their dancing. As with the Papua New Guinea Kaliai cargo cults described by Andrew Lattas, the living engage in a dialogue with the dead through various mimetic practices that Lattas calls "mirroring" (1998:131).[9] The dead constitute a productive ground for bringing about cultural and cosmological transformation, but for the Warm House dancers, this was dependent on specific communications from the dead in the form of visions.

The lack of visions was frustrating and caused the congregants to get "crazy," as Thompson much later told Elizabeth Jacobs (see Seaburg and Youst 2002:98–100). The real "craziness" involved not only building up the fire and the smokiness of the lodge but also communal sex among men and women in the dark smoky corners of the house. Although not central to the ritual and, indeed, apparently unconnected with the attempt to achieve visions, communal sex became an increasingly large part of the Warm House dance in its waning days (see Siikala [ch.10]). This is Thompson's description of the denouement of the Warm House religion: "At that time men and women were getting crazy. They were copulating with one another (there in the dark smoky warmhouse). Lots of men copulated with the women, even married people copulated with others because nothing could be seen; it had gotten to be dark (in there). That's the way it happened; when they danced it changed to a different way. In the daytime the women were around there naked. That's the way they did. (Hoxie [Simmons, a Galice informant,] says only 3 or 4 families, and some bachelor fellows, were in on this at the end. Everybody else kept away). That's why they finally set the Warm House on fire and it all burned up. (They baptized the people after this)" (1935 [parenthetical comments by Jacobs?]).

Gananath Obeyesekere (1990:26–29), in his psychodynamic analysis of Sri Lankan religious expression, divides rituals into two types, dromena and cathartic rites. A *dromenon* (Greek for "thing performed") is a solemn and stately rite in which cultural, religious, and philosophical values are represented in a fairly straightforward manner. Individual psychological problems are not absent, and indeed provide a basic motivation for the ritual enactment, but are transformed into idealized cultural themes and "brought in line with higher cultural values" (Obeyesekere 1990:27). That is, the relation to real emotions and dilemmas is rather attenuated. Dromena are "progressive" in that they attempt to resolve psychological problems by projecting them forward into the future and the level of the numinous. Cathartic rites, by contrast, represent these matters more directly, although in doing so they transform the cultural themes, often parodically. Thus, the Hindu gods and goddesses portrayed in these rites possess large sexual appetites and organs. These representations are the product of symbolic transformations that Obeyesekere calls "the work of culture" (1990:55). It is like dream work in that it transforms the original forms into distortions, the difference being that dream work disguises unconscious thoughts, whereas the work of culture reveals them (Obeyesekere 1990:56). Cathartic rites are thus regressive, in that they dwell on psychological conflicts without attempting to transform or resolve them.

We are now in a better position to address the "craziness" that Coquille Thompson observed in the latter days of the Warm House movement. The movement was transformed from a dromenon, which attempted to resolve the conflicts that the western Oregon Indians were experiencing in the postcontact period by transferring them onto another plane, into a cathartic rite, in which these themes were radically and parodically distorted. Reunification with dead parents becomes transformed into physical union with contemporaries. We must reject, or at least we need not accept, the Freudian theory of psychological development underpinning Obeyesekere's analysis. The Warm House dancers were not regressing in the sense of acting out infantile fantasies but, rather, turning away from the possibility of a resolution of the dilemma. As frustration at achieving a solution increased and efforts to achieve visions became more extreme, the movement was deflected toward simple catharsis. In a sense, the increasing dissolution of the Warm House dance functioned as a kind of abreaction of the process of cultural disintegration, in which even the most strongly held moral principles and the fundamental structure of society (divided into people with whom sexual relations were permitted and forbidden) were violated. Levels of social control were stripped away. The communitarian values stressed in the early dance were transformed into a parody of communitarianism: group sex.

When this reached a logical end point, the houses were burned. This resonates with the Coos and Alsea custom, probably practiced more widely on the southern coast, of burning the houses of the recently deceased, primarily chiefs (Drucker 1939:97; Jacobs 1933; Ray 1938:76). As a closure to the movement, and as an icon of the central meaning, which was death and its effect on survivors, a more appropriate symbol could not be found. After this complete symbolization of culture death, the way was paved for adopting missionary Christianity and all that went with it.

Cathartic Rites as a Response to Colonialism

There can be little doubt that religious movements such as the Warm House dance should be seen as ethnohistorical phenomena, viewed within the matrix of Euro-American invasion and forced culture change (Walker 1969). Further, it is clear that they are mechanisms for dealing with collective stress and powerful negative emotions—and not always therapeutically. They offer emotional release from the dreary reality of death, disease, starvation, and acculturation. What is more, they replace the specific qualities of each person's suffering with a collective meaning constructed in ritual. In this sense they allow for a certain forgetting of the specific past of massacres and epidemics, which is replaced with the idealized account (Fogelson 1989). At first, such movements are optimistic and future oriented. They are dromena in Obeyesekere's terminology. However, over time, as their participants are repeatedly discomfited, the focus turns away from future-oriented optimism and moves increasingly in the direction of pure catharsis. At such a point the grotesque qualities of the rite are elaborated and come to prevail.

An important distinction must be made here. Simply because a ritual is focused on death does not mean that it is inherently grotesque and cathartic. The great variety of motif and ethos of the various "Ghost Dances," "prophet dances," "earth lodge dances," and so forth bears this out. But it is possible, I think, to go further. In early stages such movements tend to be closer to the dromenon type, with an emphasis on positive images of the future. They do the "work of culture," as Obeyesekere calls it. The fact that these movements are composed of *dream* fragments contributed by congregants makes their psychodynamic quality abundantly clear. At this early stage, they might even be reasonably viewed as a type of collective talk therapy, in which dream fragments are discussed, evaluated, and recontextualized. However, participants are focused on causing specific external events to occur, usually involving the entire world, rather than providing therapy for one another. Thus, when the predicted events fail to occur or, as was the case in the Warm House, visions fail to materialize, the movement takes a new turn.

The failure of dancers to receive visions in the Warm House movement signifies repression rather than expression of latent dream contents. Presumably, this is because dream contents are too terrifying or disturbing and are blocked by the dream censor. This produces anxiety, which is expressed in the increasingly desperate quest for visions and for alternative ways to release anxiety. At this point the movement becomes a cathartic rite.

The intersection between the individual and the group becomes simplified. If original visions are lacking, then no source of potential conflict can derive from such visions. In the earlier phase, the proliferation of house "bosses" suggests that the very success of the movement was dependent on a degree of differentiation and disagreement. Everyone is in the same situation of blockage. At the same time, the possibility of positive action for the congregants and the larger community is diminished. It becomes obvious to all that the former way of life will not be restored and that, instead, the worst of possible outcomes will occur. The cathartic quality becomes more pronounced, as the rite seems to parody the culture from which it derives. Communal obligation is transformed into communal sex. To say that this represents a breakdown of the cultural order is imprecise; an inverted cultural order is actively constructed.

The purpose at this point becomes closure. Just as, according to Freud, *thanatos* is a goal of individual striving, cultural death becomes the goal of collective action. As the past way of life and its restoration become increasingly untenable, the most that can be done is to mark history's passing and achieve closure. When the Warm House movement reached its conclusion in 1880, with the burning of the houses, Christianity became the primary spiritual option. Mimesis of the dead was replaced by mimesis of whites, a potential source of spiritual power that was much more problematic (see Bhabha 1994:85–92; Lattas 1998).

Of course, this trajectory fit into the missionary discourse perfectly, although their interpretation of the events preceding mass baptism was quite different. What followed was the establishment of a pastoral regime, in which effective local authority is exercised by missionaries (Foucault 1982). In the Grande Ronde community, Roman Catholic missions took hold; in Siletz, Methodists. In both cases, boarding schools were established more efficiently to wipe out native culture (Beckham 1990).[10] It is important that native people themselves saw the Warm House movement as the historical transition point to this new cultural and political order.

Conclusion: Ritual Forms and Modalities

The many ritual forms generally associated under the term *revitalization* share a few key features. In addition to Wallace's criteria, having to do with building up and releasing systemic stress, it seems that most such movements have an explicitly mimetic function. They are miming the dead or a mode of existence glossed as "heaven" or the spirit world. In addition, they may mime whites and their cultural practices, or they may, on the contrary, attempt to exclude them entirely. This is a crucial consideration, for whether a movement entails mimetic inclusion or exclusion of whites determines whether the movement will be nativistic or accommodationist. Of course, these poles exist at either end of a continuum, and most historical movements exist somewhere in between.

One term I have avoided up to this point is *utopia*. Clearly, there are elements of utopian discourse in the Warm House movement: the reopening of a path between living and dead, the erasure of social distinction, and the establishment of an egalitarian, communitarian society, which in the end could be achieved only in parodic form. This connection is less interesting for what it says about the Warm House movement itself than for what it may say about European utopian movements. A similar underlying ritual logic exists, in which the modality of a movement changes from *dromenic* to cathartic, as, for example, the French Revolution gave way to the Terror.

It remains to be seen whether this model may be usefully applied to a wide range of social movements. It seems promising, for scholars have noted a "tipping point" in the history of these movements where they abruptly transform themselves from one state to another, states that may be viewed as dromenic and cathartic (Cobb 1987; Festinger et al. 1959; Gladwell 2000). Such transitions are not, of course, inevitable; some revitalization movements never make it but, rather, become institutionalized instead (Wallace 1970b; Wallace 1978). However, whether movements make such a transition or not is an important variable to consider in any cross-cultural analysis and may be correlated with other factors. The advantages of this model are that it connects individual and collective psychological states with the social and political goals of the movement, through the mediation of ritual.

In looking at the Warm House movement, it is clear that ritual leaders and participants acted in the only arena available to them, at a time of great stress. The creative reworking of themes from previously diverse cultural traditions, using mimesis to represent a nostalgically idealized land of the dead, stands as a powerful testament to the overwhelming effects of colonialism on native cultures and their adaptive responses. The tragic denouement of the Warm House movement speaks eloquently to the need to comprehend the political, social, religious, and psychological dimensions of these phenomena in all their specificity.

Notes

I wish to thank Robert Boyd and Raymond Fogelson for reading an earlier version of this chapter. I would especially like to thank William Seaburg and Robert Scott Byram for commenting on an earlier version and suggesting source material. Finally, my fellow panelists at the 1999 American Anthropological Association session on revitalization movements, Jim Roscoe (a discussant for that session), Lamont Lindstrom, and the University of Nebraska Press's anonymous reviewer all provided valuable comments.

1. Of course, the question of whether a movement is successful or not is open to interpretation and is politicized. Thornton (1986) has suggested that the Lakota Ghost Dance was indeed a successful revitalization movement that resulted in a demographic rebound. This interpretation has been criticized on statistical and methodological grounds (Kehoe 1988). It also is remarkable for ignoring the issue of culture, which is the linchpin of any coherent theory of revitalization. Mere population growth does not indicate cultural vitality, as the rise of First World "edge cities," Third World megalopolises, and similar social arrangements attests.

2. See, for example, Porterfield's (1987) discussion of feminism and revitalization.

3. It is essential to distinguish between cultural and demographic mortality. Many groups that saw the end to a distinctive cultural formation, based on language, religion, control of territory, and so forth, nevertheless remained demographically strong and, indeed, often successfully put forth new cultural syntheses. At the same time, some groups that practiced the Ghost Dance, such

as the Lakota, remained relatively intact both culturally and socially but suffered the closure of certain lifeways, such as bison hunting, at least temporarily.

4. "Warm House" is an early English gloss for the sweat houses (as they were called by the early 20th century), which were a prominent part of southern Northwest Coast culture (Harrington n.d.: reel 27:272).

5. It is evident that "sweat house" is something of a misnomer and that they were much different from, for example, the sweat lodges of the Plains Indians. The temperature was normally merely comfortable rather than sweltering, making it the most pleasant place in the village to be during cold and rainy weather.

6. Big Snake may be related to *sisiutl*, the wealth-bringing serpent of the Wakashan cultures. However, snakes were generally considered bad omens in coastal Oregon, especially those that, like sisiutl, were two-headed. In the myths that Elizabeth and Melville Jacobs collected, there is no mention of the wealth-bestowing aspect.

7. Nash sees the dance becoming more individualistic among the Klamath and other interior Oregon and California groups gathered at the Klamath Reservation, reflecting the individualistic bent of interior cultures. The coastal Warm House dance, by contrast, moved in a direction dissonant with the themes of Coos, Siletz, and other coastal cultures.

8. The agent at Siletz during the period of the introduction of the Warm House dance, Joel Palmer, was content to allow the dance (DuBois 1939:26; Lionel Youst and William Seaburg, personal communication). However, neighboring whites were less tolerant.

9. One major difference between cargo cults as described by Lattas (1998) and most North American revitalization movements, including Warm House, is the lack of a doubled mimesis in the latter. In cargo cults, the European or *waitskin* merges with the dead (who are believed to possess white skin), thus allowing for a mediation of the opposition between black and white. This logic is very far indeed from that of Ghost Dances, which were often nativistic and intended to drive whites out.

10. Not all traces of native spirituality were wiped out by the missionaries, however. Phenomena known as the "Dream Dance," which was probably related to Warm House, and the "Feather Dance" succeeded the Warm House in the late 19th and early 20th century. In the 1920s Indian Shakerism took hold at Siletz (Barnett 1957:75; Beckham 1990:183–184; DuBois 1939:34–36).

7. THE EVOLUTION OF REVITALIZATION
MOVEMENTS AMONG THE YANGORU
BOIKEN, PAPUA NEW GUINEA

Paul B. Roscoe

In his lively and engaging book on Melanesian "cargo cults," Lind-strom (1993) queries why these movements so fascinate the West.[1] With their themes of longing for cargo, he concludes, they perhaps echo "our own diffuse but powerful discourses of desire and love, particularly the melancholy of unrequited love" (1993:184). This is an intriguing idea, and it enshrines an important cautionary note: cargo cults are Western cultural constructions, emerging from a matrix of colonial discourse (e.g., McDowell 1988). This does not mean, of course, that cargo cults—or, at least, something corresponding to what we mean by this term—do not exist. *All* knowledge of the world—of the physical world as well as the social world—is a discursive construct (Rorty 1982:199; Roscoe 1995b:494–497). Yet this eventuality has hardly torpedoed the success of inquiry in the physical sciences, and there is no a priori reason to suppose it should undermine investigation in the social sciences. Cargo cults may have been constructed in a matrix of colonial discourse, but this does not mean that the concept therefore lacks any defensible referent, that it does not capture some regularity among humanity's social worlds and processes.

It was just such a regularity that Anthony F. C. Wallace sought to dis-cern in his classic article on revitalization movements. In Wallace's view (1956c:267), Melanesian "cargo cults" furnished the classic instance of one of three forms of revitalization movement: a type that emphasized the importation of alien values, customs, and material goods as a means of recapturing satisfaction in a culture stressed by contact with other societies. The particular virtue of Wallace's article is its holistic attempt to identify an underlying commonality among cultural differences, and it is surely a mark of his success that, half a century later, his portrayal of these movements is still very much representative of mainstream anthropological thinking on the subject.

It is no discredit to Wallace's work, however, that more recent research highlights a need to reformulate and extend his depiction of the cargo cult and, by extension perhaps, of the revitalization movement. In this chapter I use an extended analysis of the postcontact history of the Yangoru Boiken of the East Sepik Province of Papua New Guinea to review the concept of the revitalization movement. The Yangoru Boiken are especially valuable to this purpose because their postcontact history is constituted by some 80 years of ongoing engagement in millenarian (cargo) activity (Gesch 1985; Roscoe 1988, 1993). In addition, the record of these involvements can be tracked in significant detail. Yangoru contact with the West was recent, so it was still possible in the 1980s to collect ethnohistorical data from people who had witnessed events in the later part of the contact period (ca. 1905–30) and who remembered the reminiscences of their parents and grandparents about the earlier part. Complementing these memories is a comparatively rich historical record that includes a published account of the first European contact with Yangoru (Limbrock 1912–13), a partial historical record of the period from about 1930 to the end of World War II and a rich documentary record of the postwar years.

In this chapter I use these data to try to reformulate several aspects of our understanding of revitalization movements. My hope is that the findings prove suggestive for analyzing these movements in less well documented places and times. My main purpose is to demonstrate that Wallace's revitalization concept is too static. In Wallace's (1956c:268–275) model, revitalization movements represent a transitional phase between two functionally organized "steady states." A social group in a steady state encounters some kind of stressor—in the case of cargo cults, another culture. It starts to experience increasingly severe stress at environmental, organic, social, and cosmological levels, which, after a while, overwhelms existing stress-reduction techniques. The existing culture comes to seem deficient, provoking a revitalization movement that, via a gestalt shift in perceptions and an extensive reordering of social relations, creates a culture that is more satisfying because it reduces experienced stress. In the case of cargo cults, the particular means of achieving this new state is identification with an alien, European culture—a mimicking of aspects of the colonial enterprise through the importation of European values, customs, and material goods (Wallace 1956c:276).

The data from Yangoru reveal several problems in this thesis. First, the trajectory of its revitalization cults reveals an overall processual dynamic to the particular processual dynamics of its several individual movements. Successive movements were not simply reiterations of the same transitional process; instead, they underwent a significant evolutionary shift as local perceptions of Europeans developed. Second, the earliest movements in this evolutionary trajectory were in no sense a response to perceived stress, deprivation, or cultural distortion but, rather, were attempts to increase well-being in a culture already considered satisfactory. Finally, Yangoru's movements did not involve attempts to import alien values, customs, and material goods, nor did they involve gestalt perceptual shifts or reorderings of cultural relations. Rather, they rested on extensions or elaborations of preexisting perceptions and relations. Where Wallace presented cargo cults as psychocultural responses to stress, Yangoru's movements seem rather to have been interpretative attempts to extend prevailing ideas about the universe in order to encompass and deal with previously unencountered phenomena. In this sense, they were not at all unlike the interpretative exercise that we call Western science (Roscoe 1995b:494–497; see also Narakobi 1974).

"Strength" and the Millennium

In reviewing the diversity of the world's revitalization movements, Wallace (1956c:267) distinguishes three major types: the cargo cult, described above; the nativistic or revivalistic movement, which seeks change through a return to the old ways; and the utopian or vitalistic movement, which seeks to create an entirely new world. As he himself notes, these are not mutually exclusive categories: "A given revitalization movement may be nativistic, millenarian, messianic, and revivalistic all at once" (1979:423). In Yangoru, as in many other areas of Melanesia, in fact, cargo cults are typically also millenarian movements, embodying a vision that performance of the appropriate ritual procedures in proper spirit will precipitate an apocalyptic and empowering world transformation. "Cargo cult" is thus a poor representation of what motivates these movements. It is not so much that people desire cargo—Western material goods; rather, they desire what access to these goods represents—a state of *halinya*, of "strength" or "power."

Halinya was, perhaps, the foremost orienting theme in traditional Yangoru Boiken male culture: the lives of individual males, their subclans, and clans revolved around ongoing attempts to achieve and demonstrate this "strength." To be "strong" was to exhibit a dangerous potency—a spiritual, ritual, economic, political, and military power that involved not just the capability to get things done but also an edge of menace. "Strong" subclans and clans comprised "strong" men, men who were not just physically strong but also psychologically motivated, spiritually graced, and intellectually equipped to prove their "strength." These were men who were keen and able to "stand up straight in a fight" against the enemy, a capability that projected threat and thereby deterred predation on their groups as it helped them prey on others. Within the confines of their village, where the exercise of physical violence was deplored, they were men who projected symbolic rather than actual power and menace. Pigs and shell wealth being symbolic spears, they were men who could overwhelm their exchange partners and affines with gifts of pigs and wealth. They were men capable of organizing and creating spectacular works of art that evoked feelings of power and menace in themselves and unease, even fear, in others (Roscoe 1995a).

Females were not disenfranchised from this male enterprise. Women as well as men strove to demonstrate "strength." Where men manifested their "strength" through direct deployment of real and symbolic spears, however, women demonstrated it by indirect contributions to these projects. "Strong" women birthed many sons who would later become warriors and many daughters who would later be sources of bridewealth and affinal allies. They raised and tended many pigs for their husbands; and they produced plenty of food to reward relatives who gave their husbands wealth. It was no coincidence that a good wife was referred to, and often addressed as, her husband's "younger brother." Like her husband's younger brother, a wife demonstrated her "strength" by helping her husband and his descent groups to demonstrate their "strength."

Yangoru's millenarian movements have all been motivated by a concern to acquire and demonstrate this "strength." In the beginning, the desire was to demonstrate "strength" relative to other descent groups and villages. Later, however, the focus shifted to acquiring and demonstrating "strength" relative to Europeans. "What we wanted," my adoptive father and closest friend once confided in me, "was to sit down with you whites [i.e., be your equals]. We wanted to be able to travel to your country just as you travel to ours, to get cars and good food, just like you. We wanted for you to marry our sisters and for us to marry yours. We wanted to sit down with you." If we are to track the evolutionary shifts through which Yangoru sought to achieve this end, we must begin with the course of the region's history and the evolving interpretative frames within which villagers sought to place Europeans.

The Return of the Ancestors

On October 4, 1912, Fathers Eberhard Limbrock and Francis Kirschbaum, priests stationed in the little Catholic mission at the coastal village of Boiken, descended from an arduous traverse of the Prince Alexander Mountains into the territory of the northern Yangoru Boiken (Limbrock 1912–13). Numbering some 13 thousand in 1980, the Yangoru Boiken are slash-and-burn cultivators of the foothill slopes around Yangoru Government Station. Their subsistence is based on yam, taro, and sago, supplemented with pigs, banana, and a variety of bush (and now trade store) foods. The nuclei of their social life are patrilineages and clans, and their political life swirls around the activities of big men, whose prestige nowadays derives primarily from performance in ceremonial pig exchanges (for ethnographic summaries, see Gesch 1985; Roscoe 1991).

Although Limbrock and Kirschbaum were the first Europeans to enter Yangoru, the region had known for some time about whites and their powers. In the latter part of the 19th century the Wewak area had fallen into the operational sphere of the German Neu Guinea Kompanie, and by 1900 the Neu Guinea Kompanie had acquired landholdings along the coast and was recruiting laborers from Boiken territory. The Church followed hard on the heels of the company. By 1908 Catholic missionaries of the Divine Word had established missions on Yuo Island off the Boiken coast and another at the coastal village of Boiken. News of these events moved quickly along trade routes into the hinterlands. Some northern Yangoru villagers encountered these Europeans on their periodic trips to trade partners out on the coast, and at least one young Yangoru man had been recruited as a laborer by 1910 (Limbrock 1912–13:127).

As they descended into Yangoru on that long-ago afternoon, Limbrock and Kirschbaum were delighted to discover thickly populated new pastures in which to spread the Word (Limbrock 1912–13:126–127). Over the next few years, Limbrock and his coastal catechists sought to capitalize on the discovery, returning from time to time to Ambukanja, the northern Yangoru Boiken village from which some of the villagers at Boiken drew their hinterland trade partners. In 1914 the presence of the cloth assumed tangible form when Limbrock purchased a plot of land in the Ambukanja hamlet of Hwerenimpo and constructed a priest's house, a church, and a small school (Gesch 1985:116). With this as their hinterland base, missionaries and their catechists continued periodically to tour Yangoru through the 1920s (e.g., Gerstner 1929–30:229).

When asked to recall in the 1980s what their parents and grandparents had told them about these first European visitors, people stressed first and foremost that their forebears were unsure quite what to make of them. A common view was that they were perhaps *kamba*—spirits of the dead—returned to visit their living relatives. On Limbrock's first visit, an elderly woman in the Soli area had cried out upon seeing him, "O Jova, O Jova!"—"Eh father, father!" As a Catholic priest, Limbrock understandably presumed that she was using his clerical honorific; in light of modern testimony that the two priests were returned ancestors, it seems more likely that she intended it literally.

A second, related opinion held that the pair were *walankamba*. When people die, their kamba are believed eventually to become a part of their clan's *wala* spirit. Wala spirits are ubiquitous in Yangoru's ritual culture and take several forms. As *walazaiyi*, they are the culture heroes, who nowadays are incarnated in the mountain peaks that loom above Yangoru. As lesser wala, some are believed to inhabit lakes or large rocks and are sometimes totemically identified with a village. The most common wala spirits, however, are those believed to reside in the bush— in dark pools in the streams and rivers, or, occasionally, in patches of sword grass, or in trees hung thick with lianas. Like all wala, these bush wala may be male or female. Female wala are considered vengeful of trespassers on their abode, whom they punish with sickness. Male bush wala are considered more benign, and every clan claims one of them as a totem, believing it to be made up of a mystical union of the clan's kamba. Because these clan wala occasionally appear in dreams as ghostly white human figures, it is perhaps not surprising that some people held Limbrock, Kirschbaum, and other Europeans to be walankamba—bush wala that embodied many kamba.

The significance of Yangoru's first encounter with Europeans lay in the status of kamba as the spiritual font of prosperity and, hence, of the "strength" that Yangoru culture covets. Kamba are believed to watch over, protect, and empower their descendants. Through the agency of insects such as fireflies, crickets, and birds, for example, they warn of impending ambush or sorcery attack, they direct game onto their descendants' spears or into their traps, and they enter and fatten up their pigs and yams. As unions of these powerful and protective beings, clan wala spirits are considered emblematic of their descent groups' "strength," powerful and protective of those under their aegis, and menacing to those who are not (Roscoe 1995a:15–16).

In the normal course of events, kamba are believed to empower and protect their descendants as a matter of course or, in some instances, in answer to their ritual entreaty. In contrast to groups in some areas of Africa and Highland New Guinea, there is no feeling that the ancestors are somehow capricious dealers of misfortune or that they must be cajoled into dispensing favor. They are believed to assist their children out of affection, much as they did when they were alive. Thus, when ancestors reappeared in the form of Limbrock and Kirschbaum, it was presumed that they and other Europeans had returned to help empower their descendants. Their fabulous goods, their firearms, and their large metal ships, which occasionally appeared off the coast, were all believed to emanate from the nether world, and Yangoru waited eagerly for their newly returned ancestors to provide them with access to these goods and powers.

The evidence strongly suggests that these expectations fuelled and shaped Yangoru's early cargo movements. These were clearly already under way when the first Europeans entered Yangoru. By Limbrock's (1912–13:127, 142) own account, he and Kirschbaum were greeted by throngs of friendly, delighted villagers who eagerly pressed them for their blessings. To the two priests, this unexpectedly warm reception was welcome evidence that the mission's teachings had spread to a receptive audience in the hinterlands: "One sees it, the word 'missionary' really has a good sound here" (Limbrock 1912–13:126). According to today's villagers, though, their elders saw things from a different perspective: the spirits of the dead were once again among the living.

In the ensuing years the pronouncements of visiting priests and catechists were all interpreted as ancestral blueprints for precipitating the millennium. In his little bush church in Ambukanja, for example, Limbrock probably sermonized about the importance that Christian behavior would assume on the Day of Judgment, when the dead would rise and together with the living face God, the Father. Probably, too, he spoke of the importance of prayer and church attendance if villagers were to become Christians like the white-skinned newcomers to their world. According to modern testimony, however, the congregations listening to these homilies attached an immediacy and a mechanicalism to them that Limbrock hardly could have intended, a millenarian disposition no doubt encouraged by the native catechists who accompanied him as interpreters or visited Yangoru in his stead. As a result, people flocked to Limbrock's church and dutifully prayed beneath its eaves, not from any interest in the fate of their souls in the hereafter but in the expectation that these magical actions would induce "God, the Father" to come down to Yangoru, the spirits of the dead to return, and villagers to become white skins with access to European property and power.

With the missionaries' constant talk of God, villagers soon became as curious about His nature as they were about the Europeans who preached of Him. They wondered who God was and where he lived: Was he a man, an ancestral spirit, or what? European goods had by this time begun to filter into the area along traditional trade routes, and an idea spread that God was responsible for these goods and the powers possessed by Europeans. It was believed that if villagers did as the priests counseled, then they too would assume this European estate. In response to missionary perorations that God abhorred warfare, sorcery, and initiation, for example, a movement spread through northern Yangoru in the late 1920s and early 1930s advocating the abandonment of all three in the belief that thereby villagers would "find God" in a literal sense, become white skins, and gain unfettered access to Western goods.

Revitalization movements occur, according to Wallace, when members of a population "experience increasingly severe stress as a result of the decreasing efficiency of certain stress-reduction techniques" available to them (1956c:269). The cause may be "climatic, floral and faunal change; military defeat; political subordination; extreme pressure towards acculturation resulting in internal cultural conflict; economic distress; epidemics; and so on" (Wallace 1956c:269). A revitalization movement then precipitates as an attempt to reduce or remove the stress experienced. This argument is much in line with a common and continuing theme in the analysis of Melanesia's millenarian movements: working at the psychological, intellectual, and political level, cargo cults are rituals of resistance to colonial (and, more recently, postcolonial) power and the changes it has wrought (e.g., Aberle 1962; Errington and Gewertz 1991:19–47; Lanternari 1963; Lattas 1998; Valentine 1963; Worsley 1957).

As I shall presently contend, these arguments may be applicable to the later years of Yangoru's contact with the West, but they distort the early period of this history. In these immediate postcontact years, there is no evidence that Yangoru's population felt any kind of stress in the face of the European presence or that the region's early movements were acts of resistance or stress reduction. To the contrary, villagers *identified* with the newcomers, presuming that they would acquire their powers and material wealth. They perceived the foreigners not as some alien "them" but as "us"; and they understood European powers and goods not as "theirs" but also as "ours." Rather than acts of resistance or stress reduction, Yangoru's early movements were acts of capitalization, no different in essence from people's actions before contact, when kamba or walankamba had appeared in dreams with warnings and advice about how to capitalize on the future.

To be sure, the white newcomers provoked struggles and acts of resistance, but, to the extent that these were asserted against anyone, they were not against Europeans but, rather, against other Yangoru individuals and groups. The spirits of the dead had returned to confer "strength" on their descendants, but precisely whose dead ancestors were they? Fragmentary evidence indicates that several groups in northern Yangoru, the region closest to the coast, tried to lay claim to the newcomers. Limbrock (1912–13:126, 142) notes that his first visit was a response to frequent solicitations from Ambukanja village, presumably aided by their trade friends in Boiken village. En route through Parina village, though, he and Kirschbaum were offered land for a mission station if they would just settle there (Limbrock 1912–13:142). And there is also the aforementioned old woman in Soli village who seems to have claimed Limbrock as her father.

In the event, Ambukanja prevailed, but, according to modern accounts, a struggle to claim Limbrock then ensued within the village. A man called Saramiemba, who could already speak some Tok Pisin ("pidgin English"), attempted to persuade Limbrock to locate with him, but the priest chose instead the hamlet of Hwerenimpo, possibly because the catechist accompanying him was related to its owner, Wamazaira. Wamazaira then proceeded to claim Limbrock as his deceased father, come especially from Aitape in search of his ancestral home and descendants. Subsequently, Wamazaira would spend long hours at night

closeted with the priest and his catechist, leading others in Ambukanja
to wonder to what tantalizing secrets he was becoming privy.

Of Foreign Powers and Ordinary Men

By the early 1930s two events were in train that would significantly
change Yangoru's perceptions of Europeans. The first was the arrival of
Europeans who were considerably more violent than the missionaries.
In the 1920s labor recruiters and their native henchmen and carriers
began to tour the region, conscripting young men for three-year periods
of indentured labor in the budding urban centers and plantations of the
territory. In theory, recruiters were under tight governmental regulation; in practice, in the hinterlands away from the eye of the administration, they were a law unto themselves. A number of them simply
abducted young men for labor, used dynamite and firepower to terrorize
villages into surrendering youths, and shot villagers who resisted them.
Protected by white power, their native assistants frequently raped and
plundered the villages they passed through (e.g., Beazley n.d.; Scaglion
1983; Townsend 1968:110–114).

In the environs of my field site, Sima village in northern Yangoru,
it was not so much European labor recruiters themselves who abducted
young men for labor but, rather, their armed native henchmen, who conducted illegal sweeps of northern Yangoru from the coastal plantation
of Karawop (see also Townsend 1933). By 1930 Yangoru had also fallen
within the orbit of Australian administration patrols from Wewak, and
villages found these early patrol officers, supported by their phalanxes of
native police and carriers, to be even more frightening. Patrol officers
quickly became known as *hauwalya*, "the wala spirits who strike": they
are said to have punched people who failed to line quickly for census
and to have raped and stolen from villagers.[2] To the people of Yangoru,
this was hardly the behavior to be expected of the returned ancestors
they had taken Europeans to be. A perception began to spread that Europeans were not spirits of the dead or bush wala spirits after all; rather,
they must be foreign wala spirits, spirits who were akin to the walazaiyi
incarnated in the region's mountains and lakes but who had come from
"outside," from abroad—most notably from a mysterious place known
as "Sydney."

The second event to change perceptions of Europeans occurred as
Yangoru entered the 1930s: the young men recruited to urban centers
and plantations in the 1920s began to return from their indentured ser-

vice. These men had left their homes believing that they were going to the lands of the dead. They returned after three to six years of observing whites at close quarters, declaiming that Europeans were neither kamba nor wala but merely human.

By the mid-1930s, in sum, village perceptions of whites had changed radically. Although their evident material wealth and power clearly bespoke that they were either of the spiritual world or had secured access to it, Yangoru was much less inclined to consider them returned ancestors and much more inclined to believe that they were foreigners. Accordingly, conceptions of how to achieve the millennium changed. Europeans were no longer "us," returned ancestors obligated and willing to empower their descendants. Instead, they were a physical or spiritual "them," with access to spiritual powers but no motive to share these secrets with local people. Movements thus shifted from passive enactments of a millennial blueprint dictated by returned ancestors to movements predicated on beliefs that Europeans had to be induced, seduced, or deceived into yielding up these secrets.

What may have been the first of these new movements occurred in the late 1930s, when the area was sufficiently under government control for Mt. Hurun, the prominent peak overlooking Yangoru, to be included among several Wewak area mountaintops set ablaze one night with bonfires. In 1930 the Wewak administration had honored the birth of Princess Margaret with similar beacons on prominent points along the coast from Wewak to Aitape (Fleetwood 1986:32), and it is possible that this later event was a celebration of King George VI's coronation in May 1937. Alternatively, it may have been the clearing and firing of Hurun's summit by District Officer G. W. L. Townsend in order to install a trigonometric marker for mapping the Sepik Basin (Gesch 1985:32). Whatever the reason, it escaped the people of Yangoru. They believed instead that the village of Ambukanja, which owned Mt. Hurun, had secured Western assistance though its privileged trade contacts with the coast to mount an event that would bring about the millennium (see also Gesch 1985:32). *Luluais* and *tultuls* (government-appointed village officials) from throughout Yangoru converged on Ambukanja to witness the firing of the summit. For the remainder of the night they participated in a *lumohlia*—a festival of song and dance in honor of the dead and celebration of the political triumphs of the living—and at dawn they returned to their villages in expectation that now "the good times would come."

Several scholars have noted the important role in revitalization efforts such as these of individuals who present themselves as having privileged access to colonial powers and imply that they have secured or stolen knowledge of these powers. In Melanesia, Burridge has noted: "The vast majority of effective prophets have had a relatively wide experience of the white man's world. . . . Most of them have been mission teachers, men selected on account of their character and qualities of intellect, and then given a special training denied to others. They have usually been well travelled men, who have rubbed shoulders with all sorts and sizes in the hurly-burly of the greater commercial community. . . . To their own communities, if not to Europeans, they have been men whose general acquaintance with the wider environment and larger community is evidence of the fact that they can understand and cope with it" (1971:156–157).

Tommy Kabu, head of a Purari Delta movement, is a case in point. A member of the native constabulary before World War II, Kabu effectively became an officer's orderly in the Royal Australian Navy during the war. Upon his return, "he consistently emphasized his connections with the European or new way of life and played down his experience with the old. . . . He also kept up a correspondence with his war-time employer. . . . By emphasizing this relationship, Tommy transmitted the impression to his followers that he had connections in the powerful European world which were above the heads of the government officials who were closer at hand. . . . [I]t was said that Tommy was married to a daughter of the King of England and that they had two children. The source of this story has never been satisfactorily identified, but Tommy remained passive in the face of the widespread acceptance it had for a time" (Maher 1958:79).

I do not know whether similar individuals were at work during the firing of Mt. Hurun in the 1930s, but there is evidence that they were important in some postwar movements. Around 1949 a "New Times" movement emerged under the leadership of Yauiga, a man from the Nagam region east of Yangoru. Yauiga had been awarded a medal for heroic service with Australian forces in World War II, and after the war he was instrumental in spreading Catholic teachings to the hinterland (Gerstner 1952:800). These teachings penetrated East Yangoru under the leadership of ex-army sergeant Beibi from Toanumbu village (Yangoru Patrol Report 1949–50:3); it was perhaps because of the expectations raised by this movement that an "airstrip" was cut through the forest near Musuwagen (Yangoru Patrol Report 1949–50:8). Yauiga's motivations in this movement are unknown, but both he and Beibi had spent time in Australia, where Yauiga had received a blue Australian eye to replace his own, which had been destroyed on active duty (Fleetwood 1986:36–37; Wewak Patrol Report 1949–50: attached note). The unusual enthusiasm with which his message was received (Gerstner 1952:800) and the close connections to Europeans that he was believed to enjoy by virtue of his military service and position with the Catholic mission suggest that people believed that he and Beibi had used their privileged access to induce Europeans to surrender their millenarian secrets.

Within a couple of years Yangoru was again acting on a belief that Europeans had been induced to divulge the secrets of their "strength." Australian agricultural officers had begun to tour the region advocating the virtues of "development" in general and of growing rice as a cash crop in particular as a means of obtaining Western goods. At least two prominent local men, Paulus Hawina from Ambukanja village and Wundawabie from Ninduwi, helped propagate this message, claiming (according to modern testimony) that they had brought rice growing to Yangoru. I know little about Wundawabie, but Hawina had by this time clearly secured privileged access to the foreign world. He had risen to prominence during the war as a native official under the Japanese. According to today's villagers, he achieved sufficient influence with his Japanese commanders to ensure that soldiers who abused their village hosts were executed. Following the war, he managed to escape punishment for his wartime collaboration and achieved governmental favor as a "constant supporter of the administration" (Yangoru Patrol Report 1954–55:5). Under his and Wundawabie's tutelage, Yangoru plunged enthusiastically into rice growing (Yangoru Patrol Report 1954–55:5) in the belief that the pair had become privy to the secret by which Westerners generated their enormous wealth. Vastly inflated estimates circulated about the cash remuneration to be expected on a bag of threshed rice, and when actual returns failed miserably to meet these expectations, enthusiasm for rice plummeted as quickly as it had risen (Roscoe 1983:101–102).

In 1959 another movement sprang up around Neigrie mission station focused on a recruitment drive by the local Catholic priest and his village catechist. A series of festivals celebrating the opening of village churches drew thousands of followers to the enterprise of symbolically renouncing sorcery and actually renouncing polygyny. Although the Catholic mission apparently interpreted these events from a Christian perspective, the catechist and Yangoru's villagers imbued them with great eschatological significance. By virtue of his office in the Catholic Church and his status as one of the first in the area to receive a Western education, the catechist claimed privileged access to Western knowledge. To bolster his claims, he showed paintings of Christ and a small, hand-cranked movie of the Crucifixion, presenting them as actual photographs and footage of the scenes. Under this tutelage people came to believe that they had secured the secrets of access to "God-Jesus" and that, by their actions in renouncing sorcery and polygyny, they could induce him to return and usher in an eternal bliss in which food, housing, and money would appear spontaneously (see also Gesch 1985:122–126).

After Yangoru's early enchantment with Europeans, in sum, the decades that followed were a period of disillusionment. By their actions, white visitors proved themselves to be foreigners not natives, to be humans or spirits from abroad not from home. Even so, Yangoru has never entirely surrendered a hope that *some* light-skinned visitors, at least, might one day prove to be the spirits of the dead returning to empower their descendants. In December 1942, when the Japanese took the provincial capital of Wewak, they discovered an Ambukanja man called Hombinei in the town jail, where the Australian administration had imprisoned him for prewar millenarian activities. The Japanese released him, and Hombinei returned to Ambukanja, where he set about rebuilding his millenarian following by claiming that the Japanese were returned ancestors. In this enterprise he was no doubt assisted by the Japanese policy of purposely claiming to be ancestral spirits to ensure village support for their war effort (Aitape Patrol Report 1943–44; Gesch 1985:120). Following Hombinei's instructions, people brought the occupying soldiers pigs and food in the expectation that a new "Law" would thereby come. Within months Hombinei had become influential with the Japanese, who rewarded him with money and other gifts. Before too long, though, the occupiers were betraying their claims to "ancestorhood" by beating and shooting those who failed to obey them, and soon thereafter Hombinei's following disintegrated.

As late as 1980, however, people were still willing to believe that, among the general dross of European humanity, there might be a few who would prove to be returned ancestors. In the late 1970s, for example, when Canadian missionaries from the quasimillenarian New Apostolic Church arrived in Yangoru (Gesch 1985:106–114; Roscoe 1993), it was believed that they might be the returned ancestors of local New Apostolic functionaries. Principally, though, people reserved the status of ancestor spirit for those few Europeans, such as SIL missionaries, my wife, and myself, who acted *as though* they were ancestors. These Europeans came and settled in a village: They gave gifts; loaned goods and cash; provided rudimentary first aid and occasionally transport; and, when villagers fell ill or died, were visibly saddened and came to mourn. My wife and I were named Kwanjane and Yundaningai, after the returned ancestors we were taken to be. And, in 1981, we unwittingly became the focus of a minor millenarian movement: Shortly before our departure, rumors began to circulate that we would be returning to the land of the dead, taking with us those whose hands we had shaken at our farewell feast.

Resistance and the Millennium

As Yangoru entered the 1950s, a third form of millenarian activity emerged that fell much more into the classic anthropological mold that analyzes cargo cults as a form of resistance to European domination. By this time, a perception had emerged that whites were actively working to impede local access to the millennium. The reasons for this shift are unclear to me, but the failure of so many earlier movements to realize the millennium may have focused attention on the possibility that local efforts were being systematically undermined. Movements began to emerge that advocated displacing whites from the local scene. Perhaps the first of these occurred in June 1953, when the Yangoru Patrol Post again had the summit of Mt. Hurun cleared and fired, this time to celebrate the coronation of Queen Elizabeth II. Villagers organized large amounts of food, and a protracted pig festival was organized in Ambukanja. This time around, villages recognized the connection with royalty but again misunderstood the purpose. The firing, it was believed, would remove the Australians and their administration and effect the accession of New Guineans to their positions and estate.

In the late 1960s another movement began to coalesce that was to reach a crescendo in the well-known Peli movement. Beginning in the 1930s, colonial mapping teams had sunk a number of cement trigonometric markers into the summit of Mt. Hurun, the highest peak in the Wewak region and one that affords an excellent triangulation point (Gesch 1985:31–33). In pursuing their mapping tasks, these teams were not to know—they had not cared to inquire—that they had created an unfortunate conjunction of two Yangoru beliefs. The first is a belief that Mt. Hurun incarnates Yangoru's supreme walazaiyi, Walarurun, nowadays often identified as "God-Jesus." Like bush wala, Walarurun is believed to be a mystical union of kamba—the union, in fact, of kamba from the entire Yangoru region.[3] Kamba being the font of prosperity and "strength," Europeans thus had chosen to meddle with the most important entity in the Yangoru cosmos. A second belief made matters worse: one can destroy the fertility of land by burying bespelled stones on the heights overlooking it. If Yangoru people had not already begun to suspect Europeans of undermining their access to the millennium, it was hard for them to avoid such a conclusion now: Europeans had buried cement stones in the mountain summit that embodied the very font of Yangoru's "strength."

In 1969 a man from Marambanja village, Daniel Hawina, began to garner followers from as far afield as Lumi, 150 kilometers to the west, for an attempt at removing the markers from the summit of Mt. Hurun (Gesch 1985:30–37). In the spectacular, better known Peli movement of 1971, Hawina again toured widely, this time under the banner of Matius Yaliwan—the Peli movement's "prophet"—attracting a membership estimated at between 50,000 and 200,000 to a second attempt on Hurun's cement markers (Gesch 1985:27–95). Amid newspaper headlines warning of human sacrifice, some three hundred men removed the blocks and carried them down to the Yangoru Patrol Office, where they were deposited before a waiting crowd of about six thousand. By these actions, it was believed, the malevolent ritual obstacles that Europeans had erected to local participation in the millennium had been removed. The fertility of the bush and streams was now restored, it was said, a metaphoric reference to the "strength," prosperity, and material wealth people associated with the millennium. Yet there was also in these actions an element of resistance to the white presence. Yaliwan claimed on many occasions that he (not the Australian administration) was God's divinely sanctioned leader of Papua New Guinea (Gesch 1985:40–41). Within a year, in fact, the movement had gone on to elect him to the National House of Assembly, where, in the middle of a debate on a speech by the governor general, he proclaimed himself the country's leader and declared that immediate self-government and independence be instated (Gesch 1985:81–83).

By 1980 Hawina and the Peli movement were again using Yaliwan's name to attract a Sepik-wide millenarian following, this time under the badge of the New Apostolic Church (NAC). Again, a theme of resistance to Europeans was present. The NAC movement went through several crescendos, guided by a general belief that Yaliwan would usher in a cataclysm and then appear resurrected as the black counterpart of the white Jesus. Between them, the two Jesuses would then judge the living, white and black, admitting only members of the NAC to a paradise of material wealth in which the races would live together in emancipated and harmonious perpetuity.

Vitalization, Revitalization, and the Millennium

Although cargo cults are commonly analyzed as emergent phenomena of the engagement of Western and Melanesian worlds, Wallace makes it clear that revitalization movements have no necessary connection to Western or colonial influence. In New Guinea there is ample evidence of precontact movements that sought to reverse perceived declines in the prosperity of the universe. Before contact, for example, the Hulis of the Southern Highlands had come to believe that their physical and social worlds were in decline—that crop yields were falling, pigs were becoming thinner and sicker, and immorality—especially among the young—was increasing. To counteract these effects, they had deployed a ritual cycle called *dindi gamu*, which they believed would stimulate a flow of revitalizing magical power into the area (Allen and Frankel 1991:94–97). At contact, in fact, a progression of ritual "fertility" complexes was diffusing up into the Central Highlands through the Southern Highlands, fuelled by a perception that they conferred prosperity (for a summary, see Strathern 1994).

In precontact Yangoru, similar revitalization rituals were conducted when the prosperity of the universe seemed to be in decline. Perhaps the crops had failed or game had vanished from the bush. Perhaps villagers had suffered a number of military defeats, or there had been an unusual number of deaths. Whatever the case, the perception that something was amiss prompted the performance of counterritual. Occasionally, this ritual was mounted in isolation: I observed one such in 1980, when people discovered that their gardens had been "sorcerized" with bespelled stones. More commonly, it was performed as the culminating rite of the *walahlia*, the final ceremony of the mortuary sequence.

In New Guinea at least, many such cults were more than the restorative responses to stress that Wallace envisions; in addition, or instead, they attempted to ensure or enhance well-being *in the absence of stress or the perception of decline*. Thus, the Yangoru Boiken sometimes performed their revitalization ritual not because they thought the universe was in decline but simply to ensure or enhance descent group "strength." In other areas of the Sepik, head-hunting seems to have had a similar aim. Among Sepik River groups such as the Iatmul, there was a belief that successful head hunts would bring prosperity to the village—good health, plenty of children, and the creation of fine ritual art (Bateson 1958:139–141).

There is little evidence, moreover, that head-hunting or the performance of the walahlia "fertility" rite wrought the kind of gestalt transformation in local perceptions and the reordering of cultural relations that Wallace (1956c:267) proposes as criteria for revitalization movements. He might argue, of course, that, lacking these components, these were not therefore revitalization movements, sensu stricto; but gestalt perceptual shifts and reorderings of cultural relations were no more a part of Yangoru's cargo cults, to which Wallace could hardly deny the name "revitalization movement." In mimicking European values and customs, Yangoru's movements might look as though they were attempting to transform preexisting perceptions and relations, but in actuality they were simply extending or elaborating them.

This was the case of Yangoru's early movements. Catholic priests were considered the spirits of the dead returned, and their advocacy of prayer and exhortations to abandon war, sorcery, and initiation were believed simply to be new types of *kworbo*, magical rites that would enhance "strength." For a more recent example, the actions taken in the Peli movement were but extensions of the precontact ritual that restored the fertility of lands sorcerized by buried stones. In this ritual, the bespelled stones would be located, unearthed, and carried away to be discarded in the watery abode of a nearby wala spirit. For several hours afterward, everyone had to keep deadly quiet in the belief that noise would undermine the ritual's efficacy. The culmination of the Peli movement reenacted this ritual. The cement trigonometric markers buried in Mt. Hurun were uprooted and then carried down in total silence to be deposited outside Yangoru Patrol Office, the local administrative center and, hence, the abode of the white wala (Roscoe n.d.). In a rite conducted under the aegis of the NAC, families throughout the region gathered to mount little feasts under the benediction of local New Apostolic officials. These feasts were conducted in the conviction that Yaliwan's crucifixion and resurrection were imminent, and they bore a striking resemblance to the Last Supper. But they were also simply extensions of the *tuahrung hieri*, a ritual to ensure group and ancestral acquiescence before any important group action can proceed (Roscoe 1993:297, 299).

I have sketched in this chapter how revitalization movements in 20th-century Yangoru followed a distinctive evolutionary trajectory. In the beginning they were predicated on identification with Europeans: whites were taken to be returned ancestors, and movements coalesced around the execution of what was believed to be their magical blueprints for achieving "strength," represented by the millennium. After European behavior demonstrated that these people could not possibly be ancestral spirits, villagers reoriented their movements. Though not themselves ancestors, Europeans were still viewed as beings with access to ancestral or spiritual power, and movements now attempted to solicit or suborn them for the secrets that would yield the millennium. Only later, perhaps in response to the continued failure of earlier attempts to achieve the millennium, did movements eventually emerge that portrayed Europeans as inimical to local aspirations and sought to resist or displace them.

The value of this case study, I hope, is the illumination it might provide for understanding revitalization movements in other, less well documented parts of the world. It underscores, for example, that conceptions of ancestral power can be of great importance in precipitating and shaping revitalization movements. Thus, as Hill (1944) suggested many years ago, the Navajo may have rejected the Ghost Dance because of their unusual fear of the dead. For another example, resistance to the white presence is a commonly reported theme of the Ghost Dance (e.g., Harkin [ch. 6]), but the Yangoru data suggest that it might be worth exploring whether this was a later evolution of an earlier pattern in which Native American populations first identified with whites.

It is, of course, a matter for other scholars to judge how useful the Yangoru case may be to the analysis of revitalization in different regions of the world. Suffice it to say, the evolution of revitalization movements elsewhere is useful for contemplating their future development in Yangoru. As several contributors to this book document (Nesper [ch. 10], Henry [ch. 11], McMullen [ch. 12]), revitalization has taken a new turn among many indigenous peoples, involving a secularization of the process of assertion and resistance. Among Tahitian and Native American populations, movements have emerged that deploy material, social, or spiritual elements of received cultural heritages as symbols of identity to revitalize local groups and advance their contemporary, secular political struggles.

In parts of Island Melanesia with a much longer postcontact history than Yangoru and a more intimate interaction with Europeans, there is evidence of a similar turn. *Kastom* (custom)—the self-conscious deployment of cultural heritage as an element of identity—has become a significant force in provincial, national, and even international politics. This is a phase that Yangoru has yet to enter, but the chapters in this book help us imagine how it might progress. Harkin (ch. 6) analyzes the Ghost Dance as a psychodynamic transition from *dromena* to *catharsis* that effects closure on a past way of life. Some of Yangoru's movements might be similarly analyzed. In the Peli movement and the earlier 1959 movement centered around the Negrie Catholic mission, for example, ideas circulated that pottery, carvings, and shell wealth had to be smashed as a necessary precursor to the millennium.

A more profound process effecting Yangoru's transition from millenarian movements to identity politics may prove to be more straightforward: generational succession in the face of increasing encapsulation by the industrialized world. As late as the 1990s, the older generation still clung to a magico-religious view of the cosmos. In the 1980 national elections, for example, they understood that they were voting to select a "boy" (i.e., the prime minister) who would periodically venture down to Sydney, the land of the dead, and bring back the ancestral spirits' "orders" for the country. In 1987 the national election was described as the "last" election, the election that would institute "Fritan [Freedom] Independens," a millennial era in which the black and white peoples of the world would settle down together in equality.

As an increasing number of Yangoru youths graduate and go on from school, however, this "false consciousness" cannot prevail indefinitely. Some of Yangoru's sons and daughters already have held prominent positions in the country's government, university system, museums, national airline, and even its mission to the United Nations. As more of the region's youths are exposed to Westernized educational curricula, as this elite interacts with its relatives back home, and as the older generation passes away, it seems inevitable that Yangoru will eventually move from a ritualized to a more profane worldview, one in which the secular nature of political process, the region's subordination to global capitalism, and the value in these arenas of symbols of cultural heritage will become ever more apparent.

Notes

1. For good reason, the term *cargo cult* has fallen into disfavor in anthropology, not least because it badly distorts the aspirations of these movements (see below). In the Yangoru Boiken case examined in this chapter, *millenarian movement* would be a better (albeit imperfect) term. However, because this chapter takes issue with aspects of Wallace's analysis of these movements, and because Wallace uses *cargo cult* to refer to them, I have no option but to use the term from time to time to avoid confusing the referent of my argument.

2. Though Australian patrol officers are known to have used physical violence against villagers, there is little evidence that they themselves raped and stole. Villagers exposed to these patrols appear to have made little distinction between the actions of the European officer and those of native police and carriers, who seem to have been considered as, in a sense, the officer's refractions (see also Gerstner 1929–30:229).

3. When queried by a pestilential anthropologist about how kamba can incarnate both their clan wala and Walarurun, people reply that the kamba divide their time between the two positions.

8. RECONTEXTUALIZING REVITALIZATION

Cosmology and Cultural Stability in the Adoption of
Peyotism among the Yuchi

Jason Baird Jackson

During summer 1993 I had the great fortune to begin a personal and
research relationship with members of the Yuchi tribe, people of Woodland Indian heritage who live today in the region south and west of
Tulsa, Oklahoma. My initial studies of Yuchi ethnography were focused
on the recent history of community social institutions, particularly the
ceremonial ground organizations in which distinctly Yuchi ritual and
religious life persists (Jackson 2003). Despite this initial focus, my discussions with Yuchi elders ranged over a wide array of topics, and, as
my years of involvement with Yuchi life and people have lengthened, I
have had the additional benefit of seeing Yuchi community life through
the lenses of history and personal experience. This chapter draws on
these experiences in an effort to consider the Native American Church
within the context of Yuchi culture and the anthropological study of
revitalization movements.

Prominent among those Yuchi elders who have expended considerable effort in sharing Yuchi cultural values and history with me is Jimmie
Skeeter. For most of the 20th century, Mr. Skeeter had been an active
participant in and keen observer of the life of his people. During the final
year of his long and fruitful life, I had the honor of spending time with
him. Like most of the Yuchi elders I have known, he possessed broad
interests and an active intellect. He not only taught me much about his
people but also coached me through my initial struggles with the strange
anthropological business of actively learning an unfamiliar culture.

In June of my first summer in Oklahoma we sat together in the
shade outside his home in the Yuchi community of Duck Creek, seeking to escape the midsummer heat. We were enjoying the breezes that
thankfully come at sunset during the Oklahoma summer, and we talked
intermittently between silent pauses that were normal for him and still

unnatural for me. The Native American Church emerged as a topic after I commented to him on seeing what I thought was a set of tipi poles in his backyard. He indicated that they were tipi poles and that they were used when he sponsored Native American Church meetings at his home. In the context of this discussion he related an informal telling of the account that follows. After his thoughts had wound around to another pause, I jumped in, excited by the detail and richness of Mr. Skeeter's account. I made a request for a retelling, this time for my tape recorder. He agreed, and as is evident from the framing techniques he used, his audience for the second telling was no longer me but was instead the Yuchi community that he thought might one day find his narrative useful. Mr. Skeeter began:

> The year I don't know, but I might get pretty close to the year. I'll just tell it in English because a lot of them don't understand the Yuchi language.
>
> Alright, I am going to say a few words regarding the Native American Church, to the Yuchi people. The story I got [was] that when my grandfather Big Mosquito had a service at his home, Sac and Fox Tribe of those people conduct[ed] a service at my grandfather's home. It must have been during the time of World War I, the years when it [the Native American Church among the Yuchi] started. So this [peyote] service was for my uncle. He was going into the [military] service, so they had a service for him at my grandfather's home. So in the service, they went through, [they] stayed up all night, and my grandfather sat outside and listened to what went on. And the reason [that] he could understand what was going on in there [was] that he understood the Sac and Fox people's language. He understood what those people were talking about. So when the service was about to end the next morning, they have [a ritual] breakfast in[side] the service, in the morning. They invited [him] into that service. [When] it was [time for the] breakfast they was going to have.
>
> And so him and another old man [had] sat out [and] listened all night. The other old man was named Long Hair Tiger. He didn't go in, just my grandfather went in. So when they had breakfast they opened the room [to see] if he wanted to say something on behalf of what had went on that night. So, he had a chance to talk. So he talked to our tribal people, the Yuchi, and he talked to the Sac and Fox people: "Every tribe has their own custom ways." And he told the Yuchi people: "The Indian ways, [it] seem to me, in the Yuchi Tribe was fading away." He knowed it. So, he told the Yuchi people what [it was that] went on [there] that night. He observed, at that point in the

time that "the day may come that our Yuchi's custom ways might fade away complete."

And so on that, Native American Church [that] had a service there at his home, he told the people that that was the next best [thing] for them to rely on to continue the Indian custom ways. That's the word he give to the Yuchi people and the Sac and Fox people. And that was the word that he give us. I understand that a witness of that . . . two or three parties have told me that. At the time I didn't know he talked Sac and Fox, understood [the] Sac and Fox language, but later I learned that he talked that Sac and Fox language. That's why he understood what was going on there. So he really first gave permission to hold services in his home.

That's during, [what] must [have] been 1916, or '17, or '18 . . . somewhere in there. I don't know the year, but that [was] the way during that World War I. That's what he told the people.

So, myself, I go by that. So, I try to think about the ways that he told the people. That [is what] I was told on that. So today, I still try to follow that way. [I] try to follow our custom ways. But [what] my grandfather had said that, I think about that. I'm still going. And I think about things that have been said [way] back, not just [by] him, [but by] other elder people. What they used to say to us, talk to us younger ones. They said: "You must try to uphold your Indian tradition, your custom ways, as long as you live. Take care of it." They have told us: "Don't abuse it." Said: "That was yours, our custom ways." That was the way. Every tribe of Indians got their own custom ways, but that was ours, that what was the word that was given. As they said: "Don't abuse your ways, you must take care of it, that's yours."

That's the way the word came out later, so that's what I am saying. That's what I go by today. So, maybe there is a lot of things to talk about, but on that occasion that's about all I have to say. I am going to thank each and everyone that hears what I said, just now. So that's all I have to say. Thank you.[1]

For purposes of studying Yuchi speaking practices and cultural values, Mr. Skeeter's text is valuable in and of itself. At a broader level it points to a number of significant issues long at the center of Americanist ethnography. My general interests have tended toward the study of such narratives and their role in constructing a public "traditional" culture in Yuchi society, but in this chapter I wish to use Mr. Skeeter's history as a starting point for exploring the nature of American Indian revitalization movements as they diffuse and are brought into dialogue with preexisting cultural frameworks. Classic ethnological problems relating to the nature of American Indian cosmologies as well as collateral topics, such as realistic theories of diffusion and American Indian understandings of intellectual property, are all productively raised through a study of Yuchi adoption and incorporation of the peyote religion. Based on its history of development among western groups, particularly on the Plains and in the Great Basin, peyotism is widely recognized and well documented as a revitalization movement. At what points in its ongoing spread does it cease to be recognizable as such and become a distinctly different phenomenon? If such a transformation is possible, then what social processes account for the integration of peyotists from different backgrounds into a larger interactional world signified by the denominations of the Native American Church and the remarkably intertribal character of its religious practice? Such considerations prompt a reassessment of the revitalization movement paradigm along lines that emphasize the complex local nature of those revitalization movements that break free of their initial contexts and become successively recontextualized in new cultural settings.

The Peyote Religion

Because of its vitality and wide geographic spread, the peyote religion (and its associated organizational bodies constituting various branches of the Native American Church) is arguably the best-documented and most intensively studied North American Indian religious tradition. [2] Along with the Ghost Dance and the teachings promulgated by the Iroquois leader Handsome Lake, the peyote religion has served as a core case study for the development of a general theory of cultural revitalization (Aberle 1991:315–342; Swan 1990:13–30; Wallace 1956b, 1956c). Like the Ghost Dance, the peyote religion is an intertribal faith that arose among the native peoples of western North America during the great social stresses that accompanied forced settlement on reservations in the 19th century. Despite this fact and a number of other similarities, peyotism is unlike the Ghost Dance in many of its tenants and in the fact that it has never, as a national institution, experienced a period of decline and obsolescence. [3] Although never universally embraced by the members of any particular American Indian community, the religion has continue to spread and flourish throughout the 20th century and into the 21st. For hundreds of thousands of American Indian people today, the Native American Church provides a rich system of spiritual purpose, a comprehensive outlet for aesthetic and creative energies, and a focus for both distinctly tribal and more generally "Indian" social life (Swan 1999). For practitioners, past and present, the faith offers solutions to personal difficulty and social trauma through ritual, prayer, and communion.

Basic to the peyote religion is the sacramental use and veneration of the peyote cactus (*Lophophora williamsii*). The basic ceremony of the religion is an all-night service combining prayer, singing, the consumption of specially prepared peyote, and the completion of a series of ritual gestures under the direction of an experienced ritual leader often referred to as a "roadman." Peyote services (also called "meetings") are emotionally rewarding, ritually complex, and physically demanding undertakings. They are typically held through the sponsorship of an individual or family seeking prayer and support in the face of a particular difficulty or seeking to acknowledge a positive achievement, such as the birthday of an elder or the graduation of a child. Very active and devoted peyotists might attend services several times a month, even weekly, but most individuals practicing the faith attend services less frequently. Because they occur under different sponsorships, services are ad hoc events taking place at various family "fireplaces." The composition of attendees at meetings will vary considerably, and participants cultivate far-flung friendships that lead to patterns of reciprocity and, sometimes, distant travel. In the absence of single stationary congregations that serve a fixed group of practitioners, the local level of organization within the Native American Church is a "chapter." In Oklahoma, chapters usually correspond with tribal groups, though this need not always be the case. Chapters constitute localized groups of peyotists who actively support one another by providing assistance in the organization of services. Chapters also represent local interests at the state and national level.

Despite the extensive (some native people would say excessive) attention that anthropologists have devoted to the peyote religion, some important questions of a more general sort have gone unexamined. Here I seek to reassess the nature of the Native American Church as a revitalization movement through an examination of the religion among a Woodland Indian people residing in Oklahoma, the region that anthropologist Omer Stewart has identified as "the cradle of Peyotism" (1987:53).

Beyond the fact that Yuchi peyotism has never been the subject of a published account, this case has several features that give it special interest. The Yuchi are customarily thought of as a "southeastern" people, meaning that their aboriginal homeland was in the southeastern Wood-lands region of North America and that, on this basis, their cultural practices have been viewed as conforming to a general regional pattern. From this point of view, the adoption of peyotism by the Yuchi is notable because the members of no other southeastern Indian community have accepted the faith in significant numbers. Various casual observations have been made to explain this later fact, but none does justice to the issues involved. This same fact is significant from the perspective of Yuchi ethnography because their adoption of peyotism is another piece of previously unconsidered evidence revealing the extent to which they are neither a typical southeastern Indian group nor culturally homogenized with their Muscogee (Creek) neighbors. Analysis of the manner in which the Yuchi incorporated the ritual use of the peyote cactus into the fabric of their tribal culture and society broadens the ways in which peyotism in general, and as a revitalization movement in particular, should be understood. In many tribal contexts, the peyote religion has very clearly served as a revitalization movement of the classic sort, but the Yuchi case suggests that this need not always be the case. How, then, can the same religious tradition be a revitalization movement in one community and not one in another, even when the members of these two communities are neighbors and participate together in shared ritual events? The solution to this puzzle is central to understanding peyotism and to better understanding American Indian cultures and cultural revitalization. It is also a central fact explaining the success that the Native American Church has had in its spread across Indian Country. Before introducing and exploring Yuchi peyotism in these contexts, I begin with a brief introduction to the Yuchi community and its ethnographic situation in the 20th century.

Yuchi Culture and Society

The Yuchi are a Native American people who reside today in three settlements south and west of Tulsa, Oklahoma. Largely enrolled as members of the Muscogee (Creek) Nation, the Yuchi are a culturally and linguistically distinct people who live intermixed with neighbors of European, African, and Native American ancestry. As throughout Oklahoma, "Indian Country" in the Yuchi settlement area comprises a patchwork of native-owned land intermixed with holdings now controlled by nonnatives. Prior to Oklahoma statehood, the United States pursued a policy of allotting tribal land to individuals. For this reason, the reservation system, which is familiar to Indian communities elsewhere in the United States, is absent in Oklahoma.

Prior to the era of ethnic cleansing that is better known in U.S. history as "Indian removal" and to native Woodland people as the "Trail of Tears," the Yuchi resided in politically autonomous towns located in the present-day states of Georgia, Alabama, South Carolina, and Tennessee. In the 100-year period prior to removal in 1836, the Yuchi towns participated, to a greater and lesser degree, in a multiethnic confederacy dominated by towns in which Muskogee (a.k.a. Creek) was spoken as a first language. Through this alliance, the Yuchi became entwined with the history and fate of the ethnic amalgamation that has come to be known as the Creek Confederacy (later the Creek Nation and today the Muscogee [Creek] Nation). Prior to about 1700 the Yuchi were most often found in settlements quite distant from those of Muskogee-speaking peoples, and at the period of European contact in the Southeast, the Yuchi homeland was in eastern Tennessee, where they were bounded by Cherokees to the east and Koasati-speaking peoples to the west.

In their earliest known homeland, the Yuchi were in regular contact with neighboring groups that have come to be classified as "northeastern," particularly their longtime allies and friends, the Shawnees. The classificatory cases of the Yuchi and the Shawnees point to the limits of the culture area approach for dealing effectively with groups situated at areal boundaries (Howard 1975). If Yuchi culture is treated (in the fashion of early-20th-century American anthropology) as a configuration of cultural traits, then they stand in an intermediate position between the northeastern Shawnees and the Muskogean-speaking peoples of the Southeast. From a Yuchi point of view, of course, their culture is a distinct and unique whole. This view is supported by the uniqueness of the Yuchi language (an isolate) and by beliefs and practices that are not found among their neighbors. In terms of shared cultural background, the Yuchi illustrate the manner in which the northeastern and southeastern Woodlands are better thought of as two parts of a common cultural region. Throughout the Woodlands, cultures and environments change gradually along north-south and east-west gradients.

In this regional matrix the Yuchi of the historic era shared (and share) many similar patterns with their neighbors. Among these are common modes of music and dance, an economy built around corn horticulture, a social organization focused on autonomous permanent towns led by local chiefs, and a common cultural style expressed in sacred narrative, ritual, and cosmology. Differences in culture are perhaps subtler, but as the considerations below reveal, at times they can be crucial to the flow of historical change.[4]

In contrast to the worries expressed by Mr. Skeeter's grandfather, Yuchi "custom ways," while not unchanged by the experience of the 20th century, are rather robust today. Ceremonial grounds are presently active in all three Yuchi settlements, and the number of Yuchis participating in them continues to rise from a low ebb that occurred around 1965. Within this context, only a minority of Yuchis are active peyotists. While difficult to assess, peyotists probably constitute about 10 percent of the tribe's population. This is comparable to the level of participation occurring in Big Mosquito's lifetime (see Stewart n.d., discussed below). The Methodist Church represents a third sector of religious life among the Yuchi. Two historically Yuchi congregations exist in the community. Although their Yuchi memberships are larger than the number of active peyotists, they have experienced a loss of members as Christians, particularly those living away from Yuchi settlements, have joined an array of congregations in the general population.

The Peyote Religion and the Anthropology of Revitalization

Other authors contributing to this book have surveyed the anthropological literature on revitalization movements in the Pacific (where cargo cults provide the model example) and the Americas (where this role is filled by the Ghost Dance and the transformations of Iroquois society carefully studied by Anthony F. C. Wallace). The Native American Church has been a crucial secondary case study (Aberle 1991; La Barre 1975; Swan 1990; White 2000).

Looking at the anthropology of peyotism more broadly, Daniel Swan (1998:52–53) has observed that three basic explanatory frameworks have been used to understand the emergence and spread of the religion. All three view peyotism as a means of adjustment to social change, with the faith helping ease the difficulties faced by Indian communities coping with the ramifications of the colonial experience. The nativistic view places emphasis on indigenous aspects of peyotism and frames the faith (like the Ghost Dance on the Plains) as a counterresponse to colonialism. In other words, peyotism is taken as a mode of resistance. The acculturational view sees peyotism as a bridge to fuller participation in the dominant political and cultural order. This view tends to emphasize the Christian aspects of the faith and its intertribal organization on the model of Christian denominations. The mediate position is an accommodative view in which peyotism is framed as a syncretic religion positioned midway on a continuum from distinct tribal religions at one end to the complete abandonment of native cultural forms on the other. This view of peyotism is in keeping with the theory of pan-Indianism, which sees the emergence of generically "Indian" cultural forms as a correlate of detribalization and progressive acculturation to the dominant society. Before offering a reassessment of these views, I should note that none of them is particularly appealing to peyotists. Formulated by outsiders, all obviously miss the very special and personal meanings religious life holds for the faithful.

The need for anthropological reassessment of these revitalization theories is not new. The leading scholar of the Native American Church, who was also one of its most sympathetic supporters, was Omer Stewart. In the 1940s he warned (as Swan [1998:52] has cautioned more recently) that these broad interpretive frameworks have been accepted without having been tested against individual cases. Stewart writes: "So satisfactory have appeared the interpretations based on these postulates that they have almost become truisms in ethnology. Although no one has assumed they explain everything, they have been employed almost exclusively, either because data for more detailed analysis was lacking, or it was assumed that the problem seemed adequately solved" (cited in Swan 1998:52).[5] Although both comparative and ethnographic studies of a sophisticated sort have examined the details of peyotism and its history in the Great Basin and Southwest, fewer studies have achieved an equal level of sophistication for the Plains and Woodlands. Thus, it seems appropriate that a reassessment of theorizing about peyotism be launched from the position that Michael Harkin jokingly characterizes in his introduction as the "not in my village" method. Swan's study of Osage peyotism inaugurated this work in a particularly complex and interesting context, and study of peyotism in various Woodland communities should prove illuminating. My contention here is that none of the models explaining peyotism on the basis of social deprivation, revitalization, or acculturation fits the Yuchi case well.

All Roads Are Good: You Don't Want to Mix Nothing
Two rather different perspectives on culture and religion crystallized in Indian Country during the 20th century. In thinking about these two perspectives, I associate each with a catchphrase that encapsulates its

essence. In my interactions with Native American people today, I have found that both views exist in stronger and weaker forms, sometimes within the same community. The first, but not necessarily older, perspective is the view that native North American cultures are integrated wholes and that an individual can only fully and properly live within one such system at a time. I associate this view especially with the opinions of Northern Paiute elder and former opium addict Corbert Mack. In his biography, he repeatedly discusses the various paths or ways that were available to the Paiute people, particularly the Ghost Dance, the peyote religion, old-time Paiute doctoring and witchcraft, opium addiction, and alcoholism. What is most interesting about Mr. Mack's account is his characterization of the varied but exclusive life paths available to Paiute people. These options conflate choices that outsiders and many Paiutes would regard as social ills with varieties of "traditional" religion. Setting this issue aside, the point to be made here is that he subscribes to a widespread view that individuals have a choice as to which way to follow but that one choice precludes the others. He repeatedly comments that illness, madness, and death come to those who try to "mix" these alternatives (Hittman 1996: ch. 7).[6]

The alternative view is ecumenical. I associate it with the phrase "all roads are good," spoken most often by Native American intellectuals when characterizing the diversity of American Indian cultures and religious traditions. In this view, all of the traditional teachings and beliefs of Indian Country share the same epistemological status. All are rooted in the experiences of worthy elders and ancestors. All derive ultimately from the power of the Creator and her or his ultimate concern for the fate and well-being of native people. Although this view is most often expressed in generalizing and public discourses (consider *All Roads Are Good*, the inaugural exhibition of the National Museum of the American Indian), it also represents a common response in traditional, "grassroots" American Indian communities.

In Oklahoma, most Yuchi people live in Tulsa and Creek counties. The county directly to the north of these is Osage County. Modern Osage County corresponds to the political boundaries of the Osage Nation and is the home to the Osage people and their collective community life. Comparison of Yuchi and Osage peyotism clarifies the distinction I am making here.

The history of Osage peyotism has been well documented and analyzed by Swan (1990, 1998), who has worked closely with Osage people, particularly peyotists, continuously since 1984. In understanding the history of Osage peyotism, Swan has sought to balance attentiveness to issues of culture change, as represented by revitalization theory, with an understanding of the local and unique political, economic, and social changes that correlate with such revitalization. He has also focused attention on the role of community leaders in actively organizing and directing social change. Osage conversion to peyotism happened during a very short time window (1898–1906), was relatively complete among the Osage as a whole, and, in their case, displaced the older Osage tribal religion, which was already becoming moribund at this time. The tribal religion, because it was founded on cultural practices that had become infeasible to maintain, particularly buffalo hunting and intertribal warfare, had become impossible to sustain. Continued practice of the tribal religion was further complicated and compromised (in this colonial historic context) because linkages existed among social hierarchy, tribal demography, economic change, and the possession and transmission of complex bodies of esoteric ritual knowledge. During the 19th century, Osage society, economy, and demography had changed in ways that meant that this religion, which had focused on complex ceremonies organized around sacred bundles, could not be perpetuated as an integrated cultural system and was no longer meeting the needs of Osage communities and individuals.

The Osage case, as analyzed by Swan, has already contributed in important ways to a reexamination of revitalization theory in connection with political-economic issues and a refined consideration of individual, local, and population-wide levels of analysis. My purpose in reviewing this case is to illustrate the alternative responses I introduce at the beginning of this section. The Osages adopted peyotism and "put away" their old religion. The last generation of Osage leaders knowledgeable in its forms and meanings made a conscious choice to end its practice. Becoming active peyotists in the "Big Moon" tradition, they came to view the religion of their ancestors as incompatible with their new faith, while they maintained a positive attachment to the memory of their ancestors and a respect for their spirituality in a general sense. One of the many processes this view produced was the sale of many Osage ceremonial objects to museums. Today, older Osages urge their tribe's people to avoid contact with these objects because they are dangerous and incompatible with modern Osage life.

A short distance to the south, the Yuchi response to peyotism during this era was quite different. As Mr. Skeeter's narrative reveals, they adopted the "all roads are good" perspective, incorporating the Native American Church into community life in an additive manner. Peyotism has never engaged the participation of the whole of the Yuchi community, but it has never been perceived as something to displace the practice of the Yuchi ceremonial ground religion. This differential experience is made clear in a more detailed examination of Yuchi peyotism, one that builds on Mr. Skeeter's account of the process.

The History of Yuchi Peyotism

Although no published sources document this topic, the fate and future of the Native American Church among southeastern Indian communities were considered by an earlier generation of scholars, most fully by Stewart (1908–91). He was an anthropologist whose name remains well known and honored among peyotists throughout the West (for his biography, see Howell 1998). Stewart's long involvement with members of the church led to decades of legal activism on behalf of peyotists and culminated in an important book that recounts the history of the religion (see 1987). Considering the peyote religion throughout native North America, Stewart's history documents the main themes and patterns in the development of the religion and its formalization within the organization of the Native American Church.

Stewart's professional papers at the University of Colorado reveal that some of the less charted streams of this history had also been his concern. A draft chapter that was edited out of the published book but which has been preserved in Stewart's manuscripts is an account, with associated documents, of peyotism among the Yuchi (see n.d.). While less rich in context and data than one might wish, the manuscript is especially useful when studied in consultation with Yuchi people.

Although his broader goal was to trace the general history of the diffusion and adoption of the peyote religion, Stewart was struck by the manner in which the Yuchi in particular represented a countervailing case running against conventional wisdom about southeastern Indians. Opening his never published chapter, he comments: "To start this chapter to review what is known of Peyotism among the Five Civilized Tribes with the name Yuchi (also known as Euchee and Uchee) may appear strange to historians of Oklahoma Indians inasmuch as the Yuchi are a minority separate language group included as part of the Creek Nation. Focusing on Peyotism of the Five Civilized Tribes, the Yuchi have been outstanding for at least fifty years. Were it not for the Yuchi the Five Civilized Tribes could be passed over with the comment that a very few of their individual members became Peyotists" (n.d.:1).

Stewart begins his review of Yuchi peyotism with an analysis of a series of government documents from 1919. In response to a government questionnaire aimed at documenting the spread of peyotism, agents among the Five Civilized Tribes reported that the religion had not been adopted among them with the exception of about 10 percent of the Yuchi. Follow-up investigation by the Bureau of Indian Affairs produced a census indicating the names and addresses of the 49 known Yuchi peyotists. Stewart notes that 39 of these clustered under nine family names. Stewart interprets this in light of the common pattern he had observed of peyotism being adopted at the family level. My own familiarity with Yuchi family histories suggests that these individuals were densely linked by family ties but also by patterns of marriage and of deep involvement with the most traditional sectors of Yuchi community life. Many were active leaders or participants in the Yuchi ceremonial grounds. Among those enumerated in this group is Albert Big Mosquito, the grandfather at the center of Mr. Skeeter's narrative.

When Frank Speck visited the Yuchi for the final time in 1909, they had not yet received the peyote religion. On this subject, Speck writes (reflecting the confusion among outsiders at the time between mescal bean ceremonialism and peyotism): "There is, in fact, some reason to believe that the mescal worship may spread among the Yuchi if it continues eastward, as it has already gained a foothold among the conservative Pawnees and Osages" (1909a:130). As Mr. Skeeter and the documents obtained by Stewart indicate, the Yuchi first came into contact with the religion between 1910 and 1918, probably in 1915–16. When anthropologist Günter Wagner visited the Yuchi in 1928–29 to pursue linguistic research, peyotism was an established part of community life. Wagner even lived briefly with a leading peyotist, Larry Brown, one of the Yuchi identified in the 1919 list. Unfortunately, Wagner's ethnographic notes related to this work were lost in Europe during World War II and were never published in detail, although bits and pieces of Yuchi information appear in the published version of his dissertation (1932), a general overview of the development and spread of peyotism.

The person most closely associated with the early period of the peyote religion among the Yuchi is John James. Reporting Mr. James's views on the significance of peyote, Wagner published the following account.

This is a translation based on the published version, given in German: "Peyote is good for everything. It heals the brain, ears, joints, toothache, and also moral diseases. It makes us a good human being. It causes us to love everyone. It makes us tolerant. There was a medicine man (Peyote) who was without fault. God had granted him power. He could heal a child without causing it pain. He speaks to our hearts. He tells us about God. Peyote points the way to God and Christ. Peyote knows everything. Peyote is holy. Peyote can talk about everything in the Bible, but the Bible cannot speak about Peyote. Peyote will tell you who you are. Because of that, Peyote is good. Peyote demands faith. Peyote will help you, like Christ. Peyote is the best physician. Peyote makes us work and plant corn. Peyote is perfect and pure, the devil has no power over it" (Wagner 1932:68).[7] It is interesting that Mr. James is identified by Wagner as a Shawnee Indian living in Kellyville, Oklahoma. Kellyville is a municipality in Creek County at the center of the Yuchi settlement area. Yuchi people in this area are considered to be members of the Pole-cat town, and most are affiliated with the Polecat ceremonial ground, which is located in this district. Mr. James appears at the top of the 1919 government list of Yuchi peyotists. Yuchi people, together with later fieldworkers, have likewise considered him to be a Yuchi. Stewart's manuscript includes a report, based on an uncited Oklahoma Historical Society document, that Dawes Fife (probably a Creek fieldworker for the "Indian and Pioneer" oral history project spearheaded by historian Grant Foreman) contacted John James, an "elderly Shawnee and Euchee Indian, living 12 miles northwest of Sapulpa . . . who belongs to the Native American Church" (n.d.:5). Mr. James was not unique in being of both Shawnee and Yuchi heritage. Many Yuchi people possess Shawnee ancestry, while numerous Shawnee likewise acknowledge Yuchi ancestors. This is a reflex of a long history of alliance and friendship maintained between the two groups, a pattern that goes back to the Ohio Valley before European contact.

One topic that has preoccupied previous students of peyotism in Oklahoma is the question of which groups or individuals were responsible for introducing the faith into particular communities. Though probably somewhat spurious because adoption of peyotism most often takes place at an individual or family level, this focus is a natural confluence of anthropological interest in diffusion and local Indian interests in history and in the provenance of particular cultural practices and teachings. From an Eastern Delaware man, Mr. James Webber, anthropologist

Vincenzo Petrullo learned that Mr. James (who was also known as Jimmie Johns) introduced peyotism to the Loyal Shawnees, living near the town of White Oak, sometime between 1922 and 1929. According to what Weber learned from the Loyal Shawnees, the Yuchi had learned about peyote from the Cheyennes (Petrullo 1934:71–72). This is a different source than the Sac and Fox, as identified by Mr. Skeeter.

In a May 1937 oral history interview conducted by Mr. Rufus George (a Yuchi fieldworker for the Indian and Pioneer history project), another Yuchi peyotist, Mr. Jacob Rolland, discussed the significance of the Native American Church. Along with an account of the benefits of peyote and the nature of the ceremony, he reported: "The Indians here in the Creek Nation, and many other Indians in other nations, have what is known as a Peyote religious worship. It is called the Union Native American Church. This religious worship was handed down to the Euchees here by the Caddo Indians" (Works Progress Administration 1937). Like Albert Big Mosquito and John James, Mr. Rolland appears on the 1919 census. The fieldworker, Mr. George, also belongs to a family represented in the 1919 list.

Attributed sources for Yuchi peyotism are thus quite diverse—Absentee Shawnees, Sac and Fox, Caddos, Cheyennes. The role that Yuchi people have played in spreading the faith to other groups is also complex. Mr. James has already been identified as a source bringing it to the Loyal Shawnees. This history is supported by Yuchi and Shawnee people I have consulted with in recent years. Of further interest in this regard is a report that Stewart obtained from David Aberle, an anthropologist who worked among the Navajo for many years. Aberle wrote to Stewart from the Navajo Reservation in August 1949 indicating that John James, "a Yuchi from Oklahoma," had been running meetings at Sawmill, Arizona. Later Aberle attended a meeting that he ran for the Navajo in August 1951, the same year in which Mr. James died. Here we see a Yuchi leader in the Native American Church active in taking the faith to the Southwest (Stewart n.d.:5; see also Aberle 1991:172, 216).

This role was continued in the 1960s and 1970s by Mr. Walter Thompson and Mr. George Watashe. Mr. Thompson was a man of African American heritage who grew up among the Otos and who later lived among the Yuchi, learning to speak Yuchi and participating fully in Yuchi community life. Among his close friends was Watashe, a Yuchi ceremonial ground leader and an officer in the Native American Church of Oklahoma. Stewart himself met these men during peyote meetings in western Oklahoma and among the Northern Cheyennes. From various friends active in the church, Stewart learned in the 1970s what I was later told in the 1990s. Both men were active in leading peyote meetings throughout the West and in teaching it to those seeking to adopt it. A Cheyenne peyotist who married into the Navajo community at Sawmill told Stewart in 1972 that "Walter Thompson was very popular with the Navajo. They invited him often and when he was roadman, the meeting was crowded. Often he came with George Watashe, and they drummed for one another, his singing was greatly admired" (n.d.:7). Stewart learned from Mr. Watashe that he had also conducted meetings for the Jicarilla Apaches, Southern Utes at Ignacio, and Ute Mountain Utes at Tawoac. I never had the opportunity to meet either man, but Watashe's wife and daughters have become close friends. They report that he was active in conducting services throughout both western Oklahoma and among the Paiutes, in addition to those groups mentioned by Stewart. His career as a cross-country truck driver facilitated these contacts throughout the West.

This history of involvement in the spread of peyotism suggests the significance that the faith has had for those Yuchi people who have embraced it. Yuchi have consistently played a role in the faith beyond their local communities. They have regularly served as officers in the Native American Church of Oklahoma, attended and led services beyond their home communities, and participated in the church at a national level.

This involvement, nonetheless, retained a Yuchi character. I have already noted that, when they adopted the faith around 1915, it was incorporated as an ancillary activity supplementing communal ceremonialism. As Mr. Skeeter noted, the first generation of peyotists saw the Native American Church as a worthy thing, a form of Indian religiosity that might endure, even if the tribal religion someday waned. Though grounded in worry about cultural loss, this response was different from the Osage one. The Yuchi did not wish to replace their tribal ceremonials and, unlike the Osages, did not feel compelled by changing economic and demographic circumstances to do so. What is more, they instituted an informal rule that peyote meetings should not be held during the summer ceremonial season when they would conflict with community-wide ritual obligations. This ruling, which continues to be acknowledged by most Yuchi peyotists today, served to maintain harmony among those traditional people who incorporated the faith into their lives and those who did not. It also maintained the strength of the ceremonial ground religion while admitting the new faith into the seasonal round of community life.

Peyotism and the Cosmology of Woodland Religions

The religious and cultural milieu within which peyotism originally developed was substantively different from contexts into which it was later adopted as an established set of practices. The Yuchi provide a case in point. The 19th century in western North America was a time of great religious ferment. New religions found particularly fertile ground in part because the native cultures, particularly the cosmological views, of the peoples of the Basin and High Plains were open to such possibilities. Fundamental in this region was (and is) a conception of power that is located in particular individuals, often charismatic men. Suitable individuals could obtain power (viewed here broadly), in part at least, through direct contact with the spiritual powers of the world—animals, spirit beings, and the broader creative force(s) controlling the world. The vision quest is the most well known manifestation of this worldview in action (Benedict 1922). When successful, such quests provided individuals with instrumental power (often glossed as "medicine"), and, whether taking the form of songs, charms, personal bundles, or ritual techniques, such power was a form of knowledge of a very esoteric kind. While conforming to general cultural outlines, it was rather unique at an individual level, having been communicated directly from spiritual being to human recipient.

Eastern Woodland societies, particularly those of the Southeast, as Raymond Fogelson (1977) has noted in discussing Cherokees, operate with a rather different cosmology of power. Although it would be in error to see southeastern Woodland cultures as unchanged by the influence of individuals, they fit into the social and cultural order very differently than in the West. Power in the Southeast is embodied in knowledge, particularly of the esoteric but codified sort that is transmitted between generations of ritual specialists. Although found in a reduced form among some Northeast Woodland peoples, the vision quest as practiced in the West is unknown in the Southeast. Likewise, although willing in extreme cases to acknowledge the potential significance of dreams and of prophecy, southeastern people, in my view, are rather skeptical of such power.[8] The power to heal, the power to cause harm, and the power to command love or loyalty—these are capacities that reside within knowledge that is obtained by individuals through study or apprenticeship with those already in possession of such knowledge, usually elders. Rather than fasting alone on a remote butte hoping for a unique transcendental moment, the person seeking power in the Southeast spends years learning medical botany, complex spoken formula and songs, and particular techniques for assessing, managing, and channeling the forces of the world. Among the Yuchi, this process included what are known in English as "doctors' schools," in which (usually) men began their formal training under the direction of one or more recognized practitioners. This process included fasting for purification but focused specifically on memorizing large bodies of formulaic knowledge.

I contrast these two approaches to spiritual power because they seem to me to relate to the ways the Native American Church has succeeded, failed, or changed as it diffused eastward from its origins in western Oklahoma. As Stewart (n.d.:1) has noted, the Yuchi are unique among southeastern groups in adopting peyotism in significant numbers. Among the Cherokees and Choctaws, for instance, there are only a handful of peyotists among tens of thousands of tribal members. As Wagner (1932:81–82) has observed, the longtime establishment of organized Christianity in these communities certainly played a role. In its history, well-established Protestant communities in which tribal religions had been lost or abandoned have not often taken up peyotism.

In the case of the Yuchi, demographics are also a factor. The Yuchi are a small tribal group, and they were (and are) located at the northwest margins of the Muscogee (Creek) Nation. In this location they were in direct contact with the Sac and Fox and in broader contact with a host of other small prairie and northeastern groups. Added to this are their long-standing ties to the Shawnees, who played a central role in the diffusion of peyotism in central Oklahoma. The other southeastern groups (Choctaw, Chickasaw, Creek, Cherokee, Seminole) were large enough to sustain relatively closed societies, whereas the Yuchi participated (and continue to participate) in a different social network, one more tied to other small groups like the Shawnees, Delawares, and Sac and Fox. It should be noted, too, that those Woodland groups with which the Yuchi have sustained the most contact, particularly the Shawnees and Sac and Fox, share their orientation to peyotism as an additive practice that does not (and should not) conflict with the practice of tribal ritual. James Howard notes: "The Peyote religion has adherents in all three Shawnee bands and does not seem to militate against traditional ceremonialism in any way. The leaders at all three ceremonial dance grounds, in fact, are also Peyotists and attend Peyote meetings (ceremonies) regularly during the fall, winter, and early spring when the traditional Shawnee ceremonial cycle is dormant" (1981:301).

Reflecting again on cosmology, it is hard to justify seeing the Yuchi adoption of peyotism as a revitalization movement. In the era before they took up peyotism, they rejected other Plains religious movements to which they were exposed, most notably the Ghost Dance. In my view, these religions tended to be grounded in ecstatic experience and personal revelation, sources of power foreign to Yuchi culture. Because they were new, they also reflected a view of religion out of step with Yuchi beliefs, in which knowledge, truth, and ritual were provided to the tribe at Creation. Existing since the beginning, religious truths and ritual forms are to be conserved and passed on through time—but not invented. Peyotism succeeded on this point because it does not command a radical alteration of the existing views of its adherents. It does not promise wholesale transformation of the world or of the social order. Open to those with both "all roads are good" and "no mixing" perspectives, some peyotists are Christians and some are not. Some also practice tribal religions, whereas others either choose not to do so or belong to communities where this is no longer an option. Among the Yuchi at least, peyotism can transform individuals in different ways, but it does not seek to transform society as a whole or alter the fundamental fabric of the world. The ways in which its public rituals unfold—the consumption of a plant medicine, spoken prayer to the Creator, and the singing of songs of thanksgiving and petition—were already basic features of Yuchi religious life. For this reason, they were acceptable adjuncts to existing religious practice.

When confronted with peyotism, Yuchi elders chose to fit it into an existing cultural and social framework. This framework did not change appreciably, and peyotism has provided what they had envisioned—an additional means of praying to and thanking the Creator, one that benefits those individuals for whom it is a meaningful choice. In coming to this view of Yuchi peyotism, I am neither categorically denying its potential as a revitalization movement nor questioning the broad usefulness of the general revitalization model. I do think that consideration of the case of peyotism and its spread into new social and cultural contexts can open up a more nuanced view of such movements. What Wallace's model identifies as the (relatively) steady state of cultural equilibrium that follows a successful revitalization may be hard to differentiate from

the case of a relatively stable, functioning society that has adopted someone else's revitalization movement without having undergone a process
of revitalization itself (cf. Wallace 1956c:275). Only closer consideration
of particular cases will reveal the facts of the matter.

I think that it is reasonable to interpret the emergence of peyotism
as a revitalization movement in some communities, particularly those
groups on the Plains, that experienced extensive and measurable deprivation coupled with rather radical cultural and socioeconomic change
during the mid–19th century. If, in other contexts, peyotism can be
adopted without this backdrop, then a broader question is opened up. If
Yuchi ceremonial life, during the early 20th century, had collapsed, was
on the verge of disappearing, or was out of step with the economic and
social realities of lived experience, then we can easily imagine peyotism
being adopted and reconfiguring spiritual life among the Yuchi, as it
did among the Kiowas, Osages, and other Plains groups. The actual
history of its adoption suggests that this process, for the Yuchi, was
a more common kind of cross-cultural transmission, one that Boasian
anthropologists have described as diffusion and contemporary theorists
are exploring from new angles as processes of "cultural flow" (see, e.g.,
Appadurai 1991). The movement of cultural materials—beliefs, behaviors, objects—is not in itself remarkable. What is of interest is how
a specialized package of cultural materials, one group's revitalization
movement—spawned by individual innovators operating in a complex,
particular cultural context—can become flexible enough to serve new
ends in new circumstances. Although it is less satisfying at the level
of generalizing social theory, such a conclusion is in keeping with the
Americanist tendency toward theoretical modesty grounded in an appreciation of the complexities of history and ethnography located in
actual places and times.

I am fortunate to have been invited to join Yuchi friends in prayer
in many settings. Participation, as a non-Indian guest, in Yuchi peyote
meetings suggests to me something of what Mr. Big Mosquito and his
generation thought and felt when they first experienced peyotism. It is
a flexible faith that centers not on dogma but on individual piety and
self-betterment while providing the support and encouragement of a
community of worshipers. Peyote meetings are aesthetically remarkable,
providing a picture of an ideal social order (through the ritual movement
of people who care for one another) and images of individual and collective beauty. These aspects, together with the room that individuals

have to craft their own religious identities within a collective effort, underlie the appeal that the faith has for Yuchi and, I think, for most other peyotists. Such an interpretation does not negate the revitalizing effect that the religion had in the communities of its origin or discount the real ways in which it helps individuals of all backgrounds to revitalize their own individual lives. The success that the Native American Church has had in spreading can be understood as a by-product of the flexibility that became a design principle woven into the fabric of the faith at the time of its origin. This flexibility has enabled it to be a source of revitalization at a community and individual level in certain settings and, at the same time, to meet other needs in other lives.

Notes

Acknowledgments. Not all Yuchi people embrace peyotism, but Yuchi of all backgrounds have made considerable efforts to help me understand what is important about the history and culture of their community. I am grateful to all my Yuchi friends for this immense courtesy. In connection with this chapter, I am especially appreciative of the families of Mr. Jimmie Skeeter and Mr. George Watashe, especially Mrs. Mary Watashe, who has included me in celebrations and peyote services at her and her late husband's home. Joseph Rice (Sac and Fox), Herman Henderson (Shawnee), and many other peyotists from central and eastern Oklahoma have been generous in sharing their thoughts and experiences with me. Study among the Yuchi during 1995–96 was supported by the Wenner-Gren Foundation for Anthropological Research. Gilcrease Museum and the University of Oklahoma have facilitated my research in numerous ways. Omer C. Stewart's advocacy of the rights of peyotists is a model of anthropological responsibility to one's friends and teachers. His manuscript on Yuchi peyotism was crucial to my effort here. I hope he would appreciate the use to which I put it. I am grateful to Daniel C. Swan for providing access to Stewart's manuscript, for introducing me to the literature on peyotism, for sharing his field experiences among peyotists, and for encouraging my own work. I accept sole responsibility for errors of fact or interpretation.

1. In transcribing Mr. Skeeter's account I have used standard English spellings. Editorial insertions for clarification appear inside brackets. Though they are not my focus here, I have elsewhere discussed aspects of Yuchi oral tradition in linguistic anthropological terms (see Jackson 1996, 1997, 2003; Jackson and Linn 2000).

In speaking of breakfast, Mr. Skeeter was describing the common practice of inviting supporters who have come to the site of a peyote meeting to offer support, but who have not participated in the meeting throughout the night, to come inside for the final ritual acts that take place inside the service in the morning. Among the most important of these is the consumption of a ritual breakfast involving special foods and blessings. This service, like most held in Oklahoma, took place inside of a canvas tipi. Big Mosquito had stayed awake all night outside the tipi listening to what took place inside. In this manner, he could evaluate the form and meaning of the new faith.

When Mr. Skeeter's grandfather spoke to the tribal people, this was also another basic feature of the peyote meeting. At its conclusion, the "roadman" gives all who wish to do so the opportunity to speak to the group about their feelings and concerns. Typically, participants will express thanks to those involved and testify to the spiritual success of the gathering. Big Mosquito's comments would have been in accord with such a moment.

Note, in addition to his active involvement in the Yuchi ceremonial grounds, Mr. Skeeter was an active peyotist who participated in the organizational activities of the Native American Church, having at one time served as the president of the Yuchi chapter. In his role as a public orator, Mr. Skeeter was frequently called on to speak at public gatherings, not only on the ceremonial square grounds but also at community events and secular political meetings. Although he showed little hesitation about talking on a range of subjects with me, he consistently discouraged me from audio taping our conversations. His reasons for readily agreeing to record this story are uncertain to me.

2. Evidence of the size of the peyote literature is available in a recent selected bibliography annotated and published by Phillip White (2000). It contains close to five hundred sources, mostly drawn from anthropology.

3. The faith has declined in particular communities but continues to grow and expand in North America. Much of this growth is attributable to continued adoption among Navajos.

4. The basic anthropological sources for the Yuchi include Frank Speck's (1909a) ethnography, the linguistic studies of Günter Wagner (1931), ethnographic and linguistic work by W. L. Ballard (1978), and recent studies by Pamela Wallace (1998, 2002), Mary Linn (2001), and myself (Jackson 1996, 1997, 2000a, 2000b, 2003; Jackson and Linn 2000).

5. This quotation appears in Daniel Swan's study of Osage peyotism, where it is used to illustrate the same point I am making here. My own comparative knowledge of peyotism beyond the Yuchi case is quite limited, and I owe much to Swan for helpful conversations and the detailed information he has provided relative to this topic.

6. Michael Hittman is to be commended for his work in compiling Corbert Mack's biography; it is an outstanding contribution to the American Indian life history literature.

7. I wish to thank Ursula W. Ekren and Gertrud Schmidt, volunteers at

the Gilcrease Museum, who during 1996 translated Wagner's monograph into English for my use and that of my colleague, Daniel Swan. Their translation of this passage matches in essence that which Stewart independently produced and incorporated into his unpublished manuscript (see n.d.:3a).

8. My views of this matter are in contrast with those of Joel Martin (1991 [see also ch. 2]), whose analyses of southeastern religion and cosmology (relatively) emphasize such phenomena and downplay the power of codified cannons of traditional ritual knowledge. My own view is grounded in my fieldwork among southeastern ritualists and 20th-century ethnography, whereas Martin has focused on the case of religious nativism among the Creeks in the late 18th and early 19th century.

9. NEW LIFE FOR WHOM?

The Scope of the Trope in Marshall Islands Kūrijmōj

Laurence Marshall Carucci

I have written extensively about Kūrijmōj, a four-month celebration performed each year by the people of Ujelang and Enewetak Atolls in the Republic of the Marshall Islands (see Carucci 1980, 1993, 1997b). This lengthy cycle of feasting and reverie draws on components of local cosmology and elements from a complex colonial past, and I have argued that Kūrijmōj is an extremely productive cultural domain that Marshall Islanders use to shape and project a vital sense of identity at several different levels. I have noted that, while the celebration is a classical cyclical rite of renewal and regeneration, its meanings are many layered, both semantico-referentially and pragmatically. In the broadest sense, the celebration can be seen as a type of revitalization movement in Anthony F. C. Wallace's terms because it represents a "deliberate, conscious, organized effort by members of a society to create a more satisfying culture" (1956c:279). Of course, although these terms are, in some senses, appropriate descriptions of what occurs during Kūrijmōj, this is not how local people talk about the event. In other ways Kūrijmōj is not very much like the classical revitalization movements Wallace describes. In particular, it is a yearly renewal celebration co-organized, in large part, as a standardized communal event. Its form is dynamic, changing gradually through time, but it is certainly not an event inspired or headed by a single charismatic leader, much less by one who receives insights through hallucinatory visions. Nevertheless, Kūrijmōj is a "special kind of culture change phenomen[on]" and is certainly one that has arisen under colonizing circumstances that, in Wallace's matrix constancy, organismic model, have produced "internally distorted" conditions (1956c:265, 269).[1] Wallace, of course, recognizes that grand classificatory schemas, like revitalization, present taxonomic problems in terms of how well or poorly the observed social phenomena "fit" the explanatory templates. Indeed, the fact that Wallace's (1956c:267) analytic subtypes are not mutually exclusive creates a dilemma for him. Nevertheless, mere classification—Handsome Lake as revitalization personified—equated with explanatory potency in 1956. The shift to a semiotic or hermeneutic approach has led to a substantial rethinking of this equation. Not only has the explanatory potency of various classifications come under attack, but the way in which the analytic categories are intimately intertwined with discourses of the colonizers has become far more apparent.

The issue of "whose meaning," therefore, forms the central topic of this chapter. And the celebration that Enewetak people call Kūrijmōj provides an adequate example. Though I give a brief overview of the celebration, my intent is not to reanalyze the complex ritual as a whole. Instead, I wish to explore the range of interpretative frames that local people use to describe what Kūrijmōj means to them, as well as to consider the degree to which these interpretations allow us to consider the celebration as a type of "revitalization," "renewal," or "regeneration" and to what degree local people's perspectives on the festivities point in other directions. In this quest, I express my debt to Lamont Lindstrom (1993), who has explored the cargo cult motif in New Guinea, the Solomon Islands, and Vanuatu in an attempt to discover the contextual frames of its construction. Although the revitalization motif has never had the same populist appeal as its subgenre, "cargo cult," at the same time, I believe that our intellectual discussions construct the category through a reliance on the comparative method. We then impute meaning to local practices out of all proportion to the significances that those pursuits have to local people by abstracting meanings from their relevant use contexts. These essentialized, absolute meanings take on a life of their own. Through a sleight-of-hand re-presentation—a shift from token to type, from performative process to inscribed representation—once pragmatically and semantico-referentially pregnant polysemic processes are reduced to "examples of": representations recontoured to lend central emphasis to the "distinctive features" of revitalization at the cost of sacrificing the multiplicity of representative and performative values they may have at the moments of their initial enactment. The meanings they convey as instances of revitalization are neither the same as nor often particularly consonant with those performative processes. This, in any case, is true of Marshall Islands Kūrijmōj.

An Outline of Kūrijmōj
Historical Background

Kūrijmōj forms the core event of the ritual cycle on Enewetak Atoll. In its elaborated form, the celebration was developed during the 30 years that Enewetak people spent in exile on Ujelang Atoll while the United States conducted nuclear tests and other military exercises on Enewetak following World War II. There is little doubt that the long history of colonial encounters on Enewetak provides many of the raw materials out of which Kūrijmōj is fashioned, though these materials are fully reshaped to serve local contours of empowerment (Carucci 1997a). Nuclear detonations compete with 19th-century missionary vessels, Spanish designated jails, and Japanese self-defense in this celebration of local design. None of the four colonial tidal waves that swept over these atolls beginning in 1529 and intensifying in the 19th century—first Spanish, then German, Japanese, and American—goes unrepresented.

Although the Spanish were the first Europeans to sail through the area, they traveled through the western Pacific to get to valuable treasures that lay beyond. Concomitantly, ritual materials in Kūrijmōj hewn from Spanish ores are relatively few. In 1857 American Congregationalist missionaries representing the American Board of Commissioners for Foreign Missions first entered the Marshall Islands. After some lean years, several chiefs finally welcomed the mission and its influence spread, though it was not until the late 1920s that a Kosraean-trained mission teacher finally reached distant Enewetak. Along with the missionaries came Christmas, which some Enewetak residents recall from the 1930s as a time when people sang translated seasonal hymns, shared food, and contributed to a church offering. It was not until their post–World War II exile on Ujelang that local people would envision Kūrijmōj, an elaborated local response to Christmas.

Prior to the mission's arrival on Enewetak, however, Germany gained control of the Marshall Islands in 1885, consolidated the copra trade under a state business authority, and transformed the chieftainship into a largely static hierarchical regime to support copra production (see Carucci 1997a:202–203; Hezel 1983: ch. 8). Within 30 years, however, Germany found itself too embroiled in World War I to maintain its colonial interests. Japan seized control of the region and began to impose its own imperial designs. This was a much more comprehensive colonial plan that included Marshall Islanders as low-class citizens of the Japanese Empire, that transported many Japanese to island outposts as residents, and that incorporated copra and fishing enterprises as a much more broadly based social and economic plan for the area (Peattie 1988). Ultimately, of course, Japan included its South Seas empire in a much larger expansionist vision that led to the Pacific War, and through its involvement in that event, Enewetak became ever more deeply implicated in the course of international affairs (Poyer et al. 2001).

Indeed, by the early 1940s Japan had begun to fashion Enewetak into a military facility to support several more thoroughly developed bases in the Marshall Islands. Following the battle for Midway and the Gilberts, however, the United States developed an island-hopping strategy that would bypass, isolate, and then contain most Japanese military facilities in the Marshall Islands. Only Kwajalein and Enewetak would be core battlegrounds in the Marshall Islands, and Enewetak's location as a far western outlier in the Marshall Islands would transform it into an ideal reconnaissance and trans-shipment base for Allied forces. Enewetak people were displaced onto small islets in the northern quadrant of the atoll after the battle, and they remained there after the war as Enewetak became a support facility for the first atomic tests on Bikini Atoll. Late in 1947, Enewetak people were informed that they would have to move to Ujelang Atoll, a move that would allow the United States to expand the nuclear tests to Enewetak. They remained on this tiny atoll for 33 years under marginal subsistence conditions, suffering in behalf of humanity so that the United States could (as they were told), through the nuclear testing program, secure peace and well-being for all of humankind.

In local people's somewhat less clouded imagination, the war did not end in 1945; rather, it simply shifted its focus to new battlegrounds (Carucci 1989). Enewetak was a critical practice grounds for new battlefields, from Korea to Cuba, from Vietnam to the showdown with Gadhafi. As Ujelang people faced repeated famine and dealt with the fear that their homeland had been vaporized by nuclear tests, they turned the superhuman potency of these forces to positive ends in the design of Kūrijmōj. By 1976 Ujelang residents had negotiated the return of their homeland, and in 1980 they were able to move back to that land. But they returned to a "new Enewetak," one barely recognizable as the place they had left behind. As they have adapted to this old/new land they have dealt with numerous contradictions and with new forms of suffering. These experiences have contributed to shifting contours of the celebration they call Kūrijmōj, contours that represent new articulations with the kaleidoscopic experiences through which we have since lived.

Ritual Renewal

In its performative contours, Kūrijmōj is a four-month celebration that starts in mid-September or early October with the community dividing into *jepta* (songfest groups) and beginning evening practices to develop and memorize a repertoire of locally composed songs and locally choreographed dances. After about a month of practice, the jepta begin to compete with one another, holding *kamolu* (songfest competitions) where one group brings food, speeches, and increasingly fine-tuned chorale performances to challenge another songfest group in small symbolic battles that are "won" by the group that most thoroughly overwhelms its opposite competitor. Soon after the beginning of kamolu, other competitions begin to subvert the success of the songfest competitions: *karate* and *kalabūūj* (though only karate continues as an active pursuit in recent years on Enewetak). These are gender-differentiated "games" in which the sexual focus of the interjepta battles is foregrounded. Through the inversion of everyday demeanor, karate (from the Japanese mode of self-defense) allows women to travel into the men's domain (bushlands) and steal the uncooked seafoods that men from an opposite jepta have collected in preparation for a kamolu. A lot of ribald banter is exchanged as the women feast with the men from a different group. Not uncommonly the banter ends with decisive action, as the cross-gender pairs from the different metaphoric marriage groups end up thoroughly soaked after pulling, shoving, or carrying one another into the sea. Kalabūūj, the opposite men's game, also uses inversion, placing men in a cookhouse in the women's domain, the village space, where they capture women from opposite songfest groups on their return from the bushlands with *pandanus* or coconut fronds to make mats and handicraft as gifts for December 25. Appropriating the fronds, the men promise to fulfill the women's every desire during their extended "incarceration" with the opposite group. (*Kalabūūj* is derived from the Spanish for "jail.") The focus of the banter in the cookhouse "jail" is on gustatory and sexual fulfillment. After three to ten days of indulgent captivity, the women are returned to their own group—but dressed as men.

The kamolu-kalabūūj-karate cycle continues until the "25th day" nears, but on Sabbaths prior to December 25, each songfest group presents its performance in the church and feasts the minister, chiefs, and entire community following the songs. The highlight of the celebrations, however, occurs on the 25th day, when all of the songfest groups present their full repertoire of songs and dances, prepare enormous quantities of food to exchange with other jepta, and present their *wōjke* (Christmas tree), which is more like a giant piñata, filled with money and gifts of soap, matches, and cloth, that must be magically exploded from afar. After this huge feast, with its accompanying purification of performers and of ritual space, everyone rests for a moment in exhaustion and apprehension during the week between the 25th day and New Year's. Once again, on New Year's Sunday, each group re-presents the highlights of its songs and dances, and on New Year's Eve the children "keep the night ablaze" with their singing and frolicking visits from house to house, accompanied always by a lantern. Not unlike the case on Halloween, the children must be welcomed at each house with smiles and applause, even at 3:00 A.M., given a treat, and sent on their way. Male and female softball and volleyball contests engage the various songfest groups on New Year's Day, to be followed by a week or ten days of Maan Yiō, "the face of the year" prayer services at the break of dawn each day. During this period each person should be on his or her best behavior. Following these activities, Kūrijmōj is at an end, and the community returns for a few weeks to its "ordinary" routines.

Alternative Experiences: From Familiar Words to Important Words
Again, my intention is not to reanalyze this extensive ritual event, which I have done previously, but, rather, to think about its polysemic character in order to consider closely how the shape of the event is transformed by its very consideration as a fragment of cultural activity, amenable to inscription and, thereby, to reification. Indeed, in my earlier analyses I have made due note of issues of multivocality, following through on the two most prominent interpretations of the event on Ujelang and Enewetak Atolls. But even in my attempt to draw attention to the fact that multiple interpretations exist, in the act of writing and then of rewriting to the normative standards of a publishing house, I radically reduce the number and range of interpretations. Moreover, in the process of transforming Kūrijmōj from performance to text, I inscribe a certain logos that is certainly not apparent in the performance but, equally, is far less disparate and more patterned in the written text than it was in the divergence of exegetical interpretations of Kūrijmōj that were given to me.

It certainly is true that a number of local people see the central theme of Kūrijmōj as having to do with renewal or regeneration. Their descriptions range widely. One common theme among church members deals with the way in which love and caring for others, a product of the new (Christian) way of life, produces peace and good fortune, whereas the murderous ways of the past resulted in death and ill will. Other church folk have noted that adherence to God's word will cause a new and better life to come into being in the future as compared with the current day. While common, these renewal themes offer limited historical insight. As I have stressed in my published work, they contrast the times of light with the times of darkness and elide memories of the past in favor of an amorphous recollection of pre-Christian evil. Although I certainly take account of these views, in my anthropological attempt to get beyond the limitations of the current range of Christian themes of renewal, I rely on a contrarian minority of local oral historians, many of whom are socially marginalized either because they are not members of the church or because their dedication to the church is minimal. There is no doubt that I was taken much farther along interpretational paths that I found exciting and highly elaborated by this group of marginalized ethnohistorians than by core church members. The local historians suggested that Kūrijmōj has a lot to do with human reproduction because the perpetuation of local clans is critical. Two of the most knowledgeable pointed out for me how Kūrijmōj is connected to the celestial constellations and noted the connection between the movements of the stars and the yearly growth cycle of plants and seafoods. For this small group of elite historians, Kūrijmōj plays an important role in bridging between the dry season times of scarcity and the wet season times of abundance. From them I learned that behind the Christian pantheon stands another ancient Marshallese pantheon whose movements are far "thicker," deeper, and more highly elaborated than the accounts of many church members.

In spite of their differences, these two interpretative themes were still translucently similar: one a restricted code, and the other, elaborated. Nevertheless, in their telling I could discern enough commonalities to fashion them into a powerful story about renewal and regeneration. But the thematic continuities of other interpretations were not so apparent. Their wild (dis)array did not fit the renewal theme. They did not suggest the type of cohesive story, balanced contrast, or isomorphic structure that pleases the anthropological mind. Such non-normative interpretations of Kūrijmōj were certainly not as common as the mainstream church members' view. But, of course, the insightful perspective of the local ethnohistorians was equally an infrequent view. Ultimately, the views I would like to now foreground, with their wildly divergent character, are simply views that did not fit my own search for order or did not fit another reader's or editor's requirements for cohesiveness.

As Margaret Trawick notes, "In stressing the private and the particular, one runs the risk of being accused of anecdotalism, and of one's informants being accused of atypicality" (1992:151). Admittedly, the interpretations of Kūrijmōj to which I turn now are certainly not typical, but they are no less common than the elaborated view of the local historians on whom I rely for insight. Indeed, these interpretations are hardly anecdotal, for like all discursive accounts, they are meaningful pieces of discourse that can be understood as counternormative symbolic pleas for recognition and power or emotive pleas to validate a particular person's or group's contradictory social dilemmas. Each of the following accounts uses Kūrijmōj as an important semiotic device. If they lack a clear focus on revitalization, this should not lead to their exclusion. Indeed, in the same way that I have relied on the socially marginalized group of Ujelang and Enewetak historians to allow me to explore an elaborated view of Kūrijmōj, a consideration of other marginal interpretations constitutes more than a plea for polysemy. They, too, can lend insight into the multifarious ways in which this complex ritual is related to and intertwined with local people's lives and with my writings about those lives.

The first set of narrowly topicalized perspectives came from persons other than vital, mature adults. Nevertheless, the perspectives of young people are important because, as a group, they participate as a songfest group: Naan Aorek, "Important Words." Their perspectives give a glimpse of age variation in the conceptualization of Kūrijmōj. Because of space limitations, the examples I select are suggestive, not exhaustive. For one young member of a neighboring household on Ujelang where I spent considerable time, the entire raison d'être for Kūrijmōj was "grandmother." During this particular year, the young girl was between three and a half and four years old, and with every mention of Tijemba (December), "Christmas," or the "25th day," she would respond with an inquiry about grandmother.[2] Grandmother was the entire universe she had associated with Kūrijmōj this particular year inasmuch as her own genealogical grandmother had just died, and her other important grandmother (her grandmother's older sister), a favorite of this extended family, was to arrive on the government supply ship prior to December. As was typical on Ujelang, the supply ship had been delayed several times, and the young girl, I believe, eager to have the favorite grandmother fill some of the gap of her recently deceased grandmother, could think of nothing else. Any mention of Kūrijmōj brought queries about grandmother or about the ship or the trip that would bring her grandmother. In subsequent years her vision of Kūrijmōj changed, but her contextual frame in 1977 led inexorably to "grandma."

On Ujelang many of the other children used to overelaborate certain favorite segments of the larger ritual, and, often sequentially, two or three of these foci would come to define the experience for them. Not unusually, one song would become inordinately popular, and, unlike the case with adult members of jepta, who attempted to keep their songs secret, the refrains of one children's composition would dominate children's singing throughout the village area. Work on the "Christmas tree" (the exploding piñata) and the skit that accompanied it and talk of tōbtōb (to tug on)—a game that accompanied each jepta's presentation of its dances on the 25th day in which audience members could rush up and tug on a piece of a favored dancer's clothing, forcing the dancer to sacrifice it to the admirer—were other focal topics of children that came to dominate their discussion of the entirety of the celebration. Once the community had returned to Enewetak, a new children's favorite, pānuk, tossing treats into the audience during a jepta's dance performance, joined the other focal interpretative sites that dominated children's talk of Kūrijmōj. Although the foci differed somewhat from year to year, many children used specific segments of the larger Kūrijmōj performance as condensation symbols to metonymically represent the whole. The condensation events were more emotively saturated, perhaps, than other ritual activities in the celebration. Hence, many children's meanings exude a greater luster than those of adults. In many adult's eyes, children represent the fulfillment of pleas for the regeneration of Enewetak clans, and, because the festivities are commonly said to be focused on "creating happiness," the presence of children also helps fulfill that aim. For many children, the happiness-generating moments of Kūrijmōj define the larger whole. It seems to me that children's ability to define the whole in terms of the most exciting fragments reinforced the adult's placement of children at the center of the celebration.

Mature Words

The opposite end of the age spectrum presents another array of variations on the significance of Kūrijmōj. On Ujelang, and during the first years after the community was repatriated on Enewetak, people noted that Kūrijmōj was for everyone. Not only church members but all Enewetak and Ujelang people were expected to participate in the celebrations. Yet the oldest members of the community participated in a far more restricted way than others, largely on account of their lack of mobility. For the major presentations on the 25th day, all but the most feeble were transported to the church, but even then the truly aged watched from the sidelines. They could not actively participate. And for most Kūrijmōj events they remained at home, at most observing from an outdoor lanai. In listening to their interpretations of Kūrijmōj, particularly three elderly "grandmothers" I witnessed firsthand (while grandmotherly in demeanor and grandmothers to many community members, these women were all my mothers by adoption), the most obvious generalization about the relationship between meaning and social context became clear to me. That is, the meanings that any particular person attributes to this complex ritual are directly linked to each person's experience.

For two of the grandmothers, one in 1976 and a second in 1982, Kūrijmōj was interpreted through the food. Food came into each household and went out of each household with regularity, and in increasing quantity, during the entire four-month span of the celebration. Being highly respected on account of their age and rank in this society of matriclans, these women had a right to request the highest ranked foods. And in the comings and goings of household members, these women's requests always included queries about the most highly ranked foods.

In 1977, on Ujelang, the high-ranked requests were for pig and *peru*, a pandanus-based food mixed with arrowroot. Anytime a pig was killed, this particular mother would ask, "Is there [a pig's] head?" The heads of pigs (and fish) are thought best suited to respected matriarchs. If they are consumed by men, then the heads are said to make men bigheaded: hence, the taboo. On Enewetak in 1982 the edibles had changed radically (because of the required cleanup of nuclear waste on the atoll), and all local foods were at an extraordinary premium. In these conditions, the elders craved any local food, and my elderly mother consistently asked for drinking or sprouted coconut. Higher ranked staples, like pandanus, were entirely unavailable. Her incessant requests for bird eggs, a personal favorite, were seldom fulfilled, but this did not decrease the frequency of her requests.

In addition to their common focus on the food itself, both of these women monitored the propriety of the exchanges to ensure that there was some balance in what went out of the cookhouses and what came back into them. They spoke disparagingly of households that provided inferior foods (either in quantity or in the rank of the components) in relation to what had been transported out of the cookhouse that same day. Although a few families were consistently sanctioned by other village members for failing to provide ample food, in large part the frequent and widely dispersed disparaging comments of these elderly women reflected as much their own social situation as it did a negative commentary on certain stingy or slovenly families. Like chiefs, these elderly women were supposed to receive far more than they gave, and they should receive as much of whatever food they might desire. Their seemingly incessant quips and grumbling were particularly loud when the food gifts that came into the household not only failed to account for their distinguished status but did not even balance the food that had gone out of the cookhouse. In contrast, many adult men and women of middle age, eager to increase their own rank, worked hard and without complaint to ensure that they gave away far more than they received in return. Indeed, in their view, such generosity was at the core of Kūrijmōj and formed the basis for their increased rank.

The image that these two elderly women had of Kūrijmōj was not only shaped by their current experiences of the celebration as mediated by the exchange of food; when I asked one of them about the specially composed songs she fondly recalled the compositions of years past, when she was still a vital member of one of the jepta. For her, those songs were "extraordinarily good," and when they were sung, the jepta members were particularly *beran*, "strong" or "forceful," in their presentational style. This struck me as ironic at the time, for other mature adults recalled the songs of the past as quite feeble in relation to the much more sophisticated songs of the current day. Indeed, the mature adults of the 1970s and 1980s talked about the women's performances of the past in very humorous terms because they used to sing in screechy, high-pitched tones made by overconstricting the vocal cords. This was a style, they claimed, derived from ancient styles of women's chants. In any case, for my elderly mother, these fond recollections were part of her idealization of the event, part of the way in which her own identity

fashioning and her entire interpretative frame were drawn from an experiential past that was no longer shared with more than a handful of
other living community members.

Performances of the past are consistently woven into stories of Kūrijmōj by all but the youngest of community members, but the way in
which certain extraordinary performances of the past come to be over-
represented in the minds of a particular generation of participants has
become more apparent to me throughout the 28 years since I first participated in Kūrijmōj on Ujelang. A half dozen senior community members
in their sixties or seventies, who were in their prime performative years
when I first danced during Kūrijmōj in 1976, now use one particularly
popular jepta dance that my group performed that year, Neika kōmkōm
elekejroro, as an overly idealized prototype in terms of which they depict
the entire era of mid-1970s Kūrijmōj performances as the "best ever."
Thus, the interpretative frameworks in terms of which Kūrijmōj comes
to make sense, at one level, represent a sliding scale of differential significance that relates to the life experiences of particular persons who
envision themselves at the core of a certain generation of performers.

Indeed, the array of interpretative frames for the celebration of Kūrijmōj is ever changing and, in some respects, as diverse as the audience
of performers and observers. The way in which Kūrijmōj has depended
in an important way on sexual themes and, in the abstract, on the importance of human reproductive success was first brought out for me
by one of the oldest community members in the 1970s. Because he had
been a committed pagan throughout his life, a smoker, a drinker, and one
who proclaimed the virtues of marital infidelity—all very anti-mission
themes—he felt entirely comfortable in continuously joking about the
liminal sexual freedoms of Kūrijmōj. Indeed, a good part of his counter-
cultural, tricksterish social identity derived from his ability to bring the
contradictions between what he considered to be real Marshallese custom and church-inspired repressions to the surface.

In many ways the sexually focused significances of Kūrijmōj brought
to light by this aging elder's quips are shared by many unmarried young
men and women who also see the celebration as an opportunity to pursue amorous affairs. Yet the cantankerous elder expressed absolutely no
shame in his sexual remarks because he was raised to adulthood in the
pre-Christian era. In contrast, the youths of the 1970s, 1980s, and 1990s
are highly embarrassed by any public mention or display of sexuality.
During the dances on the 25th day many youths are sent running from

the scene as an older audience member comes forward to "play the trickster." In this tricksterish miming of the dancers, the dance steps of the performers are accompanied by overexaggerated hula-style hip movements, drawing shouts and uproarious laughter from the audience.[3] This proves too embarrassing for youths, in part on account of their immaturity but equally on account of a repressed view of sexuality that was almost certainly inspired by the mission. There were never any shades of this sexual inhibition in the demeanor of the church-boycotting elder mentioned above.

In addition to the relationship between the varied interpretations and social contexts of particular actors, major changes in the structural arrangements of the community have a substantial effect on processes of interpretation. Perhaps the event that most disrupted the interpretations of Kūrijmōj occurred when the Assembly of God sect was brought to Enewetak in the late 1980s. Though I was not on the atoll during that year, it remained a major source of contention for the next several years. Even now, well over a decade later, it is a point of severe disruption in the community (see Carucci 2000). Such a source of social reordering could not help but have important effects on the interpretation of Kūrijmōj.

Although Christmas was originally introduced as religious celebration, Kūrijmōj as developed on Ujelang was a response to the missionary form designed for everyone (ñan aoleb), not just church members. If the Congregationalist introduction provided a format for all Christian converts to come together and sing Christmas songs in the late 1920s, by the post–World War II era the entire community was involved. No one was excluded because all community members were either church members, aspiring members, or persons who had fallen from grace. Ujelang jepta included all adult members of the community, as well as a children's jepta (Naan Aorek). Until the arrival of the Assembly of God group on Enewetak in 1988–89, the question of "which church" never arose. After the highly contested arrival of the new church no longer was the community "of a single piece." For four months of the year, part of the community was not included in the activities that occupied most people's minds and, for the last two months, occupied every waking moment of people's time. Not surprisingly, even one and a half years after the arrival of "Assembly," people's interpretations of Kūrijmōj were seriously affected by the change. Having been largely invented between the 1930s and 1950s when religious and community identity were being molded into a relatively cohesive package, the entire set of symbols and practices of Kūrijmōj that were designed to create and perpetuate a well-aligned Enewetak identity had to change. While people continued to say that Kūrijmōj was "for everyone," that everyone excluded Assembly.[4]

The set of newly introduced contradictions was readily apparent on Lopāt land parcel, where I lived. There were now two extended family groups that had become members of Assembly. One had a breadfruit tree that, on occasion, had a few edible breadfruits. Although the breadfruits were freely shared among land parcel members in past years because all had belonged to the same songfest group, the members of my own household now groused about not having access to the breadfruits that normally would have been their own. They pointed out that one of our household members had helped plant the tree and should have rights to some of its fruit. But now "it was of no value." A closer relative to the new Assembly members snuck over at night to steal breadfruits from his brother's tree several times during the year. After one such theft, the conversation turned to comparisons with Japanese times during World War II when people had to steal their own produce at night under the watchful eyes of the Japanese. All of this talk was quite atypical among members of the same jepta at Kūrijmōj. Talk of happiness and solidarity-building discourse were frequent within a songfest group. Talk of stealth and metaphors of battle were reserved for interactions with members of other songfest groups. Now, however, with a new, more distant "other" in the community, the Assembly of God church members, interactions within and among songfest groups were twisted to account for the new social conditions. Equally, during food distributions the entire community had once been involved. Now, as food came into the household, it was redistributed only among members of the "real church" (United Church of Christ) group. One evening, members of my household waited until after dark to take food across to a neighboring house so that the relatives who lived in the Assembly household nearby would not see the transfer of food. At the other end of the village an outspoken close sibling of mine adopted just the opposite tactic. He had been one of the staunch opponents of allowing the Assembly group to "land on" Enewetak, and each time he received food from Kūrijmōj he claimed that he purposefully walked directly past a neighboring Assembly cookhouse with a large basket of food intended for his mother's younger brother on a nearby land parcel. And, breaking all Marshallese food distribution rules, following a huge food distribution on one of the Sundays prior to the 25th day, one branch of my own family decided to feed extra

food to the pigs rather than share it with other family members on their
land parcel who belonged to Assembly.

Especially during the first few years after the arrival of the new religious group, discourse and social practice during Kūrijmōj were substantially altered. The community, once the same as the participants in
Kūrijmōj, now had to develop a more complex way of constructing identity. Exclusionary practices, including a great deal of discourse focused
on constructing a group of "others," had to be fitted into a discourse and
social practices that previously had as their ultimate aim the welfare of
the entire community in mind. Although the games among jepta had
long included competition and exclusionary strategies in their repertoire, these constructions of "otherness" were humorous and superficial
and always ritually succumbed to larger universal community aims. Such
was not the case in the 1990s when the arrival of Assembly created an
other presence within the larger community that has yet to be resolved
with new discourses, which now must find a way to allow community
unity to trump religious difference. To date, symbols of exclusion have
prevailed.

Reflections on Revitalization

Anthony Wallace's concept of revitalization extends an analytic tradition in anthropology that goes back at least to Lewis Henry Morgan's
reliance on interpretative categories based on the comparative method.
Although Wallace explicitly includes practices of peyotism in revitalization, by 1966 David Aberle, in his detailed work on peyotism among the
Navajo (1966:341), had suggested that peyotism should not qualify as a
form of revitalization inasmuch as it is a passive ritual form that does not
foresee the disappearance of white men. Peyotism, Aberle argues, should
be considered a "redemptive movement," whereas revitalization should
be reserved for so-called transformative movements such as the Ghost
Dance and, particularly, practices like Handsome Lake (1966:350). Of
course, Aberle had identified a real problem. In his terms, this problem arose on account of the "assumption that peyotism is accepted and
retained because it resembles a familiar prototype" (1966:40), and, of
course, the prototype has absolutely nothing to do with the motivations
for the practice of peyotism. Nevertheless, his solution continues to
rely on aligning diverse practices with prototypical forms. In that sense,
Aberle's solution is simply a displacement, not a solution at all. On the
other hand, Aberle's recognition that peyotism entails a set of practices

"adapted to and adaptive for [certain] contexts" (1966:351) is suggestive of a different approach that might seek to model a variety of local
meanings in relationship with a certain set of social practices. This more
fruitful approach is what I recommend in this chapter.

Of course, I have not discussed the full variety of interpretations of
Kūrijmōj, and such a task is undoubtedly impossible. My aim in the
preceding pages has been only to indicate something of the diverse
range of meanings and to note the dynamic, ever emergent, character of
new meanings that, of necessity, will derive from Kūrijmōj as fashioned
by the Ujelang/Enewetak community. As I have attempted to indicate,
the array of meanings is unlimited, as the very process of constructing
meanings, that most productive human capacity, is linked to social conditions and to lived experiences that are, themselves, dynamic and ever
changing. I would like to return to the meanings that I have, in the past,
chosen to select out and inscribe, meanings that are common but not
exhaustive.

To see Kūrijmōj as a rite of renewal and regeneration is certainly
not misguided or wrong. Closer to the ground than *revitalization*, these
terms do summarize fragments of local descriptions of what Kūrijmōj is
all about. On the other hand, these *designata* do not exhaust the interpretations that either have been or will be placed on this event. Having
participated in the celebration five times and having heard numerous
stories of other Kūrijmōj seasons on Ujelang and Enewetak, I continue
to see themes of regeneration and renewal laced through the celebration. Having been made aware by Ujelang storytellers of the connections
between the story of the primordial activities of Jebero, the younger
sibling usurper of chiefly control, and its themes of love and generosity,
it is now difficult for me to see the celebration other than through the
interpretative lens that this primordial tale provides. But these, I readily
admit, are my interpretations as an anthropologist who has intertwined
his own experiential interpretative biases with the multiple opportunities I have had to participate in Kūrijmōj. Perhaps a half dozen Enewetak
residents have read parts of my interpretation of Kūrijmōj, and they
agree that it is acceptable: "It has meaning (or sense)," as they would
say.

Nevertheless, in writing about Kūrijmōj as a ritual of renewal and
regeneration, I can do nothing other than lend credence to its stereo-
typing. I can do nothing other than transform the multifaceted elements
of a ritual performance into two-dimensional linearized text. I privi-

lege the perspectives of certain community members over those of others, reinforcing a certain image of center and periphery, criticality and marginality. And this, certainly, reifies and essentializes the cultural form by giving it a new, momentary fixity with only encapsulated indexical links to its rich performative pasts. Moreover, as Bourdieu (1991) notes, the process of inscription further overdetermines a particular version of lived reality, for the "text travels" in ways very unlike the performance itself (Clifford 1983). *Nuclear Nativity* is a very different intertextual phenomenon than are the "intersubjectivities in process" that made up the many moments of Kūrijmōj in 1976, 1977, 1982, or 1990 (Kristeva 1996: ch. 17).

Each chapter in this book faces this contradiction, for the vision of revitalization, like all processes of anthropological representation, involves multiple layers of reclassification and overdetermination. In rethinking revitalization, it is critical to reassess the complex linkages between textual representation and the multifaceted interactions and symbolic practices that local people use to make sense out of their world. As Wallace recognized, to talk of revitalization is to confront issues of classification, both for local people and for an academic audience. But Wallace's (1956c) concern is with organismic holism and with the way in which stress may be leveraged against a social system as an instrument of culture change. From a more semiotic perspective, however, revitalization looks more like a series of ritual strategies to resolve the contradictions of locally reified views of a valorized past in relation to an undervalued vision of life in the current day.[5] The fact that these dissatisfactions typically arise in colonial encounters should hardly be surprising. Yet, as I suggest elsewhere, in the case of Kūrijmōj the specific meanings that are placed on the celebration depend on differently positioned understandings of the event. In the 1970s and 1980s, core church members often envisioned Kūrijmōj as a way to reinvigorate practices that had grown degenerate since the early years of Christianity. At the same time, local Ujelang historians saw Christian practices as a subplot in a more ancient cosmological schema that was set in motion by the founding activities of the ancient deities who first inhabited the Marshall Islands. And in this chapter I suggest that the array of such meanings is much more diverse, changing substantially depending on the varied social and historical interests of local residents.

In the fashion of Lacan, Lindstrom (1993:174) suggests that "cargo cult" makes sense as a performative strategy to address unrequited desire fixated on illusory objects. While less evocative in phonological shape and semantic appeal, revitalization is little different. But the contour of those desires differs considerably from place to place, not only as they are continuously reformulated in places like Ujelang and Enewetak but also as they provide the inspiration to develop innovative forms of representational potency in very different contexts of use, including the once-hallowed halls of academe. Therefore, if I have worked harder than normal in this chapter to bring out the obtuse, it is to remind us, as anthropologists, to keep our own desire to revitalize revitalization in close contact with local practices that provide the most critical context from which one can address the question: "Vital for whom?"

Notes

1. More recently, of course, social theorists such as Homi Bhabha (1990) and Martha Kaplan (1995) have suggested that revitalization movements are, in fact, fragments of a discourse that emerges in the context of colonialism. Wallace's article appears in a special issue on acculturation, yet Wallace is more concerned with revitalization as a means of confronting "interferences with the efficiency of a cultural system." Such interferences can have a variety of sources, such as climactic, floral, and faunal change; military defeat; political subordination; extreme pressure toward acculturation; economic distress; and epidemics. Although several of Wallace's sources are intertwined with colonial forces, Wallace is unclear about the precise locations where revitalization movements articulate with his full array of cultural inefficiencies. Nevertheless, he notes that "the situation is often, but not necessarily, one of acculturation, and the acculturating agents may or may not be representatives of Western European cultures" (1956c:269).

2. Although these terms have distinct referents, *December* and the *25th day* being more narrowly focused than *Christmas*, the three were presented to the young girl as virtual synonyms. And, indeed, Ujelang and Enewetak people do frequently use *Christmas* to refer to the entire four-month period as well as smaller segments of the celebration, including (though rarely) the 25th day.

3. Some of this repression is disappearing among Enewetak residents now living on the Big Island of Hawaii, where tricksterish-like dances are becoming more frequent and widespread.

4. The fact that Kūrijmōj is a fully fashioned response to Christmas rather than "a Marshallese version" is particularly evident in the way that the Euro-American Christmas *includes* Christians of many different stripes, whereas Kūrijmōj both extends beyond the bounds of church membership to include evil-

doing pagans (*di kabuñ* or *di nana*) and *excludes* non–United Church of Christ Christians. As I have pointed out elsewhere, in the Ujelang and Enewetak view of the 1970s and 1980s, "Christian" equated to the forms of religious practice introduced by American Board of Commissioners for Foreign Missions teachers, whereas Catholics and Baptists were thought to be members of distant, non-Christian religions. By 1995 some Enewetak people were beginning to consider Assembly of God as a type of Christianity, but at the time of the group's arrival on the atoll, only those who were members of Assembly entertained such blasphemous ideas.

5. While I have explored a similar motivational schema in my analysis of Kūrijmōj (Carucci 1997a), I owe the inspiration for this formulation of the issue to Michael Harkin, who provided useful comments on an earlier draft of this chapter.

10. *OGITCHIDA* AT *WASWAAGANING*

Conflict in the Revitalization of Lac du
Flambeau Anishinaabe Identity

Larry Nesper

On January 23, 1983, the Seventh Circuit Court of Appeals in Chicago found that the off-reservation hunting, fishing, and gathering rights that the Chippewa bands in Wisconsin had stipulated in the treaties of 1837 and 1842 were in tact in *Lac Courte Oreilles v. Voigt.* The case had been in the courts for nine years and had begun when the Tribble brothers at Lac Court Oreilles were arrested for being in possession of a fishing spear off the reservation on Chief Lake out of season. The event had been staged. The brothers protested to the arresting state game warden that the State of Wisconsin had no jurisdiction over this practice and presented copies of the treaties in their defense. These band members were cited three weeks after the Boldt decision that upheld the treaty fishing rights of the Washington State tribes in *United States v. Washington* (see Cohen 1986).

The Voigt decision stunned the state Department of Natural Resources, the non-Indian communities in northern Wisconsin, and especially those people most committed to tourism in the area of Lac du Flambeau. Predictions of the end of the tourist economy and whole way of life filled the cafés, taverns, radio talk shows, television newscasts, and editorial pages of local newspapers. The fear was motivated in collectively imagining the consequences of the sudden loss of unilateral state control of how hunting and fishing would be conducted in the region. For more than a century, state law regarding natural resources had been crafted to facilitate a tourist economy. Since the mid-1970s, however, the society in the North Woods that depended on this economy was imagined by its members as increasingly fragile and vulnerable.

Rapid economic and residential development in the 1980s undermined the ongoing project of credibly representing Wisconsin's North Woods to metropolitan consumers as pristine and desirable, with the lakes full of fish. There were perceivable and measurable shifts in how the region was being used recreationally now that the area was reachable in a few hours via a highway that is four lanes most of the way. Additionally, it had been known for a number of years that demand for certain species of game fish in the northern part of the state had already outstripped supply. And there was growing concern over shoreline degradation. An emergent, politicized subsistence activity undertaken by the local indigenous population was thought to have the potential to do irrevocable economic damage, especially as the meaning of the court's decision was embodied in what appeared to be an anarchistic practice.

Some Indian people at Lac du Flambeau got the news of the court's decision via the short-wave scanners they use to monitor police, fire department, and game warden activity. While it planned a response to the decision, the Wisconsin Department of Natural Resources directed its wardens not to arrest Indians for violating the state's game laws. Within hours of the decision, a few Indian people ventured off the reservation to hunt. Previously, this was referred to as "violating" and formed an important dimension of local Indian identity. Violating represented the endurance of the collective memory of the retained right to hunt, fish, and gather on the ceded lands over a century of domination. Many Indian people survived the effects of social and economic marginalization by violating. This rather decentralized "exercise of our rights," as they would come to call it, immediately after the Voigt decision, resonated with some of the worst general fears that non-Indians had about Indians in the area.

Over the course of the next half a dozen years after the Voigt decision and a series of tribal-state negotiations and federal court cases, the rights would come to be defined as the possession of the bands collectively and not of individual tribal members. Regulation, therefore, would fall to the bands' governments. Furthermore, the state would be awarded most of the management authority over fish, game, and plants, but sustainable harvest levels and, therefore, length of seasons and bag limits would be negotiated with the bands. Concurrent with the legal process, however, a grassroots protest of treaty rights with connections to national anti-Indian organizations emerged in the area and actively contested the harvesting practices of Indian people off their reservations.[1] As these treaty rights were rooted in a historical cultural distinction, the conflict focused on the presence and legitimacy of genuine cultural differences between Indians and non-Indians.[2] Because the stakes were so high, the conflict produced a nativistic movement.

Before the Voigt decision, the differences between Indians and non-Indians were largely understood and represented by non-Indians in the symbolism of socioeconomic class. By and large, whites looked down on Indians, assuming that they had alcohol problems and were lazy, poor, and dependent on transfer payments.[3] Although these opinions were typically expressed sotto voce, the stereotype was condensed in a number of different jokes that were circulating in 1989, one of which asked, "How do you starve an Indian?" It answered, "Hide his food stamps under his work boots." Indicative of the tacit cooperation that is required for the maintenance of ethnic boundaries, as well as the appropriation and revaluation of negative stereotypes by the stereotyped, I first heard the joke told by an Indian man to a group of other Indian people, all of whom found it quite amusing.[4] Nonetheless, disproportionate high school truancy, dropout, arrest, and incarceration rates were taken as definitive of the difference between Indians and whites. These rates, too, were taken by Indian people simultaneously as measures of racism and as signs of resistance.[5] The conflict over fishing, however, revitalized symbols of difference via practices that would constitute a difference and has had the somewhat ironic outcome of integrating Lac du Flambeau more deeply in the region even as the community rehabilitated certain other traditional practices that distinguished it from the "surrounding society," as the proximate non-Indian world is referred to at Flambeau.

There is a sense in which people at Lac du Flambeau have always sought what the Supreme Court asserted in 1954 in *Brown v. Board of Education* to be impossible: a separate but equal collective existence. Historically, people at Lac du Flambeau sought recognition as distinct even as they attempted to appropriate practices from the dominant culture on their own terms. In the late 19th and early 20th century they sold their labor as woodsmen working seasonally for the lumber industry in a variety of capacities. They also sold "country food": venison, berries, and wild rice. Men worked as hunting and fishing guides, thus valorizing Indian knowledge of the land and lakes, and women sold crafts in a complementary undertaking that perpetuated identification of the local Indian people with the particular and local natural resources. In the middle of the 20th century the tribe cooperated with local business interests in building an amphitheater in which Indian people would dance for tourists and sell crafts. The site became the locus for the reproduction of local Indian identity (Nesper 2003). All of these practices served to retain a sense of community identity, but the strategy did not work to command respect for most people in the eyes of the local non-Indians in the region. Instead, the community was racialized and economically marginalized as it was incorporated into the region mostly as a flexible source of cheap labor.

The Voigt decision was a windfall. In the minds of some Flambeau tribal members who had traveled far enough from the reservation to see the community in its larger context, the decision presented the opportunity for them personally to gain prominence within the community as well as gain for the whole community that long-sought recognition from non-Indians in exercising power via the culturally specific and historic practice of spearfishing, now possible to undertake well beyond the borders of the enclave. The court decision created the conditions for the possibility of generating or energizing what Jocelyn Linnekin calls a "summarizing symbol." Typically, such a "self-conscious formulation of [a] cultural model . . . is inherently a selective and creative process" (Linnekin 1990b:158) and is undertaken in a political context. This is a point noted by Ralph Linton in an article entitled "Nativistic Movements" nearly half a century before: "What really happens in all nativistic movements, is that certain current or remembered elements of a culture are selected for emphasis and given symbolic value. The more distinctive such elements are with respect to other cultures with which the society is in contact, the greater their potential value as symbols of the society's unique character" (1943:231).

Linnekin adds that Roger Keesing points out that summarizing symbols "don't carry meanings as they evoke them" (Keesing 1982b:299). The paradox—that the distinctive practice of spearfishing was legitimated by the dominant society's embrace of the principles that underlay property law—not only produced the circumstances for this "nativistic," "rational" movement that has embraced both "perpetuative" and "revivalistic" elements, in the words Linton (1943:231) uses in his seminal article on movements, but also reiterates the fact that the production of ethnic differences is dialogical, negotiated, and provocatively cooperative.

Spearfishing and the Torch in a Colonial Context

Nicholas Thomas (1992a, 1992b) has written about processes of the production of symbols of ethnicity in the Pacific. Following his lead, the fact that spearfishing spawning walleyed pike at night would come to symbolize local identity can only be understood in terms of the history of the relationship between the tribal and non-Indian communities. A measure of the ongoing impact of an internal colonialism in northern Wisconsin, and elsewhere for American Indian people, is that they have had to "couch their identity and resistance in terms made available by the dominant: they celebrate and affirm what colonialist discourse and practice subordinate and denigrate" (Thomas 1992a:216). For example, the widely spread and general American Indian inclination represented in groups of four—such as the seasons, the directions, and the stages of human life—as well as what we might call circle ideology and subsistence self-sufficiency, should be regarded as unselfconscious customary practices become resistant responses. Insofar as the West prefers triads, linearity, and production for exchange, all implicitly and explicitly imposed on Anishinaabe people, as well as others, in the 19th and 20th centuries, identity and resistance would be cast in these registers of meaning.[6] As a result, the number four, the circle, and the indigenous practices that made for economic independence have all become Indian ethnic symbols in an intercultural dialogue of ideas and images that seeks to maximize differences via opposition. Following the same logic, it is because both Indians and whites have an interest in walleyed pike that spearing them at night had the potential to become a symbol of a total difference between the two groups in northern Wisconsin.

"How Winaboozhoo Learned to Firehunt" is a neotraditionalist story written by Ernie St. Germaine, educator and chief tribal judge at Lac du Flambeau, at the time of the conflict between the Indian community and its neighbors over the exercise of treaty rights. In the story, spearfishing spawning walleye at night with a torch is foregrounded as the motive for the ethnonym and, thus, the definitive sign of local specificity. A half-blind old man makes himself a torch to fish at night with his spear. *Oka*, the walleye, is both curious and vulnerable. Because their eyes are so big, they will be illuminated by the torch's light and speared all the easier. The old man teaches the method to Winaboozhoo, the Woodlands trickster, world transformer, and cultural innovator who taught it to the Anishinaabe people: "Other *Anishinaabeg* who came to visit here noticed this unusual way of catching fish with torches. So they called these people who lived by Bear River, *Waswaaganan*, or People of the Torches. And this place became known as *Waswaaganing*, or the Place of the Torch People" (St. Germaine 1990:61–62).

Previous versions of the story give the honor of naming the local community to the French, who are said to have seen the use of torches for fishing here first and named the location after the practice (Valaskakis 1988:270; Warren 1984:192). These versions were effectively a nod to the notion that identity is dialogical and negotiated. Indeed, the subsequent geographical term *Waswaaganing* was thus derived from "Lac du Flambeau" (Torch Lake), a kind of indigenization of the international point of view. St. Germaine's postcolonial version reverses the historical sequence and has other Indians naming the locals, concordant with the themes of self-sufficiency and autonomy that had emerged in reaction to the depredations of Anglo-American domination beginning in the 19th century. The perspective, therefore, that the Algonquian-speaking groups in the last quarter of the 18th century, who were beginning to be called and to call themselves "Ojibwe," had been incorporated into the expanding European world system for more than a century by the time they advanced into the area south of Lake Superior is demoted in importance by, if not entirely eclipsed in, a claim about historical self-sufficiency. Importantly, however, the transformation does reflect the local effort to continue to see the community as a consequential center of the production of meaning.

In Algonquian metaphysics generally, harvesting resources is necessary for their reproduction, in that relations of reciprocity obtain between communities of humans and communities of nonhuman spirits realized as animals and plants (see Brightman 1993). As far as Indian people were concerned, the hunting and gathering that they were able to do was the work they did in the ongoing process of creation. Spearfishing at night had always been, therefore, an activity of cosmic proportions.

Over the course of the 20th century, the flaming birch bark torch became one of the symbols of local specificity even as the method for spearing at night evolved.[7] Lanterns replaced birch bark torches, and rowboats replaced birch bark canoes. Then flashlights replaced lanterns. Finally, automobile headlamps duct-taped to construction helmets powered by 12-volt batteries replaced flashlights, and motorized boats replaced rowboats. The symbol of torch illumination, however, survived these changes, as it is exotic, quaint, clever, and elemental, at least from the perspective of the increasingly metropolitan non-Indians who sought engagement with natives and their resources in validating regenerative encounters. That perception was not lost on the local brokers, attuned to the exchange value of local ethnicity, who mediated the relationship between the indigenous locals and the tourists elaborating differences.

The torch was a valuable emergent symbol to both local Indians and non-Indians because it proposed such a thorough and multifaceted opposition. First of all, it evoked the encompassing opposition of night and day, consigning Indians to the former and granting non-Indians the latter. In a related register of meaning, the torch was anachronistic, and as such it juxtaposed a people who possessed a past with a group of people who claimed to possess the future. The torch condensed a class difference. It opposed Indian people who worked at fishing at night during the spawn, maximizing their technological assistance using homemade lights and spears, to whites who hunted and fished during the day after the spawning season for sport, handicapping themselves with minimally adequate mass-produced equipment.

The difference had a long if not well-known history. Indigenous spearfishing at night with torches was widespread in the region of the upper Great Lakes and beyond (Rostlund 1952:293). The Jesuit father LeJeune (1897:311) described it in 1634 near Quebec; David Thompson (1916:267–268) recorded it in Minnesota in the late 18th century; Johan Georg Kohl (1985:328) wrote about it among the Lake Superior bands in the middle of the 19th century; and Kuhm (1928:74) recorded it among a number of the Wisconsin tribes drawing on 19th- and 20th-century sources. It would be recorded by Densmore (1979:149–150) in the 1920s, by Jenness (1935:15) and Hilger (1951:127) in the 1930s among the Parry Island Ojibwa and Wisconsin and Michigan bands, and by Sister Clarissa Levi (1956:357) in the 1940s. The practice has left its mark on the local geography as well, there being three Torch Lakes in the Upper Midwest alone, not including this one named in French. An incorporating practice that transmits the past in skilled bodily movements and activities (Connerton 1989:72–104), widely shared and with great continuity, spearing would be substantivized as a sign of local specificity (Thomas 1992b) largely over the course of the 20th century as the local people expressed their own distinctiveness in terms of discourses that were made availed to them by the dominant society.

In 1912 the lumber mill that had run three shifts for 18 years closed— but not before its owners had built a dam to create a chain of lakes on the Lac du Flambeau reservation to transport the logs. "The Flambeau Chain," as it would come to be called, facilitated extensive access to much good fishing. The mill had employed scores of the reservation's working-age men as the community undertook a multidimensional articulation with the regional social and economic order. In 1913 the mixed-blood Gauthier family rebuilt the hotel that they had built when the mill arrived in anticipation of the benefits of the Indian agent's new policy encouraging tourism. They named the hotel The Flame, referring to torches, and the objectification of the spearing at night was ratcheted up a notch or two. The annual report to the Commissioner of Indian Affairs in 1914 predicted that "an increased number of tourists, and the location of summer resorts, will provide better markets for their produce, increase the value of their lands, and provide more work of various kinds. It has been my policy to encourage the tourist business, and partly with this end in view, I established a fish hatchery during the present year as a means of improving fishing conditions. . . . [T]he output was estimated at 7 million pike all of which were planted in the reservation lakes. . . . These lakes should become the most popular fishing resorts in America" (Annual Reports 1914:11–12). Those "pike" were oka.

More than 20 years later the president of the newly formed Tribal Council declared: "Our task in furthering the development of the Reservation is a large and responsible one and we hope, with cooperation of all concerned, that *we can make this Reservation the greatest recreational center of our state*" (Brown 1937:41, emphasis added). The result was that torch symbolism proliferated in tribal and private advertising and signage as Lac du Flambeau asserted its place among the fishing tourist destinations in the Upper Midwest.

Some of the fish that were being produced by the hatchery that was rebuilt in the late 1930s for sportsmen were caught by Flambeau people with rod and reel, and some were netted; but more were speared. In the conflict that ensued in the 1980s when a group of tribal members took the practice off the reservation in organized nighttime fishing expeditions, spearing became a resistant sign of the self-sufficiency and autonomy that had always been predicated of them, now introjected as the essential diacritical mark of nativeness and autochthony.

Spearing in the Conflict
The revitalization of local cultural identity via off-reservation spearfishing depended on a conflict over who was going to control the meaning of a symbol that had emerged in a colonial context as Flambeau

was articulated as periphery of the core Midwestern cities. Non-Indians downgraded the political significance of the fact that there had always been a separate society in their midst. Indians had been valuable as labor and as malleable living signs that gave credibility to the image of the North Woods as an authentic, pristine, and therefore purifying and regenerative tourist destination. The tribal members who were pushing for and taking advantage of the interim agreements with the state to spear walleye in the spring, however, were contesting this marginalization.

The full value of Lac du Flambeau's specific spearfishing practice, as a sign of their own distinction, only appeared in the mid- and later 1980s in relationship with other Anishinaabe and in relationship with the non-Indians who contested it. Soon to be known as "the Flambeau Style," the technical practice and complex that Flambeau had evolved condensed a history of appropriation.

Some Flambeau people had bought cars in the first decade of the 20th century, paid for with wages from the lumber mill. With their demise, the cars would be cannibalized for materials from which to make spearheads and torches. They had iron-working skills that they learned in the boarding school that sought to integrate the reservation into the region's working class. They had been operating the boats owned by the resorts, whose cosmopolitan clientele they had guided since the turn of the 20th century. And they knew lakes or, at least, how to recognize the rock bars where walleye spawn when the water reaches 43 degrees by the topography of the shorelines.

This accumulation of symbolic capital contrasted with that of some of the other bands, members of which used the shorter spears that Flambeau people used for fishing through the ice with decoys in the winter. These bands rowed boats and used an underwater lighting system that was less detectable by the game wardens, as they had fewer walleye lakes on their reservations and knew those wardens' habits less well than Flambeau people, who knew them from their guiding days and those of their forebears. Flambeau even claimed that they had invented this method but that it became obsolete with increasing access to motored boats.

The value of spearfishing as a substantivized practice derived largely from the fact that it was the target of non-Indian acrimony. It came to be a symbol of a total and ramifying difference. When it was said that the practice was not sporting, Indian people said that they were taught not to play with their food, something they also said of non-Indian sportsmen's practice of catch and release. The idea of a harvest ethic emerged in the writings of James Schlender (1991), a Lac Courte Oreilles member and executive director of the Great Lakes Fish and Wildlife Commission. Denounced for occasionally, inadvertently, and illegally leaving mortally wounded fish on the surface of lakes and piles of cleaned fish carcasses in the woods—as many Indian people had come to prefer filleted wall-eye, a legacy of their ancestors who worked as fishing guides and made "shore lunch" for non-Indian clientele—Indian people elaborated their historical polytheistic ideas about reciprocal relations among the "persons" of men, eagles, fish, and crayfish, who look after each other in a complicated network of exchange.

According to Thomas, it is "a reactive process of positive collective self-identification within which a local group distinguishes itself and expresses its own worth, by articulating and elaborating features of local practice which contrast with attributes of wider social relations. . . . Culture contact of all kinds does produce, and in a particularly powerful manner, essentialized constructs of selves and others within which particular customs and practices are emblematic" (1992b:79). This process of "positive collective self-identification" took place on the boat landings of the lakes within 100 miles of the reservation when a group of previously marginalized tribal members suppressed their own inclination to fight as individuals and fought in the symbolic hybrid domain of subsistence politics. "It ennobled them," in the words of the tribal attorney, recently reflecting on that time, who watched the shift with the tribal community from accommodationism to resistance (James Jannetta, personal communication, 1999). The leader of the faction at Lac du Flambeau, tribal judge and businessman Tom Maulson, was able to guide the fiercely independent tribal members' inclination to engage in dangerous activities wherein one's honor is perpetually at stake to a particular political end. In this way he was a kind of prophet, in Anthony F. C. Wallace's (1956c) sense, but only by degree, as there were others who brought their own understandings of the meaning of the project to the activity. By virtue of the social and cultural capital that had accrued to him as the son of a full-blood, fully bilingual tribal member and a first-generation immigrant father, however, Maulson understood the dynamics of lower-class Indian cultural identity as well as how that identity was located in a larger set of relations.

The boat landings themselves amassed resources that might be organized by the encompassing idea of spectacle. Hundreds of non-Indians drove to remote boat landings in the North Woods lit by gas-generator-driven police lights, where snow fence was stretched nightly to accommodate fishermen putting their boats into the water and to hold back the protesters. Sheriff's police by the score, TV and radio crews, newspaper reporters, scores of antitreaty activists singing patriotic songs, and dozens of non-Indian supporters surreptitiously tape-recording incidents of racist speech—all commingled in a volatile mix. As protesters yelled, ad hoc choirs sang; an occasional firecracker, or M-80, or gunshot (who knew?) crackled in the distance; the generators droned, backgrounded by a monotonic tree frog cacophony. It was alternately frightening and tedious.

It was under these circumstances that the spearing became warfare, condensing all the value of extracting resources from nature with the value of war, two historically related and preeminent modes of the male contribution to the reproduction of society. In 1987 Maulson began wearing, and distributing to spearers, a baseball cap with *Walleye Warrior* printed on it that his wife purchased for him in a Minneapolis sports shop. Of course, the cap was intended for the sports fishing market, but Maulson redesigned the cap, adding *Lac du Flambeau* to it in a paradigmatic and unselfconscious act of appropriation. The fishermen became warriors, and the fish became trophies for the most definitive of human undertakings. At the biggest confrontation at Butternut Lake in 1989, supporters sang love songs to the drum, while spearers took one fish each, typically a large female, full of spawn.

Spearers would be mocked in the newspaper and by local non-Indians for identifying themselves as warriors and would be lauded as such by religious leaders such as Edward Benton-Banai, a Lac Courte Oreilles tribal member, early American Indian Movement leader, and grand chief of the Three Fires Midewiwin Society, whose members he referred to in Ojibwemowin as *ogitchida*.[8] The terms *ogitchida* and *ogitchidakwe*, meaning warrior and female warrior, respectively, began to gain currency at Lac du Flambeau in 1989. A loose ogitchida society or association of sorts would follow in the early winter of that year. *Ogitchida* referred to individual Indian people who fought for the preservation of Ojibwa distinctness and rights to self-determination. After the 1989 season, "spearfishermen" were said to be ogitchida; their mothers, wives, and sisters who waited on the landings for them to return were said to be ogitchidakwe, as were Flambeau women tribal members who spearfished.

Even some non-Ojibwas were said to be ogitchida by some. The term denoted a disposition and an attitude that were signs of a motivation more than it did a particular practice.

The role had a history. The term *ogitchida* was used and described in the American Board of Commissioners for Foreign Missions missionary Boutwell's journal in the 1830s (Hickerson 1962:56). It had been revitalized at the turn of the 20th century and used to refer to the officers of a Big Drum (Rynkiewich 1980:92; Vennum 1982:76), a ceremonial complex that emerged in the 19th century. Its current connotations evoked the community policing and protection work that was being done by the members of the American Indian Movement. But it was a contested term, especially because *ogitchida* could also be used to refer to service veterans. Ernie St. Germaine reported that some older members of the community felt that "it was absurd for anyone to say that spearers were veterans because they 'faced the enemy'—a bunch of rabble-rousers who tossed insults and rocks at them. They regarded it as a disgrace and insult to those who died, bloody and torn in the mud on foreign soil, so that these spearers could one day understand the freedom and right to spear and hunt" (personal communication, 1999). The very presence of a debate on the reservation over the relationship between categories of warriors indicates that the role complex had a long, continuous, though contested history. And this was not the only debate.

Even as litigation proceeded and interim agreements that permitted harvests were worked out between the state and the bands, the Tribal Council at Lac du Flambeau recognized that only a small fraction of the community was using the newly recognized rights. In an effort to realize the rights' value more extensively, the council entered into negotiations with the state to lease the rights for per-capita payments and state programs. In 1989 the tribal members who had been spearing for a few years by then coalesced as the Wa-Swa-Gon Treaty organization, symbolized the faction with a torch, and asserted by their actions that the entire community—represented by that same symbol habitually, traditionally, and essentially—speared spawning walleye at night in the spring. Spearing became a "summarizing symbol," and the outcome was a revitalized community, for the boat landings lent themselves to being thought of as microcosms of the entire history of the relationship between Flambeau people and their non-Indian neighbors.

In the early years after the Voigt decision, small age- and gender-heterogeneous groups of Indian people attempted to quietly but now proudly go about what was left of a historical way of life that they previously had ambivalently valued simultaneously as a sign of a cultural past and a sign of poverty. They were regarded with curiosity and a growing sense of outrage by non-Indians. By the late 1980s much larger groups of mostly Indian men descended on lakes in a defensive and defiant assertion of what they referred to as their "treaty rights." They were harassed, obstructed, laughed at, denied their emerging particularity via stereotypes, threatened, and physically assaulted by larger and larger numbers of local non-Indians. Indian perseverance, tenacity, cooperation, and cleverness, however, had allied the federal government to the point of creating conditions in which a display of cultural value on the part of both sides to the other was possible. What had previously been surreptitiously undertaken as a criminal act before the court decision was now done under the lights. In this circumstance it became clear to Indian people that the non-Indians did not really want to fight for the fish; they wanted to snipe verbally and with a variety of projectiles consistent with their previous relationship of domination.[9] They desired a conflict on their own terms.

They would not get one. Though the state successfully negotiated a lease of the rights with the band's Tribal Council, the membership defeated it in referendum in October 1989. Then the leadership of the spearing faction at Lac du Flambeau and the Tribal Council joined together and sued the protest leaders and the sheriffs in 1991 for violation of their civil rights, and the protests subsided. The process left a community that was both renewed and internally divided.

The Revitalization Paradigm

In their very useful article on ethnic reorganization, Joanne Nagel and Matthew Snipp (1993) offer a comprehensive taxonomy of how the dialectical relationships between ethnic identification and ethnic ascription are worked out as social, economic, political, and cultural strategies by American Indian peoples. The last, cultural reorganization, "involves the modification, addition, or elimination of the content, practice, or transmission of material or ideational culture" (Nagel and Snipp 1993:221). The authors regard these strategies as responses to "assaults on, and threats to, group and cultural survival" (1993:221) and analyze cultural change as a mechanism of ethnic persistence. Ceremonies are modified; new forms are adopted; and groups revise, blend, and revitalize. The sense and communal imaginary of a group are retained by virtue of a capacity to represent itself to itself and others in a succession of symbolic forms. The implicit conception of culture here has been made explicit by Comaroff and Comaroff: Culture is "a historically situated, historically unfolding ensemble of signifiers-in-action, signifiers at once material and symbolic, social and aesthetic. Some of these, at any moment in time, will be woven into more or less tightly integrated, relatively explicit worldviews; others may be heavily contested, the stuff of counterideologies and 'subcultures'; yet others may become more or less unfixed, relatives freefloating, and indeterminate in their value and meaning" (1992:27). Preeminent among these weaving projects, if I may extend their metaphor, is revitalization.

In 1956 Anthony Wallace defined the concept of revitalization as "a deliberate, organized, conscious effort by members of a society to construct a more satisfying culture" (1956c:265). He concedes that the analytical idea requires accepting "an organismic analogy" and then goes on to say that we all live effectively in society to the extent to which our experience concords with "a mental image of the society and its culture" (1956c:266), an imaginary, in the current vocabulary. The discourse circulating about treaty rights and Anishinaabe tradition that describes, interprets, and motivates social processes *is* a collective reimagination of society and, as such, is an effort at revitalization.

If the necessary conditions for revitalization include periods of "increased individual stress" and "cultural distortion," in Wallace's terms, these were satisfied in northern Wisconsin when the appeals court decision in 1983 created the possibility of a whole new relationship between the tribes and the state vis-à-vis the use of natural resources. Stress and distortion were the result of the sudden implosion of a framework that had been shaping relations between the bands and the state for over a century. Also recognizing the possibilities inherent in the Voigt decision, important sectors of the local non-Indian population sought to deny them by mobilizing the media and organizing protests to conserve the status quo ante. The tension and competition between the forces of Indian and non-Indian imagination destabilized the antecedent hegemony. As McMullen (ch. 12) points out, "Revitalization . . . is—at its heart—about power and the relationship between superordinate and subordinate and not about cultural difference."

The stress induced by possibility also tore the Indian community apart in the memory of some people who lived through it. Along with the anxiety over whether or not all the spearers would come back alive came a series of questions: Was this worth it? Were some people exploiting "the culture" for personal political projects? More generally, what could and would the community and all the Wisconsin Anishinaabe people become given the Voigt decision and their elevated legal status in relation to the state? What would the personal, social, and economic costs of exercising this power be over the long term?

The periods of disorientation and of the consolidation and competition of visions took place simultaneously, not serially as Wallace has noted for the Seneca. Flambeau did not have to die in order to be reborn. In fact they went through a rather lively internal conflict, intensely debating the implications and value of their newly recognized rights over the course of the 1980s and well into the 1990s. As a measure of the intensity of the internal conflict over the value of Voigt, the staff members of the George Brown Jr. Ojibwe Museum and Cultural Center were only beginning to think about an exhibit on the 1983 Voigt decision and subsequent conflict in the late 1990s, years after the Wisconsin Historical Society had already mounted an exhibit.

No single vision emerged to reorganize the collective "mazeway," or conception of "nature, society, culture, personality and body image" (Wallace 1956c:266), of the Wisconsin Anishinaabe now in possession of federally recognized treaty rights to legally exploit resources off their reservations and negotiate the terms of that usufruct. There was no single prophet in this revitalization partially because of the general suspicion of authoritative totalizing visions among these historically egalitarian people and partially because all of these bands were in conflict with local non-Indians to greater and lesser extents. Though most Indian people had relatives on other reservations, thus articulating a transreservation social network, as political and economic entities, all of these bands had rather different histories and relationships with the non-Indian communities that they perceived as surrounding them. [10] As a result there were multiple and synergetic "prophetic visions" in a complex multiband division of symbolic labor.

The different leaders of the movement, who were exercising and articulating the meaning of treaty rights, had some qualities in common that concord with Wallace's prophetic leaders. They were cosmopolitan. They were all cultural brokers of one sort or another who had investments in the maximization of the cultural differences between the enclaves of which they were members and the surrounding society in which they had navigated with various degrees of success. All of these leaders, visionaries, as it were, were within a few years on both sides of 50 years old, so they had seen a great deal of change on the reservations over the course of their own lives. They had come of age when the dominant culture's assimilative forces were at their peak, given force and shape by the federal policy of termination. They were young adults when a worldwide cultural revolution began to challenge long-standing power relations between the dominant and the dominated. As a result, when the Seventh Circuit Court of Appeals upheld the tribe's stipulated rights in the ceded territories, they variously cooperated and competed with each other to recruit followers to their understandings of the meaning of both the Voigt decision and the local non-Indian reaction to it.

Perhaps as a consequence of their relatively broad social and multi-cultural experiences, these leaders also understood a number of things about Indian identity in the late 20th century. They knew that Indian people have a culture and that it is "worthy of respect, commitment and defense" (Sahlins 1995:13). This culturalism is "the mark of the dissolution of modernist identity" (Friedman 1987:164) and is coordinate with a diffusion of power to what were formerly hinterlands of metropolitan cores, which these leaders instantiated. Corollary to this, and in different ways and in different measures, these leaders knew that Indian culture and identity live or die on a far larger stage than their opponents were envisioning. [11] They understood that the Anishinaabe are both unique and also a *kind* of people who have a great deal in common historically and structurally with other North and South American Indians, Hawaiians, Maoris, and other so-called Third and Fourth World peoples in their view.

They understood that they are a colonized people but that they also have allies among their erstwhile oppressors: critical or alienated intellectuals and activists motivated by a general desire for social justice and nostalgic for communities organized along the lines of something more enduring and satisfying than personal choice. The material resources that these non-Indians possessed were valuable to these leaders. But these non-Indians were also valuable as signs of Indian virtue and the credibility of prophetic voices to their own communities.

It is this social process that James Clifton (1994) challenges so provocatively, if also cynically, in his recent work. He purports to segregate so many cultural constructionist undertakings as inauthentic, embracing a rather essentialized conception of North American Indian peoples, and is impatient with the complexities, ambiguities, and ambivalences inherent in decolonization and the decentralization of authorial voices.[12] The attempt to "reclaim the power of self definition" (Turner 1997:359) and the project of self-identification, as a people with a distinct culture that represents consciousness of the value of such distinction on the world stage, interacted synergistically to valorize what could credibly be represented as "tradition," "custom," or "culture" as what was at stake and as the most salient resource in this conflict.

Flambeau businessman and tribal judge Tom Maulson envisioned a coherent Indian community fully equal to the communities that surrounded and often exploited it. Walt Bresette, of the Red Cliff band and cofounder of the Wisconsin Greens, imagined indigenous stewardship as the salvation of the Lake Superior basin and ceded territories in the face of only nominally regulated post-Fordist capitalism (see Whaley and Bresette 1994). Edward Benton-Banai performed ceremonies, acted as a kind of spiritual adviser to the other leaders, and interpreted the escalating political conflict in prophetic terms in *The Mishomis Book: The Voice of the Ojibway* (1988), in which he articulates the Neesh-wa-swi' ish-ko-day-kawn' (Seven Fires) prophecy of a reemergence of the Anishinaabe people recommitted to traditional ways. Flambeau member Nick Hockings, a cultural entrepreneur and self-appointed ambassador, spoke in mystical terms of the gifts given to the four races of man and the appearance of a New People with the Seventh Fire, as he synthesized the fundamentals of his own Baha'i faith with the writings of Benton-Banai. Gibby Chapman, a Flambeau member, ex–police officer, and ex–tribal prosecutor, called for a kind of apartheid guaranteed by a willingness to take dramatic action to remind the surrounding non-Indian communities of the power and resources Flambeau could command. James Schlender (1991), a Lac Courte Oreilles tribal member, executive director of the Great Lakes Indian Fish and Wildlife Commission, lawyer, and pipe carrier, articulated a practical sovereignty and a broad political and social critique of Indian–white relations.

For about half of the 19th century and most of the 20th, Lac du Flambeau had been a dominated periphery in world systems terms. When it could no longer export furs, it exported logs, labor, and some finished goods in the form of crafts, country foods, and indigenous knowledge of wildlife. It did not control the terms of the exchange. Two weeks before the fall of the Berlin Wall, in a referendum, the tribal membership made a collective decision that marked their reimagining of Flambeau as a local center of the world. The decision was taken in a global atmosphere of modernistic decline: a dehegemonizing dehomogenization, in Fried-man's (1994) inelegant if very efficient terms. Flambeau's decision was the culmination of a process that had begun at least 15 years before, so its own proximity to events half a world away is fortuitous but not incidental. The membership rejected the opportunity to exchange off-reservation hunting, fishing, and gathering rights, a symbol of differ-ence, for a ten-year period for $50 million in cash, employment oppor-tunities, and social programs. If there is an irony here, then it is that the decision to reject the state's offer produced the conditions for acquiring that same capital by other means, and thus the community could con-tinue to credibly imagine itself significant, valuable, and important and as socially and culturally distinct.

More than half a century ago, Ralph Linton pointed out that move-ments tend to arise "when members of the subject society find that their assumption of the culture of the dominant group is being effec-tively opposed by it, or that it is not improving their social position" (1943:240). Because the central symbols of this revitalization—treaty rights and spearfishing—represent modes of resistance negotiated in terms of the dominant society's structures and categories, the outcome of the conflict over spearfishing has been a broader and deeper articula-tion with the dominant society, though the local community has asserted greater control over that process of articulation. Lac du Flambeau has an exemplary Tribal Court that has taken over a number of categories of civil law and is leading the other Public Law 280 Wisconsin tribes in taking back criminal jurisdiction from the state. It has adopted and adapted state code, though it is being applied in a way that is nuanced by local values. Lac du Flambeau is the first tribe in the state to implement a tribal Child Support Agency. As a symbol of its comprehensibility as a single totality, it has a museum that presents an idealized version of local culture and caters mostly to the region's schoolchildren and non-Indian tourists. Lac du Flambeau is now the biggest employer in Vilas County because of its casino, convention center, and hotel, which was established on such favorable terms because the tribe learned so much negotiating and fighting with the state over the Voigt decision in the 1980s. The tribe is the first in the United States ever to be chosen by the National Trust for Historic Preservation to develop the idea of heritage tourism. Lac du Flambeau sells state fishing, boating, and all-terrain vehicle licenses and keeps the proceeds in exchange for leaving credible bag limits of walleyed pike on the lakes using its government-to-government relationship with Washington as leverage in bargaining with the state. The tribe publishes a monthly newspaper.

But it has also revitalized indigenous historic "material and symbolic, social and aesthetic" forms (Comaroff and Comaroff 1992:27). In addition to spearfishing, these are the movement's "perpetuative" dimension, in Linton's (1943:231) terms, but perhaps are better thought of in the way in which Roger Keesing discusses *kastom* in Melanesia, with people "resuming old rituals, reviving traditional dress, music, and dances, and reactivating old patterns of feasting and exchange" (1982a:357). The tribe supports language classes for adults as well as language classes for children in the public grammar school. The Big Drum has returned to the reservation and is meeting weekly in the Tribe's Round House— built on the site of an earlier Big Drum structure in the Old Village. Sweat lodges and divinatory shaking tent ceremonies have also returned to the reservation.

Engaging the relationship between power and representation, the linguist Max Weinreich has been associated with the formulation that a language is a dialect with an army and a navy.[13] In the cultural register, Marshall Sahlins has distinguished the invention of tradition discourse and revitalization discourse in parallel terms, reminding us that the credibility of a historical interpretation is a function of who commands the modalities of attributing significance:

> For it happens that in the fifteenth and sixteenth centuries a bunch of indigenous intellectuals and artists in Europe got together and began inventing their traditions and themselves by attempting to revive the learning of an ancient culture which they claimed to be the achievement of their ancestors but which they did not fully understand, as for many centuries this culture had been lost and its languages (Latin and Greek) had been corrupted or forgotten. For centuries also these Europeans had been converted to Christianity, but this did not prevent them from now calling for the restoration of their pagan heritage. . . . All this came to be called the Renaissance in European history, because it gave birth to "modern civilization."
>
> What else can one say about it, except that some people have all the historical luck? When Europeans invent their traditions—with the Turks at the gates—it is a genuine cultural rebirth, the beginnings of a progressive future. When other peoples do it, it is a sign of cultural decadence, a factitious recuperation, which can only bring forth the simulacra of a dead past.

On the other hand, the historical lesson could be that all is not lost.
[1993:3]

In his introduction to the collection of essays *The Invention of Tra-dition*, Eric Hobsbawm points out that it is important to distinguish between invented traditions and customs: " 'Custom' is what judges do; 'tradition' (in this instance invented tradition) is the wig, robe and other formal paraphernalia and ritualized practice surround their substantial action" (1983:2–3). Spearfishing off the reservations among the Amer-ican Ojibwe bands is a customary practice, not an invented tradition. The thousands of walleyed pike that the band spears each year over a couple of weeks in the spring are testimony to cultural continuity, in that the past is "sedimented" in the body's "habitual memory" (Con-nerton 1989:72). Spearfishing is not ritualized or formalized. In fact, it is contested as a legitimate practice by non-Indians, in part, by virtue of the fact that it is so strikingly pragmatic, with tribal members using the most efficient means available no matter their provenance. No one would claim that it is done in a way that is unchanging. Hobsbawm's analytical rubric might aid in understanding the difference between the customary practice of dancing and the emergence of the category of Men's Traditional Dancing at powwows, for example, but it does not illuminate what is at stake here.

The ogitchida is not an invented tradition either. It is a revival or repatriation of a historic social role and ideology that emerged when "violating," a dominated people's preeminent resistance practice, was effectively decriminalized by the Voigt decision but violently contested by powerful groups that could not comprehend the legality and morality of collectively held inherited rights to property.

Spearing does represent the revaluation of a historic practice as a sign of cultural identity in a political arena where that distinction was being demeaned or denied. As such, spearing became "traditional," in native rhetoric, but meaning "customary" in Hobsbawm's sense, referring to long-standing historical practice. The current practice, historically con-tinuous with some of the very earliest descriptions of Indian people throughout the upper Great Lakes, has been substantivized, "set up as [a] definite entit[y] to be reflected upon and manipulated by the people in the situation under consideration" (Thomas 1992b:64). As such, it is also a project, "a series of actions directed toward accomplishing a particular goal" (McMullen [ch. 12]), an idea embedded in Wallace's concept of revitalization and the source of its long-lived explanatory utility.

What took place at Lac du Flambeau and at the other communities of Lake Superior Anishinaabe, and to some extent continues to take place, is a revitalization in Wallace's sense to the extent to which the communities went through a self-conscious process that eventuated in their thinking of themselves and the story of their relationship to the encompassing society in a different way. There *is* a new "mazeway" in Wallace's terms, and to some extent it has been imposed on the non-Indians' neighboring communities. In Bruner's (1986:139) terms, more extensively discussed by McMullen (ch. 12), a paradigmatic shift in the narrative structure took place wherein the past was no longer thought of as glorious but, rather, as exploitive. The present is no longer thought of as only disorganized, in that a consciousness of action as resistance movement supersedes that former negative evaluation. The future is not imagined to hold assimilation but, rather, ethnic resurgence.

Notes

For an extended treatment of the issues discussed herein, see Nesper 2002.

1. For a history of the recent anti-Indian movement, see Ryser 1995.

2. For a discussion of the history of treaty rights activism, see Prucha 1994: 409–428.

3. Bobo and Garcia's *The Chippewa Indian Treaty Rights Survey* (1992:18) indicates that 42 percent of non-Indians in the area held a negative view of Indians. Thomas Heberlein (1993) cites unemployment rates on the reservations of northern Wisconsin in the late 1980s ranging between 49 and 85 percent. In 1991, 44 percent of the potential labor force was unemployed at Lac du Flambeau (Bureau of Indian Affairs 1991). In 1993, 43 percent of the cases in Vilas County were from Lac du Flambeau. In 1980, almost 30 percent of Indian students left high school before graduation (Applied Population Laboratory 1985).

4. While in the field in the early 1990s I heard a number of jokes about Indians told by Indian people, most of which implicitly valorized some trait that non-Indians denigrated.

5. Asked why so many Flambeau students dropped out of high school, the administrator of Flambeau's elementary school told me, "If they fail, at least they can't be accused of being white." According to a lay advocate in the Tribal Court at Lac du Flambeau, the chief judge of the court is criticized for not being harder on delinquent youths by people who do not understand that scoring time

in jail is exactly what these youths are seeking to establish the authenticity of their Flambeau Indian identity.

6. Meyer's *The White Earth Tragedy* (1994) stands out as an exemplary account of this process. Danziger's *The Chippewas of Lake Superior* (1978) offers a more general chronology of the same processes.

7. In 1929 Densmore (see 1979) noted that there were five different kinds of torches for different kinds of activities. Just as *waswewin*, fishing at night with a torch, as marked practice is well described, so also is hunting deer at night from canoes with torches as the animals traversed the shorelines and shallows, attempting to escape the flies in the woods. In fact, the only deer that George Copway—"the Celebrated Kah-Ge-Ga-Gah-Bowh, Chief of the Ojibway Nation," and author of histories in 1850 and 1860—ever killed with a bow and arrow, he shot from a canoe at night by the light of a candle: "We placed in a three-sided lantern; opening one side, the light was thrown upon the deer only" (1850:35–36).

8. In Frederic Baraga's *A Dictionary of the Ojibway Language*, originally published in 1878, *ogitchida* is defined as "a brave warrior, a brave, a hero" (1992: 318). In Eugene Buechel's Teton Dakota dictionary, *akicita* is defined as "a head warrior, one next to a chief, a warrior soldier, a policeman" (1970:71). The term may be derived from the Dakota "*akita*, v.a. Seek for, hunt for, as something lost, make efforts to get," in that "*akicita*, v. (of *akita*). Hunt for another" (Buechel 1970:75, 71).

9. Identifying with the fish, whites now imagined the Indians as agents of distant and alien centers of governmental power, a model of social relations that had been lurking under the discursive radar for more than a decade at this point.

10. Heberlein (1993) offers an account of the difference between the protests in the areas of Lac Courte Oreilles and Lac du Flambeau based on the difference in the ways in which the Indian communities were nested within a configuration of non-Indian communities.

11. In general, the leaders of these Indian communities were more cosmopolitan than the leaders of the non-Indian communities, commonly having lived in the poor, multicultural sectors of large cities for some part of their lives and then having gone abroad in the armed services.

12. For a more extended discussion of Clifton's perspective, see V. Deloria 1998.

13. I thank my colleague Carolyn MacKay for telling me that the folklore among linguists has it that Weinreich was told this after a lecture he gave in New York on dialects of Yiddish.

11. EXPRESSIONS OF IDENTITY IN TAHITI
Lisa Henry

Ann McMullen (ch. 12) discusses the relationship between revitalization and the invention of tradition. She suggests that invented traditions are embedded in Anthony F. C. Wallace's (1956c) theory of revitalization, in that both ideas "involve conscious, internal efforts to direct culture change" (McMullen [ch. 12]), usually unifying socialization in response to colonial power. Inventions of traditions are essentially "by-products" of the revitalization process, in that they involve organized, conscious reconstructions of culture to develop social and ethnic identities, which then become manipulated for the advancement of contemporary nationalist agendas.

This chapter examines the context of revitalization and the politics of culture in the territory of French Polynesia. As mentioned by Jolly and Thomas (1992), the concepts of invented tradition and revitalization have been discussed and analyzed throughout numerous studies in the Pacific literature, though differences in interpretation are reflected in the varying regional experiences with colonialism and decolonialism. What they lack, notes Thomas, is a historical perspective that contextualizes change as part of local, regional, and colonial articulation: "Reifications of tradition have frequently been seen as cultural phenomena that stand essentially on their own. It's not that historical interactions with other populations, and particularly colonial experiences, are denied or left undiscussed; it is rather that these are not effectively integrated analytically" (1992a:213). This chapter offers such a historical perspective by linking contemporary inventions of Tahitian tradition with the rise and fall of Pouvana'a, the "Father" of Tahitian nationalism. This linkage is crucial to understanding the political nature of Tahitian culture that developed during the 1990s and which has informed nationalist rhetoric concerning identity, independence, and power. Specifically, I locate health care behavior at the center of this negotiation of identity as a point of articulation at which resistance to rapid social change may be expressed.

Early Nationalism as Revitalization

Wallace (1956c) discusses two conditions in which revitalization movements occur—increased stress for members of the society and a period of internal cultural distortion. In order to reduce the existing stress, a movement occurs toward "mazeway reformulation," in which ideological changes occur among certain members of the society, leading to the eventual construction of a more satisfying culture. Although Wallace contends that most revitalization movements are inspired by a supernatural revelation of a prophet or leader, he suggests that some movements may be considerably more political in nature.

Resistance to the French presence in the Pacific is not a recent phenomenon in French Polynesia. Pouvana'a a Oopa is known as the "Father" of nationalism throughout the territory. His effort to lead the Tahitian people to independence in the 1940s and 1950s was remarkably well supported by the populace. Pouvana'a, born on Huahine in a rural Polynesian village, was known for his opposition to France. His half-European descent was evident through his light skin and blue eyes, but his lifestyle and behaviors portrayed his Polynesian values, one of which was a faithful following of the Bible (Newbury 1980).

Sent to France in 1914, with scores of other Tahitian youths, to fight for France in World War I, Pouvana'a returned with progressive and worldly ideas for his small island in the South Pacific. His eagerness was supported by other war veterans and intensified with the support of returning soldiers from World War II. This new crop of war veterans remarked bitterly on the injustice they felt upon returning to Tahiti. They felt that their sacrifices for liberty and democracy in Western Europe were not appreciated by the French settlers, who successfully avoided seeing a battle during the war. In addition, like Pouvana'a, they returned from war with progressive ideas about democracy and the knowledge that "democracy" in the colonies was quite different than that in Europe. They saw in Pouvana'a a leader and flocked to his movement (Danielsson and Danielsson 1986; Newbury 1980).

The Polynesians turned to Pouvana'a for advice—every kind of advice—from marital disputes, to the correct interpretation of the Bible, to the best way to dry cobra. They saw in him the wisdom that only comes with age—they called him *metua*, "father" (Danielsson and Danielsson 1986). Danielsson and Danielsson liken Pouvana'a's role among the Tahitians to that of a latter-day prophet, "almost a messiah": "For the first time since the islands became French in 1842, the Polynesians had found in Pouvana'a a leader and a spokesman who was one of them, who understood them, and was understood by them, not only in the narrow sense that he spoke Tahitian but in the broader sense of sharing their very special way of thinking and doing things" (1986:25, 24). Not only was Pouvana'a leading the people toward independence, his movement was an effort to restore the identity of the Polynesian people within French Polynesia, where foreign leaders and institutions held the key to political and economic power (Stevenson 1992; Tagupa 1976).

The political activism and outspokenness of Pouvana'a's movement resulted in his detainment by French officials several times. Yet these conflicts with the administration only heightened his reputation as a leader among Tahitians. Pouvana'a won a seat in the French National Assembly in 1949 and established the Rassemblement Démocratique des Populations Tahitiennes (RDPT, or Democratic Assembly of the Tahitian People) the following year. Pouvana'a was reelected to the French National Assembly in 1952 and 1956. The party advanced further when it won the majorities in the local assembly in 1953 and 1957. Yet, despite his popularity on the islands, Pouvana'a had little political success in either the national or the local assemblies in seeing his visions for independence become reality (Newbury 1980).

Wallace discusses that a revolutionary movement will almost always experience opposition or resistance: "Resistance . . . is held either by a powerful faction within the society or by agents of a dominant foreign society" (1958:274). Strong opposition to the RDPT mounted among the French, demi-, and Chinese businesspeople, as well as the French administration. In 1957, as part of widespread reform throughout the French colonies, the powers of the territorial government were expanded, and the RDPT, in favor of secession, held the majority of the seats. The following year the party passed a bill for a progressive income tax that was violently opposed by local businesses. They saw the tax as Pouvana'a's way of beginning to finance his goal of independence at their expense. Shopkeepers demonstrated at the Territorial Assembly, forcing party members to seek refuge at the governor's residence. The protesters demanded the immediate abolition of the bill, and the Territorial Assembly eventually complied, without the vote of the RDPT party (Newbury 1980).

The following year General Charles de Gaulle made the announce-ment that all overseas possessions would vote to decide the future of their relationships with France. Before the Tahitians was the opportu-nity of independence, yet there were only two options: vote yes and French Polynesia would remain part of the French commonwealth, to later decide its degree of "independence," or vote no and France will cut all ties to the island, morally and economically. Pouvana'a was com-mitted to independence and fought hard to bring his message to the voters in the outer islands. At that time the French controlled all radio transmissions to the outer islands; thus any relayed messages about the vote or the Pouvana'a movement largely reflected the interest of the French administration. Unfortunately for Pouvana'a, his efforts were not enough to sustain the RDPT party: Tahitians voted yes in favor of remaining part of France (Newbury 1980).

Pouvana'a and a group of supports were later arrested on suspicion of plotting to burn down Papeete. They spent one year in jail awaiting trial, and despite some questions about the validity of the evidence pre-sented against him, Pouvana'a was convicted and sentenced to 15 years of banishment. His efforts toward cultural transformation and social re-vitalization (Wallace 1958) were effectively squelched by the prevailing colonial government.

What is interesting about the Tahitian case during the next two de-cades is the apparent lapse from nationalist discourse. Tahitians rarely spoke of independence in the 1960s and early 1970s. In 1962 they began to feel the onslaught of significant economic development when France started construction of its nuclear testing facility, Centre d'Expérimen-tation du Pacific (CEP), in the Tuamotu Archipelago. The CEP project generated an era of economic growth and associated social change by creating thousands of jobs for those seeking wage income (Finney 1973; Lockwood 1993b). French Polynesia took a giant step toward the mod-ern world with the implementation of new military bases, a major public hospital, expanded shipping facilities, and a modern transportation and communication system (Lockwood 1993a). Any opposition to the CEP was curtailed by increasing amounts of French aid and French social ser-vices, such as education, health care, communication, and public works projects. The infusion of foreign capital into the territory created a number of high-paying jobs in the public sector. As these jobs increased in number, people from the outer islands began migrating to the urban center of Papeete. Such urbanization resulted in decreased participation in "primary productive activities" (agriculture, fishing, and crafts) and decreased dependency and reliability on extended families: "Government salaries become the major source of income and are used to finance a lifestyle in which imported Western foods and consumer items have supplanted local products. In sum, islanders become dependent on external foreign funds for their jobs, social services, and an inflated standard of living which they would be unable to achieve on their own" (Lockwood 1993b:82). Thus, the trade-off of such intense development and modernization efforts was a welfare state colony characterized by a neocolonial dependency relationship and artificial prosperity (Lockwood 1993b:82).

Tahitian Inventions

As noted by Stevenson (1992), contemporary Ma'ohi identity varies from the postwar vision of Pouvana'a and his followers. Rapid modernization and Western acculturation have created challenges to the cultural values of Tahitians that had never before been questioned. Thomas (1992a) argues that the social awareness and construction of culture most often occur in opposition to others, particularly colonial influences. Stevenson reports that "the creation of a contemporary Ma'ohi identity is not only a new manifestation of a cultural heritage integral to Tahitian society, but also a manifestation of an identity in contradistinction to the French" (1992:120). As Elliston (1997) describes, the cultural revitalization movement resulted in part from the large-scale, rural-to-urban migrations experienced in the 1960s through the 1980s. For the first time in French Polynesia's colonial history, large numbers of Tahitians were exposed to metropolitan French and were forced to cope with "cultural chauvinism," metropolitan French attitude toward Polynesians, which "both presumed and asserted French cultural superiority, and denigrated as inferior to that the culture and history of Polynesians" (Elliston 1997:104). Thus, the Tahitian cultural revitalization movement is a response to these attitudes in effort to rediscover and reclaim a sense of pride and accomplishment in Tahitian cultural heritage, as well as to establish a Tahitian national identity.

The foundation for the Tahitian cultural revitalization movement began with the reinterpretation of the cultural festival known today as *heiva* (Stevenson 1992:121). The heiva is a celebration of Tahitian culture that has persisted since 1881. It began as a French celebration in honor of Napoleon III's victory over Italy in 1859 and continued as the official celebration of French independence. Although the celebration originated as a French holiday, Tahitians interpreted the festival as an official sanctioning of public song and dance, the latter having been banned by early missionaries. Over the years the celebration reinforced both colonial and traditional culture. The festivities have remained a mixture of French heritage, to reinforce France's colonial position in the territory, and Tahitian culture, as an expression and affirmation of the value of Tahitian culture (Stevenson 1990, 1992).

The heiva has become the main venue for the expression of Tahiti's neotraditional cultural identity. As various aspects of Tahitian culture become reconstructed, reinvented, and reborn, so too does the heiva adapt and transform to these new expressions of Tahitian identity. Dance groups, for example, had been competing in the cultural festival for many years. Yet it was not until 1952, as Stevenson reports, that "the respectability of dance was heightened by the standardization of the art form through the creation of a semiprofessional dance troupe by Madeleine Moua" (1992:121). The formation of Moua's dance group, called Heiva, marks the rebirth of traditional dancing in French Polynesia. Since the 1960s the heiva has become increasingly more Tahitian, as seen by the greater number of Tahitian events than French events. This shift in cultural emphasis occurred during the same time that France was building the nuclear testing facility and profoundly impacting the territory with the infiltration of military personnel, economic development, and Western culture. As French intervention increased, Tahitians turned to the heiva as both a meaningful representation of the past and a tool to reeducate the populace and reinterpret the past for contemporary agendas (Stevenson 1990).

In addition to the heiva, many other developments occurred during the initial institutionalization of Tahitian culture. Marco Tevane, the minister of culture during this time, overtly promoted the culture of Polynesia and founded the Club Ma'ohi in 1965. This association was committed to the reinterpretation of cultural values and created the Tane Tahiti—a male contest that emphasizes Tahitian values such as "strength, agility, ability in subsistence activities (fishing, paddling, copra production), and proficiency in the Tahitian language" (Stevenson 1992:122). L'Académie Tahitienne was established in 1967. Its mission is to protect and enrich the Tahitian language, as well as to give back to the Tahitian language the respectability it has earned as an ancient tradition. The academy changed its name in 1975 to Te Fare Vana'a, signifying French acceptance of Tahitian as a joint official language in the territory. The Centre Polynésien des Sciences Humaines, which includes the Musée de Tahiti et des Icircumflexles, and the Office Territorial d'Action Culturelle (OTAC), both founded in the late 1970s, are institutions devoted to the preservation, production, and development of Tahitian culture. The establishment of OTAC signaled the official desire of the government to develop the Ma'ohi culture in addition to the French culture.

Tahitian healing is also an integral part of the cultural revitalization movement in the territory. The reconstruction of Tahitian healing has become a major component in developing a Tahitian cultural identity. Government support of Tahitian healing began in the early 1980s during the same era in which many Tahitian customs were actively reconstructed and revitalized. In 1980 the district of Papeete sponsored and organized a cultural manifestation, called "Tahiti aux temps anciens" (or "Ancient Tahiti") whereby they invited the public to rediscover ancient Polynesian traditions, including Tahitian healing. Much support for Tahitian healing comes from OTAC, which works with the associations of Tahitian healers to organize healing expositions for the public. Each year Tahitian healing is honored at the Territorial Assembly in the form of a three-day exposition. Such expositions are held to reeducate the public on the methods of Tahitian healing and provide Tahitian massage therapy (and some internal medicine) to patients in need of treatment. By exhibiting Tahitian healing at the Territorial Assembly, healers provide a venue for the public to become familiar with the system of healing in an open environment. Although indigenous healing has persisted over the years, there are people (Tahitians and Europeans) who are skeptical of its efficacy and prefer to trust biomedical doctors. The expositions provide a venue for discussion, collaboration, and education about the Tahitian system of healing for all territorial residents.

The South Pacific Commission encouraged the healers of Tahitian medicine to form associations to protect the heritage of local healing, to ensure the authenticity of healers and their practice of local medicine, and to share information and healing techniques. During his term as minister of health (1987–91) Drollet strongly supported the promotion of Tahitian healing and the collaboration of local healers with biomedical doctors, as well as with other indigenous healers from other regions in the Pacific. He also encouraged healers to remain associated, for associations encourage Tahitian medicine to be practiced in public view. According to Drollet, opening the practice of Tahitian medicine to the public view provides an opportunity to "do the housecleaning" and so on, to examine more clearly its good qualities and its potential problems, and to sort out the authentic healers from the charlatans.

Associations also provide a venue for collaboration, cooperation, and innovation among healers. For many years healers were banned by the French government from practicing their ancestral medicine, yet they continued treatments in hiding. They constantly feared visits from the gendarmes and those in opposition to their healing techniques. Associations now provide healers with the security of a group identity and the knowledge that arises from close collaboration. This ultimately provides better and more innovative care for patients. One healer explained that collaboration within his association has led to creative solutions for treating patients who are difficult to heal. Many healers will conjoin to discuss a patient's condition until they have compiled enough information to understand the symptoms and origin of the illness. They will then work together to prepare a medication. If this medication does not cure the patient, then they will continue to collaborate until an effective medication is discovered. Finally, because students of Tahitian healing are taught through apprenticeships, efforts to share knowledge of treatment procedures greatly benefit the education of future generations of Tahitian healers.

Legitimization and regulation efforts are also inspired by the associations of healers. In 1988 healers proposed to Minister of Health Drollet to establish a school of massage. Drollet supported this development, in particular because healers agreed to exclude the preparation of internal medicine from the massage school because this was considered a higher risk for support by the government. Drollet was attentive to the preparations for the school of massage, and it was agreed that some regulation of this practice and profession would benefit the general public. Since Drollet's time, however, nothing has been done to realize the massage school. According to Drollet, a conflict developed between the Tahitian masseurs and the biomedically trained physical therapists. The physical therapists argued that Tahitian masseurs did not have state-approved diplomas to practice massage and therefore had no legal rights to practice. Healers appealed to the Ministry of Health about the possibility of creating work certificates similar to the credentials of biomedical doctors, but Drollet was opposed to this formal legitimization. Holding the opinion that Tahitian healers desired certification only to "play doctor," to copy biomedical doctors, he encouraged those healers instead to turn inward and examine their system of healing in order to improve it, not make it more similar to biomedicine (personal communication, 1998).

It is clear that the cultural revitalization movement is well under way in French Polynesia. The construction of a Tahitian identity, as well as the reinterpretation and reconstruction of cultural tradition, is symbolic of cultural pride and commitment to the reeducation process. Since European contact such traditions have been undergoing tremendous change and constant innovation, which have strengthened the cultural and artistic heritage of Tahiti. What is less clear, and what the next section explores, is that many of these reconstructions have political meanings and ulterior subtexts that can be manipulated in public discussions of identity and resistance. Stevenson (1992:117) hints at this when she points out the irony that many of these re-created traditions have been financed by the same colonizing government that was responsible for their demise.

The Politicization of Culture

The notion that tradition is "reconstructed," "reinvented," or "reinterpreted" for its symbolic political power is discussed throughout the current literature in the Pacific (see Babadzan 1988; Hanson 1989; Jolly and Thomas 1992; Keesing and Tonkinson 1982; Lawson 1990, 1993, 1997; Linnekin 1983, 1990a, 1992; Linnekin and Poyer 1990; Otto and Thomas 1997). Oftentimes these reinvented traditions are different than those recorded by early explorers, navigators, and missionaries, and yet these same writers and even scholars are also responsible for some of the misrepresentations of ancestral cultures that are filtering back to the community through the reeducation process (Hanson 1989). Keesing states that this "mythmaking" in the Pacific has powerful symbolic and political forces that "refashion the past to advance the interests of the present" (1989:35). Linnekin furthers this point in her discussion of Pacific anthropology: "[This] cultural objectification has been explored particularly in discussions of colonial history and nationalism. Much of this literature makes the point that models of culture, *kastom* and tradition are politically instrumental in the construction of anticolonial and national identities" (1992:253, citing Babadzan 1988; Keesing 1989;

Keesing and Tonkinson 1982; Linnekin 1990a; Linnekin and Poyer 1990).

Linnekin (1983, 1992), for example, discusses nationalists' attempts to define or create a social identity in Hawaii. She argues that tradition is inevitably invented, or reconstructed, as people consciously use past lifeways in the construction of their social identity: "In nationalist movements, tradition becomes a rallying cry and a political symbol. Cultural revivalists search for an authentic heritage as the basis for ethnic distinctiveness; as they rediscover a culture they also create it" (1983:241). Linnekin (1983:241) argues that the urban Hawaiian cultural revival movement molds and reformulates tradition to meet demands of ethnic politics. She writes: "Cultural construction implies . . . that tradition is a selective representation of the past, fashioned in the present, responsive to contemporary priorities and agendas, and politically instrumental" (1992:251).

The politicization of culture has recently been discussed in the context of French Polynesia. Jones (1992) addresses the use of invented tradition from both sides of the political debate in French Polynesia—pro-French and pro-independence. She suggests that each political power emphasizes different aspects of *tradition* in order to mold the image it would like "authentic" Polynesian tradition to represent. The pro-independence side emphasizes precolonial traditions—such as the art of tattoo and the science of canoe voyages. The pro-French side of the political debate emphasizes aspects of traditional culture that have evolved as a result of colonial influences. Jones (1992:137) states that this emphasis of tradition—one that stresses Christianity and centers on the home, garden, and sea—is the tradition most familiar to urban and rural islanders. The arts representative of this period are those with foreign influences, including the cloth pareu, *tifaifai* bedspreads, and plaited hats. Jones (1992:137) argues that pro-French politicians support traditional *artisanats* and local craft associations in order to construct and reinforce their political identity as Polynesia.

Stevenson (1992) also discusses the politically charged debate in French Polynesia over what is authentically traditional and what is not. She states that the institutionalization of culture is necessary to reeducate the population but claims that "the politics of culture in Tahiti lies in the government support of artistic and cultural activities, not in an overt attempt to manipulate this identity as a political tool" (1992:134). Contrary to Jones, Stevenson dismisses the political use of Tahitian cultural identity and suggests that "Tahitian politicians are using their artistic heritage to heighten the awareness of a cultural past and to create a cultural identity for a Tahitian future" (1992:134, see also 1990). She contrasts the Tahitian cultural expression of identity to the politicization of cultural identity within "Hawaiiana" in Hawaii and the "Maoritanga" movement in Aotearoa, or New Zealand: "Hawaiians use this cultural-political identity to fight political battles concerning land rights, sovereignty, and even the definition of what or who is Hawaiian. The Maori are also using their identity to assert their cultural and political unity, and to gain for it the recognition of the New Zealand government" (1992:134, citing Hanson 1989:894; Linnekin 1990a).

Although Stevenson (1992) maintains that cultural knowledge and pride are currently driving the objectification of tradition, she recognizes Oscar Temaru (1988) and the Tavini party's use of "La Culture Ma'ohi" to advance their independence platform. The Tavini party has experienced rising popularity in the past 15 years—winning 8.4 percent of the votes in 1986, 13.8 percent in 1991, and 35 percent in 1997 (*La Dépêche de Tahiti* 1997). I suggest that the rising popularity of the Tavini party in the 1990s resulted in a heightened political use of La Culture Ma'ohi. Temaru's actions and ideals as mayor of Faa'a and leader of the Tavini party express his commitment to Tahitian identity and the revitalization of Tahitian culture. Yet this presents some dilemma for would-be nationalists members. How can they actively express their commitment to a Tahitian cultural identity through use of reconstructed traditions? McMullen (ch. 12) suggests that today's revitalization is reflected more in maintaining identity through narratives than actually "practicing" culture. I suggest that some reinvented traditions, such as local healing methods, are a point of articulation between expressive representations of the past and adaptive actions for the future success of a nationalist movement. The Tahitian healing system provides an interesting representation of this perspective, in that ethnomedicine often provides a location for native resistance in opposition to dominant cultures or governments.

Everyday Resistance and Nationalism

Talk of revitalization and inventions of tradition address periods of cultural stress and their effective reduction through cultural movements. Several studies have shown that contemporary ethnomedicine can be a forum through which resistance to rapid social change can be expressed

(Janes 1995, 1999; Nichter 1981; Ong 1987; Parsons 1984; Quintero 1995). Although biomedicine has gained tremendous success in becoming the dominant medical ideology in most cultures, local cultures rarely completely subordinate themselves to the power in which they are embedded. Such communities act as agents in resisting the loss of local control. Local medicine and healers who have enjoyed cultural and social legitimacy "serve as a vital and salient context for the legitimizing of various forms of distress" (Janes 1995:8). Lock and Scheper-Hughes argue that "physical distress and illness can also be thought of as acts of refusal or of mockery, a form of protest (albeit often unconscious) against oppressive social roles and ideologies" (1996:64). They go on to argue that "of all the cultural options for the expression of dissent, the use of trance or illness is perhaps the safest way to portray opposition—an institutionalized space from which to communicate fear, anxiety, and anger because in neither case are individuals under normal circumstances held fully accountable for their condition" (1996:64).

Janes's (1995, 1999) study of Tibetan medicine demonstrates that contemporary Tibetan medicine is a font of ethnic revitalization and resistance to the modernization policies of the Chinese state. This is particularly evident in "a class of sicknesses that, collectively, have come to symbolize the suffering inherent in rapid social, economic, and political change" (Janes 1995:6). His analysis shows that the transformation of Tibetan society and medicine has prompted a reconstruction of explanatory models of disease that include corruptive and disruptive forces of the Chinese state. Thus, local healing systems may have an adaptive value in constituting a cultural arena in which particular forms or idioms of distress may be expressed (Janes 1995).

Ong's (1987) study of rural Malaysians suggests that spirit possession among factory women is the manifestation of protests against labor discipline and male control in the women's industrial situation. The transformation of the Malaysian economy into modern capitalism, as well as the feminization of the labor force, contributed to the reconstructed meaning of Malay female gender and sexuality. Eruptions of spirit possession are expressions of anguish and cultural struggle felt by women being reconstituted both as instruments of labor and as new sexual personalities. Such possessions may be dealt with through the efforts of indigenous healers.

Clark (1993, 1994) claims that Tahitians see French culture as a dangerous threat to Tahitian ethnic identity. Following Scott's (1985) analysis of peasant societies, Clark asserts that Tahitians embody their own ethnicity through everyday forms of expression, such as Tahitian dress, hygiene, diet, and health-seeking behavior: "Choosing Tahitian therapy over that provided by the French government is a means of affirming one's membership in the Tahitian community and one's belief in its value" (1993:198). Clark (1994) implies that because Tahitians, particularly rural Tahitians, do not have opportunities to directly assert their opposition to the French presence in the territory, the "embodiment of ethnicity" is an arena for resistance to French culture. She argues that "the talk of Tahitian indigenous medical encounters serves as an idiom to express Tahitian cultural solidarity against the threat posed by French influences and to address anxieties caused by the French presence" (1993:181).

Although I support the theory that seeking Tahitian healing is a way of expressing cultural solidarity, I suggest that framing health care decisions within the discourse of everyday resistance implies that health care decisions are unavoidably political. If choosing Tahitian medicine is an expression of Tahitian cultural solidarity against the suggested "threat" of French culture, then how can one then opt to utilize the biomedical system without suggesting support for the ongoing presence of French culture? The politicization of health care decisions implies in this case that those who choose Tahitian healing automatically oppose French presence in the territory or that those who choose biomedicine implicitly support it.

My own research shows that supporters of independence are more likely to support Tahitian healing than biomedicine when considering health care options. However, with regard to the Tavini party's political uses of Tahitian culture, I suggest that Tahitian healing is not politicized in the same manner. Tamaru and the Tavini party hold approximately 35 percent of the vote in French Polynesia. Tahitians who currently do not support independence fear the loss of economic support from France (see Lockwood 1993b). Many Tahitians believe that independence means a step backward in terms of modernization and technology (see also Elliston 1997), which includes the loss of or reduction in widely available and inexpensive biomedical services in the territory. There are many aspects of French or Western culture, such as biomedicine and formal education, that Tahitians see as beneficial to their society. I argue that if members of the Tavini party incorporate Tahitian healing in their political platform, many Tahitians, who already fear the economic consequences of independence, would interpret the promotion of Tahitian healing as a substitute for biomedicine. Temaru promotes and defends La Culture Ma'ohi, including indigenous medicine. Yet, in taking a political stance in favor of Tahitian healing, the benefits of biomedicine are subject to the same opposition the Tavini party holds for the French presence in the territory. Temaru (personal communication, 1998) and supporters of independence do not deny the progress and technological advances of the biomedical system. Drollet comments that an independent French Polynesia must continue to use and recognize biomedicine. The country must maintain its modern existence yet at the same time not forget its ancestral roots. According to Temaru (personal communication, 1998), Tahitian healing has its place in the health department and both medical systems should be supported equally. This would imply support for the evolution of a system in which practitioners from biomedicine and Tahitian healing collaborate and patients have the benefits of both systems working together toward effective cures.

Through expressions of Tahitian culture, including the choice of indigenous medicine, nationalists must assert cultural solidarity and identity while negotiating the realities that would accompany a modern independent nation. Lucas (1989), a local advocate for La Culture Ma'ohi, states that young Tahitians must learn the advances of modern science and technology but, at the same time, must consciously recognize their cultural heritage. I conclude that health care behavior among nationalists is embedded within this process—within the negotiation of past and future, local and global—and that indigenous healing provides one context for reeducation and discovery.

12. "CANNY ABOUT CONFLICT"

Nativism, Revitalization, and the Invention of Tradition in Native Southeastern New England

Ann McMullen

A hundred years ago, native peoples in southeastern New England were largely considered extinct or represented only by mixed-blood individuals with few cultural survivals. Yet today the same area is home to numerous tribes whose members participate as native people in local economies and social contexts through cultural events, gaming complexes, and other enterprises. How are we to reconcile these two images? Where were the ancestors of New England's modern tribes during the early 20th century? What were they doing, and how did they maintain the cultures that they proudly proclaim and display today? And if they are so obviously alive now, then how had earlier anthropologists missed them? Alternatively, if accounts about the demise of New England's native cultures were correct, then where have modern native people, and what they call "culture," actually come from? Were their traditions the result of revitalization (Wallace 1956c) or invention (Hobsbawm and Ranger 1983)?

As terms, both *revitalization* and *invented traditions* are problematic: one implying a phoenix-like rise from ashes, and the other, a fictitious continuity (Hanson 1997). At the very least, both imply discontinuity where native people themselves see a seamless transition from past to present. And in explaining the disparity between past and present in southeastern New England, are "revitalization" and "cultural invention" valid characterizations? Are they, in fact, the same thing?

In brief, I explore nativism, revitalization, and the invention of tradition to articulate similarities and differences and explore them as indigenous strategies to gain power. I provide examples from southeastern New England and suggest that native people have long been cognizant of social opposition and use inventive, reconstructive strategies to position themselves with regard to nonnative society. Southeastern New

England (east of the Connecticut River and south of Boston) includes approximately 25 thousand self-reported Native Americans, about half of whom are indigenous to the region. Tribes include the Mashantucket Pequot (Ledyard CT), Paucatuck or Eastern Pequot (North Stonington CT), Mohegan (Uncasville CT), Narragansett (Charlestown RI), Nipmuc (near Worcester MA), and the Wampanoag groups in Massachusetts (Mashpee, Gay Head, Assonet, Herring Pond, and Nemasket). The federal government recognizes the Mohegan, Mashantucket Pequot, Eastern Pequot, Narragansett, and Gay Head Wampanoag; all others remain unrecognized.[1]

A Review

Discussion of "invented traditions" has become popular, emphasizing the ideological manipulation of heritage. For Eric Hobsbawm (1983:1), the invention of tradition includes that which is consciously invented and arises rapidly to establish continuities with the past. Although the invention of tradition literature is relatively recent, its roots lie in studies of nativism and revitalization, both of which involve conscious, internal efforts to direct culture change. Ralph Linton (1943) and Anthony F. C. Wallace (1956c) have described situations much like those now seen in the Pacific and North America, yet modern studies of invented traditions seldom refer back to Linton and Wallace.

Linton's (1943) nativism involves conscious, organized attempts to revive or perpetuate selected aspects of culture, arising where a society became conscious of other cultures that threatened its existence. Thus, nativism occurs where groups' ideas of the world and their place in it change. If this is a natural result of colonialism and postcolonialism, then it may suggest that all indigenous people today are nativistic: They have become conscious of culture and its potential for self-representation (Asad 1991; Hanson 1989; Keesing 1989; Turner 1991). Selecting aspects of culture to be revived, perpetuated, and given new symbolic value is pragmatic and based on things that may actually *work* in the present (Borofsky 1987; Hanson 1989; Keesing 1989; Linnekin 1983; see also Harkin [ch. 6]).

Today we would call this "resistance" according to Edward Bruner's (1986) paradigms, but Linton felt that *nativism* characterizes acculturative or assimilative contexts. Nonetheless, real or perceived political inequality is the basis of nativism. Where the past appears brighter than the present, a return to some semblance of the past reestablishes self-respect.

Wallace's revitalization is closer to the modern notion of invented traditions, for it may involve rapid innovation, what he calls "a . . . conscious effort . . . to construct a more satisfying culture" (1956c:265). Elsewhere, he likens revitalization to "cultural mutations" (1956a:626), which gave way to mechanisms to maintain the new order (1961:378). Thus, nativism and revitalization may be episodes of rapid culture change in what might otherwise be a *longue durée* (Braudel 1980; Wolf 1982). But because Wallace focuses on efforts to alter subordinate/superordinate relationships, he does not distinguish invented traditions as *by-products* of revitalization. Examining revitalization *and* its by-products helps us explore social action rather than simply identifying invented traditions. Wallace's model also accounts for traditions reclaimed via nativism *and* adopted or invented traditions, even where adopted traditions are not identified by those using them (see also Powers 1995).

So, does identification of traditions as reclaimed, adopted, or invented mean that native cultures are "inauthentic," or does it suggest that our conceptions of culture are too rigid to account for such change? In his Kayapó studies, Terence Turner (1991) has suggested that in postcolonial situations, the nature and meaning of culture change radically. Older models of culture as internally focused, relatively isolated societies with self-centered worldviews fail to account for societies that find themselves but one acculturated group in a multiethnic situation.

As Turner describes them, the Kayapó have shifted from being ethnically and historically "unaware" to being concerned with cultural preservation as political action and Indian identity in opposition to whites. Their struggles have made them self-conscious: *They think about culture* and in doing so also act in ways that they feel best serve the survival of that culture.[2] Obviously, the Kayapó are not alone in shifting from an internally focused cultural system to one that must be realigned to maintain identity in relation to vastly different "Others" (Sahlins 1993). Turner's notion of culture—with its built-in need for social action for identity's sake—fits many societies in the rising global tide of postcolonial ethnic autonomy and nationalism (Anderson 1983; Friedman 1994; Handler 1991; Kohl 1998), including those who are the subject of this chapter.

The Role of Individuals and Research

Following postcontact wars, many Indians in southeastern New England sought to escape identification as Indians and pretended assimilation by "covering" identity, abandoning visible aspects of culture (McMullen 1994b). This tactic was successful until emancipation and changes in racial labels merged Native Americans and African Americans in an undifferentiated "colored" underclass. Native people ultimately resented not being recognized as distinct and sought to reestablish "Indian" in a two-part—black and white—society (Hicks 1964; Hicks and Kertzer 1972; McMullen 2002). Alternatively, Brasser (1971) has suggested that early-20th-century anthropologists in southeastern New England—James Mooney, Frank Speck, and others—spurred cultural revivals and public events to reinforce local Indians' worthiness as academic subjects and purchase artifacts for museum collections.[3] And although native people were expected to be ignorant of what was written about them, I have suggested that anthropological writings triggered revivals by implying that Indian cultures were extinct or that few cultural survivals existed (see McMullen 1996a). Individually or as a whole, these factors account for growing stress, which spurred revitalization.

In the early 20th century, growth of pan-Indian organizations and public events led non-Indians in southeastern New England to recognize that native people had survived. However, public attention focused on individuals who mediated between native and nonnative worlds as culture brokers (Clifton 1989) or "beaches" (Dening 1980) or who—via public cultural performances, informal teaching, and scouting—acted as bridges between the two worlds. These often flamboyant individuals sought acceptance as Indians and recognition for their ability to represent local Indian consciousness and survival. Through involvement with western Indians—who lent authenticity—local native people learned to present themselves in ways recognizable to nonnatives. Linking themselves to a national Indian whole, they spoke publicly about the value of Indian traditions and hopes for peaceful coexistence with nonnatives.

Some individuals were also influential in sparking revitalization. Although none can be called a prophet (Linton 1943; Wallace 1956c), their charismatic discourse spurred changes in native attitudes about Indian–white relations and ideology or a "collective reimagination of society" (Nesper [ch. 10]). For each tribe, one individual seems to have undertaken this role, resulting in popular movements of growing Indian identity. LeRoy Perry, a Wampanoag instrumental in the Indian Council of New England and the newly developed Wampanoag Nation, encouraged revivals and powwow culture at Mashpee in the 1930s (Campisi 1991; McMullen 1994a, 1994b; Speck 1928); and at Mohegan, Gladys and Harold Tantaquidgeon and the Fielding family continued longstanding traditions of the Mohegan Wigwam Festival. James L. Ciscoe and his daughter Sarah led Nipmuc cultural preservation and activities. Atwood I. Williams (Paucatuck Pequot) and William L. Wilcox (Narragansett) founded the American Indian Federation in the early 1930s and later led cultural revivals for their respective tribes (McMullen 1994a, 1994b, 1996a). Through pan-Indian organizations, these individuals all worked with one another, and revival strategies spread rapidly.

Having begun their climb to recognition through pan-Indianism, these individuals continued to use traditional dress and rhetoric drawn from western tribes to promote versions of local Indian culture and to be publicly recognized. However, in putting forth images of themselves as connected to the Indian past, they had to acknowledge—at least to themselves—that they often knew little about it or the cultures that they supposedly embodied. Having successfully reintroduced the symbolic Indian into nonnative consciousness, they faced the necessity of making themselves and their communities into "real Indians" who met public expectations and appeared to grow out of earlier cultures. The gap between the 17th and 20th centuries had—somehow—to be filled, and native people sought knowledge via research and attempted to reconcile the results with traditions still held by some local native people (cf. Rappaport 1990).

Following patterns of cultural reconstruction used by early anthropologists, native people looked to historical accounts and anthropological studies to shape what they ought to have, seeking cultural survivals in their own and other communities.[4] Although many Indian public figures were male, research was more often undertaken by women, whose higher education levels and more flexible work schedules allowed them to visit regional libraries and archives. Ella Glasko Peek (Princess Red Wing) exemplified this work, which was the basis for Narragansett revivals in the 1930s (McMullen 1996a). New ideas were fit into cultural wholes to be acted out publicly to inform nonnative consciousness. Focusing on visible, performed traditions such as dress, dance, and ceremonies helped create fetishized cultures (cf. Keesing 1982b, 1989). However, these intentional constructions were not revealed to other tribal members, and success depended on concealing tactics of fictive "cultural continuity" and routinizing the practice of culture. Younger tribal members, lacking any sense of what came before, cannot identify how present practice differs from that of the past (cf. Harkin 1997b).

The Role of Public Practice

Through early-20th-century regional contacts and involvement with nonlocal Indians, native groups learned to position themselves within regional and national frameworks of Indian symbols. The most significant was the growth of powwows and other public events. For native people, powwows are cultural celebrations that provide a sense of community (Boissevain 1959), keep culture alive (Fixico 1989; Horse Capture 1989; Roberts 1992), and provide opportunities for public presentation of native views of culture and history (cf. Rappaport 1994). While powwows are outwardly focused and convey messages to the public, they also encourage group solidarity and ethnic kinship (McDonald 1986) in opposition to a nonnative public.

Unlike informal social situations, southeastern New England powwows are constructed cultural performances scripted by "traditional ceremonies coordinators" to control information about the group and make it appear seamlessly connected with the past, even when specific powwow traditions result from invented and reclaimed traditions (Wallace 1956c). As a result, this powwow culture was invented explicitly for instrumental purposes, becoming a fetishized composite of what once might have been viable traditions (cf. Handler and Linnekin 1984; Keesing 1989; Linnekin 1983; Sahlins 1993; Volkman 1984, 1990). Because New England powwows are aimed at tourist audiences, they also combine "authentic experience" with structured schedules and programs and employ masters of ceremony who self-consciously elucidate the meaning and significance of action (cf. Volkman 1984, 1990). [5] As in other invented rituals, powwow participants are self-conscious in explaining the gravity of action and its importance to culture (G. White 1991).

Use of ceremonies at local powwows and participants' obvious enjoyment help conceal strategic action, especially overt contradiction of the public's ideas about "what Indians look like." Intermarriage with whites and African Americans has yielded a population of "brown" people not readily identified as Indians by members of the public (McMullen 2002). By denying nonnative assumptions about phenotype, powwows also focus attention on *cultural* differences enacted through performance.

Sacralization of powwows in southeastern New England sets them apart from typical western powwow practice that penetrated New England after 1970. To connect with the past, tribes must show that actions at their powwows are *theirs*: Specific local cultural practice cannot correspond with powwow practice elsewhere. Tribes also use public events to speak about their own culture and history. Their goal is to transform nonnative opinion through use of ethnic symbols—ceremony, dance, dress, and language—and discourse on Indian stereotypes, identity, oral tradition, national Indian issues, sovereignty, ecology, land, and culture and history. What is at stake is their recognition as Indians—with concomitant effects on personhood, ego, and status—as well as their identification as sovereign tribes, with ramifications for potential gaming and other business ventures, maintenance of a land base and tribal housing, health and education benefits, and much more. Tribes may be recognized as sovereign nations by the federal government yet not enjoy acceptance as Indians by their nonnative neighbors, thus leading to continual challenges to personal and group identity that breed continued performed proofs of identity.

Opposition, Ethnicity, Autonomy, Nationalism, and the Power of Narratives

Creation of identity through discourse and ideology reformulation is fundamental to postcolonial politics today. These dynamic identities often function through reactive processes that continually redefine tradition as opposite to dominant or majority values (Hanson 1989, 1997; Thomas 1992a, 1997). This accords with Wallace's suggestion that "the revitalization movement . . . occurs under two conditions: high stress for individual members of the society, and disillusionment with a distorted cultural *Gestalt*" (1956c:279), with changes in relationships between groups leading to shifting ideological ideas, in effect, changes in worldview. Because ideological changes are primary to nativism and revitalization, cultural change and the emphasis or invention of traditions are essentially by-products of revitalization, which is—at its heart—about power and the relationship between superordinate and subordinate and not about cultural difference.[6]

However, this begs the question of whether culture or the representation of culture is at issue. Where Linton's (1943:232) nativism included emulating ancestors, today's nativism and revitalization focus more on how culture and history are *talked about* than on how they are enacted.

Where the Ghost Dance and other early revitalizations were very much about action—dancing the world back to normalcy or returning to traditional lifeways—modern indigenous nations rely more on nationalist rhetoric in proving links to authentic cultural pasts: "Modern nations . . . generally claim to be the opposite of novel, namely rooted in the remotest antiquity, and the opposite of constructed, namely human communities so 'natural' as to require no definition other than self-assertion" (Hobsbawm 1983:14). This is certainly true in southeastern New England, where native people today speak far more about maintaining *identity* than about maintaining or practicing *culture*. Traditional knowledge and cultural practice—and their transmission—seem secondary to identity claims, and this is revealed in the necessity of calling oneself "traditional" when it implies only that one *values* tradition (Clifton 1997; Haley and Wilcoxen 1997).

While native identity comprises *who they are*, it also emphasizes *who they are not*, especially in defining Indians as the antithesis of Americans (Spicer 1971). Although Linton focuses on behavior, he suggests that "elements selected for perpetuation become symbols of the society's existence as a unique entity" (1943:233). Today these are history, culture, sovereignty, spirituality, and environmentalism, all of which function as critiques of Western society. Use of these themes depends on postcolonial contexts and what Bruner (1986) calls "dominant narratives." Although Bruner coined the term for North America, it is equally appropriate to indigenous or subaltern histories that shift perspective and interpretation as postcolonial situations and ideologies change (Chakrabarty 1992).

For earlier "master narratives" or paradigms of historical interpretation, tribes were fit into a continuum of assimilation. Commenting on Linton's (1940) acculturation studies, Bruner (1986) states that assimilation was assumed because no known force could stop it: "Directed culture change" (Spicer 1961) was presumed to be unidirectional and to have its own momentum. What Linton did not foresee is that "contact" replaced "directed culture change" as the characterization of colonial situations (Clemmer 1972) and that Native Americans did not completely assimilate. While master narratives of Indian history—written by nonnatives—still emphasized past glory, native consciousness shifted to include colonial domination, oppression, resistance, and an emphasis on the future. By the 1970s the nonnative master narrative also emphasized resistance (Bruner 1986). Rather than focusing on the accommodation or peaceful coexistence envisioned earlier, native people characterized their own efforts as articulated opposition to white society.

Broadly, indigenous or ethnic histories initially oppose dominant narratives: "Historical interpretations of the past first become recognizable, they first acquire their identity, through the contrast with *other* interpretations; they are what they are only on the basis of what they are *not*" (Ankersmit 1984:142), with the intent of counterbalancing and critiquing Western history (Vickers 1990:160). Nationalist rhetoric joins with created identities and histories to illustrate the inevitable rise of ethnic nations—in this case, tribes.

Refashioning the past can be problematic, especially the period between the idyllic ethnographic present and the real present: Change must be confronted, and the maintenance of tradition must be explained (Bruner 1986). Although indigenous historians must confront change in explaining links between past and present and in rationalizing themselves as historical actors, others may believe in static native cultures if it is in their best interest to "minimize the perception of change" (Schieffelin and Gewertz 1985:2). In these situations, past and present are simply juxtaposed, avoiding discussion of *how* things changed to minimize perception of change and deny inconvenient aspects of the past (Bruner 1986; McDowell 1985; Peel 1984; Rappaport 1990).

Talking about History

Reclaiming traditions and maintaining flexible historical narratives are integral to public presentations of culture, especially powwows. These historical recitations stress identity rather than culture and tradition: What is said about cultural practice is inextricably bound to explanations of identity. Cultural authorities—who perform historical addresses, provide historical "scripts" for others, or act as "ceremonial coordinators"— pull together surviving and reclaimed traditions, reinterpret written histories, and explain local history through national or regional contexts. And in contrast to earlier trends that encouraged native publications to counter nonnative histories, native New England historians today avoid overt self-contradiction by "regaining orality" (McMullen 1996a, 1996b): maintaining flexible histories by not putting them into writing. By differentiating "texting" and "writing," history can be rapidly edited and rewritten to serve instrumental purposes in the same way that film scripts are "fixed" by "script doctors," experts in particular media who understand the effects of particular actions on both sides of the camera.

Because native people see themselves as tribal members *and* as part of a national native culture, linking themselves to broader issues and histories assists identity. Native people create links between local and Western Indian histories, equating the Narragansett Great Swamp Massacre (Rhode Island, 1675) and the Wounded Knee Massacre (South Dakota, 1890). They also speak about boarding schools destroying native culture (although few New England Indians attended), criticize federal assimilation policies (which never affected New England), and call detribalization of the Gay Head and Narragansett "Termination."

By resorting to morally contextualized versions of ethnic history (McDonald 1986) created in opposition to nonnative histories, native people create their own truths and use them to negotiate identity (cf. Borofsky 1987; Bruner 1986; Hanson 1979). Calling native discourses of culture and history "truth" makes them unassailable and encourages nonnatives to accept them as valid. By casting doubt on nonnatives' preconceptions and establishing the legitimacy of native interpretations, alternative histories set the stage for other interpretations and meanings, including those about culture.

Talking about Culture

Today Americans recognize Indian survival via highly visible reservation enterprises and gaming. Yet what remains problematic for many is just how "Indian" these tribes are. Popular images of native cultures are drawn from and feed back on public expectations. Films such as *The Last of the Dogmen* (1995) bring to life the hyperromantic fantasy that, somewhere, Indians sheltered from white society exist as they did centuries ago. Ultimately, these fictional Indians are more desirable than modern Indians, who suffer by comparison and are burdened to explain these differences through histories of change.

As a result many tribes have shifted their rhetoric to culture rather than history. Historical discussions remain valuable to link past and present, but, following federal recognition of some New England tribes in the 1980s and 1990s, proving cultural difference has become more important. Cultural differentiation also helps validate federal policies that guarantee native rights, seen as unfair by non-Indians who feel that Native American people integrated into modern society no longer deserve "special treatment." Native histories that documented the survival of individuals and tribes have given way to discussions of culture itself, often based on claims such as "This is our culture." This may signal another ideological change that focuses on creating a verbal *continuity of meaning* for symbols rather than a *consistency of meaning* (Spicer 1971). Thomas aptly illustrates this strategic rearticulation: " 'Customs,' 'traditional culture,' and related labels do not refer merely to a set of beliefs and practices . . . but to a selective construct defined partly in opposition to foreign ways. . . . The practices or attitudes that become significant may obviously not be 'traditional' . . . but their authenticity . . . is less important than what people may make of them" (1997:64).

Social action and public practice are subject to public interpretation, but discourse works more directly toward proving continuity: Links to the past are more often created through words than through deeds. As Clemmer (1972) suggests, revitalization movements appear quite visionary but are actually pragmatic and reactive. This brings us back to Wallace: "If the organization cannot predict successfully the consequences of its own moves and of its opponents' moves in a power struggle, its demise is very likely. If, on the other hand, it is canny about conflict, or if the amount of resistance is low, it can be extremely 'unrealistic' and extremely unconventional in other matters without running much risk of early collapse" (1956c:279).

Growing consciousness of culture and what it should be accompanies cultural and traditional losses, spurring reclamation and invention to deny the reality of loss. Those who realize that loss of culture and tradition is too advanced for nativist reclamation satisfy themselves with invention, often through nationalist ideologies that rely on visions of the traditional past as different from the present (cf. Tonkinson 1982).

At the base of nationalism is cultural difference (Handler and Linnekin 1984), and, as Keesing suggests, culture is a powerful symbol. Although his remarks focus on *kastom* in Melanesia, everything Keesing says can refer to "culture" for Native America, particularly that culture is "an apt and powerful symbol precisely because it can mean (almost) all things to all people," with a "hypnotic power to help people believe, at least temporarily, they are what in fact they are not" (1982b:297, 299). Culture can be made into almost anything the speaker wants because "such symbols do not carry meanings: they evoke them" (Keesing 1982b:299; see Hobsbawm 1983; Spicer 1971).

Symbols are constantly evoked during cultural presentations, especially powwows, and, over the past few years, discourse about nationalist themes—language, land, and sovereignty issues—has grown. Discussion of land brings together symbols and issues on the sacrality of native lands, freedom of religion, and access to sacred sites, concepts that are bound to a national Indian identity that has developed rapidly since the 1960s and 1970s.

Because many tribal powwows are held on tribal lands or at significant historical locations, discussions of land are prominent within powwow discourse. Histories of land loss through mismanagement, long-term land leases, and state-sanctioned sales by white reservation overseers (e.g., Campisi 1991; Conkey et al. 1978; Hauptman and Wherry 1990) are often used to show historic white opposition to tribal self-maintenance. As in nationalistic movements elsewhere, speakers also emphasize native stewardship of land and environment, drawing on examples of environmental devastation to show that the land itself has also been victimized by colonialism (cf. Keesing 1989).

Native languages are also primary ethnic and nationalistic symbols often used at powwows. Native language in ceremonies and prayers at powwows and other public events suggests perfect continuity with the distant past and is part of ongoing resistance to assimilation. However, powwow speakers do not admit that language proficiency results from recent, individual efforts to reclaim traditional languages or that their proficiency is confined to the Lord's Prayer or other texts recorded by 17th-century missionaries.

Discussion and Conclusions

The New England situations I discuss above can be characterized as cultural renewal or revivals in the lay sense, but the question remains whether revitalization—as described by Wallace (1956c)—occurred. The key factors defined by Wallace—stress, altering the relationship between the superordinate and subordinate, and the potential combination of nativism, adopted traditions, and invention—are all salient in New England, although changes in these native societies bear little resemblance to other phenomena called revitalization movements. In some sense, processes in New England might not be identified as revitalization because they happened over a longer period of time. However, this points to an undefined aspect of revitalization movements: whether they are events (Fogelson 1989) or processes. What seems apparent is that revitalizations can also be "projects" or a series of actions directed toward accomplishing a particular goal (Kaplan 1995).[7] In addition, the role of prophets and the potential for violence or social disorder are largely lacking in New England, but they are also absent from other revitalizations, including the Handsome Lake religion (Wallace 1969) and others (Nesper [ch. 10]).

We must also ask whether anthropological recognition of only the most radical and revolutionary revitalization movements stems from their perceived danger. Martha Kaplan (1995) has argued that the implication of danger was a matter of the colonial imagination in Fiji. Revitalization movements such as the Ghost Dance and the Vailala Madness were based on what Redfield calls "prospective mythology," with charters that laid out drastic means to change the world or its inhabitants (1953:126, 136). Given this, we must also question whether the Ghost Dance, cargo cults, and the like were perceived as dangerous because they directly contradicted prevailing paradigms of acculturation and assimilation: Indigenous people took actions inexplicable within colonial models, and thus some extraordinary force must be at work. But we must also remember that Wallace's formulation of revitalization was developed toward the end of the paradigmatic insistence on static, ahistorical indigenous cultures.

I am not suggesting here that Wallace subscribed to a static notion of culture, but certainly his conception was far from a notion of culture as constantly changing and continually invented (Wagner 1981). Juxtaposing and comparing diachronic images of societies, rather than seeing them as a trajectory, are common and are, indeed, how I began this chapter and the research on which it is founded. But if revitalization was defined by Wallace within a paradigm of assumed eventual acculturation—and if we have moved beyond that to notions of culture as ever changing—can Wallace's concept of revitalization still have any validity?

What remains remarkable about Wallace's work is his definition of revitalization as intentional action to alter social position. Although I may be accused of ignoring Wallace's other ideas, this seems the point at which his work presages our current state of recognizing and explaining indigenous agency. As he has stated, "Revitalization movements are evidently not unusual phenomena, but are recurrent features in human history. Probably few men have lived who have not been involved in an instance of the revitalization process" (1956c:267). Revitalization thus remains a common process to achieve "a more satisfying culture."

For Indian people in southeastern New England, satisfaction revolves around being recognized as Indian, first through work as individuals, via development of recognizable tribes, and most recently in maintaining and proving cultural difference from American society. As the context—American society itself—has changed, so too have native articulations with it: Different stresses and challenges have been addressed to create images of cultural and social continuity.

And what of invented traditions? I have suggested that invented traditions are by-products of revitalization. To date, the invention of tradition literature has focused largely on reifications for public consumption. Through objectification of observable traditions, participants prove—to themselves and to the public—the existence of their "living cultures," although there is little discussion of how these "fetishized cultures" (Keesing 1989) metonymically represent the broader aspects of culture that create and support them. This has its costs: As cultural performances of objectified culture are established as practice, they create an impassable gulf between the past and present that makes the former almost invisible (Keesing 1989), inculcating in some members only reduced understandings of heritage (Clifton 1997).

Unfortunately, global contexts encourage inventions and reifications via the rise of tourism in remote and not-so-remote locales, as tourists strive to collect culture through their experiences (Volkman 1990). Indigenous committees devise traditional yet public rituals to fit external expectations, for both tourism and nationalist politics. Traditional practices are selected as convenient objects for the tourist gaze and are edited, made to look ancient, and—furthering cultural objectification—groups charge admission to public rituals and ceremonies and hire masters of ceremony or announcers to ensure "correct" understanding (Volkman 1990). Through cultural performances, indigenous history, ethnicity and identity, and culture and tradition are woven together, thus reifying cultural difference and culture itself. Via routinization, invented traditions are also rendered inseparable from what went before.

Articulating context in understanding revitalization movements is of singular importance. As Kaplan (1995) has illustrated for cargo cults, preconceived categories may fall apart under scrutiny. Obviously, this should warn us that emphasizing classification may ultimately lead to oversimplification (Carucci [ch. 9]). However, I suggest that it remains valuable to think broadly about revitalization to explore its fundamental principles. For instance, the difference between cultural invention and nativism (Linton 1943) may be the need to create a new world instead of reviving an old one (Martin [ch. 2]), but the issue is still to achieve a change in relative status with regard to Others. Similarly, much has been made of revitalization movements that focus on the extermination of colonialists and the return of the dead, such as the Ghost Dance, but in such cases we must ask what impact the return of the dead might have. Are such cases truly about the return of physical persons, or are they about recharging a cultural world with the traditional knowledge and moral and spiritual state that the dead represent? In groups traumatized by epidemic and war-related losses compounded by introduced technologies and religions, return of the dead would symbolize the rebirth of a traditional world, and the death of the colonizers would allow native worldviews to return to their original state. As above, these revitalization movements are also about changing the status of those involved.

All revitalization movements create new models of culture to live by, redefining the past and its value as it is created. The ability of indigenous people to make this process or other cultural changes appear connected to the past is, as Wallace suggests, a matter of being "canny about conflict." Besides articulating the past, Native Americans in southeastern New England have also had to consider their future and how to achieve it, even as they are working on and in the present. In working on ethnic and national projects, native people continually create their own reality, which in turn is simultaneously allied with and opposed to the realities created by those around them. As with all anthropological understandings, these realities are relative, and we must understand them as products of the colonial constructs that surround them and the postcolonial worlds they reflect.

Notes

Acknowledgments. In working on this chapter and casting back to earlier writers, I was continually reminded of lessons learned from George L. Hicks (1935–98). One of the most important of these is that, as anthropologists, we will never see very far or very clearly unless we recognize and admit that we stand on the shoulders of giants. I dedicate this chapter to George's memory.

My thanks go to Ray Fogelson and Jim Roscoe for comments on the version presented at the 1999 American Anthropological Association Annual Meeting and to Lamont Lindstrom and an anonymous reviewer for their comments. I would also like to thank Michael Harkin, Jason Baird Jackson, and Dan Odess for discussions on earlier versions, as well as Tiger Burch for suggesting that I reread Roy Wagner's *The Invention of Culture*.

Data and conclusions presented here are dealt with in greater depth in my dissertation "Culture by Design: Native Identity, Historiography, and the Reclamation of Tradition in Twentieth-Century Southeastern New England" (1996a), based on ethnographic and ethnohistorical fieldwork from June 1990 to May 1994. Research was funded by the Haffenreffer Museum of Anthropology, Brown University; the Wenner-Gren Foundation for Anthropological Research; and the Center for the Study of Race and Ethnicity in America, Brown University. I gratefully acknowledge this assistance.

1. In July 2002, the Bureau of Indian Affairs acknowledged the tribal status of the historic Eastern Pequot Tribe (McCaleb 2002), combining the hitherto distinct Paucatuck Eastern Pequot Indians of Connecticut and the Eastern Pequot Indians of Connecticut. The new entity is known as the Eastern Pequot Tribal Nation. As of May 2003, the Nipmuc Nation (a.k.a. Hassanimisco Band of Nipmuc Indians) and the Webster/Dudley Band of Chaubunagungamaug Nipmuck Indians have received "Proposed Negative Findings" with regard to their petitions to the Bureau of Indian Affairs for federal acknowledgment (McCaleb 2001a, 2001b), overturning earlier proposed positive findings (Miner 2001). As of this writing, these cases are under normal review pending issuance of "Final Determinations."

2. Although Wagner sees culture as constantly invented, he also maintains that this work is largely unconscious: "The logic of a society where 'culture' is a conscious and deliberate thing, where life subserves some purpose, rather than the reverse, and where every fact or proposition is required to have a reason, creates a strangely surrealistic effect when applied to tribal peoples" (1981:29).

3. Mooney visited southern New England to research tribal and historical entries for the *Handbook of American Indians North of Mexico* (Hodge 1907–10). Speck began professional research there before 1903 (Prince and Speck 1903a, 1903b, 1904; Speck 1903a, 1903b, 1903c, 1903d, 1904a, 1904b, 1909b). Mark Raymond Harrington was active in museum collecting during the same period.

4. This process is dealt with in greater detail in McMullen 1996a. For further discussion on the effect of anthropological research and writings on Indian people, see Haley and Wilcoxen 1997.

5. Throughout the country, powwows are quite different, both in their structure and in their purpose. What is said here refers only to powwows in southeastern New England. I am grateful to Jason Baird Jackson for this reminder, which reinforces the Boasian critique of diffusion: Like institutions do not necessarily arise from the same circumstances and must therefore be contextualized to elucidate their individual meanings and significance.

6. In examining the transformation of folk society by colonialism and urbanism, Redfield (1953) also makes clear that cultural crises arise from threats to the "moral order" of a society rather than cultural difference from others.

7. Use of different terms to describe triggers for revitalization also suggests different scopes of time: Where Wallace's *stress* can imply a long period of buildup, use of the word *trauma* (Harkin [ch. 6]) may imply a single event as a trigger.

REFERENCES CITED

Abel, Charles
  1902   Savage Life in New Guinea. London: London Missionary
                  Society.
Aberle, David F.
  1959   The Prophet Dance and Reactions to White Contact. South-
                  western Journal of Anthropology 15:74–78.
  1962   A Note on Relative Deprivation Theory as Applied to Mil-
                  lenarian and Other Cult Movements. *In* Millennial Dreams
                  in Action: Studies in Revolutionary Movements. Sylvia L.
                  Thrupp, ed. Pp. 209–214. The Hague: Mouton.
  1965   A Note on Relative Deprivation Theory as Applied to Mil-
                  lenarian and Other Cult Movements. *In* Reader in Com-
                  parative Religion: An Anthropological Approach. William A.
                  Lessa and Evon Z. Vogt, eds. Pp. 537–541. New York: Harper
                  and Row.
  1966   The Peyote Religion among the Navaho. Chicago: Aldine.
  1982   The Peyote Religion among the Navajo. Chicago: University
                  of Chicago Press.
  1991   The Peyote Religion among the Navajo. 2nd ed. Norman:
                  University of Oklahoma Press.
Adas, Michael
  1979   Prophets of Rebellion: Millenarian Protest Movements
                  against the European Colonial Order. Chapel Hill: Univer-
                  sity of North Carolina Press.
Adelbai, Clarissa
  N.d.   The Modekngei Religion. Electronic document, http://
                  www.geocities.com/SouthBeach/palms/6757/modekngei.
                  html.

Adorno, Theodor
  1973   Negative Dialectics. E. B. Ashton, ed. New York: Seabury
              Press.
Aitape Patrol
  1943–44   Aitape Patrol Report 4-43/44. National Archives, Port
              Moresby, PNG.
Allen, Bryant J., and Stephen Frankel
  1991   Across the Tari Furoro. *In* Like People You See in a Dream:
              First Contact in Six Papuan Societies. Edward L. Schieffelin
              and Robert Crittenden, eds. Pp. 88–124. Stanford: Stanford
              University Press.
Anderson, Benedict
  1983   Imagined Communities: Reflections on the Origin and
              Spread of Nationalism. London: Verso.
Anderson, Rufus, ed.
  1825   Memoir of Catharine Brown, a Christian Indian of the Cher-
              okee Nation. 2nd ed. Boston: Crocker and Brewster.
Andrew, John.
  1992   From Revivals to Removal: Jeremiah Evarts, the Cherokee
              Nation, and the Search for the Soul of America. Athens: Uni-
              versity of Georgia Press.
Ankersmit, F. R.
  1984   Historiography and Postmodernism. History and Theory:
              Studies in the Philosophy of History 28(2):137–153.
Annual Report
  1914   Annual Reports to the Commissioner of Indian Affairs.
              Washington DC: Government Printing Office.
Aoyagi, Machiko
  1987   Gods of the Modekngei Religion in Belau. *In* Cultural Uni-
              formity and Diversity in Micronesia. Senri Ethnological
              Studies, 21. I. Ushijima and K. Sudo, eds. Pp. 339–361. Os-
              aka: National Museum of Ethnology.
  2002   Modekngei: A New Religion in Belau, Micronesia. Tokyo:
              Shensenha Press.
Appadurai, Arjun
  1991   Global Ethnoscapes: Notes and Queries for a Transnational
              Anthropology. *In* Recapturing Anthropology: Working in the
              Present. Richard G. Fox, ed. Pp. 191–210. Santa Fe: School
              of American Research Press.
Applied Population Laboratory
  1985   American Indians in Wisconsin, 1980: Population Notes.
              Madison: Applied Population Laboratory, Department of

Rural Sociology Cooperative Extension Service, College of Agricultural and Life Sciences, University of Wisconsin.

Archivo General de la Nación (Mexico)

1785–87   Provincias Internas, Tomo I (Californian) 120:31 47. Diligencias; Expediente; Ynterrogatono sobre la sublevación de San Gabriel, 25 Octubre de 1785. Microfilm copies, Bancroft Library, University of California, Berkeley. Partial MS transcription, Thomas Workman Temple II Collection, Seaver Center for Western Historical Research, Los Angeles County Museum of Natural History.

Asad, Talal

1991   Afterword: From the History of Colonial Anthropology to the Anthropology of Western Hegemony. *In* Colonial Situations: Essays on the Contexualization of Ethnographic Knowledge. History of Anthropology, 7. George W. Stocking Jr., ed. Pp. 314–324. Madison: University of Wisconsin Press.

Axtell, James

1988   The Power of Print in the Eastern Woodlands. *In* After Columbus: Essays in the Ethnohistory of Colonial North America. Pp. 86–99. New York: Oxford University Press.

Babadzan, Alain

1988   *Kastom* and Nation-Building in the South Pacific. *In* Ethnicities and Nations: Processes of Interethnic Relations in Latin America, Southeast Asia, and the Pacific. Remo Guidieri, Francesco Pillizzi, and Stanley Tambiah, eds. Pp. 199–228. Austin: University of Texas Press.

Ballard, W. L.

1978   The Yuchi Green Corn Ceremonial: Form and Meaning. Los Angeles: University of California, American Indian Studies Center.

Bancroft, Hubert Howe

1886   History of California, vols. 1–2. San Francisco: History Co.

Baraga, Frederic

1992   A Dictionary of the Ojibway Language. St. Paul: Minnesota Historical Society Press.

Barker, John

1998   Tangled Reconciliations: The Anglican Church and the Nisga'a of British Columbia. American Ethnologist 25:433–451.

Barnett, Homer G.

1949   Palauan Society: A Study of Contemporary Native Life in the Palau Islands. Eugene: University of Oregon Publications.

1957   Indian Shakers: A Messianic Cult of the Pacific Northwest. Carbondale: Southern Illinois University Press.

1979   Being a Palauan: Fieldwork Edition. New York: Holt, Rinehart and Winston.

Barnley, George

1843   Summary Report to the Committee and Secretaries, Wesleyan Missionary Society, September 23. Courtesy of John S. Long.

1844   Journal, January 20. Courtesy of John S. Long.

Barnston, George

1842   Letter to James Hargrave, November 23. Hargrave Correspondence, MG19, A21. Public Archives of Canada, Ottawa.

Barrowman, Clover Brown

1937   Interview by S. R. Lewis, November 24. Indian Pioneer Papers, Oklahoma Historical Society, Tulsa.

Bateson, Gregory

1958   Naven. Stanford: Stanford University Press.

1972   Steps to an Ecology of Mind. New York: Ballantine Books.

Bean, Lowell, and Florence Shipek

1978   Luiseño. *In* Handbook of North American Indians, vol. 8: California. Robert Heizer, ed. Pp. 550–563. Washington DC: Smithsonian Institution Press.

Bean, Lowell, and Charles Smith

1978   Gabrielino. *In* Handbook of North American Indians, vol. 8: California. Robert Heizer, ed. Pp. 538–549. Washington DC: Smithsonian Institution Press.

Bean, Lowell, and Sylvia Vane

1978   Cults and Their Transformations. *In* Handbook of North American Indians, vol. 8: California. Robert Heizer, ed. Pp. 662–672. Washington DC: Smithsonian Institution Press.

Beazley, R. A.

N.d.   New Guinea Adventure. Unpublished MS, Fryer Library, University of Queensland.

Beckham, Stephen Dow

1990   History of Western Oregon since 1846. *In* Handbook of North American Indians, vol. 7: The Northwest Coast. Wayne Suttles, ed. Pp. 180–188. Washington DC: Smithsonian Institution Press.

Beckham, Stephen Dow, Kathryn Anne Popel, and Rick Minor

1984   Native American Religious Practices and Uses in Western Oregon. University of Oregon Anthropological Papers, 31. Eugene: University of Oregon Press.

Behar, Ruth

1989   Sexual Witchcraft, Colonialism, and Women's Powers: Views
                from the Mexican Inquisition. *In* Sexuality and Marriage in
                Colonial Latin America. Asunción Lavrin, ed. Lincoln: Uni-
                versity of Nebraska Press.

Benedict, Ruth Fulton

1922   The Vision in Plains Culture. American Anthropologist 24:1–
                23.

Benton-Banai, Edward

1988   The Mishomis Book: The Voice of the Ojibway. St. Paul: Red
                School House.

Bhabha, Homi

1984   Of Mimicry and Man: The Ambivalence of Colonial Dis-
                course. October 28:125–133.

1994   The Location of Culture. New York: Routledge.

Blackburn, Thomas

1974   Ceremonial Integration and Social Interaction in Aboriginal
                California. *In* Antap: California Indian Political and Eco-
                nomic Organization. Lowell Bean and Thomas Kings, eds.
                Pp. 93–110. Ballena Press Anthropological Papers, 2. Ra-
                mona CA: Ballena Press.

1975   The Chumash Revolt of 1824: A Native Account. Journal of
                California Anthropology 2(2):123–127.

Bloom, Harold

1992   The American Religion: The Emergence of the Post-Chris-
                tian Nation. New York: Simon and Schuster.

Bobo, Lawrence, and Garcia Estela B.

1992   The Chippewa Indian Treaty Rights Survey. Working Paper,
                9. Madison: Robert M. LaFollette Institute of Public Affairs,
                University of Wisconsin.

Boissevain, Ethel

1959   Narragansett Survival: A Study of Group Persistence through
                Adapted Traits. Ethnohistory 6(4):347–362.

Bolton, Herbert

1930   Anza's California Expeditions. 5 vols. Berkeley: University of
                California Press.

Borofsky, Robert

1987   Making History: Pukapukan and Anthropological Construc-
                tions of Knowledge. New York: Cambridge University Press.

Boscana, Geronimo

1978[1933]   Chinigchinich: A Revised and Annotated Version of Alfred
                Robinson's Translation of Father Geronimo Boscana's His-

torical Account of the Belief, Usages, Customs and Extravagancies of the Indians of This Mission of San Juan Capistrano Called the Acagchemem Tribe (1846). Phil Townsend Hanna, ed. John Peabody Harrington, annotations. Banning CA: Malki Museum Press.

Bourdieu, Pierre
1991   Language and Symbolic Power. Cambridge, MA: Harvard University Press.

Brainerd Mission
1820   Journal of the Brainerd Mission, May 24. American Board of Commissioners for Foreign Missions Papers. Houghton Library, Harvard University, Cambridge.

Brasser, Ted J.
1971   The Coastal Algonkians: People of the First Frontiers. *In* North American Indians in Historical Perspective. Eleanor B. Leacock and Nancy O. Lurie, eds. Pp. 64–91. Prospect Heights IL: Waveland Press.

Braudel, Fernand
1980   On History. Sarah Matthews, trans. Chicago: University of Chicago Press.

Braund, Kathryn E. Holland
1993   Deerskins and Duffels: The Creek Indian Trade with Anglo America, 1685–1815. Lincoln: University of Nebraska Press.

Brereton, Virginia Lieson
1991   From Sin to Salvation: Stories of Women's Conversions, 1800 to the Present. Bloomington: Indiana University Press.

Brightman, Robert A.
1989   Acaoohkiwina and Acimowina: Traditional Narratives of the Rock Cree Indians. Mercury Series Paper, 113. Ottawa: Canadian Museum of Civilization, Canadian Ethnology Service.

1993   Grateful Prey: Rock Cree Human–Animal Relationships. Berkeley: University of California Press.

Brown, Catharine
1819   The Converted Cherokee, a Missionary Drama, Founded on Fact, Written by a Lady. New Haven: S. Converse.

Brown, George H.
1937   A Word from the Indian Tribal Council. *In* The First Annual Flambeau Blue Book of the Flambeau Taxpayers Association. Minocqua WI: Minocqua Printing Co.

Brown, Jennifer S. H.
1977   James Settee and His Cree Tradition: An Indian Camp at the

Mouth of Nelson's River, Hudson's Bay. *In* Actes du huitieme congrès des algonquinistes. William Cowan, ed. Pp. 36–49. Ottawa: Carleton University Press.

1980   Strangers in Blood: Fur Trade Company Families in Indian Country. Vancouver: University of British Columbia Press.

1982   The Track to Heaven: The Hudson Bay Cree Religious Movement of 1842–1843. *In* Papers of the Thirteenth Algonquian Conference. William Cowan, ed. Pp. 53–63. Ottawa: Carleton University Press.

1988   Abishabis (Small Eyes). *In* Dictionary of Canadian Biography, vol. 7: 1836 to 1850. Pp. 3–4. Toronto: University of Toronto Press.

Brown, Jennifer S. H., and Robert Brightman

1988   The Orders of the Dreamed: George Nelson on Cree and Northern Ojibwa Religion and Myth, 1823. Winnipeg: University of Manitoba Press.

Brown, John

1813   Letter to Andrew Jackson, December 28. Andrew Jackson Papers, Reel 8, Ser. 1, Vol. 15, 368. Library of Congress, Washington DC.

Brown, Michael

1991   Beyond Resistance: Utopian Renewal in Amazonia. Ethnohistory 38(4):363–387.

Brownlee, Kevin, and E. Leigh Syms

1999   Kayasochi Kikawenow, Our Mother from Long Ago: An Early Cree Woman and Her Personal Belongings from Nagami Bay, Southern Indian Lake. Winnipeg: Manitoba Museum of Man and Nature.

Bruner, Edward M.

1986   Ethnography as Narrative. *In* The Anthropology of Experience. Victor Turner and Edward M. Bruner, eds. Pp. 139–155. Urbana: University of Illinois Press.

Brutti, Lorenzo

2000   Afek's Last Son: Integrating Change in a Papua New Guinea Cosmology. Ethnohistory 47:101–112.

Bucko, Raymond

1998   The Lakota Ritual of the Sweat Lodge: History and Contemporary Practice. Lincoln: University of Nebraska Press.

Buechel, the Reverend Eugene

1970   A Dictionary of the Teton Dakota Sioux Language: Lakota–English, English–Lakota with Consideration Given to Yankton and Santee. Paul Manhart, ed. Pine Ridge SD: S. J. Red Cloud Indian School.

Buff, Rachel

1995 Tecumseh and Tenskwatawa: Myth, Historiography and Popular Memory. Historical Reflections/Reflexions Historiques 21(2):277–300.

Burridge, Kenelm

1971 New Heaven, New Earth: A Study of Millenarian Activities. Oxford: Basil Blackwell.

Butrick, Daniel Sabin

1820 Letter to Samuel Worcester, September 7. American Board of Commissioners for Foreign Missions Papers. Houghton Library, Harvard University, Cambridge.

N.d. Journals. American Board of Commissioners for Foreign Missions Papers. Houghton Library, Harvard University, Cambridge.

Calloway, Colin

1997 New Worlds for All: Indians, Europeans, and the Remaking of Early America. Baltimore: Johns Hopkins University Press.

Campisi, Jack

1991 The Mashpee Indians: Tribe on Trial. Syracuse: Syracuse University Press.

Carucci, Laurence Marshall

1980 The Renewal of Life: A Ritual Encounter in the Marshall Islands. Ph.D. dissertation, Department of Anthropology, University of Chicago.

1989 The Source of the Force in Marshallese Cosmology. In The Pacific Theater: Island Representations of World War II. Geoffrey M. White and Lamont Lindstrom, eds. Pp. 73–96. Hawaii: University of Hawaii Press.

1993 Christmas on Ujelang: The Politics of Continuity in the Context of Change. In Contemporary Pacific Societies: Studies in Development and Change. Victoria S. Lockwood, Thomas G. Harding, and Ben J. Wallace, eds. Pp. 304–320. Englewood Cliffs NJ: Prentice-Hall.

1997a *Irooj Ro Ad*: Measures of Chiefly Ideology and Practice in the Marshall Islands. *In* Chiefs Today: Traditional Pacific Leadership and the Postcolonial State. Geoffrey M. White and Lamont Lindstrom, eds. Pp. 197–210. Stanford: Stanford University Press.

1997b Nuclear Nativity: Rituals of Renewal and Empowerment in the Marshall Islands. DeKalb: Northern Illinois University Press.

2000   *Mōn jaar eo*: The Church as an Embodiment and Expression of Community on Wōjlan and Āne-wetak, Marshall Islands. Paper presented at the Annual Meeting of the Association for Social Anthropology in Oceania, Vancouver.

Castañeda, Antonia

1998   Engendering the History of Alta California, 1769–1848: Gender, Sexuality, and the Family. *In* Contested Eden: California before the Gold Rush. Ramon Gutierrez and Richard Orsi, eds. Pp. 230–259. Berkeley: University of California Press.

Castillo, Edward

1978   The Impact of Euro-American Exploration and Settlement. *In* Handbook of North American Indians, vol. 8: California. Robert Heizer, ed. Pp. 99–127. Washington DC: Smithsonian Institution Press.

1991   Native American Perspectives on the Hispanic Colonization of Alta California. Spanish Borderlands Sourcebook, 26. New York: Garland Publishing.

Chakrabarty, Dipesh

1992   Postcoloniality and the Artifice of History: Who Speaks for Indian Pasts? Representations 37:1–26.

Champagne, Duane

1992   Social Order and Political Change: Constitutional Governments among the Cherokee, the Choctaw, the Chickasaw, and the Creek. Stanford: Stanford University Press.

Clark, Sheila Seiler

1993   Anxiety, Cultural Identity, and Solidarity: A Tahitian Ethnomedical Encounter. Ethos 21(2):180–204.

1994   Ethnicity Embodied: Evidence from Tahiti. Ethnology 33(3): 211–227.

Clemmer, Richard O.

1972   Truth, Duty, and the Revitalization of Anthropologists: A New Perspective on Cultural Change and Resistance. *In* Reinventing Anthropology. Dell Hymes, ed. Pp. 213–247. New York: Vintage Books.

Clifford, James

1983   On Ethnographic Authority. Representations 1:118–146.

1997   Routes: Travel and Translation in the Late Twentieth Century. Cambridge: Harvard University Press.

Clifton, James A.

1989   Alternate Identities and Cultural Frontiers. *In* Being and Be-
              coming Indian: Biographical Sketches of North American In-
              dians. James A. Clifton, ed. Pp. 1–37. Chicago: Dorsey Press.

1994   The Indian Story: A Cultural Fiction. *In* The Invented In-
              dian: Cultural Fictions and Government Policies. James A.
              Clifton, ed. Pp. 29–47. New Brunswick NJ: Transaction Pub-
              lishers.

1997   Avocation Medicine Men: Inventive Tradition and New Age
              Religiosity in a Western Great Lakes Algonquian Population.
              In Past Is Present: Some Uses of Tradition in Native Soci-
              eties. Marie Mauzé, ed. Pp. 145–158. Lanham MD: University
              Press of America.

Cobb, Richard

1987   The People's Armies: The *Armées Révolutionnaires*, Instru-
              ment of the Terror in the Departments, April 1793 to Floréal
              Year II. Marianne Elliott, trans. New Haven: Yale University
              Press.

Cohen, Fay G.

1986   Treaties on Trial: The Continuing Controversy over North-
              west Indian Fishing Rights. Seattle: University of Washing-
              ton Press.

Cohn, Norman

1970   The Pursuit of the Millennium: Revolutionary Millenarians
              and Mystical Anarchists of the Middle Ages. 3rd ed. New
              York: Oxford University Press.

Comaroff, Jean

1985   Body of Power, Spirit of Resistance: The Culture and History
              of a South African People. Chicago: University of Chicago
              Press.

Comaroff, John L., and Jean Comaroff

1992   Ethnography and the Historical Imagination. Boulder: West-
              view.

1997   Of Revelation and Revolution: The Dialectics of Modernity
              on a South African Frontier, vol. 2. Chicago: University of
              Chicago Press.

Conkey, Laura E., Ethel Boissevain, and Ives Goddard

1978   Indians of Southern New England and Long Island: Late
              Period. *In* Handbook of North American Indians, vol. 15:
              Northeast. Bruce G. Trigger, ed. Pp. 177–189. Washington
              DC: Smithsonian Institution Press.

Connerton, Paul
    1989   How Societies Remember. Cambridge: Cambridge Univer-
                    sity Press.
Connors, Sean M.
    1999   Forming Relations with Whales: The Makah Indians Kill the
                    Beloved Species according to Tradition. UC Santa Barbara
                    Daily Nexus 79(132) May 26:7.
Conser, Walter H., Jr.
    1978   John Ross and the Cherokee Resistance Campaign, 1833–
                    1838. Journal of Southern History 44(2):191–212.
Cook, Sherbourne
    1943   The Conflict between the California Indians and White Civi-
                    lization, vol. 1: The Indian versus the Spanish Mission. Ibero-
                    Americana 18.
Cook Islands News
    1988a   Gift from God. Cook Islands News, March 1: 6.
    1988b   Help Where Needed. Cook Islands News, March 4: 6.
    1988c   Aitutaki Receives Faith-Healer's Touch. Cook Islands News,
                    March 22: 4.
    1988d   Apii Piho to Return in May. Cook Islands News, March 29:
                    7.
Cooper, John M.
    1933   The Northern Algonquian Supreme Being. Primitive Man
                    6:41–111.
Copway, George
    1850   The Traditional History and Characteristic Sketches of the
                    Ojibway Nation. London: Charles Gilpin.
Crosby, Harry
    1994   Antigua California: Mission and Colony on the Peninsular
                    Frontier, 1697–1768. Albuquerque: University of New Mex-
                    ico Press.
Danielsson, Bengt, and Marie-Thérèse Danielsson
    1986   Poisoned Reign: French Nuclear Colonialism in the Pacific.
                    2nd rev. ed. Victoria: Penguin Books.
Danziger, Edmund
    1978   The Chippewas of Lake Superior. Norman: University of
                    Oklahoma Press.
Dauenhauer, Richard, and Nora Marks Dauenhauer
    1995   Oral Literature Embodied and Disembodied. In Aspects of
                    Oral Communication. Uta Quasthoff, ed. Pp. 91–111. Berlin:
                    Walter de Gruyter.

Deloria, Phil
  1998   Playing Indian. New Haven: Yale University Press.
Deloria, Vine, Jr.
  1998   Comfortable Fictions and the Struggle for Turf: An Essay Review of *The Invented Indian: Cultural Fictions and Government Policies*. In Natives and Academics: Researching and Writing about American Indians. Devon A. Mihesuah, ed. Pp. 65–83. Lincoln: University of Nebraska Press.
DeMallie, Raymond
  1984   The Sixth Grandfather: Black Elk's Teachings Given to John G. Neihardt. Lincoln: University of Nebraska Press.
Dening, Greg
  1980   Islands and Beaches: Discourse on a Silent Land: Marquesas 1774–1880. Honolulu: University Press of Hawaii.
Densmore, Frances
  1979   Chippewa Customs. St. Paul: Minnesota Historical Society Press.
Dickason, Olive Patricia
  1992   Canada's First Nations: A History of Founding Peoples from Earliest Times. Toronto: McClelland and Stewart.
Dowd, Gregory E.
  1992   A Spirited Resistance: The North American Indian Struggle for Unity, 1745–1815. Baltimore: Johns Hopkins University Press.
Drucker, Philip
  1939   Contributions to Alsea Ethnography. University of California Publications in American Archaeology and Ethnology 35(7):81–101.
DuBois, Constance Goddard
  1908   The Religion of the Luiseño Indians of Southern California. University of California Publications in American Archaeology and Ethnology 8(3):69–186.
DuBois, Cora
  1939   The 1870 Ghost Dance. Anthropological Records of the University of California 3(1):1–152.
Durkheim, Émile
  1965   The Elementary Forms of the Religious Life. New York: Free Press.
Eagleton, Terry
  2000   The Idea of Culture. Malden MA: Blackwell Publishers.

Elbert, Samuel H., and Torben Monberg
1965   From the Two Canoes: Oral Traditions of Rennell and Bel-
            lona Islands. Copenhagen: Danish National Museum.

Eliade, Mircea
1957   Time and Eternity in Indian Thought. *In* Man and Time:
            Papers from the Eranos Yearbooks, vol. 3. Joseph Campbell,
            ed. Pp. 173–200. Princeton: Princeton University Press/Bol-
            lingen.

1959   Cosmos and History: The Myth of the Eternal Return. New
            York: Harper.

1971   Patterns in Comparative Religion. New York: Meridian
            Books.

Elliston, Deborah
1997   En/Gendering Nationalism: Colonialism, Sex and Indepen-
            dence in French Polynesia. Ph.D. dissertation, New York
            University.

Engelhardt, Zephyrin
1927   San Gabriel Mission and the Beginnings of Los Angeles: The
            Missions and Missionaries of California. New Series, Local
            History. San Gabriel CA: Mission San Gabriel.

Erickson, Kirstin
N.d.   Teresa Urrea: Gender, Millenarianism, and Political Struggle
            in Northwestern Mexico. Unpublished MS.

Erikson, Patricia Pierce
1999   A-Whaling We Will Go: Encounters of Knowledge and
            Memory at the Makah Cultural and Research Center. Cul-
            tural Anthropology 14:556–583.

Errington, Frederick K., and Deborah B. Gewertz
1991   Articulating Change in the Last Unknown. Boulder: West-
            view Press.

Evarts, Jeremiah
1823   View of the Missions of the American Board of Commission-
            ers for Foreign Missions. Boston: Crocker and Brewster.

Fabian, Johannes
1983   Time and the Other: How Anthropology Makes Its Object.
            New York: Columbia University Press.

Fadiman, Anne
1997   The Spirit Catches You and You Fall Down: A Hmong Child,
            Her American Doctors, and the Collision of Two Cultures.
            New York: Farrar, Straus, and Giroux.

Faries, Richard
    1938   A Dictionary of the Cree Language. Toronto: General Synod
                    of the Church of England in Canada.
Fenton, William
    1953   The Iroquois Eagle Dance, an Offshoot of the Calumet
                    Dance. Bureau of American Ethnography Bulletin, 156.
                    Washington DC: Bureau of American Ethnography.
    1998   The Great Law and the Long House: A Political History of
                    the Iroquois Confederacy. Norman: University of Oklahoma
                    Press.
Fernandez, James
    1978   African Religious Movements. Annual Review of Anthropol-
                    ogy 7:195–234.
Festinger, Leon, Henry W. Riecken, and Stanley Schachter
    1959   When Prophecy Fails. Minneapolis: University of Minnesota
                    Press.
Feyerabend, Paul
    1975   Against Method: Outline of an Anarchistic Theory of Knowl-
                    edge. London: Atlantic Highlands.
Finney, Ben Rudolph
    1973   Polynesian Peasants and Proletarians: Socio-Economic
                    Change among the Tahitians of French Polynesia. Cam-
                    bridge: Schenman.
Fisher, Robin
    1977   Contact and Conflict: Indian–European Relations in British
                    Columbia, 1774–1890. Vancouver: University of British Co-
                    lumbia Press.
Fischer, John L. (with Ann M. Fischer)
    1957   The Eastern Carolines. HRAF Behavioral Science Mono-
                    graph. New Haven: HRAF Press.
Fixico, Michelene
    1989   The Road to Middle Class Indian America. In American In-
                    dian Identity: Today's Changing Perspectives. Clifford Traf-
                    zer, ed. Pp. 55–75. Sacramento: Sierra Oaks Publishing Co.
Flannery, Regina
    1984   Thoughts on the Cree Concept of the Supreme Being in
                    Response to Longs Interview with [Richard] Preston: The
                    Northern Algonquian Supreme Being Revisited. Unpublish-
                    ed MS, Catholic University of America, Washington DC.
Fleetwood, Lorna
    1986   A Short History of Wewak. Wewak PNG: East Sepik Provin-
                    cial Government.

Fogelson, Raymond D.

1977   Cherokee Notions of Power. *In* The Anthropology of Power. Raymond D. Fogelson and Richard N. Adams, eds. Pp. 185–194. New York: Academic Press.

1982   Cherokee Little People Reconsidered. Journal of Cherokee Studies 7(2):92–98.

1984   Who Were the Aní Kutánî? Ethnohistory 31:255–263.

1989   The Ethnohistory of Events and Nonevents. Ethnohistory 36:133–147.

1996   Sequoyah. *In* Encyclopedia of North American Indians. Frederick E. Hoxie, ed. Pp. 580–582. Boston: Houghton Mifflin.

For General Jackson's Campaign against the Creek Indians, 1813 & 1814

N.d.   State of Alabama Department of Archives and History, Montgomery.

Fortune, Reo

1963[1932] Sorcerers of Dobu. New York: E. P. Dutton.

Fossett, Renee

2001   In Order to Live Untroubled: Inuit of the Central Arctic, 1550–1940. Winnipeg: University of Manitoba Press.

Foster, George E.

1899   Story of the Cherokee Bible. 2nd ed. Ithaca: Democrat Press.

Foucault, Michel

1982   The Subject and Power. *In* Michel Foucault: Beyond Structuralism and Hermeneutics, 2nd ed. Hubert L. Dreyfus and Paul Rabinow, eds. Pp. 208–226. Chicago: University of Chicago Press.

Frachtenberg, Leo

1913   Coos Texts. Columbia University Contributions to Anthropology, 1. New York: Columbia University.

Francis, Daniel, and Toby Morantz

1983   Partners in Furs: A History of the Fur Trade in Eastern James Bay 1600–1870. Montreal: McGill-Queen's University Press.

Freud, Sigmund

1961   Beyond the Pleasure Principle. James Strachey, trans. New York: W. W. Norton.

Friedman, Jonathan

1987   Beyond Otherness or the Spectacularization of Anthropology. Telos 71:161–170.

1994   Cultural Identity and Global Process. London: Sage Publications.

Gayton, Anna

1930   The Ghost Dance of 1870 in South-Central California. University of California Publications in American Archaeology and Ethnology 24(8):57–82.

Geertz, Clifford

1973   The Interpretation of Cultures: Selected Essays. New York: Basic Books.

1988   Works and Lives: The Anthropologist as Author. Stanford: Stanford University Press.

Gell, Alfred

1992   The Anthropology of Time: Cultural Constructions of Temporal Maps and Images. Oxford: Berg.

Gerstner, Andreas

1929–30   Missionsadvent im Busch. Steyler Missionsbote 57:229–230.

1952   Der Geisterglaube im Wewäk-Boikin-Leute in Nordost-Neuguineas. Anthropos 47:795–821.

Gesch, Patrick F.

1985   Initiative and Initiation. St. Augustin, Germany: Anthropos-Institut.

Gill, Sam, and Irene F. Sullivan

1992   Dictionary of Native American Mythology. New York: Oxford University Press.

Gingrich, Andre, and Richard Fox, eds.

2002   Anthropology, by Comparison. New York: Routledge.

Gladwell, Malcolm

2000   The Tipping Point: How Little Things Can Make a Big Difference. Boston: Little, Brown.

Gould, Stephen Jay

2002   The Structure of Evolutionary Theory. Cambridge: Harvard University Press.

Grant, Campbell

1978   Eastern Coastal Chumash. In Handbook of North American Indians, vol. 8: California. Robert Heizer, ed. Pp. 509–519. Washington DC: Smithsonian Institution Press.

Grant, John Webster

1980   Missionaries and Messiahs in the Northwest. Studies in Religion 9(2):125–136.

Gray, Paul

1998   Forster vs. Pico: The Struggle for the Rancho Santa Margarita. Spokane WA: Arthur H. Clark.

Grimshaw, Anna, and Keith Hart
   1993   Anthropology and the Crisis of Intellectuals. Cambridge: Prickly Pear Press.

Guiart, Jean
   1951   Forerunners of Melanesian Nationalism. Oceania 22(2):81–90.
   1952   John Frum Movement in Tanna. Oceania 22(3):165–175.

Hackel, Steven
   N.d.   Indian Testimony and the Mission San Gabriel Rebellion of 1785. Unpublished MS.

Halbert, Henry S.
   N.d.   Cherokee and Choctaw Missions. Halbert Papers. State of Alabama Department of Archives and History, Montgomery.

Haley, Brian D., and Larry R. Wilcoxen
   1997   Anthropology and the Making of Chumash Tradition. Current Anthropology 38(5):761–794.

Hall, Edward T., and Karl J. Pelzer
   1946   The Economy of the Truk Islands: An Anthropological and Economic Survey. USCC Economic Survey of Micronesia Report, 17. Mimeograph. Honolulu: U.S. Commercial Co.

Hall, Moody
   1824   Letter to Jeremiah Evarts, February 14. American Board of Commissioners for Foreign Missions Papers, 18.3.1, v. 3. Houghton Library, Harvard University, Cambridge.

Hallowell, A. Irving
   1934   Some Empirical Aspects of Saulteaux Religion. American Anthropologist 36:389–404.

Handler, Richard
   1991   Who Owns the Past? History, Cultural Property, and the Logic of Possessive Individualism. In The Politics of Culture. Bryan Williams, ed. Pp. 63–73. Washington DC: Smithsonian Institution Press.

Handler, Richard, and Jocelyn Linnekin
   1984   Tradition, Genuine or Spurious? Journal of American Folklore 97(385):273–290.

Hanson, F. Allen
   1979   Does God Have a Body? Truth, Reality and Cultural Relativism. Man 14:515–529.
   1989   The Making of the Maori: Cultural Invention and Its Logic. American Anthropologist 91(4):890–902.
   1997   Empirical Anthropology, Postmodernism, and the Invention of Tradition. In Past Is Present: Some Uses of Tradition in

Native Societies. Marie Mauzé, ed. Pp. 195–214. Lanham MD: University Press of America.

Harkin, Michael E.

1993 Power and Progress: The Evangelical Dialogue among the Heiltsuk. Ethnohistory 40:1–33.

1997a The Heiltsuks: Dialogues of Culture and History on the Northwest Coast. Lincoln: University of Nebraska Press.

1997b A Tradition of Invention: Modern Ceremonialism on the Northwest Coast. *In* Past Is Present: Some Uses of Tradition in Native Societies. Marie Mauzé, ed. Pp. 97–111. Lanham MD: University Press of America.

Harrington, John Peabody

1933 Annotations. *In* Chinigchinich: A Revised and Annotated Version of Alfred Robinson's Translation of Father Geronimo Boscana's Historical Account of the Belief, Usages, Customs and Extravagancies of the Indians of This Mission of San Juan Capistrano Called the Acagchemem Tribe (1846). Phil Townsend Hanna, ed. Santa Ana: Fine Arts Press.

N.d. John Peabody Harrington Papers, Reels 27–28. National Anthropological Archives, Smithsonian Institution, Washington, D.C.

Hatanaka, Sachiko

1967 The Process of Cultural Change in Micronesia under the Japanese Mandate. *In* Bunka Jinruigaku. M. Gamo, T. Okayashi, and S. Muratake, eds. Pp. 65–124. Tokyo: Kadokawa Shoten.

1973–74 Culture Change in Micronesia under the Japanese Administration. Programme of Participation, 4. Paris: UNESCO.

Hauptman, Lawrence M., and James P. Wherry, eds.

1990 The Pequots in Southern New England: The Fall and Rise of an American Indian Nation. Norman: University of Oklahoma Press.

Heberlein, Thomas

1993 Conflict over the Exercise of Chippewa Indian Treaty Rights: Racism, Self-Interest, or Community Structure. Unpublished MS, Department of Rural Sociology, University of Wisconsin–Madison.

Heizer, Robert

1941 A Californian Messianic Movement of 1801 among the Chumash. American Anthropologist 43:128–129.

1968 The Indians of Los Angeles County: Hugo Reid's Letters of 1852. Los Angeles: Southwest Museum.

Hester, Thomas
    1978   Salinan. *In* Handbook of North American Indians, vol. 8:
                    California. Robert Heizer, ed. Pp. 500–504. Washington DC:
                    Smithsonian Institution Press.

Hezel, Francis
    1983   The First Taint of Civilization: A History of the Caroline
                    and Marshall Islands in Pre-Colonial Days, 1521–1885. Hon-
                    olulu: University of Hawaii Press.
    1995   Strangers in Their Own Land: A Century of Colonial Rule
                    in the Caroline and Marshall Islands. Honolulu: University
                    of Hawaii Press.

Hickerson, Harold
    1962   The Southwestern Chippewa: An Ethnohistorical Study.
                    Memoirs of the American Anthropological Association, 92,
                    vol. 64(3), pt. 2. Washington DC: American Anthropological
                    Association.

Hicks, George L.
    1964   Catawba Acculturation and the Ideology of Race. *In* Sympo-
                    sium on Community Studies in Anthropology: Proceedings
                    of the 1963 Annual Spring Meeting of the American Ethno-
                    logical Society. Viola E. Garfield and Ernestine Friedl, eds.
                    Pp. 116–124. Seattle: University of Washington Press.

Hicks, George L., and David I. Kertzer
    1972   Making a Middle Way: Problems of Monhegan Identity.
                    Southwest Journal of Anthropology 28(1):1–24.

Hiery, Hermann Joseph
    1995   The Neglected War: The German South Pacific and the In-
                    fluence of World War I. Honolulu: University of Hawaii
                    Press.

Hilger, Sister M. Inez
    1951   Chippewa Child Life and Its Cultural Background. Bureau of
                    American Ethnology Bulletin, 146. Washington DC: Bureau
                    of American Ethnology.

Hill, Jonathan
    1996   Ethnogenesis in the Northwest Amazon. *In* History, Power,
                    and Identity: Ethnogenesis in the Americas, 1492–1992. Jon-
                    athan Hill, ed. Pp. 142–160. Iowa City: University of Iowa
                    Press.

Hill, W. W.
    1944   The Navaho Indians and the Ghost Dance of 1890. American
                    Anthropologist 46:523–527.

Hinton, Leanne
  1994   Flutes of Fire: Essays on California Indian Languages. Berke-
                  ley: Heyday Books.
Hittman, Michael
  1973   The 1870 Ghost Dance on the Walker River Reservation: A
                  Reconstruction. Ethnohistory 20:247–278.
  1996   Corbett Mack: The Life of a Northern Paiute. Lincoln: Uni-
                  versity of Nebraska Press.
  1997   Wovoka and the Ghost Dance. Lincoln: University of Ne-
                  braska Press.
Hobbes, Thomas
  1987   Leviathan. London: Everyman's Library.
Hobsbawm, Eric
  1963   Primitive Rebels: Studies in Archaic Forms of Social Move-
                  ment in the 19th and 20th Centuries. New York: Praeger.
  1983   Introduction: Inventing Traditions. In The Invention of Tra-
                  dition. Eric Hobsbawm and Terence Ranger, eds. Pp. 1–14.
                  Cambridge: Cambridge University Press.
Hobsbawm, Eric, and Terence Ranger, eds.
  1983   The Invention of Tradition: Cambridge: Cambridge Univer-
                  sity Press.
Hodge, Frederick W., ed.
  1907–10   Handbook of American Indians North of Mexico. 2 vols. Bu-
                  reau of American Ethnology Bulletin, 30. Washington DC:
                  Bureau of American Ethnology.
Holland, Dorothy, and Naomi Quinn
  1987   Introduction: Culture and Cognition. In Cultural Models in
                  Language and Thought. Dorothy Holland and Naomi
                  Quinn, eds. Pp. 3–40. New York: Cambridge University
                  Press.
Hoole, William Stanley, ed.
  1986   Memoir of Catharine Brown, a Christian Indian, of the Cher-
                  okee Nation. University AL: Confederate Publishing Co.
Horse Capture, George P.
  1989   Powwow. Cody WY: Buffalo Bill Historical Center.
Horton, Wade Alston
  1992   Protestant Missionary Women as Agents of Cultural Transi-
                  tion among Cherokee Women, 1801–1839. Ph.D. disserta-
                  tion, Southern Theological Seminary.
Howard, James H.
  1975   The Culture-Area Concept: Does It Diffract Anthropologi-
                  cal Light? Indian Historian 8(1):22–26.

1981   Shawnee! The Ceremonialism of a Native Indian Tribe and
                Its Cultural Background. Athens: Ohio University Press.

Howell, Carol L.
1998   Cannibalism Is an Acquired Taste: And Other Notes from
                Conversations with Anthropologist Omer C. Stewart. Niwot:
                University Press of Colorado.

Hudson, Travis, and Ernest Underhay
1978   Crystals in the Sky: An Intellectual Odyssey Involving As-
                tronomy, Cosmology, and Rock Art. Socorro NM: Ballena
                Press.

Hudson's Bay Company Archives
N.d.   Provincial Archives of Manitoba, Winnipeg.

Huel, Raymond J. A.
1996   Proclaiming the Gospel to the Indians and the Metis. Ed-
                monton: University of Alberta Press and Western Canadian
                Publishers

Hultkrantz, Ake
1986   Mythology and Religious Concepts. *In* Handbook of North
                American Indians, vol. 11: Great Basin. Warren L. D. Azeve-
                do, ed. Pp. 630–640. Washington DC: Smithsonian Institution
                Press.

Jackson, Jason Baird
1996   Yuchi Custom Ways: Expressions of Tradition in a Southeast-
                ern Native American Society. M.A. thesis, Folklore Institute,
                Indiana University.
1997   The Work of Tradition in Yuchi Oratory. Florida Anthropol-
                ogist 50:197–202.
2000a   Customary Uses of Ironweed (*Vernonia fasciculta*) by the Yuchi
                in Eastern Oklahoma, USA. Economic Botany 54:401–403.
2000b   Signaling the Creator: Indian Football as Ritual Performance
                among the Yuchi and Their Neighbors. Southern Folklore
                57:33–64.
2003   Yuchi Ceremonial Life: Performance, Meaning, and Tradi-
                tion in a Contemporary Native American Community. Lin-
                coln: University of Nebraska Press.

Jackson, Jason Baird, and Mary S. Linn
2000   Calling in the Members: Linguistic Form and Cultural Con-
                text in a Yuchi Ritual Speech Genre. Anthropological Lin-
                guistics 42:61–80.

Jacobs, Elizabeth
1933   Tillamook (Nehalem) Ethnographic Notes Taken December
                1933 at Garibaldi, OR. Melville Jacobs Collection, Box 106,

file 7. Manuscripts and University Archives, University of Washington, Seattle.

Jacobs, Melville

1939 Coos Narrative and Ethnologic Texts. University of Washington Publications in Anthropology 7(1):1–27.

1959 The People Are Coming Soon. Seattle: University of Washington Press.

1960 The Content and Style of an Oral Literature. Viking Fund Publications in Anthropology, 29. New York: Viking Fund.

N.d. Coos Field Notes. Melville Jacobs Collection, Box 99, file 19. Manuscripts and University Archives, University of Washington, Seattle.

Jacobs, Melville, Albert S. Gatschet, and Leo J. Frachtenberg

1945 Santiam Kalapuya Myth Texts. University of Washington Publications in Anthropology, 11. Seattle: University of Washington.

Janes, Craig

1995 The Transformations of Tibetan Medicine. Medical Anthropology Quarterly 9(1):6–39.

1999 Imagined Lives, Suffering, and the Work of Culture: The Embodied Discourses of Conflict in Modern Tibet. Medical Anthropology Quarterly 13(4):391–412.

Jebens, Holger

2000 Signs of the Second Coming: On Eschatological Expectation and Disappointment in Highland and Seaboard Papua New Guinea. Ethnohistory 47:171–204.

Jeffredo-Warden, Louisa

1999 Perceiving, Experiencing, and Expressing the Sacred: An Indigenous Southern Californian View. *In* Over the Edge: Remapping the American West. Valerie Matsumoto and Blake Allmendinger, eds. Pp. 329–338. Berkeley: University of California Press.

Jenness, Diamond

1935 The Ojibwa of Parry Island, Their Social and Religious Life. National Museum of Canada Bulletin, 78, Anthropology Series, 17. Ottawa: Department of Mines.

Johnston, Bernice

1962 California's Gabrielino Indians. Los Angeles: Southwest Museum.

Jolly, Margaret, and Nicholas Thomas, eds.

1992 The Politics of Tradition in the Pacific. Theme issue, Oceania 62.

Jones, Laura
    1992   Women, Art, and the Crafting of Ethnicity in Contemporary
                    French Polynesia. Pacific Studies 15(4):137–154.
Kaplan, Martha
    1995   Neither Cargo nor Cult: Ritual Politics and the Colonial
                    Imagination in Fiji. Durham: Duke University Press.
Kay, Paul
    1987   Linguistic Competence and Folk Theories of Language: Two
                    English Hedges. *In* Cultural Models in Language and
                    Thought. Dorothy Holland and Naomi Quinn, eds. Pp. 67–
                    77. New York: Cambridge University Press.
Keesing, Roger M.
    1978   Politico-Religious Movements and Anticolonialism on Ma-
                    laita: Maasina Rule in Historical Perspective, Part I. Oceania
                    48(4):241–261.
    1982a   *Kastom* and Anticolonialism on Malaita: Culture as Political
                    Symbol. Mankind 13:357–373.
    1982b   *Kastom* in Melanesia: An Overview. Mankind 13(4):297–301.
    1989   Creating the Past: Custom and Identity in the Contemporary
                    Pacific. Contemporary Pacific 1(1–2):19–42.
    1992   Custom and Confrontation: The Kwaio Struggle for Cultural
                    Autonomy. Chicago: University of Chicago Press.
Keesing, Roger M., and Robert Tonkinson, eds.
    1982   Reinventing Traditional Culture: The Politics of *Kastom* in
                    Island Melanesia. Theme issue, Mankind 13(4).
Kehoe, Alice Beck
    1988   *Review of* We Shall Live Again, by Russell Thornton. Ameri-
                    can Anthropologist 90:190.
    1989   The Ghost Dance: Ethnohistory and Revitalization. Fort
                    Worth: Harcourt Brace College.
Kelsey, Harry
    1986   Juan Rodríguez Cabrillo. San Marino CA: Huntington Li-
                    brary.
King, Chester, and Thomas Blackburn
    1978   Tataviam. *In* Handbook of North American Indians, vol. 8:
                    California. Robert Heizer, ed. Pp. 535–537. Washington DC:
                    Smithsonian Institution Press.
Knill, Harry, ed.
    1999   Great Indians of California by Mariano Guadalupe Vallejo;
                    Colonel of Cavalry, Commandant-General of California
                    1807–1890; Padre Francisco Palou; the Father of California

History 1722–1790; H. H. Bancroft 1832–1918. Santa Barbara: Bellerophon Books.

Kohl, Johan Georg
    1985   Kitchi-Gami: Life among the Lake Superior Ojibway. St. Paul: Minnesota Historical Society Press.

Kohl, Philip L.
    1998   Nationalism and Archaeology: On the Constructions of Nations and the Reconstructions of the Remote Past. Annual Review of Anthropology 27:223–246.

Kohut, Heinz
    1977   The Restoration of the Self. New York: International Universities Press.

Kort, Wesley
    1975   Plot and Process. In Narrative Elements and Religious Meanings. Pp. 59–85. Philadelphia: Fortress Press.

Kristeva, Julia
    1996   Intertextuality and Literary Interpretation. In Julia Kristeva Interviews. Ross Mitchell Guberman, ed. Pp. 188–203. New York: Columbia University Press.

Kroeber, Alfred L.
    1905   A Ghost-Dance in California. Journal of American Folk-Lore 17:32–35.
    1907   Shoshonean Dialects of California. University of California Publications in American Archaeology and Ethnology 4(3): 65–166.
    1925   Handbook of the Indians of California. Bureau of American Ethnology Bulletin, 78. Washington DC: Bureau of American Ethnology.

Krupat, Arnold, ed.
    1994   Native American Autobiography: An Anthology. Madison: University of Wisconsin Press.

Kubler-Ross, Elisabeth
    1970   On Death and Dying. New York: Macmillan.

Kuhm, Herbert
    1928   Wisconsin Indian Fishing. Wisconsin Archaeologist 7(2) n.s.: 61–114.

Kuhn, Thomas S.
    1964   The Structure of Scientific Revolutions. Chicago: University of Chicago Press.

Kupperman, Karen
    2000   Indians and English: Facing Off in Early America. Ithaca: Cornell University Press.

La Barre, Weston

1970   The Ghost Dance: The Origins of Religion. Garden City: Doubleday.

1975   The Peyote Cult. 4th ed. New York: Schocken Books.

La Dépêche de Tahiti

1997   En 2001, Ce Pays Sera Indépendant. La Dépêche de Tahiti, May 23.

Lankford, George F.

1986   Native American Legends: Southeastern Legends: Tales from the Natchez, Caddo, Biloxi, Chickasaw, and Other Nations. Little Rock: August House.

Lanternari, Vittorio

1963   The Religions of the Oppressed: A Study of Modern Messianic Cults. New York: Knopf.

The Last of the Dogmen

1995   Tab Murphy, dir. 118 min. HBO Studios.

Lattas, Andrew

1998   Cultures of Secrecy: Reinventing Race in Bush Kaliai Cargo Cults. Madison: University of Wisconsin Press.

Lawson, Stephanie

1990   The Myth of Cultural Homogeneity and Its Implications for Chiefly Power and Politics in Fiji. Comparative Studies in Society and History 32(4):795–821.

1993   The Politics of Tradition: Problems for Political Legitimacy and Democracy in the South Pacific. Pacific Studies 16(2):1–29.

1997   The Tyranny of Tradition: Critical Reflections on Nationalist Narratives in the South Pacific. In Narratives of Nation in the South Pacific. Ton Otto and Nicholas Thomas, eds. Pp. 15–31. Amsterdam: Harwood Academic Publishers and Overseas Publishers Association.

Le Bon, Gustave

1960   The Crowd: A Study of the Popular Mind. New York: Viking Press.

LeJeune, Paul

1897   Relation of What Occurred in New France in the Year 1634. In The Jesuit Relations and Allied Documents, vol. 6. R. G. Thwaites, ed. Pp. 91–325. Cleveland: Burrows.

Lepowsky, Maria

1989   Soldiers and Spirits: The Impact of World War II on a Coral Sea Island. In The Pacific Theater: Island Representations of

World War II. Geoffrey White and Lamont Lindstrom, eds. Pp. 205–230. Honolulu: University of Hawaii Press.

1993   Fruit of the Motherland: Gender in an Egalitarian Society. New York: Columbia University Press.

Levi, Clarissa M.

1956   Chippewa Indians of Yesterday and Today. New York: Pageant Press.

Levi-Strauss, Claude

1978   The Origin of Table Manners. Mytholgiques, vol. 3. Chicago: University of Chicago Press.

Levy, Robert I.

1973   Tahitians: Mind and Experience in the Society Islands. Chicago: University of Chicago Press.

1978   Costanoan. In Handbook of North American Indians, vol. 8: California. Robert Heizer, ed. Pp. 485–495. Washington DC: Smithsonian Institution Press.

Lewis, J. L.

1967[1948]   Kusaiean Acculturation 1924–1948. Saipan: Division of Land Management, Resources and Development, U.S. Trust Territory of the Pacific Islands.

Limbrock, Eberhard

1912–13   Buschreise ins Hinterland von Beukin. Steyler Missionsbote 40(126–127):122–143.

Linde, Charlotte

1987   Explanatory Systems in Oral Life Stories. In Cultural Models in Language and Thought. Dorothy Holland and Naomi Quinn, eds. Pp. 343–366. New York: Cambridge University Press.

Lindstrom, Lamont

1989   Working Encounters: Oral Histories of World War II Labor Corps from Tanna, Vanuatu. In The Pacific Theater: Island Representations of World War II. Geoffrey White and Lamont Lindstrom, eds. Pp. 395–417. Honolulu: University of Hawaii Press.

1990   Knowledge of Cargo, Knowledge of Cult: Truth and Power on Tanna, Vanuatu. In Cargo Cults and Millenarian Movements: Transoceanic Comparisons of New Religious Movements. Gary Trompf, ed. Pp. 239–262. Berlin: Mouton de Gruyter.

1993   Cargo Cult: Strange Stories of Desire from Melanesia and Beyond. Honolulu: University of Hawaii Press.

Linn, Mary S.
  2001   A Grammar of Euchee (Yuchi). Ph.D. dissertation, Depart-
              ment of Linguistics, University of Kansas, Lawrence.
Linnekin, Jocelyn
  1983   Defining Tradition: Variations on the Hawaiian Identity.
              American Ethnologist 10:241–252.
  1990a   Cultural Invention and the Dilemma of Authenticity. Ameri-
              can Anthropologist 93(2):446–449.
  1990b   The Politics of Culture in the Pacific. *In* Cultural Identity
              and Ethnicity in the Pacific. Jocelyn Linnekin and Lin Poyer,
              eds. Pp. 149–173. Honolulu: University of Hawaii Press.
  1992   On the Theory and Politics of Cultural Construction in the
              Pacific. Oceania 62:249–263.
Linnekin, Jocelyn, and Lin Poyer, eds.
  1990   Cultural Identity and Ethnicity in the Pacific. Honolulu: Uni-
              versity of Hawaii Press.
Linton, Ralph
  1940   Acculturation in Seven American Indian Tribes. New York:
              Appleton-Century.
  1943   Nativistic Movements. American Anthropologist 45:230–
              240.
Lock, Margaret, and Nancy Scheper-Hughes
  1996   A Critical-Interpretive Approach in Medical Anthropology:
              Rituals and Routines of Discipline and Dissent. *In* Medical
              Anthropology: Contemporary Theory and Methods.
              Thomas M. Johnson and Carolyn F. Sargent, eds. Pp. 41–70.
              New York: Praeger Press.
Locklear, Heather, and Eric Elliott
  2002   From Grandma's Knees to College Classroom: Luiseño
              Comes Full Circle. News from Native California 15(3):34–
              35.
Lockwood, Victoria
  1993a   An Introduction to Contemporary Pacific Societies. *In* Con-
              temporary Pacific Societies: Studies in Development and
              Change. Victoria S. Lockwood, Thomas G. Harding, Ben J.
              Wallace, eds.; preface by Douglas L. Oliver. Pp. 1–17. Engle-
              wood Cliffs NJ: Prentice-Hall.
  1993b   Tahitian Transformation: Gender and Capitalist Develop-
              ment in a Rural Society. Boulder: Lynne Rienner Publish-
              ers.
Long, John S.
  1986   Shaganash: Early Protestant Missionaries and the Adoption

of Christianity by the Western James Bay Cree. Ph.D. dissertation, University of Toronto.

1987   Manitu, Power, Books and Wiihtikow: Some Factors in the Adoption of Christianity by Nineteenth-Century Western James Bay Cree. Native Studies Review 3(1):1–30.

1989   The Cree Prophets: Oral and Documentary Accounts. Journal of the Canadian Church Historical Society 31(1):3–13.

Lucus, Wilfrid

1989   The Cultural Identity of the Polynesian People and Its Contemporary Rebirth. Ethnies: Droits de l'homme et peoples autochtones 4:102–106.

Maher, Robert F.

1958   Tommy Kabu Movement of the Purari Delta. Oceania 24:75–90.

Malinowski, Bronislaw

1922   Argonauts of the Western Pacific. New York: Dutton.

Malone, Henry Thompson

1956   Cherokees of the Old South. Athens: University of Georgia Press.

Martin, Joel

1991   Sacred Revolt: The Muskogees Struggle for a New World. Boston: Beacon Press.

1995   From Middle Ground to Underground: Southeastern Indians and the Early Republic. In Religion and American Culture: A Reader. David G. Hackett, ed. Pp. 127–145. New York: Routledge.

Mason, William

1975   Fages' Code of Conduct toward Indians, 1787. Journal of California Anthropology 2(1):90–100.

1984   Indian–Mexican Cultural Exchange in the Los Angeles Area, 1781–1834. Aztlán 15:123–144.

1998   The Census of 1790: A Demographic History of Colonial California. Ballena Press Anthropological Papers, 45. Menlo Park CA: Ballena Press.

Matthews, Maureen, and Roger Roulette

1996   Fair Wind's Dream: Naamiwan Obawaajigewin. In Reading beyond Words: Contexts for Native History. Jennifer S. H. Brown and Elizabeth Vibert, eds. Pp. 330–359. Peterborough, ON: Broadview Press.

McCaleb, Neal A.

2001a   Proposed Finding against Federal Acknowledgment of the

Nipmuc Nation. Federal Register 66(190), October 1: 49967–49970.

2001b   Proposed Finding against Federal Acknowledgment of the Webster/Dudley Band of Chaubunagungamaug Nipmuck Indians. Federal Register 66(190), October 1: 49970–49972.

2002   Final Determination to Acknowledge the Historical Pequot Tribe. Federal Register 67(126), July 1: 44234–44240.

McCarthy, Suzanne

1995   The Cree Syllabary and the Writing System Riddle: A Paradigm in Crisis. *In* Scripts and Literacy: Reading and Learning to Read Alphabets, Syllabaries and Characters. I. Taylor and D. R. Olson, eds. Pp. 59–75. Dordrecht: Kluwer Academic Publishers.

McCawley, William

1996   The First Angelinos: The Gabrielino Indians of Los Angeles. Banning CA: Malki Museum Press/Ballena Press.

McDonald, Maryon

1986   Celtic Ethnic Kinship and the Problem of Being English. Current Anthropology 27(4):333–347.

McDowell, Nancy

1985   Past and Future: The Nature of Episodic Time in Bun. *In* History and Ethnohistory in Papua New Guinea. Deborah Gewertz and Edward Schieffelin, eds. Pp. 26–39. Sydney: University of Sydney Press.

1988   A Note on Cargo Cults and Cultural Constructions of Change. Pacific Studies 11:121–134.

McLoughlin, William G.

1984   Cherokees and Missionaries, 1789–1839. New Haven: Yale University Press.

McMullen, Ann

1994a   The Heart Interest: Native Americans at Mount Hope and the King Philip Museum. *In* Passionate Hobby: Rudolf Frederick Haffenreffer and the King Philip Museum. Shepard Krech III, ed. Pp. 167–186. Bristol RI: Haffenreffer Museum of Anthropology, Brown University.

1994b   What's Wrong with This Picture? Context, Coversion, Survival, and the Development of Regional Native Cultures and Pan-Indianism in Southeastern New England. *In* Enduring Traditions: The Native Peoples of New England. Laurie Weinstein, ed. Pp. 123–150. Westport CT: Bergin and Garvey.

1996a   Culture by Design: Native Identity, Historiography, and the Reclamation of Tradition in Twentieth-Century Southeastern New England. Ph.D. dissertation, Department of Anthropology, Brown University.

1996b   Soapbox Discourse: Tribal History, Indian–White Relations, and Southeastern New England Powwows. Public Historian 18(4):53–74.

2002   Blood and Culture: Negotiating Race in Twentieth-Century Native New England. *In* Confounding the Color Line: Indian–Black Relations in Multidisciplinary Perspective. James F. Brooks, ed. Pp. 261–291. Lincoln: University of Nebraska Press.

McNally, Michael

2000   The Practice of Native American Christianity. Church History 69:4, 834–859.

Melish, John

1818   Map of Alabama. Philadelphia.

Merrell, James H.

1989   The Indians' New World: Catawbas and Their Neighbors from European Contact through the Era of Removal. Chapel Hill: University of North Carolina Press.

Meyer, Melissa L.

1997   The White Earth Tragedy: Ethnicity and Dispossession at a Minnesota Anishinaabe Reservation, 1889–1920. Lincoln: University of Nebraska Press.

Miller, Christopher L.

1985   Prophetic Worlds: Indians and Whites on the Columbia Plateau. New Brunswick NJ: Rutgers University Press.

Miller, Jay

1984   Tsimshian Religion in Historical Perspective: Shamans, Prophets, and Christ. *In* The Tsimshian and Their Neighbors of the North Pacific Coast. Jay Miller and Carol Eastman, eds. Pp 137–147. Seattle: University of Washington Press.

Miller, Jay, and William Seaburg

1990   Athapaskans of Southwestern Oregon. *In* Handbook of North American Indians, vol. 7: The Northwest Coast. Wayne Suttles, ed. Pp. 580–588. Washington DC: Smithsonian Institution Press.

Mills, Antonia, and Richard Slobodin

1994   Amerindian Rebirth. Toronto: University of Toronto Press.

Miner, Bradford L.

2001   Feds Give Nipmuc Group Preliminary OK. Worcester Telegram and Gazette, January 21: A1.

Misima Station
    1943a   Patrol Diary, March 24. Australian New Guinea Administrative Unit, Territory of Papua.
    1943b   Patrol Report, April 3. Australian New Guinea Administrative Unit, Territory of Papua.

Mission San Gabriel
    1774–85   Baptismal Records, Church of Jesus Christ of Latter Day Saints microfilm 002643; Mission San Carlos Borromeo Marriage Number 1789, Church of Jesus Christ of Latter Day Saints microfilm 1985228. Mission San Gabriel, San Gabriel CA.

Mission Santa Barbara
    1787–88   Correspondence with Governor Fages. Santa Barbara Mission Archives, Santa Barbara.

Monroy, Douglas
    1990   Thrown among Strangers: The Making of Mexican Culture in Frontier California. Berkeley: University of California Press.

Mooney, James
    1965   The Ghost-Dance Religion and the Sioux Outbreak of 1890. Anthony F. C. Wallace, ed. Chicago: University of Chicago Press.

Moses, Lester G.
    1984   The Indian Man: A Biography of James Mooney. Urbana: University of Illinois Press.

Moulton, Gary E.
    1978   John Ross: Cherokee Chief. Athens: University of Georgia Press.

Munn, Nancy
    1992   Cultural Anthropology of Time. Annual Review of Anthropology 21:93–123.

Murdoch, John S.
    1982   Cree Literacy in Formal Education: A Problem in Educational Innovation. In Papers of the Thirteenth Algonquian Conference. William Cowan, ed. Pp. 23–28. Ottawa: Carleton University Press.

Mydans, Seth
    2000   Burmese Rebel Chief More Boy than Warrior. New York Times, April 10: A1, A8.

Nabokov, Peter
    1992   Native American Testimony: A Chronicle of Indian–White

Relations from Prophecy to the Present, 1492–1992. New York: Penguin.

Nagel, Joane, and C. Matthew Snipp

1993   Ethnic Reorganization: American Indian Social, Economic, Political and Cultural Strategies for Survival. Ethnic and Racial Studies 16:203–235.

Narakobi, Bernard

1974   Who Will Take Up Peli's Challenge? Point 1:93–104.

Nash, Philleo

1955[1937]   The Place of Religious Revivalism in the Formation of the Intercultural Community on Klamath Reservation. *In* Social Anthropology of North American Tribes. Fred Eggan, ed. Pp. 377–444. Chicago: University of Chicago Press.

Nelson, Hank

1976   Black, White and Gold: Gold Mining in Papua New Guinea 1878–1930. Canberra: Australian National University Press.

Nero, Karen L.

1989   Time of Famine, Time of Transformation: Hell in the Pacific, Palau. *In* The Pacific Theater: Island Representations of World War II. Geoffrey M. White and Lamont Lindstrom, eds. Pp. 117–147. Honolulu: University of Hawaii Press.

Nesper, Larry

2002   The Walleye War: The Struggle for Ojibwe Spearfishing and Treaty Rights. Lincoln: University of Nebraska Press.

2003   Simulating Culture: Being Indian for Tourists in Lac du Flambeau's Wa-Swa-Gon Indian Bowl. *In* Native Peoples and Tourism. Larry Nesper, ed. Theme issue, Ethnohistory 50(3).

Newbury, Colin

1980   Tahiti Nui: Change and Survival in French Polynesia 1767–1945. Honolulu: University of Hawaii Press.

Nichter, Mark

1981   Idioms of Distress: Alternative in the Expression of Psychosocial Distress. Case Study from South India. Culture, Medicine and Psychiatry 5:379–408.

Niezen, Ronald

2000   Spirit Wars: Native North American Religions in the Age of Nation Building. Berkeley: University of California Press.

Northrup, Jim

1997   Rez Road Follies: Canoes, Casinos, Computers and Birch Bark Baskets. Minneapolis: University of Minnesota Press.

Obeyesekere, Gananath

1990   The Work of Culture: Symbolic Transformation in Psychoanalysis and Anthropology. Chicago: University of Chicago Press.

1992   The Apotheosis of Captain Cook: Mythmaking in the Pacific. Princeton: Princeton University Press.

O'Connell, Barry, ed.

1992   On Our Own Ground: The Complete Writings of William Apess, a Pequot. Amherst: University of Massachusetts Press.

Ong, Aihwa

1987   Spirits of Resistance and Capitalist Discipline: Factory Women in Malaysia. Albany: State University of New York Press.

Osio, Antonio Maria

1996[1851]   The History of Alta California: A Memoir of Mexican California. Rose Marie Beebe and Robert Senkewicz, trans. and eds. Madison: University of Wisconsin Press.

Otto, Ton, and Nicholas Thomas

1997   Narratives of Nation in the South Pacific. *In* Narratives of Nation in the South Pacific. Ton Otto and Nicholas Thomas, eds. Pp. 1–13. Amsterdam: Harwood Academic Publishers and Overseas Publishers Association.

Parsons, Claire D. F.

1984   Idioms of Distress: Kinship and Sickness among the People of the Kingdom of Tonga. Culture, Medicine and Psychiatry 8:71–93.

Pate, James Paul

1969   The Chickamauga: A Forgotten Segment of Indian Resistance on the Southern Frontier. Ph.D. dissertation, Mississippi State University.

Payne-Butrick Papers

N.d.   John Howard Payne Papers. Ayer Collection, Newberry Library, Chicago.

Peach, Wesley

2001   Itineraires de Conversion: Perspectives de theologies pratique. Quebec: Editions Fides.

Peattie, Mark

1988   Nanyo: The Rise and Fall of the Japanese in Micronesia, 1985–1945. Honolulu: University of Hawaii Press.

Peel, J. D. Y.

1984   Making History: The Past in the Ijesha Present. Man 19:111–132.

Peirce, Charles S.

1998   Charles S. Peirce: The Essential Writings. Edward C. Moore, ed. Amherst NY: Prometheus Books.

Pentland, David
  1981   Synonymy [of Cree]. *In* Handbook of North American Indi-
                  ans, vol. 6: Subarctic. June Helm, ed. Pp. 227–228. Washing-
                  ton DC: Smithsonian Institution Press.
Perdue, Theda
  1998   Cherokee Women: Gender and Culture Change, 1700–1835.
                  Lincoln: University of Nebraska Press.
Petrullo, Vincenzo
  1934   The Diabolic Root: A Study of Peyotism, the New Indian
                  Religion, among the Delawares. Philadelphia: University of
                  Pennsylvania Press.
Peuch, Henri-Charles
  1957   Gnosis and Time. *In* Man and Time: Papers from the Eranos
                  Yearbooks, vol. 3. Joseph Campbell, ed. Pp. 38–84. Princeton:
                  Princeton University Press/Bollingen.
Peyer, Bernd C.
  1997   The Tutor'd Mind: Indian Missionary-Writers in Antebel-
                  lum America. Amherst: University of Massachusetts Press.
Phillips, George
  1975   Chiefs and Challengers: Indian Resistance and Cooperation
                  in Southern California. Berkeley: University of California
                  Press.
Phillips, Joyce B., and Paul Gary Phillips
  1998   The Brainerd Journal: A Mission to the Cherokees, 1817–
                  1823. Lincoln: University of Nebraska Press.
Pinker, Steven
  1999   How the Mind Works. New York: W. W. Norton.
Popper, Karl
  1966   The Open Society and Its Enemies, vol. 1: The Spell of Plato.
                  Princeton: Princeton University Press.
Porterfield, Amanda
  1987   Feminist Theory as a Revitalization Movement. Sociological
                  Analysis 48:234–244.
Powers, William K.
  1995   Innovating the Sacred: Creating Tradition in Lakota Reli-
                  gion. European Review of Native American Studies 9:21–24.
Poyer, Lin, Suzanne Falgout, and Laurence M. Carucci
  2001   The Typhoon of War: Micronesian Experiences of the Pacific
                  War. Honolulu: University of Hawaii Press.
Pratt, Mary Louise
  1992   Imperial Eyes: Travel Writing and Transculturation. New
                  York: Routledge.

REFERENCES CITED 313

Prince, J. D., and Frank G. Speck

1903a   Dying American Speech Echoes from Connecticut. Proceedings of the American Philosophical Society 42(174):346–352.

1903b   The Modern Pequots and Their Language. American Anthropologist 5(2):193–212.

1904   Glossary of the Mohegan-Pequot Language. American Anthropologist 6(1):18–45.

Propp, Vladimir

1968   Morphology of the Folktale. Austin: University of Texas Press.

Prucha, Francis Paul

1994   American Indian Treaties: The History of a Political Anomaly. Berkeley: University of California Press.

Quincy, Keith

1988   Hmong: History of a People. Cheney: Eastern Washington University Press.

Quintero, Gilbert

1995   Gender, Discord, and Illness: Navajo Philosophy and Healing in the Native American Church. Journal of Anthropological Research 51(1):69–89.

Qutb, Sayyid

1953   Social Justice in Islam. John B. Hardie and Hamid Algar, trans. Oneonta, NY: Islamic Publications International.

Raboteau, Albert

1980   Slave Religion: The Invisible Institution in the Antebellum South. New York: Oxford.

Rappaport, Joanne

1990   The Politics of Memory: Native Historical Interpretation in the Columbian Andes. Cambridge: Cambridge University Press.

1994   Cumbe Reborn: An Andean Ethnography of History. Chicago: University of Chicago Press.

Ray, Verne

1938   Lower Chinook Ethnographic Notes. University of Washington Publications in Anthropology 7(2):29–165.

Reafsnyder, Charles B.

1984   Emergent Ethnic Identity in an Urban Migrant Community in Truk State, FSM. Ph.D. dissertation, Indiana University.

Redfield, Robert

1953   The Primitive World and Its Transformations. Ithaca: Cornell University Press.

Reid, John, and John E. Eaton
1817   The Life of Andrew Jackson. Philadelphia: Cary and Son.
Richter, Daniel K.
1993   Whose Indian History? William and Mary Quarterly 50(2)
            3rd series:379–393.
Ritter, Philip L.
1978   The Depopulation of Kosrae: Population and Social Orga-
            nization on a Micronesian High Island. Ph.D. dissertation,
            Stanford University.
Roberts, Chris
1992   Powwow Country. Helena MT: American and World Geo-
            graphic Publishing.
Robertson, Tomás
1978   Baja California and Its Missions. Glendale IL: La Siesta Press.
Robles, Rhonda
2002   Whispers in the Wind. News from Native California 15(3):
            11, 13.
Rorty, Richard
1982   Consequences of Pragmatism (Essays: 1972–1980). Minne-
            apolis: University of Minnesota Press.
Roscoe, Paul B.
1983   People and Planning in the Yangoru Subdistrict, East Sepik
            Province, Papua New Guinea. Ph.D. dissertation, University
            of Rochester.
1988   The Far Side of Hurun: The Management of Melanesian
            Millenarian Movements. American Ethnologist 15:515–529.
1991   Yangoru Boiken. In Encyclopedia of World Cultures, vol. 2:
            Oceania. Terence E. Hays, ed. Pp. 388–391. Boston: Hall.
1993   The Brokers of the Lord: The Ministration of a Christian
            Faith in a Sepik Society. In Contemporary Pacific Society:
            Studies in Development and Change. Thomas G. Harding,
            Victoria S. Lockwood, and Ben J. Wallace, eds. Pp. 289–303.
            Englewood Cliffs NJ: Prentice-Hall.
1995a   Of Power and Menace: Sepik Art as an Affecting Presence.
            Journal of the Royal Anthropological Institute 1:1–22.
1995b   The Perils of Positivism in Cultural Anthropology. American
            Anthropologist 97:492–504.
N.d.   Mortuary Ritual, Revitalization, and Identity among the Yan-
            goru Boiken. Paper presented at the Annual Meeting of the
            American Anthropological Association, Chicago, November
            1999.

Rossi, Ernest Lawrence
  1972   Dreams and the Growth of Personality: Expanding Aware-
                 ness in Psychotherapy. New York: Pergamon Press.
Rostlund, Erhard
  1952   Fresh Water Fish and Fishing in Native North America. Uni-
                 versity of California Publications in Geography, 9. Berkeley:
                 University of California Press.
Roth, Randolph
  1992   Is History a Process? Nonlinearity, Revitalization Theory,
                 and the Central Metaphor of Social Science History. Social
                 Science History 16:197–244.
Rynkiewich, Michael A.
  1980   Chippewa Powwows. In Anishinabe: Six Studies of Modern
                 Chippewa. Anthony J. Paredes, ed. Pp. 31–100. Gainesville:
                 University Press of Florida.
Ryser, Rudolf C.
  1995   Anti-Indian Movements on the Tribal Frontier. Occasional
                 Paper, 16–3. Olympia: Center for World Indigenous Studies.
Sahlins, Marshall
  1993   Goodbye to Triste Tropes: Ethnography in the Context of
                 Modern World History. Journal of Modern History 65:1–25.
  1995   How Natives Think (about Captain Cook, for Example).
                 Chicago: University of Chicago Press.
Sandos, James
  1985   Levantamiento! The 1824 Chumash Uprising Reconsidered.
                 Southern California Quarterly 67:109–133.
Satz, Ronald N.
  1991   Rhetoric versus Reality: The Indian Policy of Andrew Jack-
                 son. In Cherokee Removal: Before and After. William L. An-
                 derson, ed. Pp. 29–54. Athens: University of Georgia Press.
Scaglion, Richard
  1983   The Coming of Independence in Papua New Guinea: An
                 Abelam View. Journal of the Polynesian Society 92:463–486.
Schaefer, Paul D.
  1976   Confess Therefore Your Sins: Status and Sin on Kusaie. Ph.D.
                 dissertation, University of Minnesota.
Schama, Simon
  1995   Landscape and Memory. New York: Vintage.
Schieffelin, Edward, and Deborah Gewertz
  1985   Introduction. In History and Ethnohistory in Papua New
                 Guinea. Deborah Gewertz and Edward Schieffelin, eds. Pp.
                 1–6. Sydney: University of Sydney Press.

Schlender, James

1991   Treaty Rights in Wisconsin: A Review. Northeast Indian Quarterly 8:4–16.

Schneider, A. Gregory

1993   The Way of the Cross Leads Home: The Domestication of American Methodism. Bloomington: Indiana University Press.

Schneider, David M.

1980   American Kinship: A Cultural Account. 2nd ed. Chicago: University of Chicago Press.

Schwartz, E. A.

1997   The Rogue River War and Its Aftermath, 1850–1980. Norman: University of Oklahoma Press.

Schwarz, Maureen Trudelle

1998   Holy Visit 1996: Prophecy, Revitalization, and Resistance in the Contemporary Navajo World. Ethnohistory 45:747–793.

Scott, James C.

1985   Weapons of the Weak: Everyday Forms of Peasant Resistance. New Haven: Yale University Press.

1990   Domination and the Arts of Resistance: Hidden Transcripts. New Haven: Yale University Press.

1998   Seeing like a State. How Certain Schemes to Improve the Human Condition Have Failed. New Haven: Yale University Press.

Seaburg, William, and Pamela T. Amoss

2000   Badger and Coyote Were Neighbors: Melville Jacobs on Northwest Coast Indian Myths and Tales. Corvallis: Oregon State University Press.

Seaburg, William, and Lionel Youst

2002   Coquelle Thompson, Athabaskan Witness: A Cultural Biography. Norman: University of Oklahoma Press.

Shuster, Donald R.

1982a   Islands of Change in Palau: Church, School, and Elected Government, 1891–1981. Ed.D. dissertation, University of Hawaii.

1982b   State Shinto in Micronesia during Japanese Rule, 1914–1945. Pacific Studies 5(2):20–43.

Siikala, Jukka

1982   Cult and Conflict in Tropical Polynesia: A Study of Traditional Religion, Christianity and Nativistic Movements. FF Communication, 233. Helsinki: Academia Scientiarum Fennica.

Smith, Justine
2000   Cherokee Nationalism and the Bible. Paper delivered at the
                American Academy of Religion Annual Meeting, Nashville.

Smith, Larry J., ed.
1989   Guntersville Remembered. Albertville AL: Creative Printers,
                Inc.

Sobel, Mechal
2000   Teach Me Dreams: The Search for Self in the Revolutionary
                Era. Princeton: Princeton University Press.

Sparkman, Philip
1908   The Culture of the Luiseño Indians. University of Califor-
                nia Publications in American Archaeology and Ethnology
                8(4):187–234.

Speck, Frank G.
1903a   The Last of the Mohegans. Papoose 1(4):2–51.

1903b   Mohegan Traditions of the Muhkeahweesug, the Little Men.
                Papoose 1(7):11–14.

1903c   A Pequot-Mohegan Witchcraft Tale. Journal of American
                Folk-Lore 16(61):104–106.

1903d   The Remnants of Our Eastern Indian Tribes. American In-
                ventor 10:206–208.

1904a   A Modern Mohegan-Pequot Text. American Anthropologist
                6(4):469–476.

1904b   Some Mohegan-Pequot Legends. Journal of American Folk-
                lore 17:183–184.

1909a   Ethnology of the Yuchi Indians. Anthropological Publica-
                tions of the University Museum, University of Pennsylvania,
                1. Philadelphia: University Museum, University of Pennsyl-
                vania.

1909b   Notes on the Mohegan and Niantic Indians. In The Indians
                of the Greater New York and the Lower Hudson. C. Wissler,
                ed. Pp. 183–210. Anthropological Papers of the American
                Museum of Natural History, 3. New York: American Mu-
                seum of Natural History.

1928   Territorial Subdivisions and Boundaries of the Wampanoag,
                Massachusett, and Nauset Indians. Indian Notes and Mono-
                graphs 44.

Spencer, W. Baldwin, and Frank J. Gillen
1904   The Northern Tribes of Central Australia. London: McMil-
                lan.

Spicer, Edward H.
1961   Perspectives in American Indian Culture Change. Chicago:
               University of Chicago Press.
1971   Persistent Cultural Systems. Science 174(4011):795–800.
Spier, Leslie
1927   Ghost Dance of 1870 among the Klamath of Oregon. Uni-
               versity of Washington Publications in Anthropology 2:43–55.
1935   The Prophet Dance of the Northwest and Its Derivatives:
               The Source of the Ghost Dance. General Series in Anthro-
               pology, 1. Menosha WI: George Banta.
Spier, Robert
1978   Foothill Yokuts. In Handbook of North American Indians,
               vol. 8: California. Robert Heizer, ed. Pp. 471–484. Washing-
               ton DC: Smithsonian Institution Press.
Staats, Susan
1996   Fighting in a Different Way: Indigenous Resistance through
               the Alleluia Religion of Guyana. In History, Power, and Iden-
               tity: Ethnogenesis in the Americas, 1492–1992. Jonathan
               Hill, ed. Pp. 161–179. Iowa City: University of Iowa Press.
Stern, Steve
1982   Peru's Indian Peoples and the Challenge of Spanish Con-
               quest: Huamanga to 1640. Madison: University of Wisconsin
               Press.
Stevenson, Karen
1990   Heiva: Continuity and Change of a Tahitian Celebration.
               Contemporary Pacific 2(2):255–278.
1992   Politicization of La Culture Maohi: The Creation of a Tahitian
               Cultural Identity. Pacific Studies 15(4):117–136.
Stewart, Omer C.
1987   Peyote Religion: A History. Norman: University of Okla-
               homa Press.
N.d.   Yuchi. Omer C. Stewart Collection, Second Acquisition, Box
               59, Five Civilized Tribes. University of Colorado at Boulder,
               Archives. MS consulted in the files of Dr. Daniel C. Swan,
               Gilcrease Museum, Tulsa.
Stewart, Pamela J., and Andrew Strathern, eds.
2000   Millenial Countdown in New Guinea. Theme issue, Ethno-
               history 47(1).
St. Augustine of Hippo
1961   Confessions. R. S. Pine-Coffin, trans. New York: Penguin.
St. Germaine, Ernest
1990   Winaboozhoo Adisokan: 24 Traditional Ojibwe Stories and

Legends. Lac du Flambeau Family Resource Center, Lac du Flambeau wɪ.

Strathern, Andrew J.

1994   Lines of Power. *In* Migration and Transformations: Regional Perspectives on New Guinea. Andrew J. Strathern and Gabriele Stürzenhofecker, eds. Pp. 231–255. Pittsburgh: University of Pittsburgh Press.

Strathern, Marilyn

2002   Foreword: Not Giving the Game Away. *In* Anthropology, by Comparison. Andre Gingrich and Richard G. Fox, eds. Pp. xiii–xvii. New York: Routledge.

Sullivan, Robert

2000   A Whale Hunt: Two Years on the Olympic Peninsula with the Makah and Their Canoe. New York: Scribner.

Swan, Daniel C.

1990   West Moon, East Moon: An Ethnohistory of the Peyote Religion among the Osage Indians, 1898–1930. Ph.D. dissertation, Department of Anthropology, University of Oklahoma.

1998   Early Osage Peyotism. Plains Anthropologist 43(163):51–71.

1999   Peyote Religious Art: Symbols of Faith and Belief. Jackson: University Press of Mississippi.

Tac, Pablo

1952[1835]   Indian Life and Customs at Mission San Luis Rey: A Record of California Mission Life. Minna Hewes and Gordon Hewes, eds. The Americas: A Quarterly Review of Inter-American Cultural History 9:87–106.

Tagupa, William

1976   Politics in French Polynesia 1945–1975. Wellington: Institute of International Affairs.

Taussig, Michael

1987   Shamanism, Colonialism, and the Wild Man: A Study in Terror and Healing. Chicago: University of Chicago Press.

1997   The Magic of the State. New York: Routledge.

Temaru, Oscar

1988   Maohinui (French Polynesia): The Need for Independence. *In* French Polynesia: A Book of Selected Readings. Nancy Pollock and Ron Crocombe, eds. Pp. 275–283. Fiji: Institute of Pacific Studies of the University of the South Pacific.

Temple, Thomas Workman, II

1958   Toypurina the Witch and the Indian Uprising at San Gabriel. Masterkey 32(5):136–152.

Thomas, Nicholas

1992a   The Inversion of Tradition. *American Ethnologist* 19(2):213–232.

1992b   Substantivization and Anthropological Discourse: The Transformation of Practices into Institutions in Neotraditional Pacific Societies. *In* History and Tradition in Melanesian Anthropology. J. G. Carrier, ed. Pp. 64–95. Berkeley: University of California Press.

1994   Colonialism's Culture. Princeton: Princeton University Press.

1997   In Oceania: Visions, Artifacts, Histories. Durham: Duke University Press.

Thompson, Coquille

1935   Ethnologic Text on Religion: The Ghost Dance Cult, Brought Up from the Sacramento Valley. Interview by Elizabeth Jacobs, Melville Jacobs Collection. Manuscripts and University Archives, University of Washington, Seattle.

Thompson, David

1916   David Thompson's Narrative of His Expeditions in Western America, 1784–1842. J. B Tyrell, ed. Toronto: Champlain Society.

Thompson, E. P.

1980   The Making of the English Working Class. New York: Penguin Books.

Thomson, David

2000   On the Paper Trail of the Massachusett Algonquians. Paper delivered at the American Academy of Religion Annual Meeting, Nashville.

Thornhill, Randy, and Craig Palmer

1999   A Natural History of Rape: Biological Bases of Sexual Coercion. Cambridge: MIT Press.

Thornton, Russell

1986   We Shall Live Again: The 1870 and 1890 Ghost Dance Movements as Demographic Revitalization. New York: Cambridge University Press.

Tinker, George E.

1993   Missionary Conquest: The Gospel and Native American Cultural Genocide. Minneapolis: Fortress Press.

Tonkinson, Robert

1982   *Kastom* in Melanesia: Introduction. Mankind 13(4):302–305.

Townsend, G. W. L.
1933   Diary: Entries for December 13th and 15th. Bragge Archive, Koetong, Victoria, Australia.
1968   District Officer: From Untamed New Guinea to Lake Success, 1921–46. Sydney: Pacific Publications.

Trask, Haunani-Kay
1999   From a Native Daughter: Colonialism and Sovereignty in Hawai'i. Rev. ed. Honolulu: University of Hawaii Press.

Trawick, Margaret
1992   Notes on Love in a Tamil Family. Berkeley: University of California Press.

Treat, James, ed.
1996   Native and Christian: Indigenous Voices on Religious Identity in the United States and Canada. New York: Routledge.

Trompf, Gary
1990   Cargo and the Millennium on Both Sides of the Pacific. *In* Cargo Cults and Millenarian Movements: Transoceanic Comparisons of New Religious Movements. Gary Trompf, ed. Pp. 35–94. Berlin: Mouton de Gruyter.

Turner, James West
1997   Continuity and Constraint: Reconstructing the Concept of Tradition from a Pacific Perspective. Contemporary Pacific 9(2):345–381.

Turner, Terence
1991   Representing, Resisting, Rethinking: Historical Transformations of Kayapo Culture and Anthropological Consciousness. *In* Colonial Situations: Essays on the Contexualization of Ethnographic Knowledge. History of Anthropology, vol. 7. George W. Stocking, ed. Pp. 285–313. Madison: University of Wisconsin Press.

Tuttle, Sarah
1830   Letters and Conversations on the Cherokee Missions by the Author of Conversations on the Bombay Mission. Boston: T. R. Martin for the Massachusetts Sabbath School Union.

Useem, John
1945   The Changing Structure of a Micronesian Society. American Anthropologist 47(4):567–588.
1946   Report on Yap and Palau. USCC Economic Survey of Micronesia Report, 6. Mimeograph. Honolulu: U.S. Commercial Co.

1947   Applied Anthropology in Micronesia. Applied Anthropology
                6(4):1–14.

1948   Institutions of Micronesia. Far Eastern Survey 17(2):22–25.

Usher, Jean

1974   William Duncan of Metlakatla: A Victorian Missionary in
                British Columbia. National Museum of Man Publications in
                History, 5. Ottawa: National Museum of Man.

Usner, Daniel H., Jr.

1992   Indians, Settlers, and Slaves in a Frontier Exchange Econ-
                omy: The Lower Mississippi Valley before 1783. Chapel Hill:
                University of North Carolina Press.

Valaskakis, Gail

1988   The Chippewa and the Other: Living the Heritage of Lac du
                Flambeau. Cultural Studies 2(3):267–293.

Valentine, C. A.

1963   Social Status, Political Power, and Native Responses to Eu-
                ropean Influence in Oceania. Anthropological Forum 1:3–55.

Valeri, Valerio

1985   Kingship and Sacrifice: Ritual and Society in Ancient Hawaii.
                Chicago: University of Chicago Press.

Vanderwood, Paul

1989   Santa Teresa: Mexico's Joan of Arc. *In* The Human Tradition
                in Latin America: The Nineteenth Century. Judith Elwell
                and William Beezley, eds. Pp. 215–232. Wilmington DE: SR
                Books.

1994   Using the Present to Study the Past: Religious Movements in
                Mexico and Uganda a Century Apart. Mexican Studies/Estu-
                dios Mexicanos 10(1):99–134.

1998   The Power of God against the Guns of Government: Re-
                ligious Upheaval in Mexico at the Turn of the Nineteenth
                Century. Stanford: Stanford University Press.

Vennum, Thomas

1982   The Ojibwa Dance Drum: Its History and Construction.
                Smithsonian Folklife Studies, 2. Washington DC: Smithso-
                nian Institution Press.

Vickers, Adrian

1990   Balinese Texts and Historiography. History and Theory 29(2):
                158–178.

Vidal, Silvia, and Neil Whitehead

In press   Dark Shamans and the Shamanic State: Sorcery and Witch-
                craft as Political Process in Guyana and the Venezuelan Ama-
                zon. *In* Darkness and Secrecy—The Anthropology of Assault

Sorcery and Witchcraft in Amazonia. Neil Whitehead and R. Wright, eds. Durham NC: Duke University Press.

Vidich, Arthur J.

1949   Political Factionalism in Palau: Its Rise and Development. Coordinated Investigation of Micronesian Anthropology Report, 23. Washington DC: Pacific Science Board.

1980   The Political Impact of Colonial Administration. New York: Arno Press.

Volkman, Toby Alice

1984   Great Performances: Toraja Cultural Identity in the 1970s. American Ethnologist 11(1):152–169.

1990   Visions and Revisions: Toraja Culture and the Tourist Gaze. American Ethnologist 17(1):91–110.

Wagner, Günter

1931   Yuchi Tales. Publications of the American Ethnological Society, 13. New York: G. E. Stechert and Co.

1932   Entwicklung und Verbreitung des Peyote-Kultes. Baessler-Archiv 15:59–139.

Wagner, Henry R.

1929   Spanish Voyages to the Northwest Coast of North America in the Sixteenth Century. San Francisco: California Historical Society.

Wagner, Roy

1981   The Invention of Culture. Chicago: University of Chicago Press.

Walker, Deward E., Jr.

1969   New Light on the Prophet Dance Controversy. Ethnohistory 16:245–255.

Wallace, Anthony F. C.

1956a   Mazeway Resynthesis: A Biocultural Theory of Religious Inspiration. Transactions of the New York Academy of Sciences 18:626–638.

1956b   New Religions among the Delaware Indians, 1600–1900. Southwestern Journal of Anthropology 12:1–21.

1956c   Revitalization Movements: Some Theoretical Considerations for Their Comparative Study. American Anthropologist 58: 264–281.

1956d   Tornado in Worcester: An Exploratory Study of Individual and Community Behavior in an Extreme Situation. Disaster Study, 3. Washington DC: National Academy of Sciences–National Research Council, Committee on Disaster Studies.

1958   The Dekanawidah Myth Analyzed as the Record of a Revi-
            talization Movement. Ethnohistory 5:118–130.
1961   Culture and Personality. New York: Random House.
1965   James Mooney (1861–1921) and the Study of the Ghost-
            Dance Religion. *In* The Ghost-Dance Religion and the Sioux
            Outbreak of 1980. Pp. v–x. Chicago: University of Chicago
            Press.
1966   Religion: An Anthropological View. New York: Random
            House.
1969   Death and Rebirth of the Seneca. New York: Vintage Books.
1970a   The Death and Rebirth of the Seneca. New York: A. A. Knopf.
1970b[1961] Religious Revitalization: A Function of Religion in Human
            History and Evolution. *In* Man Makes Sense: A Reader in
            Modern Cultural Anthropology. Eugene A. Hammel and
            William S. Simmons, eds. Pp. 371–383. Boston: Little, Brown
            and Co.
1990[1949] King of the Delawares: Teedyuscung, 1700–1763. Syracuse:
            Syracuse University Press.
Wallace, Pamela S.
1998   Yuchi Social History since World War II: Political Symbolism
            in Ethnic Identity. Ph.D. dissertation, Department of An-
            thropology, University of Oklahoma.
2002   Indian Claims Commission: Political Complexity and Con-
            trasting Concepts of Identity. Ethnohistory 49(4):743–767.
Wallace, William
1978   Southern Valley Yokuts. *In* Handbook of the Indians of North
            America, vol. 8: California. Robert Heizer, ed. Pp. 448–461.
            Washington DC: Smithsonian Institution Press.
Warkentin, Germaine
1999   In Search of the Word of the Other: Aboriginal Sign Systems
            and the History of the Book in Canada. Book History 2:1–27.
Warren, William Whipple
1984   History of the Ojibway People. St. Paul: Minnesota Histori-
            cal Society Press.
Weaver, Jace
1997   That the People May Live: Native American Literatures and
            Native American Community. New York: Oxford University
            Press.
Werbner, Pnina, and Tariq Modood, eds.
1997   Debating Cultural Hybridity: Multi-Cultural Identities and
            the Politics of Anti-Racism. London: Zed Books.

Wewak Patrol

1949–50   Wewak Patrol Report 10–49/50. National Archives, Port
                 Moresby, PNG.

Whaley, Rick, and Walter Bresette

1994   Walleye Warriors: An Effective Alliance against Racism and
                 for the Earth. Philadelphia: New Society Publishers.

White, Geoffrey M.

1991   Identity through History: Living Stories in a Solomon Islands
                 Society. New York: Cambridge University Press.

White, Geoffrey M., and Lamont Lindstrom, eds.

1989   The Pacific Theater: Island Representations of World War
                 II. Honolulu: University of Hawaii Press.

White, Phillip M.

2000   Peyotism and the Native American Church: An Annotated
                 Bibliography. Westport CT: Greenwood Press.

White, Raymond

1963   Luiseño Social Organization. University of California Pub-
                 lications in American Archaeology and Ethnology 48(2):91–
                 194.

White, Richard

1991   The Middle Ground: Indians, Empires, and Republics in the
                 Great Lakes Region, 1650–1815. Cambridge: Cambridge
                 University Press.

1998   *Review of* Tecumseh: A Life, by John R. Sugden. New Repub-
                 lic 219(9):45–46.

Whitehead, Neil

2001   Kanaima: Shamanism and Ritual Death in the Pakaraima
                 Mountains, Guyana. *In* Beyond the Visible and the Mate-
                 rial: The Amerindianization of Society in the Work of Peter
                 Riviere. Laura Rival and Neil Whitehead, eds. Pp. 235–245.
                 Oxford: Oxford University Press.

Williams, Francis E.

1923   The Vailala Madness and the Destruction of Native Cere-
                 monies in the Gulf District. Papuan Anthropology Reports,
                 4. Port Moresby PNG.

1934   The Vailala Madness in Retrospect. *In* Essays Presented to C.
                 G. Seligman. E. E. Evans-Pritchard, Raymond Firth, Bronis-
                 law Malinowski, and Isaac Schapera, eds. Pp. 369–379. Lon-
                 don: Kegan Paul, Trench, Trubner and Co.

Williamson, Norman

1980   Abishabis the Cree. Studies in Religion 9(2):217–245.

Wills, Gary

1999   Saint Augustine: A Penguin Life. New York: Viking Penguin.

Wilson, John A.

1880   A History of Los Angeles County. Oakland: Thompson and West.

Witthoft, John, and Wendell S. Hadlock

1949   Cherokee-Iroquois Little People. Journal of American Folklore 59:413–422.

Wogan, Peter

1994   Perceptions of European Literacy in Early Contact Situations. Ethnohistory 41:407–430.

Wolf, Eric R.

1982   Europe and the People without History. Berkeley: University of California Press.

Wolfart, H. C., and Freda Ahenakew

1998   The Student's Dictionary of Literary Plains Cree. Memoir 15. Winnipeg: Algonquian and Iroquoian Linguistics.

Works Progress Administration

1937   Interview by Rufus George with Jacob Rolland Concerning Indian Religious Worship. Works Progress Administration Project s149. Indian–Pioneer History Collection, Oklahoma Historical Society, Oklahoma City.

Worsley, Peter

1957   The Trumpet Shall Sound. London: MacGibbon and Kee.

1968   The Trumpet Shall Sound: A Study of "Cargo" Cults in Melanesia. New York: Schocken Books.

Wright, Muriel H.

1940   Springplace: Moravian Mission and the Ward Family of the Cherokee Nation. Guthrie OK: Co-Operative Publishing Co.

Wyss, Hilary E.

2000   Writing Indians: Literacy, Christianity, and Native Community in Early America. Amherst: University of Massachusetts Press.

Yangoru Patrol

1949–50   Yangoru Patrol Report 6–49/50. National Archives, Port Moresby PNG.

1954–55   Yangoru Patrol Report 4–54/55. National Archives, Port Moresby PNG.

Young, Michael

1983   The Theme of the Resentful Hero: Stasis and Mobility in

Goodenough Mythology. *In* The *Kula*: New Perspectives on Massim Exchange. Jerry Leach and Edmund Leach, eds. Pp. 383–394. Cambridge: Cambridge University Press.

Youst, Lionel, and William Seaburg

2002   Coquelle Thompson, Athabaskan Witness: A Cultural Biography. Norman: University of Oklahoma Press.

CONTRIBUTORS

Jennifer S. H. Brown is a professor of history and the director of the Centre for Rupert's Land Studies at the University of Winnipeg, Manitoba. She has authored and edited several books and has published widely on Northern Algonquian and Metis history and the fur trade. Besides continuing her long-term work on A. Irving Hallowell and his Berens River Ojibwa studies, she is collaborating with colleagues and with Cree elder Louis Bird to preserve and make available the large collection of oral histories he has gathered over the last decades.

Laurence Marshall Carucci is a professor of anthropology at Montana State University, where he has been a member of the faculty since 1985. Raised in Colorado, he earned his B.A. in anthropology at Colorado State University (1968) and his M.A. (1972) and Ph.D. (1980) at the University of Chicago. Carucci has conducted research with ethnic groups in Chicago, has worked on historical materials in Hawaii, and has lived and worked repeatedly with members of the Enewetak community and with other Marshall Islanders since 1976. He has published numerous articles on the Marshall Islands. The following books are also based on the several years of field research experience that Carucci has had in the Marshall Islands: *Nuclear Nativity: Rituals of Renewal and Empowerment in the Marshall Islands* (Northern Illinois University Press, 1997), *In Anxious Anticipation of the Uneven Fruits of Kwajalein Atoll* (USASMDC, 1997), and *The Typhoon of War: Micronesian Experiences of the Pacific War* (with Lin Poyer and Suzanne Falgout, University of Hawaii Press, 2001). He has worked closely with members of the Enewetak community as they seek compensation for damages to their atoll during years of military testing and works with several Northern Marshall Islands communities in their attempt to deal with medical problems that have resulted from their shared nuclear legacy. In addition, Carucci has been an officer and serves on the board of the Association for Social Anthropology in Oceania.

Michael E. Harkin is a professor of anthropology at the University of Wyoming.

He is the author of *The Heiltsuks: Dialogues of History and Culture on the Northwest Coast* (University of Nebraska Press, 1997), coeditor (with Sergei Kan and Marie Mauzé) of *Coming to Shore: New Perspectives on Northwest Coast Ethnology* (University of Nebraska Press, forthcoming). He is the associate editor of *Ethnohistory*. He is currently working on a book about the Lost Colony.

Lisa Henry received her Ph.D. in anthropology from Southern Methodist University. She is currently assistant professor of anthropology at the University of North Texas. Her research interests include indigenous and alternative healing systems, biomedicine and healthcare delivery, culture change, nationalism, and gender. She has research experience in French Polynesia and the United States.

Jason Baird Jackson, trained in anthropology and folklore at Indiana University, serves as the assistant curator of ethnology at the University of Oklahoma Sam Noble Oklahoma Museum of Natural History and as an assistant professor of anthropology in the university's Department of Anthropology. He was worked among the Yuchi and other Woodland Indian peoples in Oklahoma since 1993. His first book, *Yuchi Ceremonial Life*, was published by the University of Nebraska Press in 2003.

Maria Lepowsky is a professor of anthropology at the University of Wisconsin–Madison. The author of *Fruit of the Motherland: Gender in an Egalitarian Society*, she is currently writing about the histories of intercultural encounters in two distinctive regions, the Coral Sea islands of the Southwest Pacific and Southern California.

Joel W. Martin is the Costo Professor of American Indian Affairs at the University of California–Riverside (UCR), where he chairs the Department of Religious Studies. He is the author of *Sacred Revolt: The Muskogees' Struggle for a New World* (Beacon, 1991), *The Land Looks After Us: A History of Native American Religion* (Oxford University Press 2001), and other publications and is the codirector of the UCR/Pechanga Takic Language Revitalization Project.

Ann McMullen is the chief curator at the Smithsonian Institution National Museum of the American Indian. Her research and publications have focused on native people of northeastern North America, especially material culture, traditions, innovation, and commercialization; the intersection of ethnography and ethnohistory; native historiography and invented traditions; and the nature and transformation of native communities and community networks.

Larry Nesper is an assistant professor of anthropology and American Indian studies at the University of Wisconsin–Madison. He is the author of *The Walleye*

War: The Struggle for Ojibwe Spearfishing and Treaty Rights (University of Nebraska Press, 2002). In his spare time he runs marathons.

Lin Poyer received her Ph.D. in anthropology from the University of Michigan. She is the author of *The Ngatik Massacre: History and Identity on a Micronesian Atoll* (Smithsonian Institution Press) and coauthor of *The Typhoon of War: Micronesian Experiences of the Pacific War* (University of Hawaii Press). She is an associate professor of anthropology at the University of Wyoming.

Paul B. Roscoe is a professor of anthropology and cooperating professor of quaternary and climate studies at the University of Maine. He has conducted more than two years of research among the Yangoru Boiken of the Sepik Basin PNG and has archival specializations in the societies of ancient Polynesia and Sepik and Highland New Guinea. He is the coeditor (with Robert Graber) of *Circumscription and the Evolution of Society* (American Behavioral Scientist) and (with Nancy Lutkehaus) of *Gender Rituals: Female Initiation in Melanesia* (Routledge). His articles have appeared in *American Anthropologist, American Ethnologist, Current Anthropology*, the *Journal of Archaeological Method and Theory*, and *Man: Journal of the Royal Anthropological Institute*. In 1992 he won the Royal Anthropological Institute's Curl Essay Prize for his paper "Amity and Aggression: A Symbolic Theory of Incest."

Jukka Siikala is a professor of social anthropology at the University of Helsinki. He has studied the colonial history and culture of the Pacific and has done extensive fieldwork in the Cook Islands during the last 18 years. His publications include *Cult and Conflict in Tropical Polynesia* (Academia Scientiarum Fennica, 1982) and *'Akatokamanava: Myth, History and Society in the Southern Cook Islands* (the Polynesian Society, 1991). Currently he is doing research on Polynesians' presence outside of their home islands.

INDEX